HOSPITALLER MALTA AND THE MEDITERRANEAN ECONOMY IN THE SIXTEENTH CENTURY

HOSPITALLER MALTA AND THE MEDITERRANEAN ECONOMY IN THE SIXTEENTH CENTURY

Joan Abela

THE BOYDELL PRESS

First published 2018
The Boydell Press, Woodbridge

ISBN 978 1 78327 211 2

The Boydell Press is an imprint of Boydell & Brewer Ltd
PO Box 9, Woodbridge, Suffolk IP12 3DF, UK
and of Boydell & Brewer Inc.
668 Mt Hope Avenue, Rochester, NY 14620–2731, USA
website: www.boydellandbrewer.com

A CIP catalogue record for this book is available
from the British Library

To Deborah

For always being there for me

Contents

Illustrations

Figures

Charts

Maps

Tables

Foreword

As Joan Abela argues cogently in the following pages, the history of early modern Malta can truly be regarded as the epitome of the history of the Mediterranean. This authoritative and lively portrait of Maltese society and economy introduces us to a complex and diverse world in the midst of transformation. It opens exciting new areas of investigation, and is an impressive contribution to the new historiographical approach to Mediterranean history, which focuses on interaction and cross-fertilisation between different customary and legal traditions. Abela's detailed and lucid analysis brings into focus how the establishment of the Hospitaller Order in the Maltese archipelago gave rise to important structural transformations – in terms of administration, the economy and society. For the first time, the maritime economy of Malta is the focus of a sharp and comprehensive analysis which takes all these elements into account and produces a nuanced portrait of the socio-economic development of a heavily militarised society, a distinct frontier world where a crusading mission co-existed with conspicuous consumption and the challenges of provisioning an arid land which was experiencing a veritable demographic boom.

The real protagonist of this book is the population of Malta itself; not the well-known Knights of St John, the offspring of European Catholic nobility, but the local notables, merchants, seafarers and those small-scale entrepreneurs of both sexes who responded to epochal challenges with remarkable resilience and inventiveness. Joan Abela effectively demonstrates how the Maltese population, confronted with the arrival of new 'masters', found ways to negotiate their institutional and social role within this new balance of power; how they successfully took advantage both of the islands' strategic value vis-à-vis the Barbary regencies and of the multi-faceted economic opportunities afforded by the arrival of the Knights. The socio-economic consequences of corsairing activities – the foundation of the Order's existence in the fractured sixteenth-century Mediterranean – are also discussed, but with a particular focus on the ways in which, paradoxically, they gave women a greater capacity for independent action, given the men's constant exposure to the threat of captivity and relative absence from the islands.

This exciting research work builds on the recent opening of Malta's Notarial Archive to scholars and the general public, itself a wonderful story of collaborative endeavour on the part of the community to preserve its historical heritage through the establishment of a private-public partnership. Joan Abela is the true heroine of this story, because it is in great part through her own tireless efforts to preserve and share this heritage that Malta is rediscovering its own rich past.

Maria Fusaro
University of Exeter

Preface

The complexity and diversity of the Mediterranean Sea and its lands have provided fertile ground for on-going debates on a wide variety of issues, ranging from its unity to its sharp divides, from the importance of human interaction to that of its micro-ecologies. More than half a century of scholarly work and discussion has followed Braudel's monumental work on the Mediterranean,[1] yet there still remains much to explore in order to obtain a clearer picture of how seemingly opposing realities have found ways to function within an environment where politics, religion and the economy are intricately intertwined.[2] This paradox encompasses the different cultures and civilisations that have inhabited this closed space where, simultaneously, they were formally at war and trading with one another.[3]

This book presents a study of Malta, a small but strategically placed island on the central axis of the Mediterranean which in many ways could be considered as the epitome of this contradiction. Malta's central position in the Mediterranean, a few miles from the Sicilian Straits, which were crucial for control of the east–west Mediterranean passage[4] and, after 1530, the presence on the island of the Order of the Knights of St John (1530–1798), made it an active participant in Mediterranean politics and commercial networks. As in the broader context, two opposing realities played a significant part in Malta's economic performance during the early period of Hospitaller rule. One was the Order's major role as a bulwark of Christianity, mainly carried out through its corsairing activities, and the other was its constant trading activity with the 'infidels'. Malta thus lends itself to the use of case studies which are approached with a micro-historical frame to throw light on larger phenomena taking place in the Mediterranean. Through this methodological approach, which delves into what seem to be the petty details of everyday life, this study arrives at

1 F. Braudel, *La Méditerranée et la Monde Méditerranéen à l'Époque de Philippe II* (Paris, 1949, 2nd rev. edn 1966). Later translated by S. Reynolds, *The Mediterranean and the Mediterranean World in the Age of Philip II* (2 vols, Berkeley, Los Angeles and London, 1995). For a recent reappraisal of this work see M. Fusaro, C. J. Heywood & M. S. Omri (eds), *Trade and Cultural Exchange in the Early Modern Mediterranean: Braudel's Maritime Legacy* (London, 2010).

2 D. Abulafia, *Mediterranean Encounters, Economic, Religious, Political, 1100–1550* (Aldershot and Burlington, 2000), ix.

3 M. Fusaro, 'After Braudel: A Reassessment of Mediterranean History between the Northern Invasion and the Caravane Maritime', in Fusaro et al., *Trade and Cultural Exchange*, 1–22: 1.

4 D. Abulafia, *The Great Sea: A Human History of the Mediterranean* (London, 2011), 429.

conclusions which 'highlight the hiatus between the normative institutional level of history and real life on the ground'.[5] By projecting these conclusions into the wider context we can read beyond the institutional framework of economic transactions and observe them in practice.

Although there is vast literature on various aspects of the long presence of the Knights Hospitaller in Malta, comprehensive study of the commercial development of the harbour area during the first decades of the Knights' rule in noticeably absent. Despite Malta's small size, the presence of the Order of St John facilitated an inflow of foreign resources which eventually led to very dense human settlement and an international presence beyond the island's shores that was disproportionate to what would normally be the case for such a small island. The maritime nature of the Order's activities, and its heavy dependence on imports, hastened the development of an efficient maritime communication system. All the economic activity generated wealth and was a 'pull factor' for a large number of enterprising individuals, both local and foreign.[6] The result was that early modern Hospitaller Malta saw the development of an enterprising business class which, of sheer necessity, grew accustomed to operating well beyond its narrow confines. This in turn contributed to the island's becoming more open to connection with the outside world.

This book explores in detail the various economic activities that took place in Malta during the period 1530–65. The year 1565 has been chosen as an end point because the Great Siege, which took place between May and September, caused a break in the normal chain of events.[7] By concentrating on this period a portrait can be painted of socio-economic development before the onset of the 'hyper-militarisation' activities that followed the Great Siege. This is done through an analysis of the practical functioning of commerce – its agreements and disputes, its currencies, its trading posts and its nodal points. Further, it is shown how notarial evidence and the records of various tribunals set up on the island at the time help to fill in gaping holes in historical enquiry.

The chronological subdivisions adopted in the historiography of other European countries have influenced how historians of Malta have established the island's own sequential divisions.[8] They have always found the medieval period – in Malta's case running until 1530 – and the first few decades following the establishment of the

5 Fusaro, 'After Braudel', in Fusaro et al., *Trade and Cultural Exchange*, 1–22: 9.

6 Trade is not pivotal for economic upsurge; it is not a cause of economic growth, but one of its effects. C. Sabillion, *On the Causes of Economic Growth: The Lessons of History* (New York, 2008), 37–9. For a discussion on various historiographical approaches to economic systems and their effect on trade see L. Halevi, 'Religion and Cross-Cultural Trade: A Framework for Interdisciplinary Inquiry', in F. Trivellato, L. Halevi & C. Antunes (eds), *Religion and Trade: Cross-Cultural Exchanges in World History, 1000–1900* (Oxford, 2014), 24–61.

7 J. Abela, 'The Great Siege of 1565: Untold Stories of Daily Life', in M. Camilleri (ed.), *Besieged* (2 vols, Malta, 2015), vol. 2, 97–115.

8 A. Luttrell, 'Approaches to Medieval Malta', in A. Luttrell, *The Making of Christian Malta, From the Early Middle Ages to 1530* (Aldershot, 2002), paper II: 14. For a discussion on historical divisions see P. Burke, *The Renaissance – Studies in European History* (2nd edn, Basingstoke and New York, 1997).

Hospitaller Order of St John in Malta problematic. This is mostly because of the absence, dearth or inaccessibility of documentary material for the period.[9] This is alleviated only from the late fifteenth century onwards, although the documentation is still relatively sparse in comparison to data relating to the post-siege period. Although the medieval period has benefitted somewhat from a new wave of research,[10] the same cannot be said for the transitional period between the medieval phase and the early modern one of Hospitaller dominion. Most works dealing with the sixteenth century treat the first decades of the Knights' rule as a series of personal reigns of Grand Masters and emphasise particular events such as the Great Siege of 1565 and other complex politico-religious conflicts. While these are essential features of Malta's history, such studies have often neglected social and economic aspects which could provide a sharper picture of Maltese society and shed light on the broader Mediterranean picture.

This lack of interest in the socio-economic side cannot be wholly attributed to the absence of documents. Various primary sources, like notarial deeds, court records and chancery documents, which could have been exploited for such historical enquiry have been overlooked for too long. Historians of Malta have tended to focus on the history of the Knights of St John rather than on the history of a people under the Knights of St John. The result is that a vital question in Maltese historiography still awaits an answer: what were the principal factors shaping Malta's economic and social transition from the late Middle Ages into the early modern era? Does this transition merit focused attention, one which goes beyond the passing references it has received in wider historical work? Can similar economic situations be found in neighbouring Mediterranean countries?

Bearing the latter question in mind, the Introduction provides a critical appraisal of some of the landmark historical works on the Mediterranean produced since the late 1960s. This review is necessary in order to determine whether any of the hypotheses they have put forward can be applied either in whole or in part to Malta, especially with regard to economic development. The chapter invites readers to reconsider issues of economic dependency and backwardness – with which Mediterranean islands have often been associated – in broader terms. It also investigates whether these theories still hold when it is considered that in various regions which have historically been labelled as 'backward' there was commonly a preference to produce niche products over staple goods. The chapter thus sets the tone for the rest of the volume, which aims to re-assess deeply rooted historical beliefs that merit a fresh historical perspective.

Chapter One investigates issues relating to the island's institutional, legal, social and political infrastructure, and at the same time considers whether various changes in these structures affected the running of the economy. The role of the Spanish Crown in securing control over its territories is viewed in juxtaposition to the same

9 Although the chronological limits of the early modern period are open to debate, in this study the beginning refers to c. 1500 for the Europe in general, while for the Malta it is usually taken as the arrival of the Knights of the Order of St John in 1530. C. Dalli, *Malta, The Medieval Millennium* (Malta, 2006), 13.

10 Dalli, *Malta, The Medieval Millenium*, 252–6.

role which was subsequently transferred to the Knights of St John. This comparison helps to explore the effects of a change in rulership and the extent to which it ultimately affected economic performance. An important part of the analysis is the focus on the aspirations of the local merchant community, hitherto a silent voice in most studies of the period. In the initial years of their rule, the Knights faced great difficulties in setting up a strong administrative base, and this suited the aspirations of the merchant class, who seized the opportunity to take a more prominent and active role in Maltese society. Such aspirations were not exclusive to Malta but mirrored similar trends in Europe. Each of the following three chapters is dedicated to a specific case study.

The Chapter Two first case study concerns the grain trade, an important sector in the Maltese economy which brought in substantial amounts of revenue which were generated from indirect taxation. Malta's dependence on Sicily for its grain supply was a major concern throughout this period. Moreover, apart from feeding hungry mouths, the Knights knew well that they needed to act cautiously with the local representatives because it was they who held the key to duty-free concessions granted by the Sicilian Viceroy, which were proving hard to hold on to. The sources presented in this chapter have been purposely selected to reflect the great difficulties faced by the grain merchants during the import process. In line with recent trends which focus on materiality and cross-cultural trade, the chapter also examines a very unexplored aspect of local commercial trading networks,[11] juxtaposing the transfer of goods in trusted markets and prohibited ones.[12] The focus is on the clandestine re-export of duty-free grain – an issue which worried the Sicilian authorities. As is discussed in Chapter Four, other merchandise was also exported or imported to and from Muslim territories under the guise of slave ransom procedures.[13] The investigation of these mechanisms helps us to understand how the transfer of goods across cultures affected the development of societies and how, rather than observing dissimilarities, merchants of different religions acted independently of such barriers in a shared business culture. As Leor Halevi explains, 'religious and cultural boundaries cannot be drawn so neatly on maps, as if they were national borders; they are constructs. Commerce between, say, a Catholic from Venice and a Muslim from Istanbul arguably takes place within a shared Mediterranean culture.'[14]

11 Halevi argues that the economic significance of peaceful commerce in pre-modern times is debatable and thus one has to consider that most of the trade which was carried out was not only done via peaceful mechanisms but also depended on coercion and violent actions like piracy, plundering and pillaging. Halevi, 'Religion and Cross-Cultural Trade', in Trivellato et al., *Religion and Trade,* 24–61: 28–9.

12 On networks of trust see F. Trivellato, *The Familiarity of Strangers: The Sephardic Diaspora, Livorno, and Cross-Cultural Trade in the Early Modern Period* (New Haven, CT, 2009).

13 The veiling of trading enterprises under a missionary banner had parallels in other European countries. G. Marcocci, 'Trading with the Muslim World: Religious Limits and Proscriptions in the Portuguese Empire (ca. 1480–1570)', in Trivellato et al., *Religion and Trade,* 91–107: 94.

14 Halevi, 'Religion and Cross-Cultural Trade', in Trivellato et al., *Religion and Trade,* 24–61: 41.

In Chapter Three the second case study evaluates another silent voice in Maltese economic studies: women, their legal persona and how this affected their contribution to the island's economic activities. Notarial acts are a particularly helpful source when comparing the economic performance of local women with that of their Greek counterparts who, as the chapter discusses, came under a separate set of laws promulgated in Rhodes. The sources are examined in the context of legal constraints which were imposed by a male-dominated society that tended to give women sufficient privileges to enable the better functioning of male economic pursuits and interests. A delineation of these limitations at the different stages of a woman's life is essential in order to establish how society sought to profit from the participation of women while at the same time regulating their activities. The law shaped everyday life through regulations on property, dowry, inheritance, marriage and dispute settlements, making legal texts an important source for illuminating the vital processes that dictated women's actions.[15] By means of this focus the way in which women devised means to deal with constraints in a space that was shaped by norms and prohibitions is also portrayed.

Chapter Four, the third and final case study, seeks to establish how commercial links functioned between Malta – often described as the frontier of Christianity – and neighbouring Ottoman North African territories, and how merchants, both Christian and Muslim, managed to overcome the religious antagonisms which inhibited the easy flow of trade. The objective of this study is to shed light on economic activities taking place in and around Malta's harbour area during a largely unexplored period in Maltese history. It also aims to provide a better understanding of commercial relations in the Mediterranean, especially ransom processes, since the Maltese harbour was a point of intersection not just for people of different nationalities, but for people of different faiths, such as Muslims, Jews and Christians of different denominations. All were unified by a common goal – to trade and to make a profit from trade.

15 T. Kuehn, *Law, Family and Women: Toward a Legal Anthropology of Renaissance Italy* (Chicago, 1994), 2.

Acknowledgements

This book would not have been possible without the assistance of a number of people who have supported me during its preparation. As the book is developed out of my doctoral research, I wish first and foremost to express my gratitude to my supervisor, Maria Fusaro, whose unstinting assistance and enthusiasm enabled me to remain resolute even during difficult times. Her invaluable teaching, insights and intelligent criticism were indispensable for completing this project. Indeed, it was a privilege working with her. A generous full-time scholarship from the University of Exeter made this journey much easier and a financial burden was the least of my worries. For this, I am grateful to them. I am also indebted to Ann Williams, who sparked off this entire research journey. I have benefitted from the intellectual stimuli of many, among whom I must thank Charles Dalli, Stephen Spiteri and Denise Bezzina for generously sharing their profound knowledge and views in the various discussions which ensued with the beginning of each new chapter.

Generous help was forthcoming from a great many people, among whom I feel compelled to mention Maroma Camilleri at the National Library of Malta and Mario Gauci at the Cathedral Museum in Mdina. No words can express my deep gratitude for their professional help wrapped in so much kindness, and for making those painstakingly lengthy and exhausting hours far easier. I must also thank Paul Camilleri at the Notarial Archives for putting up with my incessant demands, which at times required immediate assistance, and Noel D'Anastas, who is in charge of the Legal Section at the National Archives of Malta. Deep gratitude is also due to Daniel Cilia for providing the book with the splendid images that bring the manuscript sources to life. I am most grateful to Victor Bonnici for patiently reading various passages in Latin with me and for helping me with transcriptions and translations, and to Judge Giovanni Bonello for his generous help in reading the text to produce a better version. I am also particularly grateful to my dear friend and colleague Francesca Balzan, who was always there to listen, to help, and to encourage, by offering constructive and intelligent criticism, but above all, by being a true friend throughout.

A special thank you goes to my family for always showing genuine interest in far too lengthy conversations about my research: to my sister Veronica and my late mother, Mary, for their daily prayers; to my husband, John, for his support and to my children, Sarah, Deborah and Alan. Thank you all for being so caring, understanding and patient. To Deborah particularly I owe my biggest debt. Not only has she shared household chores, cooking and shopping, but she has also lent a helping hand during various stages of this project and provided me with helpful tips. She shared not only my study space but also my anxieties, my fears, and my elation upon making new discoveries. She was always there to listen assiduously. Indeed, she was not merely a daughter, but above all, a true and loving friend. To her I dedicate this work. Finally, I would like to thank the British Commission for Maritime History for awarding me the Boydell & Brewer Prize which resulted in the publication of this book, and Horwath Malta and the Bank of Valletta plc for part-sponsoring this work to meet financial constraints.

Horwath Malta

BOV
Bank of Valletta

Abbreviations

Archival abbreviations

CAM, AO	Cathedral Archives of Mdina, Malta, *Acta Orginalia*
CAM, CEM	Cathedral Archives of Mdina, Malta, *Curia Episcopalis Melitensis*
CAM, AIM	Cathedral Archives of Mdina, Malta, Archives of the Inquisition
CAM, Misc.	Cathedral Archives of Mdina, Malta, *Miscellanea* Collection
NAM, MCC	National Archives of Malta, *Magna Curia Castellania*
NAM, ACA	National Archives of Malta, *Suprema Appellationis Curia et Tribunalis Publicae Audientiae Causae*
NAM, CA	National Archives of Malta, *Comune Aerarium*
NAM, MCC, AO	National Archives of Malta, *Magna Curia Castellania,* Acta Originalia
NAM, MCC, Reg. AO	National Archives of Malta, *Magna Curia Castellania,* Registrum Actorum Originalium
NAV	Notarial Archives Valletta
NLM	National Library of Malta
NLM, AOM	National Library of Malta, Archives of the Order of Malta
NLM, AOM, Lib. Bull.	National Library of Malta, Archives of the Order of Malta, *Liber Bullarum*
NLM, Libr. MS	National Library of Malta, Library Manuscripts Collection
NLM, Univ.	National Library of Malta, *Università* Manuscripts Collection

Other abbreviations

ab inc	*ab incarnatione*
Doc./Docs	document/documents
f./ff.	folio/folios
Fig.	figure
MS	manuscript
n.f.	no folio number
R	Register
v.	verso
vol./vols	volume/volumes

Notes

Primary sources

The primary sources consulted for this study derive from four of the main archival depositories in Malta. The main primary source is notarial registers, and these are supplemented with relevant primary documentation from the Cathedral Archives, the records of the *Magna Curia Castellania* housed at the National Archives, and records in the National Library of Malta, which range from municipal records of the town council, to various chancery and other administrative documents.

References from notarial primary sources

The great majority of notaries exercised their practice in the main centres of activity on the island, usually the town squares of Mdina, Birgu and, after the 1570s, Valletta. As shown in Table 1, prior to the establishment of the Knights Hospitallers in 1530, most notaries had their offices in the inland capital city of Mdina. The arrival of the Order and the subsequent establishment of new cities in the harbour area resulted in an ever-increasing number of notaries practising in the port city of Birgu and, later, Valletta. Thus, for the pre-1530 period the study has focused on notaries practising in Mdina, since documentation is more abundant for that city, while for the first decades of the Order's rule (1530–65), the focus is on notaries practising in Birgu, since this city experienced a major transformation and an increase in commercial activities. Furthermore, Birgu saw the establishment not only of Maltese notaries to address the increasing demand for legal services, but also that of Rhodiot notaries who served both the local and Greek communities, as well as members of the Order. Thus a wider section of society is captured in the acts of these notaries. The selection of notarial acts was also dependent on the state of preservation of the volumes.

Table 1 Notaries practising in the towns 1520–1600

	1520s	1530s	1560s	1580s	1600
Notabile (Mdina)	7	11	6	12	8
Birgu (Vittoriosa)	1	4	7	9	10
Valletta[a]	-	-	3	10	13

[a] Work on the building of Valletta started in 1565 and the knights officially transferred their seat to the new city in 1571.

Source: A. Attard, Index of Notaries 1465–1894 (Malta, 1979), 6–8, 10–19.

Notaries practising in Malta gathered and bound their registers from 1 September to 31 August, the administrative year corresponding to the Indictional year, following the style of Byzantium.[1] However, they did not adopt a uniform method of dating. Some of them, used the Florentine calendar, known as *ab incarnatione*, which took 25 March as the first day of the year, reflecting the belief that this was the day of Jesus Christ's conception. Thus, an act for 1 January 1534 would be dated 1 January 1533, and so forth up to 24 March; acts for 25 March onwards would be dated by the new year – in our example, 25 March 1534.[2] In this study, contracts with *ab incarnatione* dates are distinguished by the inclusion of *ab inc* after the date – (10.ii.1544 *ab inc*).

Other notaries used what was known as the Roman or papal Indiction, whose first day was either 25 December, better known as *nativitate* referring to Christmas, or else 1 January.[3] All the documents used for this study having this system of dating have recorded the New Year on 1 January. It is to be noted however, that at times, both types of dating feature in a volume of a particular notary. It is believed that this has occurred since very often notaries used to include *Eodem* instead of the date when drawing up contracts. This implies that a particular contract was drawn up on the same date as the one preceding it. At times, one contract can include several folios containing *Eodem* with no definite date. This must have caused some inconvenience, since one would have to go back and scrutinise a number of folios to establish the exact date to which that particular *Eodem* was referring.

Therefore, occasionally, both *Eodem* and the date feature in some contracts. A close inspection of the calligraphy and ink indicates that it is likely that the date was added at a later stage, probably to facilitate the work of those wanting to consult the documents. When such documents were analysed during this study, the dates were reproduced according to that which was added later. The acts of Notary Giuseppe de Guevara, R 224 & MS 778, are an example of such instances. Another observation related to the dating system in notarial acts is the application of religious feasts

1 G. Wettinger, *Acta Iuratorum et Consilii Civitatis et Insulae Maltae* (Palermo, 1993), 15.

2 This was not an unusual occurrence, since the French year began on Easter day until 1564, the Venetian year on 1 March until 1522, and the English year on 25 March until 1752. See B. Blackburn and L. Holford-Strevens, *The Oxford Companion to the Year* (Oxford, 1999), 103, 785, 880.

3 The series of Roman, papal, or pontifical Indictions introduced in the ninth century started from the first day of the civil year, this being 25 December in some cases, 1 January in others. This system was also common in Western Christendom, but in spite of its appellation it was by no means exclusively used in papal documents. The beginning of the year varied at different periods and in different countries. When Julius Caesar reformed the calendar (45 BC), he fixed 1 January as New Year's Day, a characteristic which it seems to have never quite lost, even among those who have chosen a different starting point for civil and legal purposes. The most common of such starting points were 25 March (Feast of the Annunciation, 'Style of the Incarnation') and 25 December (Christmas Day, 'Style of the Nativity'). In Rome and a great part of Italy, it was 25 December, until Pope Gregory XIII reformed the calendar (1582) and fixed 1 January as the first day of the year. However, the beginning of the year for the dating of papal Bulls is still Christmas Day: http://www.newadvent.org/cathen/03738a.htm (accessed 9 May 2016). Refer also to Blackburn and Holford-Strevens, *The Oxford Companion to the Year*, 770–1.

serving as time markers when referring to future dates. These often represented stipulated time markers for various obligations, such as, the repayment of a loan.

References from the notarial primary sources are reported thus:

- The main archival repository always precedes the reference to the actual acts;
- The manuscript 'MS' (original) number or the register 'R' (true copy) number is written as in the following examples, NAV, R 4/1 or NAV, MS 514/1;
- The deeds quoted are followed by the folio reference and the date in which the act was drawn;
- The letters n.f. indicate that folios were not enumerated. In this case, reference is denoted by stipulating the date of the deed.

Therefore, a typical example of a notarial register reference is NAV, R 4/1, ff. 17–18v (13.ix.1557) or NAV, MS 514/1, n.f. (13.ix.1557).

Unless otherwise indicated, all translations from original manuscripts are the author's own. Wherever possible, place names have been recorded according to their modern names. Thus, Naxar becomes Naxxar, Luca – Luqa, and so on. Words and expressions in Latin or Italian, including weights, measurements, currencies and titles, are written in italics. Whenever a question mark [?] appears in the text, it indicates that the word could not be deciphered. Since abbreviations are a common feature of the documents consulted, especially in the case of titles, hereunder is a list providing a key to abbreviations present in this work.

Don. = *Donnus* (an abbreviated form of *Dominus* meaning Master).[4]
Fra. = *Frater* (a lay brother).
Hon. = *Honorabilis* (a person who is deemed to be worthy of being honoured; often used for those who held property or were prominent merchants).[5]
Rev. = *Reverendus* (title of dignity given to ecclesiastics and religious persons).[6]
Ven. = *Venerabilis* (used for members of the higher clergy as a sign of high esteem).
Ma. = *Magnificus* (used for distinguished persons such as the town mayor, the wartime governor and notaries).[7]
Mag. = *Magister* (refers to craftsmen ranging from the town surgeon to the village carpenter)[8].
Nob. = *Nobilis* (title given to a person from the nobility and to fief holders).[9]

4 V. Mortilla, *Nuovo Dizionario Siciliano-Italiano* (2nd edn, Palermo, 1853), 310.
5 Wettinger, *Acta iuratorum*, 16. Mortilla, *Nuovo Dizionario*, 604.
6 Mortilla, *Nuovo Dizionario*, 715.
7 Mortilla, *Nuovo Dizionario*, 305.
8 Wettinger, *Acta iuratorum*, 16.
9 Wettinger, *Acta iuratorum*, 16. Mortilla, *Nuovo Dizionario*, 583.

Currency

1 *uncia*[10] or 2 ½ *scudi*	=	30 *tarì*
1 *scudo*[11]	=	12 *tarì*
1 *tarì*	=	20 *grani*
1 *grano*	=	6 *dinari*[12] or *Piccioli*

During the period under study, Sicilian coins used in Malta prior to the arrival of the Order were still in circulation. Consequently, in the documents consulted there is also reference to various other currencies, and one comes across such phrases as *pecunia argentea aquilarum*,[13] *scutis solis boni auri et iusti ponderis vel eorum iusto valore*[14] or *ducati auri*.[15] Wherever possible, any information regarding their equivalent value noted in the corresponding documents has been included in the study.

10 The *uncia* was not an actual coin; at least until the time of Grand Master Manoel Pinto de Fonseca (1741–73), it was only a unit of account. See H. Calleja Schembri, *Coins and Medals of the Knights of Malta* (London, 1966), 10; A. M. Vassallo, 'Prices of Commodities in Malta and Gozo 1530–1630' (BA Hons dissertation, University of Malta, 1976), 13.

11 The silver *scudo* was the standard coin and unit of account and was equal to 12 *tarì*, and all notarial contracts consulted for this study stipulate that the *scudo* was worth 12 *tarì*, '*ad ra[tio]nem tarenorum duodecim singulo scuto*' (at the rate of 12 *tarì* per *scudo*). NAV, MS 514/1, n.f. (27.vi.1558), to quote an example. According to Joseph Sammut, 'the first coins which appear to have been minted in Malta by the Order of St John, were the gold *zecchini* pieces struck during the brief reign of Grand Master Pietrino del Ponte (1534–35). The *Zecchino*, called by the Maltese either *zekkin* or *skud tad-deheb* [gold *scudo*] was the standard coin for the gold coinage.' J. C. Sammut, *Currency in Malta* (Malta, 2001), 35; see also M. A. Sant, 'Coinage Problems Facing the Order of St John in Malta' (MA dissertation, University of Malta, 1967), 49. At least up to the late 1630s, the Maltese *scudo* maintained a par value with its Sicilian counterpart. Sammut, *Currency in Malta*, 35.

12 For the first thirty-five years after the Order's arrival in Malta, the only copper piece minted on the island was the *picciolo* or dinar, minted by Claude de la Sengle (1553–57). However, his successor Jean de Valette (1557–68) minted a large amount and variety of copper coins; Sant, 'Coinage Problems', 90; Sammut, *Currency in Malta*, 35; S. Fiorini (ed.), *Documentary Sources of Maltese History, Part I: Notarial Documents, No. 1: Notary Giacomo Zabbara R 494/1(I): 1486–1488* (Malta, 1996), xvii.

13 NAV, R 4/1, fol. 19v (20.x.1557). On 16 May 1529, the town council of Mdina deliberated that the silver *aquile* previously circulating for 1 *tarì* 4 *grani* each, should pass current according to their weight. A *bando* dated 2 November 1536 fixed the *aquile* of standard weight at 23 *grani* each, while another *bando* dated 1 February 1537 ordered that the new *aquile* and *tarì* should *circulate* without any reference to their weight. Sant, 'Coinage Problems', 297.

14 NAV, MS 514/1, n.f. (16.v.1558), or NAV, R 224/1, fol. 49v (22.iv.1540).

15 NAV, R 4/1, fol. 7 (6.x.1557).

Weights and measures

Vital to the study of any economy are weights and measures adopted in that particular market since these provide a relation between the commodity purchased and its price, while ensuring that both parties in a commercial transaction had the necessary means to assure their proper interests. Weights and measures also shed light on whether taxes imposed on various items were light or heavy. In this study it will be noted that different provinces in Sicily used different weights and measures differing from one another, the Maltese system being very similar to that of Messina. The *tumolo* was the basic measurement used for dry goods such as the different types of grain, while the *quartuccio* was the fundamental unit used for liquid measures. The following are weights and measures used in Malta featuring in this study.[16]

Measures of capacity

For wheat, barley and rye[17]

1 *Salma*[18]	= 16 *Tumoli*	=	288.510000 litres
1 *Tumolo*	= 6 *Mondelli*[19]	=	18.031875 litres
1 *Mondello*	= 10 *Misure*	=	3.005312 litres
1 *Misura*	= 10 *Lumini*	=	0.300531 litres
1 *Lumino*		=	0.030053 litres

For other cereals (including pulses, seeds and salt)

1 *Salma*	= 16 *Tumoli*	=	334.656000 litres
1 *Tumolo*	= 6 *Mondelli*	=	20.916000 litres
1 *Mondello*		=	3.486000 litres

16 Weights were made of stone, iron or brass. All weights were inspected, adjusted and sealed by the *carapans*, the officials in charge of weights and measures. Vassallo, 'Prices of Commodities', 25.

17 All measures and their equivalents quoted from A. Martini, *Manuale di metrologia, ossia misure, pesi e monete in uso attualmente e anticamente presso tutti i popoli* (Turin and Loescher, 1883), 810.

18 'The Maltese for *salma* is *modd* worth 4 *wejbiet* and 1 *wejba* worth 4 *tomniet*. The Maltese *tomna* is worth 6 *sighan*. Although the Maltese *siegh* and the Sicilian *mondello, munneddu* are not the same fraction of a *tomna*, in Malta the *siegh* was referred to as a *mondello* in various documents.' Fiorini (ed.), *Documentary Sources of Maltese History, Part I, No. 1*, xviii.

19 According to Anthony Vassallo, the Sicilian dry measure differed from the Maltese mainly in the subdivisions of the *tumolo*, which was sub-divided into four *mondelli*. Vassallo, 'Prices of Commodities', 27.

Liquid measures[20]

Olive oil[21]

1 *Barile*	= 2 *Cafisi*	= 40.892000 litres
1 *Cafiso*	= 4 *Quarte*	= 20.446000 litres
1 *Quarta*	= 4 *Quartucci*	= 5.111500 litres
1 *Quartuccio*	= 4 *Terzi*	= 1.277875 litres
1 *Terzo*	= 2 *Casbe* or 2½ *misure*	= 0.319469 litres
1 *Casba*	= 1½ *Misura*	= 0.159734 litres
1 *Misura*	= 4 *Quartini*	= 0.127787 litres
1 *Quartino*		= 0.031947 litres

All other types of oil were sold according to weight at the equivalent of:

1 *Quintale* of 100 *Rotoli*		= 79.378714 kg

Wine

1 *Barile*[22]	= 4 *Quartare*	= 42.570000 litres
1 *Quartara*	= 9½ *Quartucci*	= 10.642500 litres
1 *Quartuccio*	= 2 *Pinte*	= 1.120263 litres
1 *Pinta*		= 0.560132 litres

Weights[23]

1 *Cantaro*	= 100 *Rotoli*	= 79.378714 kg
1 *Rotolo*	= 2.5 *Libbre* (30 once)	= 0.793787 kg
1 *Libbra*	= 12 *Once*	= 0.317515 kg
1 *Oncia*		= 0.026460 kg

Measures of length[24]

1 *canna* (for cloth)	= 8 *palme*	= 2.090038 metre

20 The Maltese system of liquid measure was rather complicated; oil, vinegar, wine and honey were measured by respective *quartuccio,* the fundamental unit of measurement used in this system. Vassallo, 'Prices of Commodities', 38–49.

21 All measures and their equivalents quoted from Martini, *Manuale di metrologia,* 810–11.

22 The *barile* was both a measure of standard capacity and a container having a barrel shape. 'A decree issued on many occasions during the sixteenth century ordered that every "*barile*" of wine had to be measured and a sign showing its capacity in *quartari* or in *quartucci* had to be put on it.' Vassallo, 'Prices of Commodities', 45–6. Refer to NLM, Univ. 14, fol. 742 (7.ix.1588).

23 All weights and their equivalents quoted from Martini, *Manuale di metrologia,* 810–11.

24 Martini, *Manuale di metrologia,* 810.

Map 1: The Maltese Islands c.1565

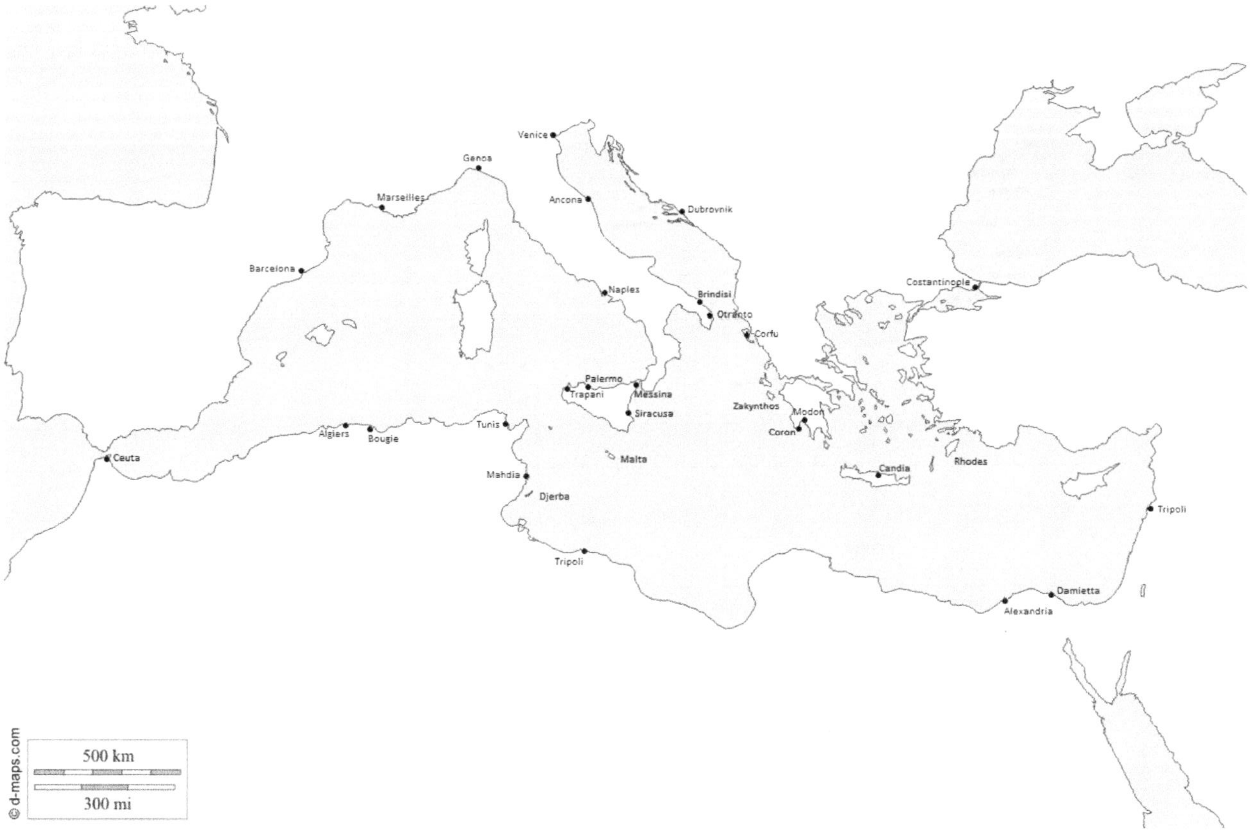

Map 2: The Mediterranean Area

Introduction

Malta and the Mediterranean context

The sixteenth century is a period of transition in European history, characterised by changes on the economic, social, religious and political level. In the long run, these changes disintegrated the old medieval order and challenged traditional and established ways of thought and action. Although Malta was slow to shed its medieval character, events in the wider European context did ultimately affect the island's society. Among other things, the century witnessed the further westward reach of the Ottoman empire and its establishment as a Mediterranean power.[1] Another significant change was the Italian maritime republics' loss of primacy and the demise of the Hanseatic League,[2] creating a void that was filled by the Habsburg–Ottoman struggle for supremacy in the central Mediterranean[3] and the rise of new economic powers like England.[4] The sixteenth century was also marked by the Habsburg–Valois rivalry,[5] which intensified as a consequence of close Franco-Ottoman relations.[6]

The spread of the Reformation to western and eastern Europe[7] saw religious orders such as the Knights Hospitaller lose substantial income from their estates.[8] An event

1 M. Kunt & C. Woodhead (eds), *Süleyman the Magnificent and His Age* (London and New York, 1995).

2 M. Ressel, 'The Hanseatics in Southern Europe: Structure and Payment of German Long-Distance Shipping, 1630–1700', in M. Fusaro, B. Allaire, R. J. Blakemore & T. Vanneste (eds), *Law, Labour and Empire: Comparative Perspectives on Seafarers, c. 1500–1800* (Basingstoke, 2015), 141–57: 143.

3 D. Abulafia, *The Great Sea: A Human History of the Mediterranean* (London, 2011), 411–13. M. Green, 'Resurgent Islam: 1500 – 1700', in D. Abulafia (ed.), *The Mediterranean in History* (2003), 219–49: 235–6. Kunt & Woodhead (eds), *Süleyman the Magnificent.*

4 M. Fusaro, *Political Economies of Empire in the Early Modern Mediterranean: The Decline of Venice and the Rise of England 1450–1700* (Cambridge, 2015).

5 H. G. Koenigsberger, G. L. Mosse & G. Q. Bowler, *Europe in the Sixteenth Century* (2nd edn, London and New York, 1992), 233–9. Green, 'Resurgent Islam', in Abulafia (ed.), *The Mediterranean in History*, 219–49: 220.

6 Abulafia, *The Great Sea*, 420–3. F. Braudel, *The Mediterranean and the Mediterranean World in the Age of Philip II* (2 vols, trans. S. Reynolds, Berkeley, Los Angeles and London, 1995), vol. 2, 921. J. F. Guilmartin Jr., *Gunpowder and Galleys – Changing Technology and Mediterranean Warfare at Sea in the Sixteenth Century* (London, 1974), 124.

7 Koenigsberger et al., *Europe in the Sixteenth Century*, 181.

8 As happened to the Order's property in Portugal, Naples and Savoy, amongst other places.

which greatly affected Malta in subsequent years was Süleyman the Magnificent's conquest of Rhodes from the Hospitaller Order of St John in 1522. For almost eight years after this loss the Knights[9] wandered from port to port, at the mercy of their various hosts.[10] They were in desperate need of a territory to rule and a base where they could consolidate and centralise not only their activities against the Muslim enemy but also communication between the conventual authority and the Order's priories. Resolving these issues was critical if they were to confirm their significance in the Christian world. The Knights were experiencing a 'crisis of identity' and thus, notwithstanding certain difficulties which will be examined in the next chapter, they viewed the possession of Malta as a positive step towards regaining their *raison d'être*.[11] Not only was the island viewed as a frontier base, due to its proximity to Muslim territory, but its superb harbours would make it an excellent base for the Knights' naval activities. The continuation of Holy War from this base would do justice to the constant flow of revenues from the Knights' commanderies across Europe.

However, in receiving the island as a fief from the Holy Roman Emperor Charles V (r. 1519–56), the Order became obliged to pay homage to the king of Spain. The Hospitallers were keen to promote their neutral status, due to their heavy dependence on the benevolent actions of European kings, and knew that they must tread very carefully in their diplomatic relations. This was especially so in the case of the king of France, from whose domains they derived most of their income.[12] In a complex scenario of political struggle, Malta's strategic location on the central axis of the Mediterranean and the use of its first-class harbours by the Spanish navy[13] propelled the island into significance within the wider Mediterranean context.[14]

As will be discussed at length in Chapter One, since 1428 Malta had enjoyed the right to direct royal government by the Aragonese crown, a privilege enshrined in King Alfonso's (r. 1416–58) charter of 20 June 1428.[15] The charter, later known

9 Throughout this book, when the word 'knights' is used on its own it refers to the Knights of the Hospitaller Order of St John.

10 V. Mallia-Milanes, 'A Trial of Hospitaller Strength: From Rhodes to Malta via Nice and Villefranche, 1523–1530', in G. Salvatore (ed.), *La Navigation du Savoir: Réseau des arsenaux historiques de la Méditerranée. Actes du Colloque: Premières journées internationals du patrimoine maritime méditerranéen, 27 au 30 mars 2003, Villefranche-sur-Mer* (Nice, 2006), 73–81; V. Mallia-Milanes, 'A Pilgrimage of Faith, War, and Charity: The Order of the Hospital from Jerusalem to Malta', in J. Carvalho (ed.), *Religion, Ritual and Mythology: Aspects of Identity Formation in Europe* (Pisa, 2006), 83–96.

11 V. Mallia-Milanes, 'La donazione di Malta da parte di Carlo V all'Ordine di S. Giovanni', in B. Anatra & F. Manconi (eds), *Sardegna, Spagna e Stati Italiani nell'Età di Carlo V* (Urbino, 2001), 137–48.

12 A. Williams, '*Sacra Militia*, the Order of St John: Crusade, Corsairing and Trade in Rhodes and Malta 1460–1631', in Fusaro et al., *Trade and Cultural Exchange*, 139–56: 150.

13 F. Braudel, *The Mediterranean*, vol. 2, 850.

14 Braudel's assessment is that the coast of Naples and Sicily, together with Malta, were 'Italy's maritime front against the Turks'. Braudel, *The Mediterranean,* vol. 2, 849.

15 Similar privileges had already been bestowed on the islands. These were a renewal of Martin I's pledge of 1397 that the islands would always be regarded as part of the royal *demanio*. C. Dalli, *Malta, The Medieval Millennium* (Malta, 2006), 211, 215, 248–9.

as *'Magna Carta Libertatis'*, was a milestone in the islands' political relationship with the Aragonese crown. While welcoming the islands into his *demanio*, King Alfonso 'guaranteed the population the right to resist with force (*manu forti*) any future enfeoffment'.[16] In fact, in later years, reports of the islands' enfeoffment were strongly resisted by the local community and regarded as a serious violation of the island's liberty and privileges.[17] From 1429 to 1530 the islands were administered by a relatively stable municipal government presided over by the royal captain, known as the *Ħakem*, and centred on an administrative team of four *jurats* (magistrates) who were elected annually and assisted by an inner circle of town councillors and municipal employees.[18]

On 10 April 1524 a meeting of the members of the islands' municipal council discussed reports that Charles V had donated the Maltese islands to the Order of St John of Jerusalem. The members of the *Università* (municipal town council) also discussed what measures should be adopted if the enfeoffment should materialise. Six years later, on 23 March 1530, the emperor and his mother, Joan, issued a charter at Castel Franco wherein Malta, Gozo and the North African enclave of Tripoli were given as a free fief to the Knights of St John.[19] The next chapter will consider the possible reasons why no signs of rebellion were recorded on the Order's arrival in the islands. However, the Ottomans' renewed advance in the Mediterranean and regular raids targeted at the poorly guarded islands by both Muslim[20] and Christian enemies of Aragon[21] must have influenced the local population to welcome their new masters with friendship rather than aggression.[22] The welcoming attitude can also to be attributed to the Order's promise to honour the privileges and liberties which the Maltese already enjoyed. Later, these were to be continually breached.

Despite the cession of Malta to the Knights of St John, politically and economically it remained closely connected to Sicily, since the presence of the military Order

16 Dalli, *Malta, The Medieval Millennium*, 211.

17 An episode which is included in the records of the municipal council dated 20 July 1450 refers to rumours that King Alphonso gave the Maltese islands to the Order of Montesa (founded in 1316 after the dissolution of the Templars), who were faithful servants of the crown of Aragon. During this meeting the majority of council members agreed that these knights should be expelled by force (*expellantur per vim*). C. Dalli, *Iż-Żmien Nofsani Malti* (Malta, 2002), 198–9.

18 For a more detailed analysis of the functions of the municipal council refer to Dalli, *Malta, The Medieval Millennium*, 217–24.

19 NLM, AOM 70. In acknowledgement of this fief the Order was commanded to deliver a falcon to the Viceroy of Sicily once a year on All Saints' Day.

20 Similar to the Hafsid invasion of September 1429, when the invaders numbered 18,000 troops aboard seventy galleys. According to one source, this raid cost 3,500 inhabitants their freedom. This figure rises to 4,500 in a report reaching Venice in October (more than one third of the population), Dalli, *Iż-Żmien Nofsani*, 175; Dalli, *Malta, The Medieval Millennium*, 235–6; and the Ottoman sack of the *Borgo* in 1488, Dalli, *Malta, The Medieval Millennium*, 240.

21 Such as the Genoese raids of the 1440s. Dalli, *Malta, The Medieval Millennium*, 232.

22 According to Braudel, the dilapidated state of most coastal and inland fortresses and fortifications in Naples and Sicily was a usual sight by the beginning of the sixteenth century, and only occasionally would there be a provision for modernisation. Braudel, *The Mediterranean*, vol. 2, 850.

suited the expansionist ambitions of the viceroys of Spanish Sicily in North Africa.[23] Grand expeditions like those of Tripoli in 1560 were primarily undertaken through the initiative of the Viceroy of Sicily, rather than that of the king of Spin.[24] As is discussed in Chapter Four, apart from joining other Christian forces, the Order was a constant nuisance to the Ottomans, since it not only attacked corsair allies of the Ottomans but also posed a constant threat to Muslim shipping routes and commerce.[25] Thus, with the establishment of the Knights Hospitaller as 'border warriors', the Maltese islanders faced two opposing realities: while they benefitted from the direct rule of the Order, who sought to enhance the island's defence, at the same time the Order's unrelenting excursions against the Ottoman fleet made Malta a prime target for Ottoman vengeance. The dramatic repulsion of the Ottomans from Malta in the siege of 1565 vindicated the Knights' losses of Rhodes in 1522 and Tripoli in 1551.[26] It was also indispensable in justifying the Order's presence in the Mediterranean, in view of Ottoman imperial designs.

The post-siege period witnessed a massive infrastructural programme that included the building of a new fortified city, Valletta. To a large extent this was made possible by the continuous flow of revenue from the Order's European priories. By the end of the sixteenth century the urban population of the island had increased considerably.[27] The harbour towns attracted people not only because of the protection offered by their fortified bastion walls but also on account of their dynamism in generating multiple commercial activities – which are well documented even in the pre-siege period in the harbour town of Birgu.[28]

The establishment of the Order of St John on the island thus brought in its wake new social and economic values, not only through the various reforms embedded in new statutes and ordinances, but also through new exigencies on the part of the Knights. Their requirements reflected their high social standing and conspicuous consumption and played a significant role in bringing an entirely different way

23 For a more detailed exposition of these ambitions up to 1525 see C. Trasselli, *Da Ferdinando il Cattolico a Carlo V: L'esperienza siciliana 1475–1525* (2 vols, Soveria Mannelli, CZ, 1982), vol. 1, 205–36.

24 Braudel, *The Mediterranean*, vol. 2, 854–65.

25 For a discussion on the definition, legal distinction and use of the terms 'corsair', 'privateer' and 'pirate' see N. A. M. Rodger, 'The Law and Language of Private Naval Warfare', *Mariner's Mirror*, 100:1 (February 2014), 5–16.

26 The 1551 Ottoman landing in Malta was not a great success: Turgut Reis the renowned and feared Ottoman corsair, found Gozo to be relatively easy prey. The latter was so ill-defended that the Ottomans managed to capture easily about five thousand inhabitants who were taken away as slaves. Afterwards, the Ottomans proceeded on their journey and succeeded in capturing the fortress of Tripoli.

27 V. Borg, 'Birgu: A Demographic Overview 1558–1658' (BA Hons dissertation, University of Malta, 1999); S. Fiorini, 'Demographic Growth and the Urbanization of the Maltese Countryside to 1798', in V. Mallia-Milanes (ed.), *Hospitaller Malta 1530–1798: Studies on Early Modern Malta and the Order of St John of Jerusalem* (Malta, 1993), 297–310; S. Fiorini, 'Demographical Aspects of Birgu up to 1800', in L. Bugeja, M. Buhagiar & S. Fiorini (eds), *Birgu: A Maltese Maritime City* (Malta, 1993), 219–54.

28 J. Abela, 'Port Activities in Mid-Sixteenth Century Malta' (MA dissertation, University of Malta, 2007).

of life to the island. As will be argued, the expansion of Malta's trade links was a direct result of the Order's establishment on the island, which led to the setting up of stronger commercial networks between Malta and neighbouring countries. Attractive trade opportunities brought together individuals and entrepreneurs acting in different locations to take advantage of Malta's ideal location in the central axis of the Mediterranean.

Does Mediterranean historiography reflect Maltese trends in economic performance?

That the Mediterranean region has been a favourite focus of study for many historians is reflected in the huge amount of literature covering the region's history from antiquity to contemporary times. The main historical themes of the Mediterranean, such as the geography and connectivity or otherwise of the region, and the impact of trade on cultural barriers, have been the focus of much debate. The aim of the following discussion is to place the questions raised in this book in the context of other debates and to highlight both the contribution which studies such as this can bring to historical enquiry and also their limitations.

Braudel's seminal study on the Mediterranean triggered intellectual debates which spread rapidly and involved several disciplines in the humanities and social sciences.[29] Reassessing Mediterranean history after Braudel's work, Maria Fusaro states that recent studies on early modern trade have shown it 'to be much more complex than has been acknowledged either by Braudel himself, or by traditional economic historiography'.[30] The almost invisible line which separated aggressive corsairing expeditions from commercial navigation is one aspect of this complexity which has only recently started to be analysed and evaluated. The present study strives to reassess not only the economic realities of Malta, but also how they can be used to decipher the daily lives of sixteenth-century Mediterranean traders and seafarers in general: their aspirations, their successes and their failures. The Maltese islands are an ideal case study, because a wealth of legal and administrative documentary sources provide an unparalleled portrait of the interplay between corsairing and trade. These documents also shed light on a variety of agreements and show how, at times, merchants, traders and money lenders from across the Mediterranean sought to circumvent the law in order to be sure of making a profit. Concern to find trading allies as near as North Africa and as far away as the Levant also compelled the Knights Hospitaller to make full use of the existing links of the Rhodiot community and of Muslim captives and merchants. The impact of institutional change on the Maltese economy, and how this affected its wider maritime trading zone, also needs to be assessed. In spite of the island's lack of essential resources, the establishment of a strong naval power that sought to make maximum use of Malta's excellent

[29] M. Fusaro, 'After Braudel: A Reassessment of Mediterranean History between the Northern Invasion and the *Caravane Maritime*', in Fusaro et al., *Trade and Cultural Exchange*, 1–22: 1.

[30] Fusaro, 'After Braudel', in Fusaro et al., *Trade and Cultural Exchange*, 1–22: 5.

harbours and strategic position provided the necessary impetus for commerce to grow in an unprecedented way.

Braudel's hypothesis of slow and almost static growth in the economy of sixteenth-century Mediterranean islands has not hitherto been tested in Maltese historiography. However, Stephan Epstein tackled this subject with regard to late medieval Sicily, which, although a fertile and much larger island than Malta, was still considered to be highly underdeveloped.[31] Traditionally, it was suggested that Sicily's underdevelopment was mainly due to 'landlord absenteeism, low investment, lack of innovation, and peasant poverty and exploitation'.[32] Braudel and Bresc[33] suggested that Sicilian agricultural workers pursued subsistence strategies that made them heavily dependent on foreign trade and that this explained the quasi-static pace of economic development.[34] Epstein dismissed this interpretation and instead suggested that although the peasants used seemingly 'archaic' tools such as oxen and scratch ploughs, 'yield ratios in Sicily up to the eighteenth century seem to have been equivalent or higher than in the most advanced northern European countries'.[35] Epstein argued further that Sicilian economic development during the late Middle Ages and early modern period was largely shaped by regional political and institutional structures which regulated access to markets. As institutions changed, so they brought about change in economic policies that ultimately affected the long-term economic development of that particular society.[36] Agricultural workers adopted what Epstein refers to as strategies of regional integration and specialisation which made them more commercialised. By such means, the production of high-value-added agricultural products such as silk, and to a lesser extent sugar, was intensified. Ultimately, this was economically rewarding and supported a much more export-oriented economy.

Does Epstein's theory hold true for the Maltese context? As is discussed in Chapter

31 See also G. Federuci & P. Malanima, 'Progress, Decline, Growth: Product and Productivity in Italian Agriculture, 1000–2000', *Economic History Review*, 57:3 (2004), 427–64; P. Malanima, 'Urbanization and the Italian Economy during the Last Millenium', *European Review of Economic History*, 9 (2005), 97–122; P. Malanima, 'The Italian Renaissance Economy (1260–1500)', International Conference at Villa La Pietra, Florence, May 2008, http://www.paolomalanima.it/default_file/Papers/RENAISSANCE_ITALY.pdf (accessed 8 August 2016); G. Alfani & S. Sardone, 'Long Term Trends in Economic Inequality in Southern Italy. The Kingdom of Napes and Sicily in the 16th–18th Centuries: First Results', http://eh.net/eha/wp-content/uploads/2015/05/Alfani.pdf (accessed 9 August 2016).

32 S. R. Epstein, *An Island for Itself – Economic Development and Social Change in Late Medieval Sicily* (Cambridge, 1992), 163.

33 H. Bresc, 'Reti di scambio locale e interregional nell'Italia dell'alto Medioevo', in R. Romano & U. T. Tucci (eds), *Storia d'Italia*, Annali, 6, 135–78; Epstein, *An Island for Itself*, 162.

34 Refer to Epstein, *An Island for Itself*, 1–24, for a treatment of the historiography and sources relating to Italy's *questione meridionale*. This refers to theory that 'the economy of southern Italy or *Mezzogiorno*-which includes Sicily and Sardinia and borders on central Tuscany to the north was permanently overtaken by that of central and northern Italy at some point during the High or Late Middle Ages'. Epstein, *An Island for Itself*, 1.

35 Epstein, *An Island for Itself*, 163.

36 Epstein, *An Island for Itself*, 1, 95, 162–8.

Two, medieval and early modern Malta had an agrarian-based economy which was highly dependent on foreign imports.[37] A striking difference between the Sicilian and Maltese peasants was that, unlike their Sicilian counterparts, the Maltese usually owned some land, even if a limited area, and were greatly disinclined to alienate their property outright.[38] Their ownership of freehold land placed Maltese peasants in a superior position to those of Sicily, where absolute ownership of property was limited.[39] In Malta, just as in Sicily, tax exemptions on the import of various staple foods such as wheat and wine, granted by the Spanish monarchs since medieval times, encouraged landholders to invest in the production of niche goods for foreign markets. These included such products as cotton and cumin, which required less land to cultivate than wheat, and which brought in better financial rewards. As a direct result of this specialisation the local wheat production diminished, thereby appearing to expose the island to a precarious life. However, as will be explained, this insufficiency must be evaluated in relation the local producers' choice to grow high-value products.

Although Epstein's theory of the Sicilian economy does not fully fit the Maltese picture, there are many similarities between the two economies. As noted above, the Sicilian preference for producing specialised goods took hold in Malta in the late Middle Ages and made Maltese farmers not only more export oriented but also more dependent on Sicilian grain imports. As in Sicily, the socio-institutional and organisational context played a relatively major role in the economic development of the island. While Malta had a high level of peasant landownership, as compared to limited peasant smallholding in Sicily,[40] from the late thirteenth century fiefs in Sicily 'began to be parcelled out as farms (*masserie*) of fifteen to forty hectares ... the size of the *masserie* seems to have been the result of bargaining between the landlord and the *massaro* based on criteria of commercial profitability'.[41] Likewise in Malta, the leasing out of parcels of land by the landowner, referred to in notarial documents as *cabella*, *incabellacio* or *gabella*, was common from medieval times.[42]

37 Here again Epstein argues that although agriculture is always assumed to be less productive than manufacturing, there are in actual fact no '*a priori* reasons for deciding whether this is the case, or even whether agriculture will be more or less capital-intensive than manufacturing at a particular level of technological development'. Epstein, *An Island for Itself*, 8.

38 G. Wettinger, 'Agriculture in Malta in the Late Middle Ages', in M. Buhagiar (ed.), *Proceedings of History Week, 1981* (Malta, 1982), 1–48: 6–7.

39 Epstein, *An Island for Itself*, 282.

40 In Sicily large proportions of arable land were under feudal lordship; however, Epstein states that 'with the law *Volentes*, promulgated by Federico III in 1296, which legalized the sale of whole fiefs to individuals of "equal or greater dignity" than the seller ... particularly from the mid-fourteenth century, and increasing during the fifteenth – [the effect of this law] was to accelerate the circulation and fragmentation of "feudal" land, at first only among the aristocracy, but increasing also among urban nobility, merchants and high government officials'. Epstein, *An Island for Itself*, 165.

41 Epstein, *An Island for Itself*, 165–6.

42 S. Fiorini (ed.), *Documentary Sources of Maltese History, Part I: Notarial Documents, No. 3: Notary Paulo Bonello MS. 588: 1467–1517 and Notary Giacomo Zabbara MS. 1132: 1471–1500* (Malta, 2005), Docs 1–2, 7, 13, 91, 98, 102, 132, 150, 168, 175, 188, 193, 202, 206.

Thus, in both islands the structure of property rights in land made it possible for land to be parcelled out and managed in a way which did not pose an obstacle to agricultural development.[43]

As in the Sicilian context, a credit system by which a lender advanced working capital, including farm animals and cash,[44] was already established in Malta before the coming of the Knights.[45] The system is defined by Epstein as one in which 'merchants advanced capital to producers, which was repaid with grain at a price (the *meta*) agreed upon after the following harvest; the *meta* embodies the rate of interest'.[46] Maltese notarial acts for the period of this study are more abundant than those for the medieval period, and they frequently document the importance of petty transactions where small amounts of cotton, cumin and wheat were traded for cash advances. At times, such agreements were entered into well before harvest time, thus suggesting that the advances helped to stimulate the economy and ensure that the farmer was provided with the necessary working capital.

David Abulafia's recent study on the Mediterranean deals more with the sea and the littoral communities that established themselves around its rim. As he writes, 'my "Mediterranean" is resolutely the surface of the sea itself, its shores and its islands, particularly the port cities that provided the main departure and arrival points for those crossing it'.[47] Islands whose inhabitants looked outward have a special mention in his history, and it is for this reason, he states, that the Maltese feature more prominently than the Corsicans.[48] But can a study of trading activities taking place in Malta during the sixteenth century shed light on supposed larger inter-group relationships in the Mediterranean? Can it provide an explanation as to how different religions and cultures traded successfully?

Maltese private and public records, such as notarial acts and chancery documents, provide historians with a good representation of both Christian and Muslim traders criss-crossing the Mediterranean. Through the issuing of official permits such as safe conducts, the government played a central role in reducing uncertainty and helping to foster trade links.[49] These documentary traces also allow for the examination of specific informal networks that infiltrated markets which were outside their geographical, political or cultural area. Francesca Trivellato explains how a recent historiographical trend has looked at the way in which 'economic exchanges occur in the absence of violence, institutional coercion or a common legal system. Using game theory and rational theory models, its advocates explain good conduct in business as a result

43 Epstein, *An Island for Itself*, 165–6.
44 Epstein, *An Island for Itself*, 166.
45 Fiorini (ed.), *Documentary Sources of Maltese History, Part I: No. 3,* Docs 13, 19–21, 24, 31, 32, 44, 47, 55, 57, 65, 66, 77, 78, 86, 88, 114, 138, 139, 201.
46 Epstein, *An Island for Itself*, 167.
47 Abulafia, *The Great Sea*, xvii.
48 Abulafia, *The Great Sea*, xxiv.
49 This same procedure was adopted by the Ottomans for foreign merchants or visitors, since these had to obtain a special authorisation or safe conduct from the sultan or local *kadi*. Islamic law permitted the enslavement of a non-Muslim foreigner who did not qualify for capitulation guarantees. H. İnalcik & D. Quataert (eds), *An Economic and Social History of the Ottoman Empire 1300–1914* (Cambridge, 1994), 193–4.

of informal elements (such as friendship, reputation, information flow, and shared beliefs) that induce self-interested individuals to commit themselves to honesty.'[50] Trivellato further suggests that 'the pursuit of economic gain was inseparable from the development of a common logic'.[51] The study of Malta's first few decades under the Knights Hospitaller makes such a study even more interesting, since to the local entrepreneurial community was added the Greek community of merchants. While serving the Order in Rhodes, these merchants had already benefitted from strong links with traders in the Levant and beyond. This issue is of great importance if one is to understand how both Muslim and Christian merchants sought to exploit each other's markets. It also highlights the need for trustworthy merchants who, even in the absence of legal constraints, could deal with foreign merchants, especially those from across the geographical, religious and cultural divides.

Political change and its impact on commercial activities

The study of specific islands of the Mediterranean can be used for comparative purposes to give a broader overview of commercial and political developments on this enclosed sea. In *A Mediterranean Emporium: The Catalan Kingdom of Majorca*, David Abulafia explores the Mediterranean kingdom of Majorca, which was established by James I the Conqueror (r. 1213–76) in 1276.[52] Abulafia offers important insights into the Christian–Muslim conflict and its impact on European expansion on the Atlantic and North African coasts. He also discusses how the Catalans contributed to this commercial and political expansion through their technical knowledge, especially the use of portolan charts and atlases.[53] Abulafia shows how the establishment of a strong political power, coupled with the commercial activities of both local and foreign seafarers in a specific region, greatly motivated and enhanced trade within the region and contributed to the strengthening of commercial relations, as I will argue happened in Malta's case. This was especially so because the 'international standing'[54] of a particular place could be enhanced through already-established links which the ruling body enjoyed with foreign countries.

Another striking similarity between the two Mediterranean islands of Majorca and Malta is the way in which the inhabitants of both, especially the trading community, may have viewed a change of ruler. The inhabitants of Majorca,

50 F. Trivellato, 'Jews of Leghorn, Italians of Lisbon, and Hindus of Goa: Merchant Networks and Cross-Cultural Trade in the Early Modern Period', in D. R. Curto & A. Molho (eds), *Commercial Networks in the Early Modern World* (European University Institute, Florence, 2002), 59–89: 63.

51 Trivellato, 'Jews of Leghorn, Italians of Lisbon, and Hindus of Goa', in Curto & Molho (eds), *Commercial Networks*, 59–89: 65.

52 D. Abulafia, *A Mediterranean Emporium: The Catalan Kingdom of Majorca* (Cambridge, 1994). This kingdom included the Balearics, Montpellier and other Catalan domains mostly east of the Pyrenees.

53 Abulafia, *A Mediterranean Emporium*, 12.

54 Abulafia, *A Mediterranean Emporium*, 75.

especially the Catalan population, perceived the change[55] as a means to better their trading prospects. This book proposes that one of the reasons for the peaceful establishment of the Knights Hospitaller in Malta may have been the support of the established merchants who, until the Order's arrival, had been prevented from holding key administrative positions. Just as in Malta's case, Majorca could not have survived without trade, due to its heavy dependence on supplies such as grain from Sicily. Soon after the conquest of Majorca both popes Gregory IX and Innocent IV granted the island's Christians special privileges to trade with the Muslims in North Africa.[56] Such concessions were not unique and where occasionally granted to various Catholic rulers.[57] As we shall see in Chapter Four, the Knights had enjoyed similar concessions while in Rhodes, and even before their establishment in Malta they petitioned the Holy See to grant them permission to trade with Muslims, due to the island's insufficient resources.[58]

The ideal geographical positions of both islands, facing the Muslim world, turned them into important centres of the international slave trade, with many slaves and captives[59] passing through the islands in transit to other European countries, the Levant or North Africa. The islands thus acted as clearing houses for the slave trade and the profitable business of ransoming captives.[60]

55 That is, from that of the James II, King of Majorca to Peter the Great of Aragon.

56 Abulafia, *A Mediterranean Emporium*, 14.

57 See for example Pope Innocent III's licence to Venice to trade with the Saracens in 1198 in J. P. Migne (ed.), *Patrologiae Cursus Completus* (Paris, 1855), vol. 214, 493, reprinted in R. C. Cave & H. H. Coulson, *A Source Book for Medieval Economic History* (Milwaukee, 1936, reprint edn, New York, 1965), 104–5. See also F. C. Lane, 'The Venetian Galleys to Alexandria, 1344', in B. G. Kohl & R. C. Mueller (eds), *Studies in Venetian Social and Economic History* (London, 1987), paper XII: 431–40.

58 S. Paoli, *Codice Diplomatico del Sacro Militare Ordine Gerosolimitano, oggi di Malta* (2 vols, Lucca, 1737), 201–2.

59 Fontenay insists that one needs to differentiate between the terms 'captives' and 'slaves' since the former had an exchange value, while slaves had a use value. The majority of captives were bought with the intent of making a good investment, while slaves were bought to reap the fruits of their labour. According to Fontenay one thus needs to distinguish between Christian or Muslim slaves who sought to redeem themselves and 'black' African slaves who were acquired from the sub-Sahara and who lived in shackles, without hope of ever being ransomed. M. Fontenay, 'Esclaves et/ou captives: préciser le concepts', in W. Kaiser (ed.), *Le commerce de captives: les intermediaries dans l'*échange *et le rachat des prisonniers en Méditerranée, XVe–XVIIIe siècle* (Rome, 2008), 15–24. Fontenay's argument has been criticised in that not all Christian and Muslim slaves were eventually ransomed (in fact the majority died in slavery) and contemporary writers used both terms interchangeably in their sources. D. B. Hershenzon, 'Early Modern Spain and the Creation of the Mediterranean: Captivity, Commerce, and Knowledge' (PhD thesis, University of Michigan, 2011), 25, http://deepblue.lib.umich.edu/bitstream/2027.42/89664/1/hershenz_1.pdf (accessed 5 April 2015). Salvatore Bono, on the other hand, has argued that only those slaves who were eventually ransomed could be termed as 'captives', and this distinction could be made only after the actual ransom had taken place. S. Bono, 'Slave Histories and Memoirs in the Mediterranean World: A Study of the Sources (Sixteenth-Eighteenth Centuries)', in Fusaro et al., *Trade and Cultural Exchange*, 97–115: 100.

60 Abulafia, *A Mediterranean Emporium*, 15.

A main argument of this study suggests that, contrary to the prevailing historical interpretation that it was only in the late sixteenth century that Malta underwent a boom in its commercial activities, the arrival of the Knights Hospitaller immediately boosted the island's trading power in the Mediterranean. Malta's trading community, which was already established prior to the Order's arrival, was small but prosperous, and ready to grasp new opportunities for growth. New prospects in turn enhanced the relationship between the commercial economy of Malta and those of other Mediterranean territories. Existing links with Sicily were strengthened, since they were essential to establishing important links with Ottoman lands and merchants as far as the Levant. The Knights brought over to Malta and cultivated a business relationship which had been tested and adopted while they were stationed in Rhodes. They made use of Greek merchants who often spoke Arabic and Turkish and served as mediators. The knowledge, skills and market intelligence of these merchants facilitated trading negotiations. Although Sicily remained the main provider of the island, other markets were sought to cater for the great increase in demand for various commodities, both essential and luxury. Therefore this book considers not only trading patterns within Malta but also the changing functions of the Maltese islands within the wider Mediterranean trading community, and how they performed in what was considered a hostile sea. In order to assess this significant change in the Maltese commercial economy, the book examines trading patterns through the surviving documents of the merchants themselves, especially commercial contracts. This approach steps back from Maltese-centred historiographical traditions and places the island's trade within the wider commercial picture of the first half of the sixteenth century.

Ottoman–Christian connectivity throughout the Mediterranean

During the thirteenth century the Byzantine empire lost all of its overseas territories, to the benefit of the Italian city-states of Venice and Genoa, on which they became economically dependent. The Latins, in turn, benefitted from a variety of incentives, including full exemption from tariffs, and monopolised the trade in foodstuffs and raw material from the Black Sea to the communes of Italy.[61] Exploitation of the indigenous people by their Catholic Latin feudal masters, and shortages of wheat, often led to insurrections by the common people, who were led by the Orthodox clergy. With the advent of Ottoman rule in the former Byzantine territories a general policy was established which aimed to abolish rights of sovereignty over the territories which had belonged to pre-Ottoman states and to deal with the colonies in accordance with Islamic rules for non-Muslim subjects or foreigners under capitulatory amnesty.[62] After Constantinople's conquest by the Ottomans in 1453, rigid measures to control merchant traffic between the Mediterranean and the Black Sea were put in place. Elizabeth Zachariadou showed how, in the middle of

61 İnalcik & Quataert (eds), *An Economic and Social History of the Ottoman Empire*, 271–2.
62 İnalcik & Quataert (eds), *An Economic and Social History of the Ottoman Empire*, 272–4.

the fifteenth century, when Rhodes was under Hospitaller rule, the Greek Orthodox monks of Patmos[63] (who were Ottoman subjects) maintained good relations with the Hospitallers.[64] She further explained that the dual protection which these monks enjoyed benefitted both Muslims and Christians in trading matters, and even for espionage purposes. Zachariadou discussed how, at times, *firmans*[65] obtained by the Greek monks to buy grain from Ottoman territory also involved spying activities on the movement of the Turkish forces. This is attested in several letters written by the abbot of Patmos to the Venetians during the Ottoman siege of Rhodes. In fact, after visiting the Ottoman sultan's camp in Rhodes and obtaining from him a *firman* to buy grain from Menteşe,[66] the abbot supplied the Venetians with various information regarding the movement of the Ottoman fleet. These monks also established similar relations with the Ottoman Turks, and by this means, in Zachariadou's words, 'Patmos got the best of the three worlds: Muslim, the Roman Catholic and the Greek Orthodox'.[67]

Emphasising the need for good links even with enemy territory, Chapter Four shows how existing business links between Rhodiots and foreigners were exploited by the Knights Hospitaller once they became established in Malta. Similar to what had happened on Rhodes, the Order aimed not simply to extend the island's trading zone, but also to spy on the enemy. The local Maltese population also tried to exploit all possible links and get the best out of the three worlds – Muslim, Roman Catholic and Greek Orthodox.

Christian and Muslim captives and merchants acted as mediators who circulated information about the enemy through their ransoming activities. Until a decade ago very few histories focused on ransom procedures and their role in the Mediterranean economy.[68] A fresh perspective was presented by Wolfgang Kaiser, who redefined redemption processes and classified them as forming an economy of ransom.[69]

63 Patmos is a Dodecanese island in the south-eastern Aegean Sea, off the coast of Asia Minor, having an area of $34.05km^2$.

64 E. Zachariadou, 'Monks and Sailors under the Ottoman Sultans', *Oriente Moderno*, new series, 81:1, 'The Ottomans and the Sea' (2001), 139–47: 144.

65 A royal edict or adminstrative order.

66 This was a Turkish beylik on the Aegean coast, revived after the Ottoman defeat by Timur in 1402. It was also an important Turkish trading state. See K. Fleet, 'Turks, Mamluks, and Latin Merchants: Commerce, Conflict, and Cooperation in the Eastern Mediterranean', in J. Harris, C. Holmes & E. Russell (eds), *Byzantines, Latins, and Turks in the Eastern Mediterranean World after 1150* (Oxford, 2012), 327–44: 330–1.

67 Zachariadou, 'Monks and Sailors under the Ottoman Sultans', 145.

68 These include *Annales* historians like J. Mathiex, 'Trafic et Prix de l'Homme en Méditerranée aux XVII° et XVIII° Siècles', *Annales*, ESC, 9 (1954), 157–64; L. Valensi, 'Esclaves Chrétiens et Esclaves Noirs à Tunis au XVII° Siècle', *Annales*, ESC, 9 (1967), 1267–88, who tackled Christian slavery in North Africa from an economic perspective by looking at prices, markets and profits. More recently, historians like Ellen Friedman analysed the activities of religious orders who were commissioned to carry out ransom procedures in the Maghrib. E. G. Friedman, *Spanish Captives in North Africa in the Early Modern Ages* (Madison, WI, 1983). The most comprehensive work to date is that by R. C. Davis, *Christian Slaves, Muslim Masters: White Slavery in the Mediterranean, the Barbary Coast, and Italy, 1500–1800* (New York, 2003).

69 W. Kaiser & G. Calafat, 'The Economy of Ransoming in the Early Modern Mediter-

This was fuelled by another important maritime phenomenon in Mediterranean countries – the *corso*.[70] Kaiser argues that the regulation of corsairing activities and the subsequent ransoming processes provided a means for rationalising trade with the 'enemy'. Following this line of thought, this book explores how ransom intermediaries interacted with institutions which in turn tried to regulate their activities through the issue of safe passages. Such practices helped to weave a web of connectivity throughout the Ottoman–Christian Mediterranean and shape the economic policies of both religions. This book shows how the ransoming of Christian and Muslim captives were not always separate processes, independent from each other. At times ransom expeditions were combined to fully exploit a round-trip voyage, taking 'home' redeemed 'infidel' captives and returning with Christian ones on the homeward journey. Thus a complicated process of negotiation took place which required mutual co-operation between the two main religions, who were constantly contesting for power in the Mediterranean.

The use of both notarial and chancery documents highlights these kinds of activity in an unprecedented way. Further, the role of Muslim captives, which is so evident in these documents, complements recent studies which have addressed the economic role of the Ottoman empire. In line with prevailing historiographical concerns, Ottoman studies which pre-dated the Second World War centred almost exclusively on political and military events. As İnalcik explains, 'the Ottomans represented for the Europeans primarily a military intrusion, requiring latter day crusades that haunted the Western memory'.[71] A growing interest in social and economic history, together with better accessibility of Ottoman archives, has made it possible to shift the discussion and expand Ottoman historiography to include debate on social and economic issues. This book follows the same path and, using notarial sources which have only recently begun to be tapped to enrich Malta's social and economic history, aims to present a somewhat different historical perspective. Breaking away from the traditional role assigned to the 'Turk' – that of the 'enemy' – this book shows the 'Turk' as a negotiator and business partner, a role which, even though limited, has been under-estimated.[72] Established historical links remained in place; thus Sicily remained Malta's main life-blood for supplies. However, it will be

ranean: A Form of Cross-Cultural Trade between Southern Europe and the Maghreb (Sixteenth to Eighteenth Centuries)', in Trivellato et al., *Religion and Trade*, 108–30; W. Kaiser, 'La exceptión permanente. Actores, visibilidad y asimetrías en los intercambios comerciales entre los países europeos y el Magreb (siglos XVI–XVII)', in José Antonio Martinez Torres (ed.), *Circulación de personas e intercambios en el Mediterráneo y en el Atlántico (siglos XVI, XVII, XVIII)* (CSIC, 2008), 171–89; W. Kaiser, 'L'économie de la rançon en Méditerranée occidentale (XVIe–XVIIe siècle), in S. Cavaciocchi (ed.), *Ricchezza del mare, ricchezza dal mare (secc. XIII–XVIII)* (2 vols, Florence, 2006), vol. 2, 689–701.

70 For an etymological explanation of the word 'corso', which literally means the 'chase' see D. Heller-Roazen, *Enemy of All, Piracy and the Law of Nations* (New York, 2009), 79.

71 İnalcik & Quataert (eds), *An Economic and Social History of the Ottoman Empire*, 2.

72 The Muslims of the Ottoman Empire were invariably referred to and grouped under the umbrella term 'Turks' by Europeans, without making any specific ethnic or regional distinction. When 'Turk' is used in this study it is because the same word is used in the original documents.

shown how alternative routes were explored and exploited by the Knights – routes which often required trade with the Turks or with subjects of the Ottoman empire.

Heavy involvement in corsairing activities during the sixteenth century led to a substantial increase in the number of slave captives of different religions.[73] Taxes on slaves and customs duties were a major source of income for both Christian and Ottoman economies.[74] As Stephan Epstein argues, medieval moralists did not trouble themselves much with what actually happened when a human being, and not just his work, became a commodity. This resulted in a developing economy that was insensitive to the use of force or fear but justified its actions through religious beliefs.[75] Men, women and children were transported like cattle in ever-increasing numbers, since they brought in a hefty profit. In fact, in his seminal study on white slavery in the Mediterranean, Robert Davis argued that for the Barbary coast alone human trafficking in the Mediterranean was such a thriving economic activity that it 'out-produced the trans-Atlantic trade' during the sixteenth and seventeenth centuries.[76]

For their part, the Knights not only permitted but even fostered the slave trade, since slaves were a crucial human commodity for the proper functioning of their naval organisation, which was built around a fleet of galleys. As well as being an essential element in both the military and economic sectors, slaves were also an integral part of society. The same may be said of Ottoman society, since here too slaves contributed in a major way to the proper functioning of the Ottoman empire. Slaves were thus an indispensable form of manpower in pre-industrial societies, and consequently a regular flow was deemed essential.[77]

In Malta's case the demand for slaves was accelerated by the coming of the Knights Hospitaller, who established an active slave market and almost immediately upon their arrival turned the island into an important centre for human trafficking. The

73 S. Bono, *I corsari barbareschi* (Torino 1964); S. Bono, *Corsari nel Mediterraneo. Cristiani e musulmani fra guerra, schiavitù e commercio* (Milano, 1993, 2nd ed 1997, French translation Paris, 1998); G. Lopez Nadal (ed.), *El comerç alternatiu. Corsarisme i contraban (ss. XV–XVIII)* (Palma de Mallorca, 1990); A. Savaglio (ed.), *Guerra di corsa e pirateria nel Mediterraneo, Atti del convegno (Crotone-Cariati 30 novembre–3 dicembre 1995)* (Cosenza, 1999); S. Bono, 'La schiavitù e la storia del Mediterraneo', in G. Fiume (ed.), *La schiavitù nel Mediterraneo, Nuove Effemeridi. Rassegna trimestrale di cultura*, 14 (2001), 4–19; H. Bresc (ed.), *Figures de l' esclave au Moyen-Age et dans le monde moderne* (Paris, 1996); M. Fontenay, 'L'esclave galérien dans la Méditerranée des Temps modernes', in H. Bresc, *Figures de l'esclave au Moyen-Age et dans le monde moderne* (Paris, 1996), 115–43; M. Fontenay, 'Pour une géographie de l'esclavage méditerranéen aux Temps modernes', in *Atti del convegno L'esclavage en Méditerranée à l'*époque *moderne*, 2002, 17–52.

74 During the fourteen-month period covering the years 1577–78 these contributed to an estimated 29% of the total revenue coming from Ottoman possessions in the Crimea. İnalcik & Quataert (eds), *An Economic and Social History of the Ottoman Empire*, 283.

75 S. Epstein, *Speaking of Slavery: Colour, Ethnicity, and Human Bondage in Italy* (New York, 2001), 150–6. Kaiser & Calafat, 'The Economy of Ransoming in the Early Modern Mediterraean', in Trivellato et al., *Religion and Trade*, 108–30: 110–12.

76 Davis, *Christian Slaves, Muslim Masters*, xxvi.

77 For a bibliographical reference to the role of slavery in European economic growth refer to http://www.oxfordbibliographies.com/view/document/obo-9780199730414/obo-9780199730414–0091.xml (accessed 30 January 2016).

meteoric profits derived from this activity were a healthy incentive for both Ottoman and Christian raiders and traders. Similar to the Islamic system of permitting slaves to work under limited service contracts, in Malta slaves were also allowed to earn their own income, small as this might have been. Such independent activity provided a means for slaves to save towards their ransom, which in many cases was agreed upon before a notary. Just as in Islamic lands,[78] Christians looked upon the manumission of a slave as a charitable act, and such good deeds are a common feature in wills, where the testator made sure to insert a clause whereby a slave, or perhaps more than one, was to be set free upon the testator's death. Other notarial acts show how manumission agreements between masters and their captives were formulated, and offer various possible terms and conditions by which the parties were bound.[79] The Mediterranean was a not only space dominated by political players, but also a space where an ensemble of intermediaries of diverse religious beliefs played an active role in building trading networks through activities such as the ransoming of slaves. As already highlighted, captured, ransomed or runaway slaves were also instrumental in the production and circulation of knowledge, not only about other captives but also on questions of military defence.[80]

78 İnalcik & Quataert (eds), *An Economic and Social History of the Ottoman Empire,* 284

79 On the moral value of manumission see: O. Patterson, *Slavery and Social Death: A Comparative Study* (Harvard, 1985); M. J. Perry, *Gender, Manumission, and the Roman Freedwoman* (Cambridge, 2013).

80 Kaiser & Calafat, 'The Economy of Ransoming', in Trivellato et al., *Religion and Trade*, 108–30: 121–5.

Fig. 1 Detailed Map of Malta. The Castle of Birgu (bottom right) is given prominence as the main defence post and harbour of the island, and Mdina, the seat of the old *Università*, has the most prominent buildings in the centre of the island. Note how Valletta, the city built after the siege of 1565, is still shown as a barren promontory between Mdina and Birgu.

Source: Giovanni Francesco Camocio, 1570, Cathedral Museum Malta

1

New Institutions and Laws 1530–65

Maltese historiography lacks a serious discussion of the development of medieval institutions.[1] However, currently available studies of the surviving documentary evidence show that already by the fifteenth century the Mdina and Gozo *Università*, or town councils, were fully developed institutions within the framework of the Kingdom of Sicily.[2] Charles V's act of cession of the islands to the Order as a free and noble fief[3] included a provision that all privileges and liberties of the Maltese were to be preserved and honoured.[4] Notwithstanding this sworn promise, it was only a few months before the Order started nibbling away at these jealously guarded rights[5] and altering the political and administrative role of the town council in a radical way.

This chapter analyses these institutional changes by focusing on the functions and privileges of the *Università* before the arrival of the Order and the subsequent gradual but significant changes implemented by the Order during the first decades of its rule. Particular attention is given to the town councils' role in controlling and conducting a variety of economic activities that were pivotal in the island's

1 C. Dalli, 'Medieval Communal Organization in an Insular Context: Approaching the Maltese *Universitàs*', *The Making and Unmaking of the Maltese Universitas* (Heritage Supplement, Malta, 1993), 1–10: 2.

2 On the development of the administrative institutions in the Kingdom of Sicily refer to A. Romano (ed.), *Cultura ed istituzioni nella Sicilia medievale e moderna* (Soveria Manelli, CZ and Messina, 1992); A. Baviera Albanese, *Diritto pubblico e istituzioni amministrative in Sicilia. Le fonti* (Rome, 1974); M. Bellomo, *Società e istituzioni dal medioevo agli inizi dell'età moderna* (9th edn, Rome, 1999).

3 The fief was granted on 23 March 1530 and accepted on 25 April 1530. The original deed of cession is preserved in the National Library of Malta, NLM, AOM 70. 'Normally a royal fief was enjoyed by the possessor for as long as he, or his heirs, survived. When, however, the possessor forfeited the fief either through rebellious conduct or behaviour unworthy of the trust placed in him by his sovereign, then the land reverted to the overlord, to be conferred on another favourite.' E. R. Leopardi, 'The Island of Gozo (1432–1453)', *Melita Historica*, 3:3 (1962), 77–80: 78.

4 Similar to the Sicilian context, starting from the first decades of the fourteenth century, a set of privileges and charters, often referring back to much older customs, was used as proof of the *libertates* enjoyed by the community.

5 Documents referring to the deliberations of the Council General of the Order with regard to accepting the island as a fief include, NLM, AOM 286, *Sacra Capitula Generalia* (1526–38), fols 5–5v (Viterbo, 23.v.1527), fols 23v–24 (Syracuse, 25.iv.1530), fols 25–28 (Messina, 10.vi. 1530).

subsistence. To date, Maltese historiography has treated this transitional period in the island's political, social and economic development in a rather isolated and Maltese-centred manner. In Braudelian terms, historians have presented the island as an isolated and self-contained world surrounded by sea.[6] Is the persistence of this isolationist view justified? Were Malta's political reforms specific to the local context, or can comparable models be found in the wider geo-historical perspective? Any attempt to answer these questions must be approached with caution, and avoid reaching arbitrary conclusions in the absence of explicit evidence.[7]

The administration of the Maltese islands prior to 1530

Study of the history of Maltese institutions in the medieval and early modern period needs to be grounded firmly in contemporary developments in Sicily, since the two islands formed part of a greater entity, the *Regno*. Notwithstanding Malta's strong connections to Sicily, as early as the mid-thirteenth century a report by the Governor of Malta, Giliberto Abbate, for Emperor Frederick II covering the decade 1230–40, highlighted the differences between Maltese customs and those of Sicily.[8] The report indicates that, although it was set within the Sicilian framework, the Maltese governing body had its own rules which were tailor made to accommodate the island's particular way of life, '*Homines insularum ipsarum vivunt aliis moribus et constitutionibus, quam alii homines regni nostrae Siciliae*' (The men of this island live under customs and constitutions which are different from those of the men of our Sicilian reign).[9]

In his seminal work on Sicilian institutions Andrea Romano asserts that the beginning of the fourteenth century witnessed an attempt to revive the juridical apparatus of the *Regno* following the crisis of the preceding century. This reorganisation defined two separate levels of jurisdiction: a peripheral, municipal one regulated by the *consuetudines* and *privilegio* (customs and privileges) of the various municipalities within the *Regno*; and a central, royal one which was likewise divided into two separate areas. At the municipal level civil and criminal authority was granted to feudal lords and officials who held royal appointments in the various towns, while jurisdiction at the royal level centred on the role of the *Regia Gran*

6 Braudel, *The Mediterranean*, vol. 1, 149–54.

7 A. Luttrell, 'Approaches to Medieval Malta', in A. Luttrell, *The Making of Christian Malta, From the Early Middle Ages to 1530* (Aldershot, 2002), paper II: 14.

8 A. Luttrell, 'Giliberto Abbate's Report on Malta: c. 1241', in *Proceedings of History Week 1993* (Malta, 1997), 1–29.

9 A. Mifsud, 'Appunti sugli archvi di Malta', *Archivum Melitense*, 2:13 (1912–13), 9–67: 34. Luttrell argues that 'Malta was attached to Sicily for many centuries, but it was also a small and barren island off the African coast, situated further south than Tunis. Malta was influenced by Spain and Byzantium as well as from Sicily and Italy, and the persistence of its fundamentally non-European language is only the most striking pointer to the unreality of many Sicilian parallels ... Maltese institutions changed slowly, often lagging well behind the developments of those who ruled them from afar.' Luttrell, 'Approaches to Medieval Malta', in Luttrell, *The Making of Christian Malta*, 1–70: 14.

Corte.[10] The latter exercised the highest jurisdictional authority in both civil and criminal cases, and also exercised competence in cases relating to feudal rights.[11]

During King Alfonso's reign (r. 1416–58) the distinction between civil and criminal jurisdictions became even more defined, each area having a distinct set-up and a tailor-made set of procedures.[12] On civil law in Malta, Giuseppe La Mantia remarked: 'As regards civil law, I would like to point out that, above all, the regulations regarding the community of property between a married couple are found in the Capitoli of 1458. As I have mentioned elsewhere, the island of Malta followed the laws of Messina on this matter.'[13] Prior to the arrival of the Order of St John in Malta, the municipal government of Mdina, also known as Città Notabile, held jurisdiction over the whole island of Malta, except the harbour area, known as *castrum maris*, which had its own Castellany.[14] Some five kilometres to the north-west of Malta the island of Gozo[15] also had its own town council, which was administered independently from that of Malta.[16]

The Maltese medieval town council or *Università*[17] was a secular institution[18]

10 During Alfonso's rule this continued to be the most significant tribunal. It was composed of four biannually appointed judges, who were chosen from among the most illustrious lawyers of the cities of Catania, Messina, and Palermo, and another from the *Regno*. A. Romano, 'Note sull'ordinamento giudiziario del Regno di Sicilia', in A. Romano (ed.), *Cultura ed istituzioni nella Sicilia medievale e moderna* (Soveria Manelli, CZ and Messina, 1992), 197–225: 217.

11 A. Romano, 'Note sull'ordinamento', in Romano (ed.), *Cultura ed istituzioni nella Sicilia,* 197–225: 211–14. Sentences delivered by this court could be appealed at the *Tribunale della Sacra Regia Coscienza*, while appeals concerning the rulings of the *maestro secreto*, who was in charge of the royal revenues, the *secreti* of the major cities, and the *maestro portulano* or harbourmaster were heard at the *Magna Regia Curia Rationum*. Romano, 'Note sull'ordinamento', in Romano (ed.), *Cultura ed istituzioni nella Sicilia,* 197–225: 214.

12 These reforms were completed only later, in 1530, under Viceroy Pignatelli, and they constituted the Sicilian code of procedure until 1819.

13 '*Per quanto riguarda il diritto civile sono qui da accennare anzitutto le regole sulla comunione di beni fra coniugi contenute nei capitoli del 1458. Come ho ricordato altrove, l'isola di Malta seguiva le consuetudini di Messina su quella materia.*' G. La Mantia, 'Capitoli e Statuti Amministrativi Dell'Isola di Malta approvati dai Re o Vicere di Sicilia 1130–1530', *Archivio Storico di Malta*, 8:1 (1936–37), 1–17: 12.

14 Dalli, *Malta, The Medieval Millennium*, 243.

15 Almost no material prior to 1551 survives for Gozo except for its *capitoli*, which in the main are similar to contemporary Maltese ones. Dalli, 'Medieval Communal Organization', 1; E. R., Leopardi, 'The Island of Gozo (1432–1453)', *Melita Historica*, 3:3 (1962), 77–80.

16 This tripartite division is mentioned as early as 1241 when Giliberto Abbate declared that the *castrum maris Malte* was one of three castles on the Maltese islands, the others being those of Mdina and Gozo. G. Wettinger, 'The castrum maris and its Suburb of Birgu during the Middle Ages', in Bugeja et al., *Birgu: A Maltese Maritime City*, 31–71: 33.

17 Extant documents produced by the town council include the records of its meetings, the *mandati* documents (authorisations for payment) and the *capitoli*. Dalli, 'Medieval Communal Organization', 1. For the relationship between the *Università* and the Crown refer to H. Bresc, *Un Monde Méditerranéen, Économie et Société en Sicile 1300–1450* (2 vols, Palermo, 1986), vol. 2, 717–19.

18 Under the laws of the Sicilian Kingdom, the clergy could not attain any of the

which performed a highly protective role in providing for the various needs of the local population.[19] It not only controlled political and military affairs but also directed and controlled the island's economy, and there was little opportunity for involvement by any who were outside its circle. The president of the *Università* was the royal captain,[20] appointed by the Crown. Royal appointments of high-ranking urban officials reflected the Crown's need to secure good relations with the various demesnes in order to establish social stability and political consensus.[21] The setting up of such groups is evidence of the Crown's continuous attempts to control its territories by means patronage, and reflects not only its concern to resist foreign invasions but also its efforts to subdue local revolts whenever the need arose.[22]

The royal captain was assisted in his duties by a group of annually elected town magistrates or *jurats*, who had to be residents of Malta.[23] The municipal records show that these members were chosen from the uppermost social echelon, the local landowning families, who sought to dominate the island's key appointments, often by establishing alliances through intermarriage.[24] The *jurats* were aided by other public officials who performed various functions within the jurisdiction of

municipal or royal offices. G. Wettinger, 'The Nature of Maltese Politics, c. 870–1964', in V. Mallia-Milanes (ed.), *The British Colonial Experience 1800–1964: The Impact on Maltese Society* (Malta, 1988), 19–34: 23–4.

19 This protective role is best expressed in a set of *capitoli* presented in 1466: '*quista Univer-sitàti comu matre et quilla che divi procurari a lu bonu et quietu viviri di lu so populu et soi figli*'. NLM, Univ. 3, Doc. 1 as quoted in Dalli, 'Medieval Communal Organization', 9. (This *Università*, like a mother, is the one who has to provide for the good and peaceful living of its population and its children.)

20 Unlike the *jurats*, since the captain was an official appointed by the Crown, he was not dependent on the municipal election mechanism. In 1416 the captaincy and its judgeships were extended to two-year terms. His appointment usually started from September. Nevertheless, if no new official was appointed from Palermo the town council temporarily extended the appointment of the existing town mayor. A similar case can be found in G. Wettinger, *Acta Iuratorum et Consilii Civitatis et Insulae Maltae* (Palermo, 1993), Doc. 137. The salary of the royal captain was the responsibility of the town council. In 1475 the Mdina town council was given the concession of having the royal captain made accountable to it for his deeds. C. Dalli, 'Capitoli: The Voice of an Elite', in S. Fiorini (ed.), *Proceedings of History Week 1992* (Malta, 1994), 1–18: 10.

21 Epstein, *An Island for Itself*, 357.

22 H. Bresc, 'The "Secrezia" and the Royal Patrimony in Malta: 1240–1450', in A. Luttrell (ed.), *Medieval Malta: Studies in Malta before the Knights* (London, 1975), 126–62: 140. As was the case in 1426 and 1427 when there was a local rebellion against Gonsalvo de Monroy to whom Malta was pawned in 1421. Dalli, *Malta, The Medieval Millennium*, 201–11.

23 Dalli, 'Medieval Communal Organization', 9.

24 A royal decree issued in 1435 stated that all municipal offices had to be annual and held by persons who had resided in the islands for at least five years. Dalli, 'Medieval Communal Organization'; see also Dalli, *Malta, The Medieval Millennium*, 216–20.

the *Università*.[25] The office of captaincy-at-arms was reserved to the royal captain,[26] which basically made him the official responsible for the public peace, the police and the citizen militia or *Dejma*.[27] From the second half of the fifteenth century this office increasingly became a separate royal appointment. The royal captain's court was distinct from the municipally controlled court and had its own assessor or judge and notary. It also controlled the town prisons, charged its own fines[28] and enjoyed criminal as well as civil jurisdiction.[29]

The Jewish community,[30] which was approximately one third of Mdina's population before its expulsion in 1492,[31] had its own governing institutions and came under the direct full jurisdiction of the captain's court.[32] The royal captain or *Ħakem* was more directly involved in town politics than were the other royal officials in Malta, since he presided over town council meetings. Other key officials,

25 Dalli, 'Medieval Communal Organization', 1. The officials of the town council consisted of the royal captain, also known as *Capitano della Verga* (Captain of the Rod) or *Ħakem* (meaning ruler in Maltese), four *jurats*, three judges of whom two were *letterati* (legally trained) and one *judex idiota* (commoner judge), a notary, a number of *acatapani*, the latter being mainly responsible for the control of weights and measures and public health, the *baiuli* whose main role was to settle agricultural disputes, the municipal archivist and the *marammerius* who supervised public works. Dalli, *Malta, The Medieval Millennium*, 217–18.

26 Dalli, *Malta, The Medieval Millennium*, 220.

27 The *Dejma* was formed of groups of villagers led by constables and was different from the organised coastal guards or *Maħras*. S. Fiorini, 'The Municipal councils in the Maltese Islands: 1530–1800', *The Making and Unmaking of the Maltese Universitas* (Heritage supplement, Malta, 1993), 13–24: 13.

28 Captains often abused their power and imprisoned people to extort fines from them. Dalli, 'Medieval Communal Organization', 9.

29 Juridical authority at times seemed to overlap. However, it must be noted that the choice of tribunal depended on the nature of the case as established in the *capitula* of the *Regno* and of the community, as well as according to the rights and duties customarily attached to each office. (Thanks are due to Charles Dalli for this communication dated 13 May 2010.)

30 Since Malta and Gozo were dependencies of Sicily, whose Viceroy was subject to the rule of the king of Spain, events affecting Spanish Jews in the fifteenth century had their repercussions on both Sicilian and Maltese Jews. G. Wettinger, *The Jews of Malta in the Late Middle Ages* (Malta, 1985), 2.

31 King Ferdinand's expulsion decree was signed in Spain on 31 March 1492 and promulgated in Palermo on 18 June 1492. All Jews were given three months to settle their affairs and were to leave the Sicilian Kingdom by 17 September 1492. Wettinger, *The Jews of Malta*, 117. However, until 1509 there still existed the post of commissioner responsible for the assets of the Jews, who charged 3 *aquile* (equivalent to 3 silver *tareni*) for each exhibited document, while the notary charged a fee of 4 *aquile*. Trasselli, *Da Ferdinando il Cattolico a Carlo V*, vol. 1, 161 n. 38.

32 Dalli, *Malta, The Medieval Millennium*, 220.

including the *secreto*,[33] the *maestro portulano* or harbour-master,[34] the vice-admiral[35] and the Castellan of the *castrum maris* attended only if they were requested to do so by the members of the *Università*. Artisan groups met with strong resistance from members of the town council when they wanted to become part of this administrative circle.[36] However, the *Università* called on a high degree of popular participation whenever it confronted issues of 'national' importance, such as rumours of possible enemy invasion, or the imposition of taxes.[37] Such gatherings were called *parlamentu generali*, and representatives from the main villages were requested to attend.[38]

The same restrictions were applied to Church participation in municipal meetings. Even though the ecclesiastical authorities were a major institutional force on the Maltese islands,[39] the clergy were beyond municipal control and as a rule were excluded from participating in the town's politics except in 'national' matters, or else in matters which directly concerned them.[40] However, the *Università* had the right to appoint proctors to ecclesiastical institutions in which it had an interest, such as at Santo Spirito Hospital in Rabat[41] and the cathedral church in Mdina. Friction between the *Università* and the Church often led to harsh rulings. One

33 The *Secreto* and *Vice-Secreto* controlled the revenues from the royal patrimony of Malta and Gozo, respectively. Bresc, 'The "Secrezia" and the Royal Patrimony', in Luttrell (ed.), *Medieval Malta*, 126–62. For a list of the revenues of the *Secrezia* refer to R. Valentini, 'Funzione storica e dispersioni del patrimonio demaniale di Malta', *Archivio Storico di Malta*, 13:1–3 (Rome, 1942), 1–39: 30–1.

34 The *portulano* was responsible for the control of measures of grain and for the importation of wheat from Sicily.

35 A number of Vice-Admirals aided the Admiral of Sicily in his duties of patrolling the seas around the realm. One of these was the Vice-Admiral of the Maltese islands. Apart from having a share from the revenues exacted out of activities like corsairs' spoils, shipwrecks, departure of vessels from port, the importation and export of various commodities, fishing and so forth, he also decided both civil and criminal cases involving seamen. The last Maltese Vice-Admiral encountered in the registers of the town council dating to September 1513 is Salvus de Falczono; see S. Fiorini, 'The Vice-Admiracia Insularum Meliveti et Gaudisii', in C. Vassallo (ed.), *Consolati Di Mare and Chambers of Commerce* (Malta, 2000), 29–44. See also C. Trasselli, *Il Mediterraneo e Sicilia all'inizio dell'epoca moderna* (Cosenza, 1977), 32–48.

36 They were banned from municipal participation in 1466. Dalli, 'Medieval Communal Organization', 9. Refer to Wettinger, *Acta Iuratorum*, Doc. 394, wherein the appointments of Antoni Xikilune and Antoni Lukis were revoked because one was a tailor and the other a cobbler, and Doc. 431, wherein Cola Xara, a tailor, argued against his removal from the post of *acatapano*, claiming that this was not contrary to one of the *capituli* which stated that artisans could not obtain the post. The Viceroy acceded to his request not to be excluded *prima facie* while at the same time instructing the municipal authorities to send their objections.

37 A. Mifsud, 'La Cattedrale e l'Università, ossia, il Comune e la Chiesa in Malta', *La Diocesi*, 2:3 (1917), 34–44: 42.

38 Mifsud, 'La Cattedrale e l'Università', 40–4.

39 The Maltese islands were a suffragan diocese of Palermo. Dalli, *Malta, The Medieval Millennium*, 244.

40 G. Wettinger, 'Early Maltese Popular Attitudes to the Government of the Order of St John', *Melita Historica*, 6:3 (1974), 255–78: 260.

41 This right was deprived to them later on in the 1600s. Fiorini, 'The Municipal Councils', 17.

such example was the bishop's[42] decision in June 1480 to excommunicate a number of persons who had attended a council meeting where there had been discussion of whether any measures should be taken against him, in view of allegations that he had pillaged the property of another cleric, namely, Don Matheus Galia.[43]

In her history of early modern Europe, Merry Wiesner-Hanks comments that 'by 1450 villages in many parts of Europe had become what were called communes, with institutions of self-governance such as councils or courts that regulated planting and harvesting, and might represent the village as a whole to outside political authorities. In some places such groups could issue ordinances and make legal decisions, either in conjunction with the local lord or on their own.' She writes further, that 'the towns and cities that won their independence from local lords and gained charters had even stronger institutions of governance'.[44]

A similar situation prevailed in Malta when, in 1428, the Maltese redeemed their island from the feudal lord Don Gonsalvo de Monroy for the sum of 30,000 Aragonese florins. On 20 June 1428 King Alfonso welcomed the islands back into his *demanio* and issued an extraordinary royal charter, known as the *Magna Carta Libertatis*, in favour of the Maltese islands. According to Dalli, not only did this event 'mark a political milestone in the relationship with the crown for the next hundred years',[45] but the fifteenth century was 'Malta's municipal age *par excellence*'.[46] The administrative duties of the now quasi-independent town council included, among others, the supervision of the town market[47] and public health,[48] the establishment and inspection of weights and measures,[49] the importation and distribution of wheat,[50] the fixing of retail prices,[51] the exacting of municipal taxes on wine[52] and other merchandise exported out of the island,[53] together with the payment and collection of various other taxes. The council also had the right to appoint Maltese consuls in Sicilian cities and to process and tackle matters relating to corsair vessels

42 Up till the arrival of the Order in 1530, Bishops of Malta did not reside on the island. In the last decade of the fifteenth century, the municipal council objected to the total negligence of Bishops and appealed to the Crown to induce them to visit the diocese at least once a year. NLM, Univ. 9, fols 170–170v, as quoted in V. Borg, *The Maltese Diocese during the Sixteenth Century* (Malta, 2009), 2.

43 Wettinger, *Acta Iuratorum*, Docs 764, 765, 770, 771. It seems that this property had to go to the cathedral.

44 M. E. Wiesner-Hanks, *Early Modern Europe 1450–1798* (Cambridge, 2006), 112.

45 Dalli, *Malta, The Medieval Millennium*, 211.

46 Dalli, *Malta, The Medieval Millennium*, 215.

47 Wettinger, *Acta Iuratorum*, Doc. 7.

48 Wettinger, *Acta Iuratorum*, Doc. 563. The official in charge of public health and orderliness was called the *accatapanum*. Dalli, 'Medieval Communal Organization', 9.

49 Wettinger, *Acta Iuratorum*, Doc. 78.

50 Wettinger, *Acta Iuratorum*, Doc. 73.

51 Wettinger, *Acta Iuratorum*, Doc. 139. These were standard pricelists issued to curb abuses in the prices of commodities and, as such, there is no concrete evidence that these were actually the prices charged by retailers.

52 Wettinger, *Acta Iuratorum*, Doc. 132.

53 The town council controlled the production of barley and cumin and the export of the cotton crop. Wettinger, 'Agriculture in Malta in the Late Middle Ages', in Buhagiar (ed.), *Proceedings of History Week, 1981*, 1–48: 13–27.

in the Maltese harbours.[54] Other important duties assigned to the town council were the organisation of the roster of night watch duties,[55] the maintenance of the town walls[56] and dealing with complaints by the town's representatives against the investigations of the royal commissioners[57] and disputes related to the bishop.

Various matters presented before the town council provide a good indication of its workings and offer excellent insight into the relationship between the institution and other royal officials, and between the Mdina *Università* and that of Gozo.[58] A typical example of the variety of matters dealt with in a council meeting is provided by a set of minutes dated 2 October 1469. One of the items discussed in this meeting related to the farming out of the wine tax known as '*trium quartuchiorum*'. The members paid special attention to the fact that revenue from this tax had been distributed among several people instead of being devoted to necessary work on the town walls. Another item on the agenda concerned updating the roster of watch duties, referred to in the minutes as *lu quaternu de la guardia*. Finally, the council tackled a particular problem concerning the shortage of wheat and the measures to be taken in respect of those caught hoarding it.[59] In another council session the members discussed the position of the Maltese consul at Licata (in Sicily), the matter of foreign wine merchants who apparently were selling barrels of wine which were not completely full and yet another matter concerning the supply of wheat. Finally, it considered an offer put forward by a Genoese merchant for the supply of arms.[60]

The council's citizen-judges were authorised by the Crown to dispense civil as well as criminal justice and had their own judge, the *judex juratorum*. It is interesting to note that consuls of the Maltese *Università* in Sicilian towns and *caricatori*[61] also enjoyed civil and criminal jurisdiction over the Maltese community who resided there.[62] However, the most distinct prerogative of the *Università* was its right to send its ambassadors with *capitoli*, or petitions and grievances, to the *Curia Regis* (the Crown). Such a petition was presented in respect of an appointment made by the Viceroy of Sicily in 1527, wherein the captain-in-arms was given the right to enjoy extended authority. The council immediately drew the Crown's attention to the

54 Wettinger, *Acta Iuratorum*, Doc. 81.

55 Wettinger, *Acta Iuratorum*, Doc. 163.

56 Wettinger, *Acta Iuratorum*, Doc. 13. This was the responsibility of the *supramarammerius*.

57 Royal commissioners were regularly appointed to report on the administration of the Maltese islands. Refer to Bresc, 'The "Secrezia" and the Royal Patrimony', in Luttrell (ed.), *Medieval Malta*, 126–62: 148.

58 The majority of the latter's legal and administrative documents preceding the year 1551 were presumably destroyed in a *razzia* which took place in the same year when almost all of the island's population was taken captive by Turgut Reis, the Ottoman corsair.

59 Wettinger, *Acta Iuratorum*, Doc. 342.

60 Wettinger, *Acta Iuratorum*, Doc. 384.

61 These date back to the times of Frederick II and were specially designated ports for the supply of grain which were mainly located in the western half of Sicily, where much of the grain was grown. D. Abulafia, 'Lo stato e la vita economica', in P. Toubert & A. Paravacini (eds), *Federico II e il mondo mediterraneo* (Palermo, 1994), 165–87. The term was also used for sixteenth-century grain stores.

62 Dalli, 'Medieval Communal Organization', 1.

fact that such an appointment breached the rights and privileges of the Maltese.[63] In another instance the town council refused to accept the appointment of a royal commissioner[64] who was assigned to hear a case regarding usury, since, they stated, this was an infringement of their privileges.[65] An inventory of these rights and charters was drawn up during a meeting held on 8 February 1471, where it was also stated that the original documents containing these privileges were kept '*intra la caxa di la Universitati*' (in the box of the town council).[66]

Andrea Romano writes that from the fourteenth century the Sicilian *Università* began to profit from a collection of privileges which were often connected to older laws and customs. Whenever it was deemed necessary this corpus of privileges was cited as proof of the town councils' rights, or else they would be presented to the sovereign, who would be requested to confirm them.[67] Cases in point in the Maltese context are the promise made in 1421 by the new lord of Malta, Don Antonio Cardona, who pledged to observe these privileges to the letter,[68] and King Alfonso's promise in 1428 to respect these rights after the Maltese had redeemed their islands from the rule of Gonsalvo Monroy.

Before the Order's establishment on Malta in 1530, and likewise during the first decades of their rule,[69] the Order was requested to promise that it would not breach such rights in any way. Ultimately, the council members of the *Università* sought such assurances because they guaranteed the power and hegemony of the ruling social class which governed Malta like a quasi-independent principality. This places Malta in a position similar to other European towns where, by the end of the fifteenth century, the majority were governed by an oligarchy composed of a patriciate of rich merchants and property owners.[70]

The holding of key positions on the administrative bodies of the islands meant that officials could often pursue their own private interests by regulating municipal politics to meet their own agendas.[71] In 1434 the town council proposed a six-month embargo on imported wine, due to a serious threat to the local viticulture. However, three members of the council, Simone de Mazzara, Angelo Vaccaro and Federico

63 NLM, Univ. 12, fols 408ff.

64 These were also known as *sindicaturi* and were portrayed by the municipal elite as oppressive intruders since they were beyond the control of the council. V. Bezzina, 'The Administration of the Maltese Islands, A Study of the Acta Iuratorum et Consilii Civitatis Insulae Maltae' (unpublished MA dissertation, University of Malta, 1999), 2.

65 Wettinger, *Acta Iuratorum*, Doc. 965.

66 Wettinger, *Acta Iuratorum*, Doc. 405.

67 Romano, 'Note sull'ordinamento', in Romano (ed.), *Cultura ed istituzioni*, 197–225: 217.

68 NLM, Univ. 3.

69 For example refer to NLM, AOM, Lib. Conc. 85, fol. 121 (7.xi.1533) (new pagination); AOM, Lib. Conc. 87 (4.v.1547); AOM, Lib. Conc. 88, fol. 120 (30.viii.1552).

70 Romano (ed.), *Cultura ed Istituzioni*, 41; H. G. Koenigsberger, G. L. Mosse & G. Q. Bowler, *Europe in the Sixteenth Century, A General History of Europe* (London and New York, 1989), 91–2.

71 R. Valentini, 'L'Espansionismo aragonese nel Mediterraneo come causa della decadenza di Malta', *Archivio Storico di Malta*, 12:2–3 (1941), 99–130: 122–7; Dalli, 'Medieval Communal Organization', 1.

Calava, were exempted from this embargo.[72] Similar preferences are reflected in the record of the town council meeting held on 6 October 1462, which discussed whether the merchant Federico Calibachi, who was also one of the *jurats*, should be entrusted with the provisioning of wheat from Sicily during his forthcoming trip to the island.[73]

In another instance the council was summoned to discuss the 'wrongdoings' of two of its members who were said to have been working against the interests of the *Università*. This grievance surfaced after the Viceroy had been petitioned to send a commissioner to investigate various abuses of the town officials.[74] In June 1475, confronted with serious allegations, the Crown appointed a commissioner, Paolo de Carcella,[75] to investigate the matter further.[76] This interference greatly disturbed the town officials, who expressed their resentment, stating that they were 'tired of repairing the walls of his [the King's] land which are dilapidated, and therefore his Highness should send help and not commissioners'.[77] In his study on Sicily and the Sicilians between 1475 and 1525, Trasselli discussed similar issues of misconduct in the Sicilian context. Similar to Malta, he notes that Sicilian *nobiles*[78] often caused trouble for the *Università* in order to improve their financial positions.[79]

The strongest secular authority which fell outside municipal jurisdiction on Malta and enjoyed freedom from certain impositions[80] was the Castellan[81] of the *castrum maris*[82] (castle-by-the-sea). From the time of its earliest known mention in 1223 the castle is depicted as being of supreme importance not only for the security of the

72 Bresc, 'The "Secrezia" and the Royal Patrimony', in Luttrell (ed.), *Medieval Malta*, 126–62: 133.

73 Wettinger, *Acta Iuratorum*, Doc. 219. Among the chief requisites for being commissioned to import wheat there were loyalty and a good representation in the town council.

74 Wettinger, *Acta Iuratorum*, Doc. 596.

75 Referred to as '*juris legum doctori consiliario et fideli regio dilecto*'.

76 Wettinger, *Acta Iuratorum*, Doc. 616.

77 '*fatigati ad fari moramma in sey locki a li mura de la terra che su isbandati et undi sua signuria si diviria mandarin ajutu ni manda commissariu*' [sic]. Wettinger, *Acta Iuratorum*, Doc. 615 (fol. 337v).

78 As regards the formation of the *nobiles* class and its political and social connotations within the framework of the *regno*, Epstein states that 'groups defined along lines of property and occupation began to form during the first decades of the fifteenth century ... Within the group as a whole, the expansion of the state and urban administration, and of the volume of resources the group managed, led to the formation during the first three decades of the fifteenth century of an increasingly strong identity as a specifically *civic* nobility, whose members began to describe themselves as *gentilhomini* or *nobiles*.' Epstein, *An Island for Itself*, 357–8.

79 Trasselli, *Da Ferdinando il Cattolico a Carlo V*, vol. 1, Premessa.

80 Wettinger, 'The Castrum Maris', in Bugeja et al., *Birgu: A Maltese Maritime City*, 31–71: 45.

81 In 1416 it was established that the castellan could not hold the office of the royal captain. He was paid from the revenues of the royal patrimony.

82 The first mention of the castle dates to 1223 in the Genoese chronicles originally commenced by Andrea Caffaro. Wettinger, 'The Castrum Maris', in Bugeja et al., *Birgu: A Maritime City*, 31–71: 33.

island, but even the safety of Sicily itself,[83] and for this reason the Castellan received special treatment from the Crown.[84] At least as early as the thirteenth century special care was taken not to combine the office of the Castellan with that of the royal captain.[85] The Castellan was supposed to exercise *de facto* jurisdiction over the *castrum maris* up to the *tagliata* or ditch, which cut the castle off from the mainland. However, the Castellan often extended this area to include the adjoining *borgo* of Birgu.[86] The latter was a small settlement, yet vital to the Maltese economy because its residents were merchants, artisans, sailors and shopkeepers, including a handful of Jewish families,[87] who took refuge in the Castle whenever the need arose.[88]

Those who came under the Castellan's jurisdiction usually did not take part in the island's roster of watch duties, and even refused to pay the taxes collected by

83 The importance attached to this post by the Crown is clearly shown in 1223 when Count Henry Piscatore, feudal lord of Malta, lost favour with the emperor. He was consequently imprisoned, and although he managed to restore his authority, he was not granted the rule over the castle. This post was later denied even to his son Count Nicoloso in 1259. Wettinger, 'The Castrum Maris', in Bugeja et al., *Birgu: A Maritime City*, 31–71: 33–4.

84 Wettinger, 'The Castrum Maris', in Bugeja et al., *Birgu: A Maritime City*, 31–71: 42.

85 '*Cap. CCCXC [Rex Alphonsus] Quod Castellani non possunt esse Capitanei Item suplica lo dicto Regno che in una medesima Terra oi Città nixuno pocza essere Castellano e Capitano (Confer Cap 2 Regis Martini); ne haviri altri offcii in la dicta Terra o Città (Cap 32 Regis Joannis)*'. F. Testa, *Capitula Regni Siciliae que ad hodiernam diem lata sunt* (Palermo, 1741), i, 351 as quoted in Wettinger, 'The Castrum Maris', in Bugeja et al., *Birgu: A Maritime City*, 31–71: 38. '(*Cap. CCCXC [King Alphonsus]* that Castellans cannot be Captains likewise in the said Kingdom or in a similar land or town *(Confer Cap. 2 Regis Martini)*, nor hold other offices in the said city or town *(Cap. 32 Regis Joannis)*.' However, there were various instances when this policy was not followed mostly due to the financial constraints of the Crown. Wettinger, 'The Castrum Maris', in Bugeja et al., *Birgu: A Maritime City*, 31–71: 38.

86 The Castellan and his men, that is, those persons falling under his jurisdiction, were restricted from carrying arms in the city. They were also obliged to submit themselves to the tribunal of the royal captain if they broke the law *extra castrum*. Furthermore, they could not extend their power, be it juridical or as an excuse for an exemption from tax, outside their territory. In addition, they could not interfere with port or corsairing activities. Finally, the Castellan had to submit to the tribunal of the town council if he was denounced by third parties or by the *jurats*. Valentini, 'L'Espansionismo aragonese', 127 n. 99. In 1458, the Mdina authorities alleged that since the Castellan and his companions were intermarried with the notables of the town, they were spending quite a lot of time there. It seems that they habitually carried weapons in contravention of the prohibitions of the royal captain, and were often involved in fights which led to the wounding of citizens, after which they sought refuge in the castle. Wettinger, 'The Castrum Maris', in Bugeja et al., *Birgu: A Maritime City*, 31–71: 46.

87 Wettinger gives some examples of the numerous business transactions which he managed to register from the records of Notary Consalvo Cancur R 140. At present, some of this notary's volumes are listed as being misplaced, a situation which was reported several years ago. Wettinger, 'The Castrum Maris', in Bugeja et al., *Birgu: A Maritime City*, 31–71: 62; Dalli, *Malta, The Medieval Millennium*, 221.

88 According to Wettinger, during the Middle Ages the castle was strong enough to resist various direct assaults and at least two long-drawn-out sieges. Wettinger, 'The Castrum Maris', in Bugeja et al., *Birgu: A Maritime City*, 31–71: 33.

the municipal government.[89] The upkeep of the *castrum maris* was financed by the incomes of the *secrezia* and from the revenues of the castle's tavern, as were the wages of the officers and men working there.[90] These special grants to the Castellan reflect that the area under his control was considered to be of the utmost importance for the safety and well-being of the entire island. This location, being the main port of the island, was also a major link connecting Malta with the outside world.[91] It provided facilities and services for the importation of victuals and other commodities, and other services related to the export of local produce. The Castellan's office therefore represented a threat to the municipal council, since its independence was a direct challenge to the council's bid for total hegemony over the island's administration. Consequently, there were frequent conflicts between these different institutions, due to their overlapping interests, especially with regard to specific areas of jurisdiction.[92]

There is an instance of this in the minutes of the town council, where it was recorded that a debate arose regarding a petition presented by some debtors from Żejtun, a village contiguous with the maritime city of Birgu. The petitioners claimed that they came under the jurisdiction of the Castellan and refused to pay the taxes which were due to the municipal council of Mdina.[93] This behaviour was judged

89 Dalli, *Malta, The Medieval Millennium*, 221. These seem to have started accumulating at least as early as 1408, when King Martin decreed that 'all the persons of the castle were henceforth freed from all new imposts'. Wettinger, 'The Castrum Maris', in Bugeja et al., *Birgu: A Maritime City*, 31–71: 45.

90 Bresc, 'The "Secrezia" and the Royal Patrimony', in Luttrell (ed.), *Medieval Malta,* 126–62: 139. Until at least 1508, the tax on wine known as *quartuchu pro quartara* went towards the expenses incurred for the repair of the castle. Wettinger, 'The Castrum Maris', in Bugeja et al., *Birgu: A Maritime City*, 31–71: 41–2.

91 The island's inhabitants set up their homes further inland, in view of recurrent corsair and pirate raids and this was the only settlement situated close to the shore. Wettinger, 'The Castrum Maris', in Bugeja et al., *Birgu: A Maritime City*, 31–71: 33.

92 Various other protests were registered, like that dated 8 September 1467 when 'Franciscu Vella alias Bercax of Birgu registers a protest against the noble Johannes de Mazara, Captain of the city and his judge and assessor, Notary Petrus Caxaro, complaining that while he (Bercax) was under the jurisdiction and protection of Johannes de Guevara (who was Castellan of the *castrum maris* between 1458 and 1487), as his servant, he and his son Thomeus were accused of insulting Antonius Bonnici but the privilege of protection, while accorded to himself, was denied to his son. He objected that it was unfair that father and son should belong to different jurisdictions'. Fiorini (ed.), *Documentary Sources of Maltese History, Part I, No. 3*, Doc. 15. A counter-protest was registered on 11 September 1467 claiming that both Mazara and Caxaro were acting within their rights. Fiorini (ed.), *Documentary Sources of Maltese History, Part I, No. 3*, Doc. 23.

93 The claim regarded the export of a horse and ten *salme* of barley. Wettinger, *Acta Iuratorum*, Doc. 101. The people of Żejtun were claiming that they had been under the Castellan's jurisdiction, and thus were exempt from payment pro rata to the royal *collecta* tax, since before 1460. The town council thought otherwise and insisted that if they did not perform guard duties and were not paid employees at the castle they could not be exempted. In 1494, the Palermo authorities decreed that the inhabitants of Żejtun were to contribute to the defence of the castle rather than participate in the island's general militia organisation. However, they still had to receive instructions from the Royal Captain and not the Castellan, unless the former proved to be negligent in carrying out his duties. Wettinger, 'The Castrum Maris', in Bugeja et al., *Birgu: A Maritime City*, 31–71: 49–50.

unacceptable by the *jurats*, and in a meeting held on 18 May 1468 the council read out a letter which had been sent by the Viceroy to the Castellan. The letter reprimanded the Castellan for sequestering a consignment of wheat on its arrival from Sicily, and for other unjust actions.[94] An extract from the letter reads:

> Through a letter sent by the town council we are informed that you, vice-castellan, some days ago have sequestrated by force a supply of wheat which was destined to provision this city and island, apart from performing other grievances by interfering with issues which do not concern you, and this against the provisions laid down in the charters and ordinances of this town.[95]

By the early years of the sixteenth century, shortly before the Order's arrival on the island, relations between the two institutions worsened to such an extent that the town council filed a case against the Castellan before the *Magna Curia Castellania*, which it eventually won.[96]

The *Secreto* of Malta and *Vicesecreto* of Gozo were also royal officials who held substantial political power, since they exercised authority in the king's name and were in charge of collecting revenues derived from the royal patrimony. The Maltese *Secreto* was often, though not always, chosen from the civic nobility who, although resident in Malta, held lands in Sicily attached to the semi-feudal nobility.[97] The *Secreti* were held personally responsible for the proper administration and regular payment of grants and salaries and for the raising of taxes, with the possibility that their personal goods would be seized if they defaulted. In view of these responsibilities it was necessary for the holder of such a position to have a personal fortune and to provide guarantors.[98] This royal official, together with that of the town council, annually negotiated a sum of money to be collected, known as *collectio*.[99] This system often led to protests from both tax-payers and town authorities, the latter insisting that due to the island's financial deficit it could not guarantee the various expenditures such as payment of salaries or the upkeep of the defence system. Such complaints led to granting of part of the royal patrimony revenues or *gabelles* to the town council to relieve them of this encumbrance. The *Secreto* enjoyed two types

94 Wettinger, *Acta Iuratorum*, Doc. 293, see also Doc. 877.

95 '*Cum licteri di quissa Universitàti simo informati vui vicecastellanu li proximi jorni vinendu certi frumenti ad opu et subiectioni di questa chitati et insula vilu prindistivu per forcza ultra zo vi haviti inferuto et continuamenti inferiti multi altri gravizii et indebiti novitati incomictendovi in cosi chi non diviti contra la forma di li capituli et ordinacioni di quista chitati.*' [sic].

96 Dalli, 'Medieval Communal Organization', 10.

97 In one instance, on 20 December 1443, Petrus de Busco, a Catalan knight and ship's captain, was granted the office of the *Secreto* for life, together with the right to all that remained from the revenues after the payment of wages and pensions to soldiers, and to holders of grants. Bresc, 'The "Secrezia" and the Royal Patrimony', in Luttrell (ed.), *Medieval Malta*, 126–62: 144.

98 Bresc, 'The "Secrezia" and the Royal Patrimony', in Luttrell (ed.), *Medieval Malta*, 126–62: 144.

99 For a deeper insight into the income of the royal revenues refer to Valentini, 'Funzione storica e disperione del patrimonio demaniale di Malta', 1–39.

of income, one derived from consumption and foreign commerce[100] and the other pertaining to the exploitation of lands held by the *regis curia*, either through direct administration or through lease.[101]

Henri Bresc's analysis of the Maltese *Secrezia* indicates that in the last quarter of the fourteenth century the taxes due from Gozo were derived mainly from a tax on gardens and fountains, while those on consumption produced a lesser income. In Malta the royal revenues seem to have depended less on the agricultural economy than they did in Gozo, since only one third of revenues came from the exploitation of land.[102] Such a low income reflected the transformation of the royal *massarie* of the thirteenth century into fiefs, which brought a census to the *Curia* by the fifteenth century.[103] By 1506 the Crown's policy of alienating these fiefs[104] and other incomes[105] led to a heavy drop in its revenue.[106] The substantial increase in the revenue of the alienated fiefs indicates the unproductive way in which they were administered by the royal authorities prior to their alienation. Clear examples of this are *Ginen el Firen* and *La Quattara*, which in 1506 registered an increase of 25 *uncie* in respect of their income of 5 *uncie* in 1439, and that of the Marsa fief, which almost quadrupled over the same period.[107] During the initial years of Hospitaller rule, the problem of low revenues from royal income was considered a major financial setback for the Knights. In fact, in a bid for the concession of extra duty-free grain quotas the Grand Master emphasised that the Order was relieving the Crown of a

100 Part of these incomes must have been enjoyed by the harbour-master (*portulano*). However, there seems to be scant information on the income enjoyed by the latter. Bresc, 'The "Secrezia" and the Royal Patrimony', in Luttrell (ed.), *Medieval Malta,* 126–62: 129.

101 According to Bresc, it is difficult 'to calculate the respective values of the *gabelles* and the incomes from the lands, gardens and water-rights of the curia'. See Bresc, 'The "Secrezia" and the Royal Patrimony', in Luttrell (ed.), *Medieval Malta,* 126–62: 129.

102 Bresc, however, also notes that the *massarie* or farms of the *curia* were administered directly and the revenue from them is not known. Bresc, 'The "Secrezia" and the Royal Patrimony', in Luttrell (ed.), *Medieval Malta,* 126–62: 129.

103 The *massarie* were vast domains of royal fiefs or *latifundia* which were devoted to the growing of cereals through the exploitation of a labour force of *vilani.* Bresc, 'The "Secrezia" and the Royal Patrimony', in Luttrell (ed.), *Medieval Malta,* 126–62: 131. The loss of these revenues led to the creation of new taxes in the fourteenth century, especially due to financial pressures created by military and political necessities. Bresc, 'The "Secrezia" and the Royal Patrimony', in Luttrell (ed.), *Medieval Malta,* 126–62: 134. For an explanation of census, see Chapter 3, n. 141.

104 Roberto Valentini compares the volume containing such alienations of fiefs, namely, NLM, Univ. 206, *De insulis Meliveti et Gaudisii eiusque secretia, feudis et iuribus. Capibrevium, concessiones et Privilegia prout in Regia Cancelleria Regni Sicilie*, with William I's Domesday Book. Refer to his analysis of same volume in Valentini, 'Funzione storica e disperione del patrimonio demaniale di Malta', 1–39.

105 Like, for example, dues on tunny-fishing, rights of passage, registration dues in ports etc. Bresc, 'The "Secrezia" and the Royal Patrimony', in Luttrell (ed.), *Medieval Malta,* 126–62: 141.

106 Bresc, 'The "Secrezia" and the Royal Patrimony', in Luttrell (ed.), *Medieval Malta,* 126–62: 131.

107 Bresc, 'The "Secrezia" and the Royal Patrimony', in Luttrell (ed.), *Medieval Malta,* 126–62: 144.

great financial burden by investing substantial sums of money in an island which contributed only 41 ducats[108] per annum to the Crown revenues.[109]

The *Secrezia* also benefitted from additional revenues, among them those derived from the rent of shops in Mdina which belonged to the curia and other buildings such as the castle at Gozo, and from extraordinary income such as the chance finding of treasure.[110] Taxes collected by the *Secrezia* of both Malta and Gozo amounted to 511 *uncie* and 200 *uncie*, respectively, in 1506. According to the Chief Notary of the Royal Crown, Giovanni Luca Barberi,[111] about 311 *uncie* of the total revenues were paid out in salaries to officials holding royal offices, such as those at the castle-by-the-sea,[112] the *Secreto* and others.[113]

Although by the mid-fifteenth century the oversimplified traditional tripartite division of medieval society overlooked various large groups, it is still relevant to highlight the significant way in which society was divided, that is, by social rank or what later came to be known as 'estate' or 'order'. This partition was highly dependent on family of birth and function in society, although other factors contributed to social mobility.[114] A citizen or member of the town council could shape relationships of power and access to wealth at the local level. Thus, by economic means, movement up or down the social scale was possible.[115] The monopolising trends in the decision-

108 The ducat was worth 13 *tari*. ACM, Misc. 440, fols 3–3v (1540). R. Valentini, 'Il Patrimonio della Corona in Malta fino alla venuta dell'Ordine', *Archivio Storico di Malta*, 5:1–4 (1934), 3–32. S. Fiorini, 'Malta in 1530', in V. Mallia-Milanes (ed.), *Hospitaller Malta 1530–1798: Studies on Early Modern Malta and the Order of St John of Jerusalem* (Malta, 1993), 111–98: 164.

109 R. Valentini, 'I Cavalieri di S. Giovanni da Rodi a Malta: Trattative diplomatiche', *Archivum Melitense*, 9:4 (1935), 137–237: 172.

110 In 1458/9 five boys discovered a hoard of 248 Byzantine gold pieces which were sent to the Viceroy. Bresc, 'The "Secrezia" and the Royal Patrimony', in Luttrell (ed.), *Medieval Malta*, 126–62: 136.

111 Barberi was secretary of state of the *Regno* and was commissioned by King Ferdinand the Catholic (r. 1479–1516) to draw up a report on the state of Royal Patrimony, which had shrunk immensely after King Alfonso's reign. For a list of the major feudal lands refer to Valentini, 'Funzione storica e dispersioni del patrimonio demaniale di Malta', 31 n. 115. See also, A. Luttrell, 'The Earliest Documents Transcribed in the Cathedral Archives Mdina: 1316–1372', in J. Azzopardi (ed.), *Archives of the Cathedral of Malta Misc. 32A: 1313–1529* (Malta, 1977), 29–52: 34–6.

112 For a breakdown of the annual pay of the Birgu garrison refer to Bresc, 'The "Secrezia" and the Royal Patrimony', in Luttrell (ed.), *Medieval Malta*, 126–62: 138, Table IV. The upkeep of the *castrum maris* also benefitted from the revenues of the castle's tavern. Bresc, 'The "Secrezia" and the Royal Patrimony', in Luttrell (ed.), *Medieval Malta*, 126–62: 139.

113 A. Mifsud, 'Papi, Fortificazioni e Tasse nel Passato di Malta', *Archivum Melitense*, 3:1 (1919), 399–430: 410. Valentini, 'Funzione storica e disperione del patrimonio demaniale di Malta', 34.

114 In the fifteenth century Europeans adopted a tripartite division of society. This division led to generalisations of large groups – such as nobles, members of the clergy and peasants – which differed greatly in their political and financial status. At the same time, they totally discarded large communities such as Jews and Muslims. Society was thus divided by social rank, or by what came to be known as 'estate' or 'order'. Wiesner-Hanks, *Early Modern Europe*, 26–7. The concept of 'class' pertains to a later period.

115 Trasselli, *Da Ferdinando il Cattolico a Carlo V*, vol. 1, 238.

making processes of the Maltese urban elites, such as Desguanes, Vaccaro, Calibachi, Burdino, Sillato, Xahica, Caxaro, Mazzara and Guevara, are evident from the town council records.[116]

The small, insular and resource-limited context of this select group of town representatives, together with the way in which they controlled the annual elections, encouraged and guaranteed the maintenance of the *status quo* in the island. Thus, Malta followed the same pattern as other medieval states in Europe, where those who were politically active acquired most of their power through the development of local judicial institutions and the protection of the property rights of the ruling class.[117]

Henri Bresc notes that the fundamental aim of the town council was to secure for itself the highest possible revenue. This it did through repeated official requests, such as its request for the abolition of privileges enjoyed by other royal offices; by compelling the dispersed population to live in Mdina and thus ensuring a better hold over it; and by trying to secure the administration and incomes of all royal offices[118] while at the same time forbidding the transfer of revenues to Sicily.[119] The political influence and hegemony of this group of socially pre-eminent people is perhaps best exemplified by their exclusion from council representation of other estates who were deemed to occupy a lower place in the social hierarchy, such as the artisans. Charles Dalli notes that 'the era of municipal administration in the Maltese islands had given them what was in practice autonomy. A local social stratum made up of municipal nobles was able to govern the rest of the population without much outside interference while acting as the supreme mediator between the Crown and the rest of the population.'[120] This fundamental reality was made possible by the

[116] G. Wettinger, 'Honour and Shame in Late Fifteenth Century Malta', *Melita Historica*, 8:1 (1980), 65–77: 68. For more insights on the origin of Maltese surnames refer to G. Wettinger, 'The Origin of the "Maltese" Surnames', *Melita Historica*, 12:4 (1999), 333–44; G. Wettinger, 'The Distribution of Surnames in Malta in 1419 and the 1480s', *Journal of Maltese Studies* (University of Malta), 5 (1968), 25–48; S. Fiorini, 'Medieval Connexions of Some Medieval Maltese Surnames', *Journal of Matese Studies* (University of Malta), 17–18 (1987–88), 104–38; M. Cassar, 'Vestiges of Arabic Nomenclature in Maltese Surnames', 22nd International Congress of Onomastic Sciences, Pisa, 4 September 2005, https://www.academia.edu/183114/Vestiges_of_Arabic_Nomencalture_in_Maltese_Surnames (accessed 21 August 2016).

[117] J. R. Strayer, *On the Medieval Origins of the Modern State: With New Forwards by Charles Tilly and William Chestar Jordan* (Princeton, 2005), 61. In spite of harsh opposition from local authorities, different forms of juridical power were at times also transferred to the direct rule of new lords when feudal privileges were conceded, as for example in 1361 when Jacobus de Peregrino was castellan as well as *capitano* of Malta. Wettinger, 'The Castrum Maris', in Bugeja et al., *Birgu: A Maritime City*, 31–71: 38.

[118] In 1427 the town council requested that the *Secreto* and all royal officials should henceforth be indigenous islanders, and in particular that the Maltese *secrezia* be freed from the control of the *maestro secreto* of Sicily. Bresc, 'The "Secrezia" and the Royal Patrimony', in Luttrell (ed.), *Medieval Malta*, 126–62: 145.

[119] Bresc, 'The "Secrezia" and the Royal Patrimony', in Luttrell (ed.), *Medieval Malta*, 126–62: 150.

[120] Dalli, 'Medieval Communal Organization', 10.

novel structure of relationships between the Crown and the domanial communities which had evolved in the Kingdom of Sicily.[121]

Sources of income

From the thirteenth to the eighteenth centuries Europe adopted a common taxation system, with local variants, that emphasised indirect, as opposed to direct, taxation. Taxes on essentials produced a large share of the regular income; port dues were followed by taxes on wine, grain, cattle and salt. The imposition of taxes on necessities rather than on luxury goods meant that the burden fell more heavily on the poor rather than on the rich.[122] Similarly in Malta, the *Università* could hope to achieve its targets and objectives only through the proper administration of income derived from various taxes and levies imposed on domestic and foreign trade, as well as from fines. The town council used these revenues not only to finance various projects and work towards the strengthening of the island's defence system, but also to pay salaries to the officials of various institutions.

Just like other communities within the *Regno*,[123] at times Malta had to bear the brunt of the Crown's fiscal crisis.[124] Such was the case under Martin I (1356–January 1410), during whose reign the *Università* of both Malta and Gozo were conceded extensive rights, including authorisation to impose new taxes or *gabelle* on imports[125] and exports, and on the sale of essential commodities like wine[126] and oil.[127] Such instances provided excellent opportunities for the *Università* to extend their reach.

Various other taxes were also imposed, as is attested in a number of *capitoli* dating to 1409 or 1410 in which the town council petitioned the Crown to revoke a set of restrictions which had been imposed on corsairing activities. Among others, these included a 20% tax payable to the admiralty, as well as payments of *tratte*[128] on

121 Bresc, *Un Monde Méditerranéen*, vol. 2, 731–2.

122 P. Spufford, 'The Role of Entrepreneurs in State Formation', in S. Cavaciocchi (ed.), *Poteri Economici e Poteri Politici Secc. XIII–XVIII, Atti della 'Trentesima Settimana di Studi', 27 aprile–1 maggio 1998* (Florence, 1999), 483–500: 485–6.

123 Epstein, *An Island for Itself*, 355.

124 Financial needs led to the pawning of Malta on 20 January 1421 for the price of 30,000 Aragonese florins, about ten times the annual royal income from both islands. Dalli, *Malta, The Medieval Millennium*, 204, 210.

125 A thirtieth *ad valorem* on all imported merchandise. Bresc, 'The "Secrezia" and the Royal Patrimony', in Luttrell (ed.), *Medieval Malta*, 126–62: 134.

126 This was set at one florin per *botta* of imported wine, two *quartucchi* on each *quartaria* of wine sold in retail. Bresc, 'The "Secrezia" and the Royal Patrimony', in Luttrell (ed.), *Medieval Malta*, 126–62: 134.

127 Bresc, 'The "Secrezia" and the Royal Patrimony', in Luttrell (ed.), *Medieval Malta*, 126–62: 150. Dalli, *Malta, The Medieval Millennium*, 189, 200, 204.

128 A *tratta* or an export licence was a special duty with an oscillating value. While one *salma* of wheat had to pay one *tratta*, the same measure of barley paid only half a *tratta*. C. Trasselli, 'Una statistica maltese del secolo XVI', *Economia e Storia*, 9 (1966), 474–80: 475.

supplies for Maltese-based galleys.[129] This process was intensified under Alfonso V (1416–58), who, according to Epstein, 'made peremptory demands for financial aid and expanded the range of financial and administrative burdens which localities had to bear, leaving it to communities to meet them as best they could and shifting the focus of conflict over allocation to the localities'.[130] Such measures led to a situation in which taxes were also used for ad hoc and often short-term purposes, including the buying back of local privileges[131] or local offices[132] which were sold outright to provide the Crown with a much-needed current income.[133] Royal finances, on the other hand, had three main purposes: to support the Crown; to finance the defence of the realm; and to be distributed as patronage or in payment for service.[134]

The island had a dire need to import essential foodstuffs and commodities, and taxes were imposed on practically all commodities. The town council also had an obligation to collect a tax for the Crown called the *collecta*, or by its Spanish name *donativo*,[135] which was handed over to the royal commissioner or *sindicaturi*. Each village had its own *gabellotto/i*, whose job was to organise and supervise the collection of royal and municipal taxes. This job carried with it the power to enforce discipline in case of default, and was delegated to the highest bidder at a public auction which was held annually towards the end of August. The *gabellotto*, usually a wealthy person, guaranteed to pay the *Università* an agreed sum of money which would have been collected from the tax-payers.[136] He acquired his salary and registered a profit by retaining a percentage of the amount collected. From the records of council minutes it is clear that auctions of tax farms were not always successful, and council members sometimes found themselves in a situation where no one had applied for the post. Such was the situation at a meeting during which the town council discussed an unsuccessful auction for the post of tax farmer in respect of the tax on imported wine, the *cabella intrate sive floreni pro vegete/butti*.[137]

Among the *gabella* mentioned in the records of the *Università* is the *gabella del maldenaro* (maldinaru),[138] which enabled the *Università* to impose a tax of two *denari* on every *rotolo* of meat sold. Although this tax continued to be exacted until the end of the Order's rule, members of the Order, who were the island's prime consumers of

129 Dalli, *Malta, The Medieval Millennium*, 200.

130 Epstein, *An Island for Itself*, 355. See also D. Mack Smith, *A History of Sicily: Medieval Sicily 800–1713* (London, 1968), 94–104.

131 This was the case with the pawning of Malta to the Castilian alley captain Gonslavo Monroy in 1421. The Maltese redeemed their island in 1428.

132 Dalli, 'Medieval Communal Organization', 9.

133 Mack Smith, *A History of Sicily*, 97.

134 Epstein, *An Island for Itself*, 379. The *Secreto* benefitted from taxes like the *dohana* or customs dues, the *mahdia* or Gozo ferry tax, the *gisia* or poll-tax imposed on Jews and other minor taxes. Bezzina, 'The Administration of the Maltese Islands', 82.

135 This name signified that in theory this was a gift by the parliament. Mack Smith, *A History of Sicily*, 96.

136 Bezzina, 'The Administration of the Maltese Islands', 75.

137 Wettinger, *Acta Iuratorum*, Doc. 50.

138 This tax was approved by the Viceroy D. Lopo Ximenes de Urrea on 17 January 1460. Vassallo, 'Prices of Commodities', 125.

meat, were exempted from this impost.[139] In an analysis of meat prices for the period 1467–1534, Anthony Vassallo illustrates how they were affected by the Order's arrival. He notes that during the period from 1467 to 1528 the prices of most types of meat registered only a slight increase, while during the early years of Hospitaller rule they registered sky-high increases, at times even doubling.[140]

After the Order's arrival on the island a tax related to the sale of local wine, called *xisa vini sive tri quartuchi per quartara*, was discontinued.[141] This was possibly done to promote the production and consumption of the local wine, which does not seem to have been renowned for its quality.[142] The *cabella baractaria*, which was a tax imposed on payments in kind and by barter,[143] also survived up to 1530. The imposition of such a tax indicates that barter must have been a common way of paying dues and in turn reflects a situation where a significant proportion of the population lacked cash in hand or found it difficult to undertake trading activities which involved cash transactions. In addition to the above taxes, owners of oxen had to contribute a specific amount of wheat known as *el-mahares* or *gius delle guardie*.[144] Other taxes were *xorta*, a tax on games of chance, *barbaria*, which was a tax and monopoly on barbers, *consura* or *cusia* on tailors,[145] *conciaria* on tanning of hides, *dohana* on imports and incomes from sales, *mahdia* on the ferry between Malta and Gozo[146] and *tintoria* on the dyeing of cloths.[147]

Table 2 provides a breakdown of taxes which were collected as part of the revenues of the Crown in 1506. The numbers indicate that, just as in the European context,

139 NLM, Univ. 202, fol. 215. Letter sent on 1 December 1565 by Commendatore Cellieus to the *jurats* of Mdina. This tax was farmed out to the highest bidder. After the issue of the September pricelist for meat, the issue of a *bando* proclaimed that retailers had to indicate the number of animals they had for slaughter and these had to pay the tax due on their meat. Butchers were required to weigh their meat in the presence of the tax-farmer in order to ensure just payment of the tax due. The penalty for tax evasion could cost the individual nine times the amount of tax evaded. NLM, Univ. 14, fol. 405 (12.ix.1582); Vassallo, 'Prices of Commodities', 126.

140 Vassallo, 'Prices of Commodities', 120–60.

141 According to Fiorini the last mention of the *cabellotto xise* occurs in 1548, see NLM, Univ. 13, fol. 251v, and Fiorini, 'The Municipal Councils', 20 n. 77. The Castellan was exempt from paying tax on wine. Bezzina, 'The Administration of the Maltese Islands', 83.

142 Wettinger, 'Agriculture in Malta', in Buhagiar (ed.), *Proceedings of History Week, 1981*, 1–48: 23.

143 Fiorini, 'Malta in 1530', in Mallia-Milanes (ed.), *Hospitaller Malta 1530–1798* 111–98: 172.

144 Prior to the construction of coastal watch towers the farmers (*massari*) contributed towards the expense and maintenance of the cavalrymen who guarded the shore. The latter would warn them if the enemy was sighted so that the farmers, together with their animals, would have ample time to take refuge in fortified zones. In 1691 the quantity to be contributed was one and a half *mondello* of meslin (a mixture of wheat and barley) for the first and second ox or cow. Mifsud, 'Appunti sugli archvi di Malta', 39 n. 122.

145 Bresc, 'The "Secrezia" and the Royal Patrimony', in Luttrell (ed.), *Medieval Malta*, 126–62: 134.

146 This was a tax on livestock carried from Gozo to Malta, and up until 1602 it was still exacted. Fiorini, 'The Municipal Councils', 20.

147 For a full list refer to Bresc, 'The "Secrezia" and the Royal Patrimony', in Luttrell (ed.), *Medieval Malta*, 126–62: 134.

taxes on imports produced the largest share of the island's regular income.[148] As already noted, with the transfer of Malta to the Knights of St John these revenues were transferred to the revenues enjoyed by the Grand Master. In addition to these there was another income of 98 *uncie* 1 *tarì* 8 *grani*, collected from a 15% tax which feudal lords residing outside the island had to pay as a contribution towards the island's security.[149] This tax was exacted until 1600, after when it seems to have shrunk considerably and eventually fizzled out.[150] It is important to note that there is only fragmented information recording the Crown's revenues from the Maltese islands. The figures reproduced in Table 2 are taken from Alfredo Mifsud's analysis of the Barberi report. Although some revenue-generating sources such as the *mahdia* tax and revenue from feudal lands are missing or incomplete, historians tend to agree that so far there is no better or fuller list, and have not disputed Barberi's report. However, these figures should not be interpreted as showing the yearly fixed income from the Maltese islands, since it is not known whether Barberi was 'giving the figures for a particular year which he regarded as an average one, or merely providing some isolated and unrepresentative statistics'.[151]

In order to relate the amounts in Table 2 to some contemporary values, an indication of the approximate prices of some commodities and salaries during roughly the same period is useful. Some salaries provide compounding differences when compared to others. A case in point was the salary paid to the Viceroy, who received 700 *uncie* per annum, as against the 30 *uncie* earned by a high-ranking official like the Castellan.[152] However, when the latter's pay is compared to the annual salary of the deputy Castellan, who got 8 *uncie*, this seems to have been quite good remuneration. A labourer's daily income between 1494 and 1496 was approximately 10 *grani*,[153] which had risen by only 2 *grani* by 1534,[154] while that of a master mason, craftsman or his assistant ranged from 1 *tarì* 8 *grani* to 1 *tarì* 2 *grani* 3 *dinari*.[155] Such figures indicate wide differences between incomes, making certain commodities on the market affordable to only a handful of people.

Stanley Fiorini calculated that the cost of supplying the basic amount of bread for a family of six amounted to 6 *tarì* per month, so that a labourer who supported

148 Spufford, 'The Role of Entrepreneurs in State Formation', in Cavaciocchi (ed.), *Poteri Economici e Poteri Politici*, 483–500: 486.

149 On 22 May 1507, King Ferdinand sanctioned a tax of 15% on the assets of those who did not reside on the island. Mifsud, 'Appunti sugli archvi di Malta', 39; Valentini, 'Funzione storica e disperione del patrimonio demaniale di Malta', 34 n. 122.

150 Fiorini, 'The Municipal Councils', 20.

151 Bresc, 'The "Secrezia" and the Royal Patrimony', in Luttrell (ed.), *Medieval Malta*, 126–62: 127.

152 Bresc, 'The "Secrezia" and the Royal Patrimony', in Luttrell (ed.), *Medieval Malta*, 126–62: 138, Table IV.

153 Fiorini, 'Malta in 1530', in Mallia-Milanes (ed.), *Hospitaller Malta 1530–1798*, 111–98: 171, Table IX.

154 Most of the salaries of the *Università* were paid in Sicilian money, thus 10 *uncia boni* was equivalent to 29 times the wage of a labourer. Fiorini, 'Malta in 1530', in Mallia-Milanes (ed.), *Hospitaller Malta 1530–1798*, 111–98: 171.

155 Fiorini, 'Malta in 1530', in Mallia-Milanes (ed.), *Hospitaller Malta 1530–1798*, 111–98: 171, Table IX.

Table 2 Revenues of the Royal Crown in 1506[a]

Type of tax	**Income in *uncia*, *tarì* and *grani*[b]**
La gabella della Cascia e del peso	
On merchandise – import[c]	93.02.00
On exports	18.18.00
On land where wheat is sown	9.20.02
On land where barley is sown	5.12.00
On cumin	0.15.00
On cotton	7.15.00
On leather	5.20.00
On linen	5.10.10
On dye	0.13.10
La tassa delle tratte sulle bestie	
On animals[d]	0.10.00
On biscuits	2.00.00
On anchorage[e]	1.00.00
On the redemption of slaves[f]	1.6.00
Le gabelle della barba e dell'ufficio del Bajulo a censo	
Income from the office of the Bailiff and the tax on barbers	20.0.00
From feudal land which was not alienated	N/A

a Under the Order's rule, these taxes were modified and gradually increased in such a way that customs revenues in 1775 amounted to 75,000 scudi per annum. For a more detailed breakdown of these taxes refer to Mifsud, 'Papi, Fortificazioni e Tasse', 410 n. 2.

b These amounts were given in Sicilian currency, usually referred to as ponderis generalis or bona moneta equivalent to the uncia of 30 tarì, the tarì of 20 grani and the grano of 6 denari. The Maltese currency, also divided into uncia, tarì, grani and denari, was worth one-seventh of the Sicilian. During the sixteenth century, the Sicilian uncia was worth half of the Neapolitan uncia. See G. Alfani & S. Sardone, 'Long Term Trends in Economic Inequality in Southern Italy. The Kingdom of Napes and Sicily in the 16th–18th Centuries: First Results', http://eh.net/eha/wp-content/uploads/2015/05/Alfani.pdf (accessed 9 August 2016). It is not known if and in what metal Maltese money was coined. Bresc, 'The "Secrezia" and the Royal Patrimony', in Luttrell (ed.), Medieval Malta, 126–62: 127, n. 4; Fiorini, 'Malta in 1530', in Mallia-Milanes (ed.), Hospitaller Malta 1530–1798, 111–98: 162–3.

c In 1646 a tax of 18 tarì per uncia was paid on all types of merchandise imported into and exported from Maltese ports. Over and above this tax there was another tax known as dritto di cascia, which amounted to one tarì per uncia on the same merchandise. A total of 7,000 scudi per year were collected from these taxes. Mifsud, 'Papi, Fortificazioni e Tasse', 410 n. 1.

d Animals exported from Malta included donkeys, horses and goats. Valentini, 'Funzione storica e disperione del patrimonio demaniale di Malta', 30 n. 109.

e This was calculated according to the number of masts. Valentini, 'Funzione storica e disperione del patrimonio demaniale di Malta', 31 n. 112.

f Under de Valette this was increased to 25 scudi per slave.

Source: Mifsud, 'Papi, Fortificazioni e Tasse', 410.

a family of six had to budget half his earnings for the supply of bread alone.[156] However, in view of Malta's agrarian-based economy this problem would have been alleviated, since most consumers were also producers. This eliminated the need to buy a variety of staple commodities, which consumers could acquire through barter. As has already been noted, this was such an important economic activity that the authorities imposed a tax on it.

The donation

Although the deed of donation of the Maltese islands to the Order of St John was issued on 23 March 1530,[157] negotiations for the cession of Malta had started as early as 1523.[158] Malta, situated at a comfortable distance from other European countries, seemed to present a good option for the Order to establish itself and consolidate its presence without any worries of invasion from surrounding countries.[159] The island was also sufficiently close to enemy territory to permit the Order to exercise its main function as *milites Christi*.[160]

Notwithstanding Malta's ideal location on the central axis of the Mediterranean, the Knights were well aware of the difficulties that this donation presented. For this reason, they pleaded with the king to grant them a three- or four-year stay in Syracuse which would permit them to fortify the island. Further, they viewed the

156 Fiorini, 'Malta in 1530', in Mallia-Milanes (ed.), *Hospitaller Malta 1530–1798*, 111–98: 170.

157 Original deed of cession is preserved at the National Library of Malta, NLM, AOM 70. For a translation of the deed of donation by Louis Mendola with additional historical material by V. Mallia-Milanes refer to https://www.orderofmalta.int/wp-content/uploads/archive/pubblicazioni/Charlesv_donation.pdf (accessed 7 March 2017).

158 The exact date and outcome of the initial discussions on the possibility of settlement in Malta is still not known. However, according to the early sixteenth-century Venetian diarist Marino Sanuto, 'on 10 April 1523 ... Grand Master Philippe Villiers de L'Isle Adam, wrote to the Signory of Venice to thank them for their hospitality and referred to his appeal to the Emperor Charles V, offering him 100,000 ducats in cash for the seaport of Brindisi or the Mediterranean island of Malta'. R. Fulin et al., *I Diarii di Marino Sanuto* (58 vols, Venice, 1879–1903), xxxiv, 98, as quoted in V. Mallia-Milanes, 'Introduction to Hospitaller Malta', in V. Mallia-Milanes (ed.), *Hospitaller Malta 1530–1798*, 1–42, 2. Refer also to Valentini, 'I Cavalieri di S. Giovanni da Rodi a Malta: Trattative diplomatiche', 137.

159 'During the XIV century the Hospital on the island of Rhodes and the Teutonic Order in Prussia and Livonia created order states which ruled over virtually independent territories. The Hospitallers developed a formula for an island-based order state which allowed it after 1530 to survive on Malta with a genuine military function for many centuries. The Teutonic Order faced mounting difficulties as almost all its neighbours became Christian so that the principal justification for its existence was eroded.' A. Luttrell, *Studies on the Hospitallers after 1306: Rhodes and the West* (Aldershot, 2007), paper I: 88.

160 'The military-religious orders were corporations of religious within the Roman Church whose special function was to oppose the infidel or the pagan.' Luttrell, *Studies on the Hospitallers after 1306*, paper I: 88. While the Order of the Templars was composed of military men with a warlike purpose from the time of its foundation, the Hospitaller Order of St John added this military activity to its charitable concerns only gradually. Luttrell, *Studies on the Hospitallers after 1306*, paper I: 80–1.

island as unable to provide for their daily needs, and so they also requested tax-free concessions on various essential commodities which would be imported from both Sicily and Naples.[161] The Viceroy of Sicily, Ettore Pignatelli,[162] who according to Bosio insisted in 1523 that the Grand Master should remain in Messina until he had sorted out the Order's affairs,[163] was motivated to support the Order's possible establishment on the Maltese islands,[164] as it would rid him of the financial burden which their defence presented to a Crown in serious financial difficulties.[165] The extent to which Pignatelli felt that Malta was a 'burden' can be discerned from the way in which he removed all duty-free quotas and, when complaints from both the Order and the Mdina *Università* reached the king, the latter ordered that these be conceded to. Pignatelli issued the quotas, but at the same time imposed taxes relating to them. Equally supportive of the cession of Malta to the Order were Pope Adrian VI (r. 1522–23) and King Henry VIII of England (r. 1509–47), who intervened with Charles V in favour of the grant.[166]

The political context played a major role in Charles V's decision to renounce direct administration of the islands and offer it to the Order, together with the Tripoli base. Malta was a frontier against Ottoman expansion, and its potential loss would inevitably bring the enemy closer, apart from providing the Muslims with excellent port facilities. But the Order's presence would ensure constant policing of the pirate-infested seas, which were a barrier to effective commercial relations with the East and with North Africa. However, the Order's request for possession of the island '*cum mero et mixto imperio*'[167] – which translated into the delegation of all powers, political, administrative, fiscal, military, judicial and feudal – met with the king's difficult terms of transfer,[168] which at first were unacceptable due to the *sine qua non* addition of Tripoli.[169] At this very early stage the Maltese town council members, hearing rumours of the possible alienation of their islands from the royal demesne,[170] decided to act.

161 Valentini, 'I Cavalieri di S. Giovanni da Rodi a Malta: Trattative diplomatiche', 144.

162 Pignatelli was appointed Lieutenant General on 22 February 1517 and then promoted to Viceroy of Sicily by Charles V.

163 G. Bosio, *Dell'Istoria della Sacra Religione et Illustrissima Militia de S. Giovanni Gerosolimitano* (3 vols, Rome, 1594–1602), vol. 3, 15.

164 A. Giuffrida, *La Sicilia e l'Ordine di Malta 1529–1530, La centralità della periferia Mediterranea* (Palermo, 2006), 13

165 NLM, Univ. 13, fol. 247. See also Valentini, 'I Cavalieri di S. Giovanni da Rodi a Malta: Trattative diplomatiche', Doc. III: 181, refers to the instructions given to the Order's ambassadors to Charles V in respect of their diplomatic mission for the cession of the Maltese islands.

166 Valentini, 'I Cavalieri di S. Giovanni da Rodi a Malta: Trattative diplomatiche', Doc. II: 180.

167 Valentini, 'I Cavalieri di S. Giovanni da Rodi a Malta: Trattative diplomatiche', 143.

168 Valentini, 'I Cavalieri di S. Giovanni da Rodi a Malta: Trattative diplomatiche', 147.

169 Bosio, *Dell'istoria della sacra Religione*, vol. 3, 77E.

170 According to Valentini these were strengthened by the meetings held between L'Isle Adam and Pignatelli in Messina. Valentini, 'I Cavalieri di S. Giovanni da Rodi a Malta: Trattative diplomatiche', 145.

Accordingly, on 10 April 1524, the council summoned the *parlamentu generali*. The assembly deemed it unacceptable that the islands should once more be given as a fief. It was further agreed that, 'in virtue of the said town's privileges the *jurats*, on behalf of the *Università* send as ambassadors *magnificus* Alvarum de Casseres, one of the *jurats*, and *magnificus* Antonium Bonellu, doctor of laws, to resist and fight against the said concession'.[171] The two men were to go directly to the Viceroy and, should their mission fail, they were to lay their complaints before the king himself.[172] The outcome of this meeting is not known, as relevant documents are not available in local archives.[173]

In the meantime, on 28 June 1524, eight months after the Order's official request to Charles V, the Knights commissioned eight of their members to visit Malta, Gozo and Tripoli and compile a report on, among other things, the state of the city and its fortresses, the number of villages or castles and the number of able-bodied men, the revenues and the annual output of agricultural produce, the quality and the quantity of potable water, wood, stone, lime and other building material which would facilitate the building of defence structures. The commission was also instructed to inspect 'that tongue or stretch of land of this island where, as has often been speculated, the Castle or fortress which would serve as residence to the Convent could easily be built'.[174] The Order thus made clear, as early as 1524, its intention to build the future fortress city of Valletta.[175]

Pignatelli, signing as El Conte de Monteleone, sent definite instructions to the Mdina town council regarding the visit of these Knights. Shrewdly, he camouflaged the expedition as one heading for Tripoli on a mission assigned by the Crown, and he instructed that the Knights were to be given 'the best possible treatment' by the local authorities and supplied with all that was required for the continuation of their journey.[176] It is clear that the Crown was seeking to keep the Maltese in

171 *'in virtute privilegii dicte civitatis magnifici Jurati nomine Universitàtis recurrant et mittant in ambaxiatores magnificos Alvarum de Cassares, unum ex Juratis, ac Mag. Antonium Bonellum ju. u. Doctorem, ad resitendum et inpugandum dictam concessionem.*' NLM, Univ. 12 (10.iv.1524). Valentini, 'I Cavalieri di S. Giovanni da Rodi a Malta: Trattative diplomatiche', Doc. V: 183–4. Three representatives were eventually chosen and in addition to the above mentioned two, Giacomo Ingeraldo Inguanez was to form part of the delegation. Valentini, 'I Cavalieri di S. Giovanni da Rodi a Malta: Trattative diplomatiche', 146.

172 Trasselli states that Charles V was not familiar with Sicily, did not hold a Latin or Mediterranean education and was thus not tied in any way to the paternalistic traditions of his predecessors. For the king, the privileges granted by the Crown did not hold any special significance and he did not in any way feel that he had to honour them. Trasselli, *Da Ferdinando Il Cattolico a Carlo V*, vol. 2, 723.

173 Research in foreign archives, such as those in Sicily or Spain, could well shed light on this important episode in Maltese history.

174 *'quella lingua o strectura de dita insole dove, speculando la carta, havemo piu' volte ragionato se porria commodamente edificare lo Castello o vero forteza per la residentia del Convento.*' Document reproduced in Valentini, 'I Cavalieri di S. Giovanni da Rodi a Malta: Trattative diplomatiche', Doc. VII: 185–7.

175 The foundation stone of Valletta was laid after the Ottoman siege of 1565 by Grand Master de Valette (1557–68) on 28 March 1566.

176 '*cum omni charicze et bon tratamento possibile*'. NLM, Univ. 12, fol. 362v (13.vii.1524).

ignorance of negotiations for the possible transfer of Malta to the Knights, in an attempt to avoid an eventual build-up to resistance from the Maltese *Università*. The captain-in-arms, Girolamo Campo, together with a *jurat*, was to accompany the Order's delegation because, it was stated, they were to have access even to the most confidential information and wanted to see the ports and other localities on the islands. Unfortunately, the official report of the eight-man commission is lost. However, a summary of the findings was noted by Bosio.[177] These reveal that, except for the excellent harbour facilities, the commissioners felt that the islands had nothing to offer.

Interestingly, according to Vincenzo Bonavita, during the course of the negotiations in June 1526 Pignatelli appointed *Fra.* Alfonso Paradal,[178] a Spanish merchant and a servant-in-arms of the Order, to be officer in charge of the defence of the *castrum maris*.[179] Bonavita claims that this was a strategic move on the Viceroy's part to facilitate the arrival of the Order, should the Maltese authorities offer any resistance. The appointment by monarchs of members of the Order of St John as Castellans in various strategic locations throughout Europe was not uncommon during the sixteenth century.[180] Why would Bonavita's claim merit further investigation? Historians have always asserted the almost total hegemony of the de Nava and de Guevara families[181] as Castellans of the *castrum maris* up to the time of the Hospitallers' arrival in 1530.[182] Even Bosio, in his history of the Order of St John, states that Alvaro de Nava had been appointed Castellan for life by the Spanish king, and that when the Order took over in 1530, as compensation for losing his office they offered him an annual payment of 32½ Sicilian *uncie*.[183] How far can Paradal's supposed appointment in 1526, and Bonavita's claim that he was stationed in Malta at the *castrum maris* as a strategic move by the Sicilian Viceroy, be substantiated from the extant evidence?

It can be ascertained from the minutes of the municipal council meeting held on 22 June 1526 that a *Fra.* Alonso [*sic*] indeed found his way to Malta in 1526 and

177 Bosio, *Dell'Istoria della Sacra Religione*, vol. 3, 29–32.

178 In a biographical note Bosio writes the following about Paradal, '*Alfonso Paradal Biscaino entra in Rodi assediato et havendo perduta una sua nave in servitio della Religione e da quella stipendiato sotto l'habito di Donato, e fu poi Gran Visconte di Malta.*' (Alfonso Paradal from Biscay sails in a besieged Rhodes and having lost his ship while in service of the Religion is by it [the Religion] rewarded by being made a Donat, and later *Vicecomite*.) Bosio, *Dell'Istoria della Sacra Religione*, vol. 2, Alphabetical Index.

179 V. Bonavita, *Dissertazioni Storico Legali su Malta e Gozo*, fols 26v–27.

180 There were other instances when members of the Order of St John were placed as Castellans in European castles. See, for example, British History Online, http://www.british-history.ac.uk/report.aspx?compid=92249 (accessed 9 May 2016), which refers to a Knight of the Order of St John in charge of a castellany in England in 1462. (Thanks are due to Stephen Spiteri for this information dated 30 January 2012.) See also Giuffrida, *La Sicilia e l'Ordine di Malta*, 21.

181 These were two of the major landowning families in Malta.

182 Wettinger, 'The Castrum Maris', in Bugeja et al., *Birgu: A Maritime City*, 31–71: 43. A. Luttrell, 'The House of the Castellan of Malta', *Heritage*, 9 (Malta, 1978), 161–5: 161.

183 Bosio, *Dell'Istoria della Sacra Religione*, vol. 3, 84.

was subsequently 'in charge of the castle of these islands'.[184] His arrival does not seem to have provoked any protests from the *Università*, since the only discussion about his arrival was related to whether he would be allowed to go to the Castle to perform his duties or be kept in '*purgazione di contumacia*'[185] for forty days for having landed at Scicli in Sicily, a town suspected of harbouring plague. Opinions differed and various councillors expressed an opinion that if, after this period, the health authorities had further reservations about his health, *Fra.* Alonso would have to remain in quarantine until he was certified free from any contamination.[186] The full name of *Fra.* Alfonso Paradal and his connection with the Hospitaller Order before 1526 are explicitly mentioned by Bosio, who notes that during the siege of Rhodes the Spaniard Alfonso Paradal had shown great courage and even lost one of his ships in the service of the Order. Bosio further states that in order to reward him for his loyalty the Order had bestowed on him the title of Donat of the Order.[187]

Various documents pertaining to the very first years of Hospitaller rule on Malta also make continual reference to Paradal, who is noted as holding important positions in the new administrative frame of the Order.[188] In fact, notarial acts pertaining to the years 1538[189] and 1545[190] refer to him as *maiorem vicecomite huius suburbi melitae*.[191] Other documents refer to him as forming part of the Confraternity of the Purification of the Blessed Virgin, which had been established in the principal

184 '*in custodia castri huius Insule*' [sic]. NLM, Univ. 12, fol. 409v (22.vi.1526). See also S. Fiorini (ed.), *Documentary Sources of Maltese History, Part III: Documents of the Maltese Universitas, No. 3: Acta Juratorum et Consilii Civitatis et Insulae Maltae, II: 1512–1531* (Malta, 2016), Doc. 917.

185 In quarantine. NLM, Univ. 12, fol. 409v (22.vi.1526).

186 NLM, Univ. 12, fol. 409v (22.vi.1526).

187 For a more detailed description of Paradol's participation in the siege of Rhodes refer to Bosio, *Dell'Istoria della Sacra Religione*, vol. 2, 698–707.

188 Paradal seems to have been very active in various economic activities as there are several references to his name in notarial registers. Some examples may be found in NAV, R 202/2, fols 150–151v (15.ii.1537 *ab inc*), R 202/3, fols 78–81 (29.xi.1538); R 202/9, fols 272v–273 (5.ii.1544 *ab inc*). See also NAM, MCC, Reg. AO, vol. 1, fol. 50 (30.ix.1536) which refers to a *Fra.* Aloysius Pardal [sic] *vicecomes* and NAM, MCC, Reg. AO, vol. 1, fol. 147 (3.ix.1538), wherein Paradol is mentioned as performing the duties of a sanitary official. See also S. Fiorini, 'The Rhodiot Community of Birgu, A Maltese Maritime City: 1530–c. 1550', in V. Mallia-Milanes (ed.), *Library of Mediterranean History* (Malta, 1994), vol. 1, 183–241: 191, 194. Fiorini lists Paradal as a member of the Rhodiot community. It is important to note that in documents he is never referred to as being Greek but listed as a *biscanio*.

189 NAV, R 202/3, fol. 78 (28.xi.1538).

190 NAV, R 202/9, fol. 272v (5.ii.1545).

191 For the duties and functions of the *Vicecomite* in Hospitaller Rhodes refer to NLM, Libr. MS 153, *Pragmaticae Rhodiae, F. Emerici D'Amboyse Magni Magistri Sacrae Religionis Hierosolymitanae*, fols 9v–10. During Hospitaller rule in Malta, this office did not experience any major changes. A. Micallef, *Diritto Municipale di Malta Compilato Sotto De Rohan G.M. Or Nuovamente Corredato di Annotazioni* (2 vols, Malta, 1841), vol. 1, 53–9. (Thanks are due to Albert Ganado for making a copy of this publication available to me.)

church of the *castrum maris* prior to the arrival of the Order.[192] If Bonavita[193] is to be believed, before the Order's arrival Paradal was not very highly regarded by the *Secreto*, since his name was the last one on the salaries list. Bonavita substantiates his claims by referring to two protests which were filed by Paradal and which, according to him, were registered in the acts of Notary Giacomo Bondino on 2 and 3 November 1528.[194] If the *Fra.* Alonso documented in the town council minutes of 1526 was in indeed the newly appointed official in charge of the defence of the castle, could his appointment have been related to the on-going negotiations for the donation of Malta?

Bearing in mind that in 1524, when rumours of the ceding of Malta to the Order first started to spread, the municipal council had already petitioned the Crown with its objections, and also considering that the Maltese had the right to bear arms against the imposition of feudal lords, was this a significant move on the part of the Sicilian Viceroy? The appointment would have taken place concurrently with another one, that of the new captain-in-arms, Johannes Ribes Altes.[195] Could such cautious manoeuvring have been intended to strengthen royal control over the port and artillery in the event of any resistance by the islanders following the donation of the island to the Knights Hospitaller?[196] Should the need have arisen, would Paradal have taken over from de Nava and facilitated the landing of the Order's troops and artillery?

192 M. Fsadni, 'The Dominicans', in Bugeja et al., *Birgu: A Maltese Maritime City*, vol. 2, 663–715: 672.

193 Bonavita, *Dissertazioni Storico Legali*, fol. 27.

194 Various lacunae in the acts of Notary Giacomo Bondino indicate that these seem to have been lost, most probably due to damage sustained through two direct hits which the *Auberge d'Italie* suffered in April 1942 during World War II. The auberge then housed the Notarial collection and, according to an inquiry report prepared by H. Jenkinson on the state of the archives of Malta in May 1944, the bombing on these two occasions resulted in the destruction or damage of some 2,000 volumes. *Report by Mr. H. Jenkinson, C.B.E. on The Archives of Malta* (May 1944). (Acknowledgements are due to Michael Ellul for providing me with a copy of this document.) The present volumes show signs of re-binding whose material indicates that it could have been done during the British period. It is thus probable that when Bonavita was writing his dissertations in the first decade of the nineteenth century, these acts were still extant and available for his perusal.

195 NLM, Univ. 12, fols 408v–409 (11.v.1526). A transcription of a copy of this letter found in the Cathedral Archives is available in J. Del Amo García, S. Fiorini, G. Wettinger (eds), *Documentary Sources of Maltese History, Part III: Documents of the Maltese Universitas, No. 1: Cathedral Museum, Mdina, Archivum Cathedralis Melitæ, Miscellanea 33: 1405–1452* (Malta, 2001), Doc. 124.

196 The reason given for appointing Johannes Ribes Altes was that there was an increase in the number of Turkish and Moorish ships in the seas of the realm. Ribes Altes was reprimanded in March 1527 by the Viceroy 'for interfering in the running of the Maltese judicial system by pretending to decide cases outside his jurisdiction contrary to Maltese privileges ... it was further stressed that the Captain at arms' jurisdiction is limited to war time and to four specific cases identified in the *capitula*'. Del Amo García et al., *Documentary Sources of Maltese History, Part III: Documents of the Maltese Universitas, No. 1*, Doc. 127.

As has been observed elsewhere, the manning of the *castrum maris* had always received the Crown's special attention, due to its great importance for the security of the whole island.[197] Having already proved his loyalty towards to Order in the siege of Rhodes, and being also of Spanish origin, would have made Paradal the ideal candidate for the post. Just how real the Knights considered the possibility of resistance by the islanders can be observed from a chancery document dated 24 July 1530 which notes the peaceful transfer of government, '*havendo havuto adesso el possesso pacifico*' [sic] (having had now the peaceful possession [of Malta]).[198] The missing link in the puzzle seems to be the lost notarial document of Giacomo Bondino, which would confirm the true identity of *Fra.* Alonso and his official designation. Perhaps the collection in the Notarial Archives will yield further surprises for historians in the future.

Negotiations for the transfer of Malta seem to have become protracted after the initial discussions,[199] even more so when the Order began to consider the prospect of reconquering its Rhodian home.[200] However, this had fallen through by 1529. Bosio informs us that Grand Master L'Isle Adam, having lost hope of generating enough funds to recapture Rhodes, was considering attacking Modon, a well-fortified city which could serve the Order's purpose since it could be made impregnable with only minor expense. It seems, however, that even this project was shelved, the Grand Master considering it to be too risky.[201] Thus, on 26 September 1529 the Grand Master once again requested Pope Clement VII to negotiate with Charles V on the question of Malta,[202] even though, '[with Malta] lacking every comfort and pleasure,

197 Wettinger, 'The Castrum Maris', in Bugeja et al., *Birgu: A Maritime City*, 31–71: 42.

198 NLM, AOM, Lib. Bull. 414, fol. 271v (24.vii.1530).

199 The General Chapter held on 23 May 1527 unanimously approved the acceptance of Malta and Gozo as the seat of the Order on condition that the Order would not be made vassals to the Spanish Crown. Diplomatic envoys were immediately sent to various European kings and princes in order to assure them of the Order's continued neutrality. Valentini, 'I Cavalieri di S. Giovanni da Rodi a Malta: Trattative diplomatiche', Doc. XXI: 202, Doc. XXIV: 204, Doc. XXV: 205.

200 Valentini, 'I Cavalieri di S. Giovanni da Rodi a Malta: Trattative diplomatiche', Doc. VII: 160–2. On 7 October 1527 the Order anchored at Nice, due to the bad political situation in Italy and the outbreak of plague. L'Isle Adam's letters from this port addressed to various European powers communicated only the Order's proposed reconquest of Rhodes and did not mention the donation of Malta. From here the Grand Master tried to mobilise the necessary forces to undertake this feat. The Maltese harbours were to accommodate the Order's fleet, which was to embark on this mission. NLM, AOM, Lib. Bull. 414, fol. 258 (13.vi.1529). Charles V offered 25,000 *scudi* for the expedition, while the King of Portugal offered 15,000 ducats. NLM, AOM, Lib. Bull. 414, fol. 271v. Valentini, 'I Cavalieri di S. Giovanni da Rodi a Malta: Trattative diplomatiche', 161–2. Accordingly, the Order's fleet left from Villefranche on 18 July 1529 and anchored in the Maltese ports on 29 August 1529. From here the Grand Master received news from his envoy Antonio Bosio that the project to conquer Rhodes had fallen through. Refer to letter written by the Grand Master to Pope Clement VII on 26 September 1529. NLM, AOM, Lib. Bull. 414, fol. 259v, transcribed in Valentini, 'I Cavalieri di S. Giovanni da Rodi a Malta: Trattative diplomatiche', Doc. XXXIII: 214–15.

201 Bosio, *Dell'Istoria della Sacra Religione*, vol. 3, 75.

202 NLM, AOM, Lib. Bull. 414, fol. 259v, transcribed in Valentini, 'I Cavalieri di S. Giovanni da Rodi a Malta: Trattative diplomatiche', Doc. XXXIII: 214–15.

we shall suffer a lot, which [suffering] we will be willing to endure since we shall be situated in a place where Christianity will benefit from our service ... and his Majesty and all the Christian princes will acknowledge this as a fact'.[203]

The Order's stay in Sicily was becoming more uneasy.[204] By mid-May 1530 the town authorities were once again discussing the donation of Malta and elected two ambassadors[205] to represent their objections to the Viceroy, giving them specific instructions to head directly to the king's court if the outcome of talks with the Viceroy was not positive.[206] The council based its objections on a juridical issue, since in 1428 the Maltese had redeemed their islands from the feudal lord de Monroy for the sum of 20,000 florins, which gave them the privilege to declare null and void any agreement that involved the transfer of Malta and Gozo to a feudal lord. This privilege had been reconfirmed by Charles V and his mother, Joan, on 22 September 1516.[207] Although the lack of documentation means that the outcome of this meeting is unknown, according to Bonavita, Pignatelli assured the Maltese delegation that this was a short-term fief, since the Knights intended to reconquer their Rhodian island and thus their stay would be temporary.[208]

Unlike the Order's invasion and subsequent occupation of Rhodes in the fourteenth century,[209] the occupation of Malta and Gozo was conducted in a peaceful manner, through a number of contracts between Charles V, the Church and members of the respective town councils of the two islands. Bonavita states that the Knights, aware of the fact that two of the most capable diplomats were away from the island, took advantage of the situation and immediately sent their procurators with the royal commissioners to negotiate terms with the remaining members of the town council. However, Bonavita's statement is not backed up by documentary evidence.[210] What is documented, and places Bonavita's claim in a stronger light, are the events that took place on 17 June 1530. On this date the Maltese

203 '*per esser priva d'ogni commodità et piacere, havremo da soffrire assai, il che faremo volentieri per essere situate in parte dove la christianità receverà servicio da noi ... et sua M.tà et tutti li principi christiani lo congnoscerano per effetto.*' NLM, AOM, Lib. Bull. 414, fol. 271. From a document containing the instructions given to *Fra.* Ludovico de Andugar the Grand Master's envoy to the King of Portugal on 24 July 1530.

204 This may be testified by a chancery document dated 21 May 1529 which sheds light on the necessity for the Order to have its own harbour in order to function properly. The reported incident states that a captured enemy ship which was now the property of the Order had anchored in Brindisi and the Castellan there had immediately taken hold of it, depriving the Order of a lucrative reward. NLM, Lib. Bull. 414, fol. 258 (21.v.1529).

205 These were G. Ingeraldo Inguanez and Antonio Bonello. Valentini, 'I Cavalieri di S. Giovanni da Rodi a Malta: Trattative diplomatiche', 168.

206 Valentini, 'I Cavalieri di S. Giovanni da Rodi a Malta: Trattative diplomatiche', Doc. XL: 224.

207 Valentini, 'I Cavalieri di S. Giovanni da Rodi a Malta: Trattative diplomatiche', 168.

208 Bonavita, *Dissertazioni Storico Legali*, fol. 28.

209 The Rhodians capitulated on terms which guaranteed their rights. A. Luttrell, 'Malta and Rhodes: Hospitallers and Islanders', in Mallia-Milanes (ed.), *Hospitaller Malta 1530–1798*, 255–284: 259.

210 Bonavita, *Dissertazioni Storico Legali*, fol. 28.

representatives[211] consented to the relaxation of the 30,000 florins (20,000 had been paid in 1428 and the other 10,000 were forgiven by de Monroy on his deathbed) to the Grand Master, hoping that when the Order left Malta and Gozo the sum would still be deposited at the *Regia Curia* and the islands would retain their place within the royal demesne.[212] This suggests that the municipal authorities indeed considered the alienation of their island to be short term in nature, while proving beneficial to the Knights since they could claim the royal demesne privileges when the need arose.[213] The following day, 18 June, the Order's procurators entered into an obligation to honour the privileges and customs of the local Church.[214]

By means of these agreements, the Order made the Maltese a party to the delivery of the islands under the feudal grant and thus succeeded in obtaining the consensus of the islands' leading institutions. They could now safely establish themselves without running the risk of being undermined. Valentini offers a different perspective on this mutual agreement. While he refers to Bosio's work, wherein the latter states that L'Isle Adam held secret negotiations with a view to conquering Modon from the Ottomans, according to Valentini this move reflected the Order's intentions to leave Malta as soon as the Modon campaign materialised.[215] However, if this was the case, why did the Knights opt to ransack the fortress-island in September 1531, barely a year after their arrival, and leave, when they could have held on to it[216] and left Malta?[217]

211 Apart from the members of the town council there were also the representatives of the villages of Naxxar, Birkirkara, Żurrieq, Siġġiewi, Birmiftuħ, Żejtun and Qormi. Valentini, 'I Cavalieri di S. Giovanni da Rodi a Malta: Trattative diplomatiche', Doc. XLI: 226.

212 NLM, Univ. 12, fol. 549v (17.vi.1530); Valentini, 'I Cavalieri di S. Giovanni da Rodi a Malta: Trattative diplomatiche', Doc. XLI: 225–6. (Note that Valentini's reference to this document has been changed because this volume, like many others in the section of the Archives of the Order which were previously part of the Library Manuscript collection, for a time was inventoried as MS 929. Thanks are due to Maroma Camilleri for this information communicated on 30 January 2012.) This agreement was ratified by the Grand Master by means of a Bull issued from Syracuse on 18 July 1530. NLM, AOM, Lib. Bull. 414, fol. 270. Valentini, 'I Cavalieri di S. Giovanni da Rodi a Malta: Trattative diplomatiche', Doc. XLII: 227.

213 As, for example, when negotiating for duty-free grain quotas.

214 Valentini, 'I Cavalieri di S. Giovanni da Rodi a Malta: Trattative diplomatiche', 169.

215 Valentini, 'I Cavalieri di S. Giovanni da Rodi a Malta: Trattative diplomatiche', 169. (Note that Valentini quotes the old reference to this document in his work, that is, Arch. Catt. MS XXVII, c. 691. This has now been reclassified and should read ACM, Misc. 28, fol. 347 – new stamped pagination.)

216 K. M. Setton, *The Papacy and the Levant (1204–1571)* (4 vols, Philadelphia, 1984), vol. 3, 352.

217 Anthony Luttrell informs us that, 'the old principle that the military orders could retain lands won from the infidel was recognized in 1307 in a papal confirmation of the Hospital's rights to Rhodes which it had conquered from enemies of Christendom, that is from "schismatic Greeks" and from "infidels" who must have been Turks'. A. Luttrell, 'The Earliest Documents on the Hospitaller *Corso* at Rhodes: 1413 and 1416', in B. Arbel (ed.) *Intercultural contacts in the medieval Mediterranean* (London and Portland Oregon, 1996), 177–88: 178; Mallia-Milanes, 'Introduction to Hospitaller Malta', in Mallia-Milanes (ed.), *Hospitaller Malta 1530–1798*, 1–42: 6–7.

The chief legal provisions of the Maltese grant, which was 'in perpetual, noble, full, and free enfeoffment',[218] were that it was a fief of the first order; that it was free, because it did not entail a duty of military service by the Order; that it was noble, because it had attached to it the prerogative of nobility,[219] which meant surmounting the coat of arms with the Marchional Crown;[220] and finally that it was *mero e misto* because full civil, criminal and political power was attached to it. The Hospitallers were bound to the annual feudal payment of a falcon or a hawk on All Saints' day to Charles V as King of Sicily, or subsequently to his successors.

On 10 June 1530 the Order received the Crown's permission to appoint persons to administrative and judicial roles, and other officials, and at the same time it had to confirm and approve the municipal laws, immunities and privileges of the Maltese or, if necessary, amend them accordingly.[221] This last clause gave the Order a free hand to embark on a policy which sought to accommodate both the islanders and its new rulers, the latter having their own laws and customs which had been tested in Rhodes for more than two hundred years. On 22 June 1530, almost four months before the Grand Master took official possession of the islands, Aurelio Buttigellis,[222] in his competence as lieutenant of the Grand Master and Governor of Malta, issued the first laws which were to regulate the feudal lands.[223] These stipulated that nobody could alienate immovable assets to foreigners or to other Maltese domiciled abroad without the written consent of the Grand Master; second, whoever possessed feudal lands and privileges had to produce proof of ownership, under pain of losing all rights.[224] Those resident in Malta were given fifteen days to comply, while those living in the *Regno* had forty days, and those posted outside the *Regno* had six months from the date of the proclamation. Lastly, the hunting and killing of partridge was declared illegal; anyone caught breaking this law would be fined 10 *uncie*.

218 '*in feudum nobile, liberum et francium.*' NLM, AOM, Lib. Bull. 414, fol. 221v. Valentini, 'I Cavalieri di S. Giovanni da Rodi a Malta: Trattative diplomatiche', Doc. XXXVII: 222.

219 If a fief had the prerogative of being noble it was thus called, otherwise if the feudal lord did not hold the right of nobility it was called *ignobile* or *plebeo*. P. De Bono, *Sommario della Storia della Legislazione in Malta* (Malta, 1897), 168 n. 2.

220 Later on, in the eighteenth century Grand Master Pinto (r. 1741–73) assumed the title of Most Serene Highness and changed the armorial emblems of the Order by substituting the Marchional Crown with the Royal Crown. He also started creating and granting titles of nobility. In 1753 he even denied Charles VII of Naples the right to send an ecclesiastical visitor to inquire about the prevailing condition of the Church in Malta. Mallia-Milanes, 'Introduction to Hospitaller Malta', in Mallia-Milanes (ed.), *Hospitaller Malta 1530–1798*, 1–42: 5.

221 Valentini, 'I Cavalieri di S. Giovanni da Rodi a Malta: Trattative diplomatiche', Doc. XXXVII (B): 220–1.

222 NLM, AOM, Lib. Bull. 414, fol. 273v. On 20 October 1531 Buttigelli appointed his brother Paolo as his procurator. See NAV, MS 585/1, fols 159–160v (20.x.1531). In the spring of 1534 he was successful in capturing three Turkish galleons in the waters off Djerba. Bono, 'Naval Exploits and Privateering', in Mallia-Milanes (ed.), *Hospitaller Malta 1530–1798*, 351–97: 354.

223 NLM, Univ. 7, fols 173v–174 (22.vi.1530).

224 NLM, Univ. 7, fol. 174ff still holds the original copies of the documents containing proof of titles produced by the various feudatories.

On 15 July 1530, on the insistence of the town council, the Grand Master ratified the promise made earlier by the Order's procurators[225] and declared that 'if the royal captain, the *jurats*, the *Università* and the people of these islands and towns promise and swear in honest in favour of us and our successors, we promise not to violate and to observe their privileges, immunities and their good customs'.[226] In the same month, the town councils of both Malta and Gozo sent the names of the new town officials who were to take office in September for the Grand Master's approval, thus indirectly confirming that they had accepted him as their new ruler.[227] The Grand Master approved these officials without any constraints,[228] thus carefully ensuring that long-standing claims to administrative posts were satisfied, and a smooth transition of power.

In any discussion of the administrative framework of the island it is essential to place the councillors of Mdina and the merchant entrepreneurs of Birgu in their separate spheres. A petition list for the opening of a Dominican friary in Birgu in 1528[229] shows that before the arrival of the Order the surnames of Birgu were mostly connected to maritime activity. At the same time, in contemporary documentation recording the members of the municipal nobility of Mdina and other royal appointments the complete absence of these same surnames – such as that of the Abelas[230] – is very noticeable.

[225] The appointed procurators were the Knights Ugo de Copons and Giovanni de Bonifaciis. Refer to Doc. XXXVII in Valentini, 'I Cavalieri di S. Giovanni da Rodi a Malta: Trattative diplomatiche', 220.

[226] '*Se capitaneo, Juratis, Universitàti et populo eiusdem insule et civitatis promisisse et iurasse in animam nostrum nostrorumque sucessorum inviolabilem observationem privillegiorum, immunitatum, libertatum, franchisiarum, jurium, laudabilium consuetudinum et bonorum morum eorundem.*' Valentini, 'I Cavalieri di S. Giovanni da Rodi a Malta: Trattative diplomatiche', Doc. XXXVII (D): 221.

[227] The *jurats* for Gozo were Giacomo Inguanez, Andriota Manara, Vito Vagnolo and Valerio d'Alagaria. Vincenzo Castillata was the treasurer. The *actapani* were Rodrigo Pontremolo and Antonio di Francesco Platamone *ex gratia*. The civil court's judges were Andriota di Santi, Nardo Manara and Massimo Falzoni, while Florio Sansone was the Civil Court's notary. Matheum Andree Sanctorum was *magistrum munditie*. In Malta's case the *jurats* were: Nardo de Bordino, Nicolo Sagona, Antonio Falzoni and Bernardo Cassar. The *acctapani* were Luca D'Armenia and Antonio Zammit and the treasurer was Mariano D'Armenia. The judges of the Civil Court were Graziano Vassallo, *letterato*, Guglielmo Ribera and Giovanni Bitirio, and the court's notary was Franchino d'Aligrito. *Nobilis* Giovanni Calavà was confirmed as *Secreto*. NLM, AOM, Lib. Bull. 414, fol. 273v. Valentini, 'I Cavalieri di S. Giovanni da Rodi a Malta: Trattative diplomatiche', 170–1.

[228] Valentini, 'I Cavalieri di S. Giovanni da Rodi a Malta: Trattative diplomatiche', Doc. XLII: 227.

[229] As Wettinger rightly points out, the list comprises the names of particular persons and is not strictly comparable to militia or *angara* records. However, those whose signature was solicited were, undoubtedly, among the leading men in the community of Birgu. Wettinger, 'The Castrum Maris', in Bugeja et al., *Birgu: A Maritime City*, 31–71: 59. The original deed is lost. Nevertheless, a copy still survives in the Dominican Archives Rabat. This was transcribed in S. Fiorini, 'Demographical Aspects of Birgu up to 1800', in Bugeja et al., *Birgu: A Maritime City*, Docs I and II; Fsadni, 'The Dominicans', 672–3.

[230] Abela was a surname that was intrinsically tied to mercantile activities in the late medieval and early modern period. Wettinger, 'The Castrum Maris', in Bugeja et al., *Birgu: A*

This suggests that at the time Birgu was a centre of commercial maritime activity which lacked social prestige, and there must have been a sharp social divide between the councillors in Mdina and the established merchants of Birgu.[231] The latter must have comprised a wealthy section of Maltese society, because their ships were considered sufficiently strong to assist the Royal fleet in 1432, and again in 1510 when King Ferdinand the Catholic conquered Tripoli.[232] In the town council meeting of 31 January 1520[233] the councillors agreed to send twelve ships, namely *grippe* and *galeotte*, to join the Royal forces in Trapani and ordered the Birgu ship owners to abide by the council's decision.[234] The *patroni* responded to such orders that although they were ready to send their vessels, they were not ready to provide the sailors since, in their opinion, this should be done by the authorities.[235] The members of the town council did not look favourably on this request and agreed only to contribute a loan towards the sailors' pay as far as Trapani. The *patroni* must have been contemptuous of the municipal authorities of Mdina for burdening them with such expenses. Their disdain may well have escalated the next day when the town crier read out a *bando* which stated that 'no skipper of *grippi* or other types of vessels should leave harbour without an authorisation from the town mayor and the aldermen on pain of death and confiscation of their goods'.[236]

This poses a number of questions. Why were the merchants not represented on the municipal council when the latter took such significant and costly decisions that affected them? Did they vie for a place in the local administrative set-up? Did they vie for a place in the higher echelons of society? This certainly was the case later on, in the seventeenth century, when Gian Frangisk Abela (1582–1655) was appointed Vice Chancellor of the Order. Would a study of the increase in title-holders, a phenomenon experienced in the eighteenth century, show any link to this new emerging elite?[237] What did the arrival of a strong naval establishment on the island really mean to these *patroni*?

The merchants must have known well that the presence of a prestigious maritime Order would translate into much greater potential for those among them who wished to enhance and develop their maritime activities. The establishment of a naval power would mean improved port facilities and better policing of navigable waters at a time when piracy was on the increase.[238] New investment opportunities could also be expected, since the Order's presence was sure to generate more work

Maritime City, 31–71: 66. For the importance of the Abelas as regards maritime connections refer to Fiorini, 'Demographical Aspects', in Bugeja et al., *Birgu: A Maritime City*, 219–54: 224–6.

231 Wettinger, 'The Castrum Maris', in Bugeja et al., *Birgu: A Maritime City*, 31–71: 58–9.

232 Fiorini, 'Demographical Aspects', in Bugeja et al., *Birgu: A Maritime City*, 219–54: 224.

233 NLM, Univ. 12, fols 232–234.

234 These orders list five Abelas in a list of thirteen names. Wettinger, 'The Castrum Maris', in Bugeja et al., *Birgu: A Maritime City*, 31–71: 66.

235 Wettinger, 'The Castrum Maris', in Bugeja et al., *Birgu: A Maritime City*, 31–71: 65.

236 Wettinger, 'The Castrum Maris', in Bugeja et al., *Birgu: A Maritime City*, 31–71: 66.

237 A. Caruana Galizia, 'The Maltese Nobility during the Hospitaller Period: Towards a Reappraisal', *Symposia Melitensia*, 7 (2011), 89–102.

238 A. Brogini, *Malte, frontière de chrétienté (1530–1670)* (Rome, 2006), 30–2.

and attract new trading partners. A list of Birgu inhabitants who used the services of Notary Nicolò de Agatiis during the years 1538–40 sheds light on the influx of people who made their way to Birgu in the early years of Hospitaller rule.[239] While the 1528 petition referred to above included only twenty-five different surnames of Birgu residents, the list of notarial acts includes 141 different surnames,[240] 58 of them belonging to foreigners resident in Birgu.[241]

As already observed, government by the Hospitallers also meant that the merchants could hope to climb the social ladder. The names of these merchants appear in the records of council meetings of the Birgu *Università* after 1530, where they were appointed to fill key administrative posts.[242] Thus, the arrival of the Order represented a break from the past for a group of Maltese who had previously been excluded from such positions. They immediately took advantage of the opportunity and began to participate in public affairs. The presence of the Knights allowed ambitious people who were closely linked to commerce, not only to enhance their trading activities, but even and to climb the social ladder. In turn, this emerging faction of society helped the Knights to establish control over an area which was crucial to the success of their governance, and were an important source by which the Knights could gauge the mood of the population. These facts present the scholar with yet another fundamental question. In view of the generation of all this new economic activity, to what degree did the Mdina town council fear the allegiance which not only the ***patroni*** but also a good section of the population might offer to the Order? Is this yet another factor explaining the smooth transition of power from the hands of the municipal council in Mdina to that of the Hospitaller Order in Birgu?

When dealing with the transfer of Malta to the Knights of St John and the reaction of the Maltese, local historiography tends to focus on the actions of just one stratum of society, the upper layer which held important municipal posts. But how far can one say that this 'one group' model encompassed the thoughts and feelings of other social groups? The municipal council was composed of a tightly knit group of nobles, lawyers and landowners who largely excluded other social groups from their circle. Did not the latter together comprise a greater force than the ruling elite? Did they not also have their own aspirations and ambitions?

An earlier study of the economic activities taking place in and around the port in the early years of Hospitaller rule[243] has shown that the establishment of the Order generated a myriad of new economic opportunities which ultimately saw both the

239 D. Bezzina, 'Early Hospitaller Birgu: A Study of the Acts of Notary Nicolò de Agatiis 1538–1540' (BA Hons dissertation, University of Malta, 2001), Appendix 1, 102–7.

240 Once again Abela (Habel, Xabela, Chabela) is the most common surname in Birgu.

241 In these Notarial registers not all contracting parties had their place of origin noted next to their name. Therefore, despite providing very good insight, this list does not represent or give details of each resident of Birgu for the period. It also excludes the knights who used the services of the notary at the time. These are listed in a separate list comprising 134 different knights. Bezzina, 'Early Hospitaller Birgu', Appendix II, 108–11.

242 NAM, MCC, Reg. AO, vol. II., n.f. (13.ix.1552); MCC, Reg. AO, vol. I, fols 101v–102 (1.ix.1537), fols 146v–147 (3.ix.1538), fols 199v–200 (1.ix.1539).

243 J. Abela, 'Port Activities in Mid-Sixteenth Century Malta' (unpublished MA dissertation, University of Malta, 2007).

local population and foreigners flocking to Birgu. Not only did merchants, traders and craftsmen enhance their economic activities, but many also discovered that life-long aspirations for their group to participate in administrative life were at last being realised. After 1530, merchants, tailors, cobblers, stonemasons and silversmiths all had representatives in official posts. Were the Knights the only real threat to the *status quo* of the nobility of Mdina, or did this elite have other 'enemies' in the form of aspiring social groups?

The early legislation and the usurpation of local rights

Although the donation of the Maltese islands to the Hospitaller Order was secured by a pact to honour existing laws and customs, the establishment of the Knights implied that the new masters were empowered to promulgate new laws.[244] The intention of such legislation was to ensure the effective administration of the islands and to give the Order the upper hand in pivotal decision making to ensure a stable government. However, just how successful the Knights were in establishing their Maltese island state remains a matter of contention. Before this question is examined, an overview is needed of the set-up of new institutions and laws promulgated by the Knights in the period 1530–65.[245]

Grand Master L'Isle Adam issued a set of laws, the *Statuti ed Ordinazioni* as early as 1533. Although they were rudimentary in nature, these laws were a pillar of the constitutional set-up that was in force during the Order's rule, not only because they were the very first laws enacted by the Hospitaller Order, but also because they remained in force for many years.[246] Among other things, they established the office

244 See A. Williams, 'The Constitutional Development of the Order of St John in Malta, 1530–1798', in V. Mallia-Milanes (ed.), *Hospitaller Malta 1530–1798: Studies on Early Modern Malta and the Order of St John of Jerusalem* (Malta, 1993), 285–96; Williams, '*Sacra Militia*', in Fusaro et al., *Trade and Cultural Exchange*, 139–56; Paoli, *Codice Diplomatico*; De Bono, *Sommario della storia della legislazione.*

245 It is interesting to note that as late as 1895 a court sentence given regarding the case of *Nobile* Formosa vs *Nobile* Attard Montalto decreed that 'the old Sicilian laws continued to apply in so far as they were not revoked or changed by contrary legislation after the occupation of the Knights, since Malta was not conquered but donated *ex munificentia*'. W.D. Barz, 'The Maltese Statuti e Ordinamenti of 1533' (trans. J. Sammut), *Id-Dritt* (official organ of the Law Society, University of Malta), 15 (1990), 5–20: 7.

246 The promulgation of this set of laws was issued on 5 September 1533 and the text is divided into six chapters. NLM, Libr. MS 148, Prammatiche Magistrali pubblicate l'anno 1640 per comando del serenissimo Principe Fra Paolo Lascaris Castellar, fols 24v–25; NLM, Libr. MS 439, Prammatiche Magistrali Lascaris 1640–1692 incluse quelle di Omedes 1553, fols 33v–36. These laws were later reconfirmed by various Grand Masters, such as Verdala (paragraph 120 of the Code of Verdala of 1598) and Lascaris in his *Prammatiche* issued in 1640. They were superseded only in 1724 by the Code of Manoel, NLM, *Leggi e Costituzioni Prammaticali, Rinuovate, reformate, ed ampliate dal Serenissmo, ed Ementissimo Signor Fra D. Antonio Manoel de Vilhena de Conti di Villaflor: Gran Maestro della Sacra Religione Gerosolimitana, e dell'Ordine Militare del S. Sepolcro, Principe di Malta, e Gozo, & c: Colle Pandette, ed Inidice de Titoli, e delle materie* (Malta, 1725). See also Barz, 'The Maltese Statuti', 5–20.

and tribunal of the *Castellania* that had formerly functioned in the city of Rhodes.[247] This court, which was of first instance, was presided over by the Castellan, who was one of the highest-ranking officials in the Order's hierarchy. He was responsible both for the internal affairs of the Order and for secular aspects of the law in the courts.[248] Thus, the newly established tribunal not only dealt with cases involving the Order but also heard appeals from the *Università* of both Malta and Gozo. The inhabitants of Birgu were subject to the tribunal, but this law also gave parties who were under the jurisdiction of the Royal Captain of Mdina the right to claim the jurisdiction of the Castellan, if they so desired.[249] This was a subtle attempt to attract the inhabitants to submit to the Order's jurisdiction rather than that of the municipal council of Mdina, and various petitions were presented by members of the *Università* on this matter.[250] A clear reference to such grievances is contained in the town council minutes of 8 June 1531, where it was resolved that the town councillors should plead in front of the Grand Master to restore to the council '*lo integra jurisdictioni civili et criminali di tutta la insula et so populu et etiam dilu Burgu come sempre fu*'.[251]

Appointments of town council officials were confirmed by the Grand Master from as early as July 1530.[252] Notwithstanding the increasing limitation of its functions, the composition of the town council remained basically the same as that of its medieval precursor. Other administrative posts which continued to function during Hospitaller rule were those of the inspector of weights and measures, the *accattapani*; the *Secreto*, who now administered the property of the Grand Master, collected related taxes and issued building permits; the *Portulano*, responsible for the control of measures of grain and the importation of wheat from Sicily; and the *Credenziero*, who issued receipts for all imported provisions. Some other offices ceased to function, including the office of Vice-Admiral and that of *Massaro*.[253]

247 For the functions and duties of Castellan refer to NLM, Libr. MS 153, *Pragmaticae Rhodiae, F. Emerici D'Amboyse Magni Magistri Sacrae Religionis Hierosolymitanae* (seventeenth-century copy), fols 5–5v. See also A. Luttrell, 'The Rhodian Background of the Order of Saint John in Malta', in J. Azzopardi (ed.), *The Order's Early Legacy in Malta* (Malta, 1989), 3–14: 5; A. Luttrell, 'The Fourteenth-Century *Capitula Rodi*', in A. Luttrell, *The Hospitallers of Rhodes and their Mediterranean World* (Aldershot, 1992), 204–11: 205.

248 Together with the Castellan, this court consisted of two judges, one of whom enjoyed a civil jurisdiction and the other a criminal jurisdiction. De Bono, *Sommario della storia della legislazione*, 171.

249 '*Qui Castellaniae Burgi praest, Ius dicere non debet extra territorium suum, quod dumtaxat nouis Burgimoenibus, continentibusque aedificiis determinamus, Religquis Melitae Incolies ad Praefecti Ciuitatis Iurisdictionem pertinenetibus, et consentient tunc protest eis, et aduersus eos Ius dici ab eo, cuius Tribunal communi consensus elegerint*' ('He who presides over the Castellania of the Borgo should not administer the law outside his sphere of office which we limit to the new fortress and its adjacent buildings. The rest of the inhabitants of Malta fall under the jurisdiction of the prefect of the community. Those who through some kind of contract subject themselves to another jurisdiction and consent to it, could be then judged by the latter tribunal which they have chosen through mutual agreement.') English version quoted from Barz, 'The Maltese Statuti', 14–15.

250 Fiorini, 'The Municipal Councils', 13.

251 NLM, Univ. 12, fol. 564v; 'all civil and criminal jurisdiction over all the island and its people, also that of Birgu, as has always been'.

252 NLM, AOM, Lib. Bull. 414 (1528–30), fols 270–270v.

253 In medieval times the *massaro* had been responsible for the income derived from customs duties. Fiorini, 'The Municipal Council', 16–17.

The Gozo *Università* suffered even heavier blows than that of Malta. In fact, after the great Turkish incursion of 1551 the Order replaced the post of Captain of the Rod with that of a Knight who also acted as Governor of Gozo, leaving in place the functions of the *jurats*, judges and *accattapani*. Further, most medieval offices pertaining to Gozo were also abolished by the Order. These included the offices of *Credenziero*, Castellan, Guardian of the Citadel Gate, Vice-Admiral and *Portulano*.[254] The disaster of 1551, which resulted in the captivity of almost all the island's population, reflected Gozo's weak defence system, a factor which must have given the Order a free hand in so radically changing the island's administrative structure. The episode must also have had serious repercussions for the population of the island of Malta, who knew that in spite of their loyalty to the Spanish Crown the latter had made little effort towards the proper upkeep of the island's defence system. The Hospitallers, meanwhile, had almost immediately started work on the defence system at Birgu and were showing commitment to the island's safety by investing considerable sums of money and undertaking a number of infrastructure projects which seemed to offer the population at least some measure of assurance.

Since the naval engagements of the seafaring Hospitallers required the transfer of the seat of government from Mdina to the Castle of St Angelo and its suburb of Birgu,[255] members of the Order and their entourage soon took over the few houses that could provide them with at least a minimum of comfort.[256] The town was distressingly small, and the shortage of suitable housing led the Knights to establish makeshift residences while undertaking their intensive building programme. As early as 1531 the first law to regulate housing was enacted in order to control lease agreements and enable the Knights and their followers to find suitable housing. The large influx of new residents led to a situation where demand exceeded supply, which proved very profitable for speculators and seemingly led to 'a black market in lodgings'.[257]

In order to address this problem Grand Master L'Isle Adam issued the *Ordinationes Domorum*[258] and, as a result, the tribunal of the *Officio delle Case* was set up. This

254 Fiorini, 'The Municipal Councils', 16–17. Unfortunately, Gozo lacks proper documentation for the period, since after the 1551 *razzia* most of the documents went missing. See NLM, Libr. MS 1214 Ragguaglio de' Pubblici Notari antichi di Malta e Gozo dei quali non si trovano i registri, per essere porzione trasportati in Constantinopoli e porzione in Catania, dall'anno 1312, con una cronologia de' Pubblici Notari i registri di quali esistono nell'Archivio della Cittàotabile, for a list of notaries whose notarial volumes were missing from the Maltese archives due to the 1551 Turkish incursion on Gozo.

255 Birgu had the added advantage of being distant from Mdina, the seat of the old Maltese feudal nobility who were, for obvious reasons, reluctant to share a home with the Order. R. de Giorgio, *A City by an Order* (Malta, 1985), 33.

256 According to Bosio '*non eran nel Borgo all'hora tante habitationi ... erano per questo costretti à far camerate, & à ricoverarsi à dieci, & à quindeci insieme in ogni piccola casetta*'. (At the time there were not many houses in Birgu ... for this reason they [the Knights] were compelled to share lodgings, and to shelter in [groups of] ten, and even fifteen in each little house.) Bosio, *Dell'Istoria della Sacra Religione*, vol. 3, 297.

257 S. R. Borg Cardona, 'The *Officio delle Case* and the Housing Laws of the Earlier Grand Masters 1531–1569', *The Law Journal*, 3:1 (University of Malta, 1951), 39–69: 42.

258 NLM, AOM, Lib. Bull. 415, fol. CCXXIII.

tribunal was composed of three Maltese residents of Birgu and two Knights. They had very wide powers, among which was the right to enforce the compulsory sale of houses, to dictate the just price of houses and to deal with disputes.[259] It could be argued that the inclusion of Maltese citizens in such tribunals was a measured step, intended to gain local support and serve as a means to assess popular attitudes. In spite of such measures, it seems that the Rhodiot community in Birgu continued to bear the brunt of exorbitant house prices, because on 26 May 1548 another ordinance regulating housing was promulgated, in view of the complaints made in this regard.[260] Among other things, the ordinance changed the composition of the tribunal, and although the two Knights were retained as commissioners, the three Maltese representatives were substituted with a Maltese and a Rhodian *jurat*.[261]

The inclusion of members from the Rhodiot community in key administrative posts alongside Maltese officials is documented in various other instances. In the records of the *Magna Curia Castellania*, Simon Exarcopulo is noted as serving in the post of *catapanus* from 1532 to 1533,[262] while Theodorus Zacharias and Stephanus Guascon were appointed *jurats* for the administrative year 1534–35.[263] Similarly, between 1537 and 1538 Johannes Callamia was one of the four appointed *jurats* of the *Università*; Theodorius Zacaria was a health official together with the Maltese Johannes and Paulus Habel; Laurentius Ros was a *catapanus* with another Maltese, Luca Vella; Petro de Vera was the government official for gold and silversmiths; Simon de Petrollo was the official for tailors; Johannes Portughes was appointed as the government official in charge of stonemasons; and Antonio de Lauda was appointed official in charge of cobblers (*sabbatero*), together with another Maltese official, Juliano Vella.[264]

The appointment of both Maltese and Rhodiot officials to the same offices ensured a healthy mix of representatives and projected the government's efforts to integrate two communities with substantial cultural differences. However, this policy is also a clear indicator that in the initial years of Hospitaller rule the administrative power at the island's commercial heart was partly delegated to people whom the Maltese still viewed as 'foreigners' resident on the island. This must have worried the elite of Mdina considerably.[265]

259 For a detailed list of the functions of this tribunal refer to, Borg Cardona, 'The *Officio delle Case*', 41–2.

260 Borg Cardona, 'The *Officio delle Case*', 43.

261 Borg Cardona, 'The *Officio delle Case*', 45. For a deeper insight into all Ordinances regulating housing up to 1569, especially those of 1555 and 1562, refer to Borg Cardona, 'The *Officio delle Case*', 39–69.

262 This refers to the administrative year, which started on the 1 September and ended 31 August.

263 Fiorini, 'The Rhodiot Community of Birgu', in Mallia-Milanes (ed.), *Library of Mediterranean History*, vol. 1, 183–241: 198.

264 NAM, MCC, Reg. AO, vol. I, fols 102v–103 (1.ix.1537), see also fols 146v–147, fols 199–200. There were other members who were appointed apart from those indicated above. However, only those who were specifically noted as being Rhodiot or Maltese have been mentioned above.

265 One must keep in mind that the port of Birgu was the major gateway linking Malta to the outside world.

Just like their predecessor, the Grand Masters who ruled after L'Isle Adam until 1565 did not promulgate any major law codes. Juan D'Homedes (r. 1536–53) issued the laws known as *Pandectae et Ordinationes*, which were mainly targeted to regulate court fees and other fees.[266] The next Grand Master, Claude de la Sengle (r. 1553–57), published his *Bandi e Commandamenti* in 1555. Of these, the most relevant law for this study is the one in which he ordered that all foreigners[267] who were not traders should be expelled from the island. This law should be viewed in the light of the great difficulties which the Order faced in providing an ever-growing population with the necessary food supplies, apart from other problems related to the defence of the island in case of siege.

The heavy influx of new arrivals in the harbour area can be gauged from an analysis of the acts of Notary Placido Abela for the administrative year 1557–58, which include eighty-eight different foreign clients.[268] This notary operated in Birgu, and although he received his notarial warrant only in 1557[269] he seems to have been a popular choice with people coming from different strata of society, both local and foreign. The number of workmen imported from Sicily, which the Order needed for its building programme, must be added to the number of arrivals.[270] The human invasion of the harbour area created serious problems of over-population. In a case of siege it would have been difficult to provide the necessary refuge to everyone within the walls of the small town. Bosio's description of how the town accommodated an influx of refugees following the raid by Turgut Reis in 1551 enables one to visualise the relation between the population density in Birgu and the town's defence.[271] The following is Abbé de Vertot's English translation of the account:

266 These were divided into six chapters as follows: *Jura indicum; Jura decretorum; Jura candelarum; Jura magistri notarii; Jura notariorum;* and lastly, *Jura advocatorum et procuratorum*. NLM, Libr. MS 148 .

267 The term 'foreigner' in this context excludes members of the Order and those of the Rhodiot community who came to Malta with the Knights of St John.

268 NAV, R 4/1 and MS 514/1 (1557–58). It is important to note the following; MS 514/1 covers the period 1 November 1557 to 1560. However, only the acts covering the same period as register R 4/1 (1557–58) have been analysed for the compilation of this list. Volume R 4/1, covers the period 2 October 1557 to 1 September 1558 and is divided into four sections. The first section holds the acts starting from fols 2–3v (2.x.1557) up to fol. 145v (31.xii.1557), while the second section contains a register of procurations commencing from fols 1–3v (7.x.1557) and ending with a deed on fol. 140–40v (18.viii.1558). In all, this section holds a total of 106 procurations. The third section is also a register containing 109 procurations and begins with the act found in fols 1–2 (5.ix.1558) and ends with the act on fols 139–142v (30.viii.1559). The fourth section starts with the act referenced on fols 143–143v (1.ix.1558), and the last noted act is in fols 173–174 (24.xi.1558). It is important to state that sections regarding procuration acts are not included in this analysis. Thus, in all probability the number of foreigners in Birgu using the services of this notary was even higher.

269 NLM, AOM, Lib. Bull. 426, fol. 188v (13.ix.1557).

270 A. Hoppen, 'The Fortification of Malta, 1530–1798: The Impact on the Maltese', in V. Mallia-Milanes (ed.), *Hyphen*, 3:3 (1980), 103–14: 104.

271 Bosio, *Dell'Istoria della Sacra Religione* (2nd impression, Naples, 1684), 297.

> There were not houses enough to lodge all this multitude, they were most of them obliged to stay in the market-places and the streets; and what added to their misfortune, was, their being exposed during all the dog-days to the heat of the sun, which rages with intolerable violence in that burning climate. The infection and stink that exhaled from the excrements of these poor creatures, thus crowded together, would soon produce contagious distempers ... and there was but little water in the cisterns.[272]

More significant changes took place during the 1550s under the rule of Grand Master de Valette,[273] who proved to be more despotic than his predecessors. He attempted to take over all the income of the Mdina *Università*, which at the time amounted to approximately 11,000 *scudi* annually, and promised in return to pay the salaries of the officials of the town council and to pay out 600 *scudi* per annum to support its functioning.[274] He also placed extensive restrictions on the petitioning powers of the Mdina *Università* by threatening to resort to harsh punishment against anyone who dared to oppose his orders.[275]

However, de Valette's repressive measures need to be examined within the prevailing context of political tension in the Mediterranean. The Spanish Crown was facing great challenges in maintaining its prime position among the contesting Mediterranean powers, and Ottoman–French relations seemed to be taking a favourable turn at a time when the Ottoman forces were expanding into Europe, the Middle East, Egypt and North Africa. Barbary corsairs, especially those stationed in Algiers, were continually attacking Christian shipping and conducting successful piratical excursions on most Mediterranean shores.[276] Malta was not spared these incursions, especially since the Ottomans knew that in order to gain hegemony in the Mediterranean they must subject the island to their rule. Thus, attacks by the Ottoman fleet were quite frequent, the most significant being those by Turgut Reis in 1547, 1548, 1550, and the worst being that under Grand Master Juan D'Homedes in 1551, when, after besieging Mdina, the Turkish fleet attacked Gozo and took almost all the inhabitants captive. From Gozo, Turgut proceeded to attack the Order's base at Tripoli and succeeded in ousting the Hospitallers from this strategic North African post. Various rumours of imminent Ottoman attacks kept arriving

272 A. de Vertot, *The History of the Knights of Malta* (London, 1728) (2 vols, facsimile edn, Malta, 1989), vol. 2, 115. In addition to these, in the lower strata of society were the slaves, whose number was on the increase due to rising demand.

273 For a reappraisal of de Valette see, V. Mallia-Milanes, 'Frà Jean de La Valette 1495–1568', in T. Cortis (ed.), *The Maltese Cross* (Malta, 1995), 117–29.

274 C. Cassar, 'La Valette bl-Assedju Riesaq', in E. Bartolo (ed.), *Min Kien Callus?* (Malta, 2003), 55–62: 55.

275 In 1561, Joseph Callus, a medical doctor, businessman and councillor in the Mdina town council was condemned to death for having tried to send a petition to the king of Spain wherein he accused the Order of usurping local rights and privileges. This petition was intercepted by the Order and Callus was immediately accused of treason. Fiorini also states that during the Order's rule there was a systematic destruction of evidence which might have shed light on this case. S. Fiorini, 'X'Nafu dwar Callus', in Bartolo (ed.), *Min kien Callus?*, 15–53.

276 See P. Earle, *Corsairs of Malta and Barbary* (London, 1970).

from abroad.[277] This must have preoccupied the ruling Grand Masters, since they could not afford to suffer yet another defeat in the eyes of the Christian world.

In 1558 de Valette further consolidated his power through a concession made by King Philip II of Spain, wherein it was decreed that cases relating to feudal lands were now to be decided by the Grand Master, and any newly elected Grand Master was also exempted from having to submit his appointment for approval by the Viceroy of Sicily.[278] Such measures must be seen in the light of the hegemony enjoyed by various feudal lords in Malta, who, prior to the arrival of the Knights had participated in what Bresc terms an 'accelerated dilapidation of the royal patrimony'.[279] The gradual spread of the Order's control over the feudal lords, and its policy of acquiring much of what had once been the property of the 'private' sphere and making it 'public' by incorporating it into the Grand Master's territory has been described by Michel Fontenay as an 'almost undeniable feature ... in line with an evolutionary process which had begun during the late middle ages, [where] there appeared everywhere a tendency to strengthen the powers of the Prince who, with the help of an important corps of officers, lawyers and other "civil servants", was supposed to work for the public weal, regardless of social antagonisms'.[280] Fontenay argues that this trend was not successful in the Mediterranean as it was in the north-west of Europe, since in the former location the nobility seem to have taken over the state by the seventeenth century. However, in Malta's case it was the state, governed by a group of European nobles, which gradually took over the local nobility and diminished its claim to participate in the island's administration.[281] Once again, the claim that for all intents and purposes Malta remained part of the *Regno* provided the nobles with a valid reason to pay allegiance to the king rather than the Knights.

The local religious-political situation was not easy. As Ann Williams argues, 'although the population was Catholic, the religious situation was much less favourable than it had been in Rhodes'.[282] The Maltese Church, which in medieval

277 The Order was constantly sending its spies to investigate the progress of the Ottoman army. See for example NLM, AOM, Lib. Bull. 418, fol. 201 (12.vii.1543), where *Fra.* de Aguila was to sail to the Levant with an armed galley, '*per sapere et intendere li progressi et nove de larmata turchesca et ritornare subito darne aviso*' [sic]. (To spy on the progress of the Turkish armada and return back immediately to give us news.)

278 De Bono, *Sommario della storia della legislazione*, 173–4.

279 Bresc, 'The "Secrezia" and the Royal Patrimony', in Luttrell (ed.), *Medieval Malta*, 126–62. Bonavita states that in view of loan advances made to the *Regia Corte*, rich families of Malta were pawned various offices and lands. The de Nava family held the Castellan's office and the rich Marsa feud; the de Guevaras enjoyed the income from the office of the *Secrezia* of both Malta and Gozo and were also lords of the Għajn Tuffieħa feud; the Inguanez family was pawned the office of the Bailiff, while the Falzons were conceded that of the Vice-Admiralty. However, he does not give references to primary sources. Bonavita, *Dissertazioni Storico Legali*, fol. 105v.

280 M. Fontenay, 'The Mediterranean 1500–1800', in Mallia-Milanes (ed.), *Hospitaller Malta 1530–1798*, 43–110: 89–90.

281 The main work on Maltese nobility is still J. Montalto, *The Nobles of Malta 1530–1800* (Malta, 1980). For a reappraisal of the subject see Caruana Galizia, 'The Maltese Nobility during the Hospitaller Period: Towards a Reappraisal', 89–102.

282 Williams, '*Sacra Militia*', in Fusaro et al., *Trade and Cultural Exchange*, 139–56: 150.

times had no say in political issues, soon became the only institution which held enough power to oppose the ruling masters.[283] It was granted great privileges by the Holy See and the Order could not impose its laws or regulations on the clergy without the consent of the pope or the bishop.[284] Before 1530 the bishop had rarely resided in Malta.[285] However, from that time he was nominated from among the members of the Order and was resident on the island.[286] According to the conditions of the grant of the Maltese islands, the appointment of the bishop had to be approved by the king of Sicily from among candidates nominated by the Grand Master. The bishop became established as a political figure on the island and, despite usually being a former member of the Order, 'on his appointment to the bishopric he generally became an opponent of the policies of the Grand Master'.[287] He tended to 'ally with the upper clergy at Mdina and represent the interest of the Maltese as against the foreign Hospitallers'.[288] However, 'neither the bishop nor the inquisitor was likely to reveal the sources of his information or the way he influenced or manipulated the political sentiment of the people. This leaves a large part of the story untold in view of the foreign extraction of both bishop and inquisitor.'[289]

A source which was commented upon by Wettinger relates to a *relazione* written in the early seventeenth century[290] by Dun Filippo Borg[291] which sheds some light on the political scene during the first decades of the Order's rule in Malta. Borg relates how 'the Order began, as foretold, by treating people well and during the first four magistracies the people lived well and happily. Then followed Grand Master La Valletta, a Gascon knight, who muzzled the people and imposed burdens on them in 1560.'[292] The clergy became strong opponents of the Grand Master's administration when these burdens affected them and usually appealed to Rome, especially when they were called upon to contribute towards the upkeep of the town walls. As Wettinger further informs us, 'Church–State dispute concerned mainly church rights, not the rights and privileges of the people and the old municipality vis-à-vis the Grand Master – it was largely a reassertion of church rights which the local

283 Wettinger, 'Early Maltese Popular Attitudes', 255.

284 G. Wettinger, 'L-Attitudni tal-Maltin Lejn il-Kavallieri', in Bartolo (ed.), *Min kien Callus?*, 7–14: 9.

285 Dalli, *Iż-Żmien Nofsani Malti* (Malta, 2002), 117–19; Dalli, *The Medieval Millennium*, 225–6.

286 Mifsud, 'La Cattedrale e l'Università', 41.

287 Wettinger, 'Early Maltese Popular Attitudes', 255.

288 Luttrell, 'Malta and Rhodes', in Mallia-Milanes (ed.), *Hospitaller Malta 1530–1798*, 255–84: 274.

289 Wettinger, 'Early Maltese Popular Attitudes', 256.

290 For a full account of this '*Relazione*' refer to Wettinger, 'Early Maltese Popular Attitudes', 255–78. This account was written by Borg with biased feelings wherein he gave his opinion of the political situation as he understood it, and not as a scholar. Wettinger, 'Early Maltese Popular Attitudes', 264.

291 Dun Filippo Borg was the first provost of the canonry of Birkirkara and held the post of schoolmaster at Mdina in his late teens between October 1583 and November 1585. He had been acting schoolmaster without pay since 1582 and in 1622 he was Vicar General. Wettinger, 'Early Maltese Popular Attitudes', 257.

292 Wettinger, 'Early Maltese Popular Attitudes', 268.

church authorities had allowed partly to lapse during the later middle ages, allowing laymen to intervene in the financial administration of the Church (Cathedral, hospital, etc.) as they had been doing at least since the fifteenth century.'[293]

Members of the Order were exempt from the bishop's jurisdiction since they had their own clergy and conventual church in Birgu, and later in Valletta. This led to the direct participation of the clergy in political affairs, which later became a recurrent feature in Maltese political history. Further, the bishop also attended the Order's Council and at times this resulted in great political tension. Matters worsened after 1574 when the Holy See appointed an Inquisitor who established his own palace and exercised his own jurisdiction.[294] Moreover, he was also empowered to try cases involving suspected abuses, including those involving the Knights themselves. In addition, from time to time papal delegates were sent to report on the state of religion on the island, with a view of implementing changes which would ensure that the island was in line with Counter-Reformation standards established by the Council of Trent.[295]

During the late medieval period the Maltese community was greatly attached to the Church, priests being the main representatives of the villages and the focus of social organisation. According to Charles Dalli, 'it seems that the Church had the means to control the population, impose orthodoxy, and reach out against any sign of deviance from the established social and cultural norms'.[296] Carmel Cassar argues that during the Hospitallers' rule the parish priest's role came to be challenged by the Knight who was nominated as the local captain of the militia in larger villages, since this position became 'a new source of patronage attracting all those who sought favours from the Hospitaller Government'.[297]

Opinions differ on the extent of the Knights' success in building on their Rhodian experience and coordinating an efficient state organisation in Malta. Anthony Luttrell argues that, once in Malta, the Order 'followed many standard practices which formed part of an extraordinary continuity of institutions and traditions which enabled the Hospital successfully to transfer its unique form of government, its "island order state", from Rhodes to Malta'.[298] Contrary to Luttrell's view, historian Ann Williams argues that it took the Knights nearly a hundred years from their arrival in Malta to adequately build on the foundations of their Rhodian state, and highlights the immense difficulties which arose due to the material losses of the westward move.[299]

Such statements need to be evaluated in the light of evidence which provides a

293 Wettinger, 'Early Maltese Popular Attitudes', 260–1.

294 Luttrell, 'Malta and Rhodes', in Mallia-Milanes (ed.), *Hospitaller Malta 1530–1798*, 255–84: 274.

295 Williams, '*Sacra Militia*', in Fusaro et al., *Trade and Cultural Exchange*, 139–56: 150.

296 Very little is known about pre-1400 religious communities on the Maltese islands. Dalli, *Malta, The Medieval Millennium*, 225–6.

297 Cassar, 'Popular Perceptions and Values', in Mallia-Milanes (ed.), *Hospitaller Malta 1530–1798*, 429–73: 437.

298 A. Luttrell, 'Hospitaller Birgu: 1530–1536', *Crusades*, 2 (Society for the Study of the Crusades and the Latin East, Aldershot, 2003), 121–50: 121.

299 Williams, '*Sacra Milita*', in Fusaro et al., *Trade and Cultural Exchange*, 139–56 147–8.

clearer picture of the actual situation. In Rhodes, during the fourteenth century, the Order had promulgated the *Capitula Rodi*,[300] and later, in 1509, much more extensive legislation entitled *Pragmaticae Rhodiae*.[301] Even though in the case of Malta the Hospitaller Order had promised to take over a regulated community which followed laws promulgated by the kings of Sicily, it was difficult, if not impossible, for them to discard their Rhodian laws and customs, which had been tested over a period of two hundred years. Things were even more complicated due to the settlement of the Greek community that followed them, since, as will be explained, these did not want to partake of their Greek customs or come under the laws and jurisdiction of the Maltese. In fact, as early as 1530, in order to attract Rhodiot settlers on the island, the Order supplicated Pope Clement VII to grant exemption to those following them from Rhodes from the jurisdiction of the bishop of Malta, and instead to place them under the ecclesiastical authority of the prior of the conventual church. This request was granted on the grounds that the new settlers did not speak or understand Maltese.[302] Such requests reflect how, even before its establishment on the island, the Rhodiot community[303] showed its concern at being governed by local laws,[304] while at the same time the Maltese town council pressed hard to ensure that long-established local laws and customs were respected.[305]

During the initial years of their stay the Knights found it increasingly hard to adopt separate rules for different people governed by the same authority. It was thus that in the Chapter General of 1555 two Knights, the Conventual Chaplain and three Maltese lawyers were appointed to examine prevailing Sicilian and Rhodian civil and criminal law and to try to formulate a common law which would suit both Greeks and Maltese.[306] The outcome of this commission is not known. However, it seems that at the time no consensus was reached, since another commission was requested to undertake the same task on 3 July 1560, but it seems that even this commission did not produce the desired solutions, or, if it did, these were not implemented.[307]

300 For a transcription of the surviving document see Luttrell, 'The Fourteenth-Century *Capitula Rodi*', in Luttrell, *The Hospitallers of Rhodes*, 204–11.

301 The recodification of the customs and statues of the town of Rhodes dated 24 February 1510 survives in a seventeenth-century copy under NLM, Libr. MS 153, and in an eighteenth-century copy under NLM, Libr. MS 740 Costituzioni di Malta 1509–1681 Luttrell, 'The Fourteenth-Century Capitula Rodi', in Luttrell, *The Hospitallers of Rhodes*, 204–11: 205–6.

302 Paoli, *Codice Diplomatico*, 201–2.

303 By 1575 there were three Greek parishes in Birgu serving seventy-four families. Luttrell, 'Malta and Rhodes', 266–7.

304 Bonavita, *Dissertazioni Storico Legali*, fol. 125.

305 Luttrell, 'Malta and Rhodes', in Mallia-Milanes (ed.), *Hospitaller Malta 1530–1798*, 255–84: 267–8.

306 NLM, AOM 89, fol. 50 (new enumeration) (24.ix.1555).

307 NLM, AOM 90, fol. 108 (new enumeration in pencil) (3.vii.1560). Occasionally, the Rhodian statutes were confirmed together with the Maltese statutes, such as in 1543, NLM, AOM 1651, fol. 121; in 1548, NLM, AOM 1651, fol. 130 and even later in 1640 by Grand Master Lascaris (1636–57) in NLM, Libr. MS 439, fol. 249v which states '*Copia delle Pragmatiche di Rodi cioé l'esecuzioni delle sentenze confirmate dalle Pragmatiche di questo dominio*'.

The privilege to import duty-free grain

A fundamental privilege enjoyed by the Maltese ever since medieval times was the grant of duty-free concessions on grain and victuals.[308] Even though the deed of donation of the islands did not mention the continuation of such tax exemptions, the Order knew that this was a vital privilege.[309] The Hospitallers not only sought to take advantage of these exemptions but even requested the Crown to make a further concession of 6,000 *salme* of wheat,[310] to be granted for its sole use,[311] in addition to the duty-free amounts which Malta, Gozo and Tripoli[312] were already allowed to import.[313]

The justification for this claim was that the Order had to invest a considerable sum of money in order to provide the island with a better defence system, and it was not prepared to pay extra duties on essential commodities as these would ultimately deplete its treasury. Negotiations on the matter proved rather difficult. In fact, the Viceroy was not even inclined to renew the established privileges relating to duty-free concessions once the terms of the donation had been agreed, let alone increase the quotas.[314] Towards the end of 1531, the Viceroy even extended trading restrictions by imposing a tax on the export of meat and biscuit from Sicily.[315] Such disagreements greatly hindered the Order's establishment on the island, especially as it was facing serious financial difficulties and could do without extraordinary fiscal

308 One of the first acts granting duty-free concessions was that of King Peter of Aragon in 1283. A. Mifsud, 'L'Approvigionamento e l'Università di Malta nelle passate dominazioni', *Archivum Melitense*, 3:5 (1918), 163–212: 170–1.

309 While still in Rhodes, Charles V conceded the Order a licence to export up to 500 ducats' worth of wheat from Sciacca, Sicily. They were, however, prohibited from getting any supplies from the wharfs at Agrigento, Termini and Licata. The first such licence was granted on 27 August 1513 and reconfirmed periodically. Valentini, 'I Cavalieri di S. Giovanni da Rodi a Malta: Trattative diplomatiche', 174 n. 1.

310 This amount was to be divided as follows: 5,000 for the use of the Order and the remaining 1,000 for Tripoli. NLM, AOM, Lib. Bull. 414, fol. 279.

311 It is estimated that after the knights' arrival there was an increase in population of about 3,000. This number included the knights, their slaves and servants and the Rhodian families who accompanied them. Fiorini, 'Demographic Growth', in Mallia-Milanes (ed.), *Hospitaller Malta 1530–1798*, 297–310: 298–9.

312 According to a supplication made by Grand Master L'Isle Adam to Charles V on 8 October 1530, during the nine years prior to the arrival of the Order the Maltese were allowed 12,000 *salme* of duty-free wheat per year, while Tripoli was conceded 2,200 *salme* of wheat. Valentini, 'I Cavalieri di S. Giovanni da Rodi a Malta: Trattative diplomatiche', Doc. XLVI: 234.

313 Valentini, 'I Cavalieri di S. Giovanni da Rodi a Malta: Trattative diplomatiche', 174. The delivery of this petition was entrusted to the Knight Francesco Nibia and to Pietro Cassar as ambassador of the Maltese *Università*.

314 According to Bosio, the Grand Master's objection to Pignatelli's claim for the rich Marsa fief in Malta provoked contempt from the latter. As a result, the Viceroy refused to grant such concessions. Valentini, 'I Cavalieri di S. Giovanni da Rodi a Malta: Trattative diplomatiche', 174 n. 1; NLM, AOM, Lib. Bull. 414, fol. 279. As regards the importance of the Marsa fief in respect of the *Secrezia's* revenues refer to Valentini, 'Funzione storica e disperione del patrimonio demaniale di Malta', 24–5.

315 Valentini, 'I Cavalieri di S. Giovanni da Rodi a Malta: Trattative diplomatiche', 174.

burdens which were above and beyond its means. The Order also knew that if the hard-won exemption was negated to the Maltese, they would regard the Order's arrival as having upset long-standing agreements – quite aside from the fact that the inhabitants would be reluctant to pay extra taxes on staple food.

By threatening to renounce the donation under such circumstances,[316] the Order eventually managed to obtain the necessary concessions, albeit at a lower quota than it had requested. Both islands were eventually granted 9,500 *salme* of wheat, 700 *salme* of barley and 300 *salme* of vegetables. This concession marked a reduction in the annual amounts of imported duty-free wheat conceded during the nine-year period prior to the Order's arrival; according to a petition presented by Grand Master L'Isle Adam to Charles V, Malta and Gozo had previously been granted 12,000 *salme* of duty-free wheat annually.[317] As is discussed in Chapter Two, the limited quotas and the increase in population, coupled with several bouts of famine, eventually induced the Order to seek alternatives to the Sicilian source of grain supplies.

The political context favoured the Order's imperative to consolidate its hold on the Maltese islands, as did its adopted policy of divide and rule. As early as 1533, and perhaps sooner, this policy was clearly being implemented through the establishment of a *Università* at Birgu[318] which eventually took over the key role played hitherto by the *Università* of Mdina.[319] This new institution was supposedly set up to cater for the needs of the urban area surrounding the Grand Harbour. However, the dominance of this new establishment, administered by members of the Order, stifled most of the functioning of the Mdina *Unversità*.[320]

Taxes and defence of the island

The Knights regarded the issue of the island's security as paramount. During the Middle Ages the upkeep of town walls and various watch posts and the proper provisioning of the town in case of a siege was the responsibility of the *Università*, which had the right to collect taxes to cover such expenses. A particular tax, the revenue from which partially[321] filled this purpose, was the tax on the sale of wine,

316 NLM, AOM, Lib. Bull. 414, fol. 279 (8.x.1530).

317 NLM, AOM 6421, fols 1–3v. '*Essecutoria del Vicere Duca di Monteleone le 26 Agosto 1532 de Diploma dell'Imperatore Carlo V data in Brusselles le 9 Marzo 1531.*' Valentini, 'I Cavalieri di S. Giovanni da Rodi a Malta: Trattative Diplomatiche', Doc. XLVI: 234.

318 Notarial documentation is testimony to the existence of the Birgu *Università* at least as early as January 1533. Fiorini, 'The Rhodiot Community of Birgu', in Mallia-Milanes (ed.), *Library of Mediterranean History*, vol. 1, 183–241: 198.

319 The Mdina *Università* included the parishes of Żebbug, Siġġiewi, Naxxar and Birkirkara. C. Cassar, *Society, Culture and Identity in Early Modern Malta* (Malta, 2000), 36–7.

320 The harbour area *Università* incorporated the parishes of Bir Miftuħ, centred on the village of Gudja, Żejtun, Qormi and Żurrieq. By 1551 the *Università* of Gozo and its decisions were taken over by a Knight of the Order. Cassar, *Society, Culture and Identity*, 36–7.

321 The income from this tax was also used to pay town council officials, and during certain periods even the upkeep of the castle-by-the-sea. Mifsud, 'Papi, Fortificazioni e Tasse', 409.

called *xisa vini sive tri quartuchi per quartara.*[322] The town council was reluctant to renounce any share of its sources of income, especially when these were rendered more profitable through commercial trading.

However, the Knights stripped the *Università* of its right to collect this tax as early as August 1530, when Governor Buttigellis, on behalf of the Order, took over the right to administer it. An agreement between the two parties stipulated that the town council was to receive an annual payment of 450 *uncie* to compensate for the loss of its privilege. Barely three years later, this amount was almost halved, to 250 *uncie.*[323] The records of the town council meeting of 8 June 1531 include a strongly worded petition addressed to the Grand Master in which he was admonished that he had 'no right to act as he was wont to do in Rhodes and usurp to himself the right of dictating regulations governing the running of the watch'.[324] It seems, however, that such petitions fell on deaf ears, even when the matter was crucial to the Knights' interests. One petition, for example, argued how unjust it was to strip the Royal Captain of his right to collect much-needed taxes to defend the island.[325] Clearly, the Knights felt that they were better suited than the local authorities to take care of defence matters.

The Grand Master even sought to look into the financial records of the Mdina *Università* and began to request statements of all the Treasurer's accounts.[326] It is interesting to note that although there were strong objections, when it came to taking important decisions about the action to be taken against such grievances the council was almost divided. The Royal Captain himself, Paulo de Naso, and another nine councillors opted to assume a conciliatory stance and opposed the confrontational approach favoured by nineteen other councillors.[327] Such divisions benefitted the Order and weakened any possibility for the *Università* to regain its rights. Why would the Royal Captain, a high-ranking official who had been deprived of his rights, reject adopting a militant attitude? Did he assume that it was futile to fight against an Order which had the support of the Viceroy of Sicily, and also of most of the kings and princes of Europe? Did de Naso and his supporters have ulterior motives which went beyond 'national' interest and translated into personal gain? Then again, who were the stakeholders when it came to 'national' matters? The masses or the select few? Why did de Naso[328] opt for self-exile later in the century?[329] Undoubtedly, from the earliest years of Hospitaller rule a good number of town council officials were aware that the Order's authority over island affairs was beyond

322 Mifsud, 'Appunti sugli archvi di Malta', 38. Also known as '*la tassa dei tre quartucci*'. Mifsud, 'Papi, Fortificazioni e Tasse', 408.

323 In 1450 it was sold at 761 *uncie* of Maltese money. Mifsud, 'Papi, Fortificazioni e Tasse', 409.

324 Fiorini, 'The Municipal Councils', 13; NLM, Univ. 12, fols 560–564.

325 NLM, Univ. 13, fols 44–45v (8.ii.1532).

326 Fiorini, 'The Municipal Councils', 14.

327 Fiorini, 'The Municipal Councils', 13.

328 Paolo de Naso was Royal Captain in 1531–32 and *jurat* in 1534–35, 1538–39, 1542–43, 1546–47, 1551–52. Fiorini, 'The Municipal Councils', 14.

329 Various members of the nobility who had also been, at one time or another, members of the town council opted for self-exile. Fiorini, 'The Municipal Councils', 14.

their control. It was now a matter of gradually ceding power, yet holding enough to survive by clutching to old privileges which were gradually disintegrating.

Although the town council's income potential was continually being weakened, it was still held responsible for the maintenance and proper upkeep of Mdina's walls, and thus it was necessary to introduce new taxes to finance such work. Already by 1536 the council had approved a tax of two *tarì* on every *salma* of wheat and one *tarì* on every *salma* of barley imported from Sicily. This tax was not imposed over the whole island, but only in Mdina, Rabat and the four parishes which were its dependencies. Throughout the sixteenth century similar taxes were imposed for the same purpose, not only on wheat but also on meslin[330] (a mixture of wheat and barley), wine, meat and other commodities.[331] Such additional expenses considerably reduced the profits of the merchants, who often filed protests against the town council because, they claimed, not only were their activities not returning any profits but also they were losing out on their investments.

Conclusion

In his analysis of the Sicilian context Epstein argues that the 'lack of widespread social conflict and anti-monarchical action in fifteenth-century Sicily was not so much the result of successful royal endeavour, as of the Sicilian upper classes' decision to abide by *pactismo* [contractual political consensus] in their own interest'.[332] Even in Malta's case, the political and fiscal power handed down by the Crown to the elite (what Bresc terms 'noblesse civique' made up of *nobiles, egregi, magnifici* and *honorabili*) gave them a primary role in the economic and social life of Malta and Gozo which enabled them to enhance their financial position. Thus, domestic political autonomy was traded for loyalty and subordination which addressed Aragonese fiscal needs. Moreover, just as in the Sicilian context, where municipal town councils profited from hard-won privileges, the local *Università* made sure to voice its concerns by continually reminding the Crown of its rights and of the various promises to honour and respect them. Pride of place among these privileges was given to the promise not to alienate the islands from the Crown demesne, and to the right to use force should this happen against the will of the Maltese.

The arrival of the Hospitaller Order of St John in 1530 threatened this political and administrative set-up. The local authorities were keen to resist the alienation of the islands, but the political context, especially the advance of the Ottoman forces, frequent incursions by the enemy and the lack of investment in the defence of the island by the Spanish Crown, weighed heavily on the decision whether or not to welcome a naval power which could protect the island and police the surrounding waters. The peaceful establishment of the Order as a naval power must also be seen

330 Also known as 'small corn', which was a mixture of wheat and barley. F. Braudel, *Civilization and Capitalism 15th–18thCentury: The Structures of Everyday Life* (Berkeley and Los Angeles, 1992), vol. 1, 109.

331 Mifsud, 'Papi, Fortificazioni e Tasse', 408.

332 Epstein, *An Island for Itself*, 392.

in the light of addressing the aspirations of a local group of prosperous merchants whose ships and crew had often mobilised to satisfy the Crown's defence strategies, but who were kept at arms' length from decision-making institutions.

Thus, after protracted discussions, the rule of the Maltese islands was transferred to the Knights of St John, subject to a number of contractual obligations. Old legal and administrative structures remained; however, in spite of the various promises to respect existing laws and institutions, municipal autonomy could no longer really be sustained because the town council's potential to act independently started to dwindle systematically. Thus, the functions of the old *Università* and its primary role in town politics and economy became considerably weakened.[333]

As is discussed in the next chapter, the Order regarded the *Università* as a potential means by which to exploit old privileges and concessions enjoyed by this institution – such as the granting of duty-free grain supplies and other victuals – and to use them to its own benefit. For this reason, although in many instances the Order acted in direct confrontation with the old town council by establishing its own institutions and administrative centre, it also gave the council a life line, knowing well that the council was the essential link by which the island could claim its share of grain concessions from the *Regno*.

The island-state model adopted in Rhodes was not easily transferable to the Maltese context because, unlike the situation in Rhodes, the Knights had legal obligations towards the Maltese. Administering the island proved to be difficult because the Knights had to please two culturally different communities, the Maltese and the Greek, who were both keen to keep their own laws and customs. The attempt to fuse the two so as to establish a functional legal and political order became ever more complicated. Added to this was the religious-political issue, with the local Church being granted special privileges and enjoying the protection of the pope. Such rights placed it beyond the Order's jurisdiction, a situation which resulted in the bishop becoming the main opposing figure and stumbling block to the Order's rule.

333 Dalli, 'Medieval Communal Organization', 10.

2

The Grain Trade

On 27 December 1554 the Mdina municipal council held a general assembly to express its concerns, 'because in the island we have a great shortage of grain'.[1] Similarly, only five months later, in May 1555 the assembly once again gathered due to the bad harvest which the island was registering.[2] Such references are a recurring feature in the municipal council's meeting minutes; hunger did not augur well for the stability and prosperity of any government. An important factor affecting the import and distribution of grain was the great influx of new arrivals in 1530. An increase in population was the most striking effect of the arrival of the Knights Hospitaller on the island, felt mostly in the port town of Birgu and eventually affecting the whole island.

Lack of reliable documentation means that historians have been able only to speculate on possible population figures. Various official reports, most of which were prepared with a view of acquiring much-needed duty-free grain quotas, need to be treated with caution since they may have reported higher populations in order to achieve the quotas.[3] A report drawn up by the Order's Commissioners in 1524 mentions 12,000 inhabitants on the island of Malta and around 5,000 on Gozo.[4] Although exact numbers for Malta before the arrival of the Order are not known, various sources point to a figure of 20,000.[5] In 1535 the envoys of the Mdina *Università* who were sent to Sicily to negotiate wheat quotas informed the Viceroy that the islands had a population of 28,500,[6] while another report drawn up in 1545

1 *'perche nella insula havemo gran mancamento de frumenti'*. NLM, Univ. 202, n.f. (27.xii.1555).

2 *'mala ricolta de grani che si demostra in questa insole de Malta'*. NLM, Univ. 202, n.f. (15.v.1555).

3 Cassar, *Society, Culture and Identity*, 122.

4 Fiorini, 'Demographic Growth', in Mallia-Milanes (ed.), *Hospitaller Malta 1530–1798*, 297–310: 297.

5 Quintin d'Autun estimated that the Maltese population in 1533 exceeded 20,000. J. Quintin d'Autun 'Insulae Melitae Descriptio (Lyon, 1536)', in *The Earliest Description of Malta* (trans H. C. R. Vella, Malta, 1980), 29; Fiorini, 'Demographic Growth', in Mallia-Milanes (ed.), *Hospitaller Malta 1530–1798*, 297–310: 298; Cassar, *Society, Culture and Identity*, 122; Wettinger, 'Agriculture in Malta in the Late Middle Ages', in Buhagiar (ed.), *Proceedings of History Week, 1981*, 1–48: 13.

6 ACM, Misc. 34, fols 351v, 366. (Old reference was ACM, Misc. 37. Refer to Azzopardi, *Archives of the Cathedral of Malta*, Appendix 3, 26–77.)

by the same *Università* informs us that with the arrival of the Knights the population had escalated to 30,000 in 1530.[7]

While this remark may represent an inflated figure, it needs to be evaluated in the light of the Mdina *Università*'s perception that the large influx of population had drastically affected local grain supplies.[8] However, the report noted further that by the time of writing the number had dwindled to 22,000, due to the fact that many people had fled from the island when faced with a serious food shortage. Was this decrease a cause of worry for the Sicilian authorities? Did the officials mention it in their report in order to project a scenario in which the island might gradually become depopulated and thus be left at the mercy of the enemy, to the detriment of the Spanish Crown? The report also noted that in addition to the 22,000, some 2,000 merchants and craftsmen had found their way to the island and were constantly commuting in order to perform various economic activities. Although exact numbers or port records relating to arrivals or departures are not available for this period, the number of 2,000 relating to merchants and craftsmen seems plausible, since fluctuations in the population, especially that of Birgu, are evidenced in the number of new names appearing in notarial acts, as mentioned in the previous chapter.[9]

The grain trade was a perennial major concern for an island where wheat production was particularly low and far from able to meet the needs of a growing population.[10] As Fontenay observes, during the sixteenth century 'the search for grain was universal', and although the island's dearth of cereal production was an intrinsic part of the problem, this was by no means exclusive to the Maltese community.[11] This chapter aims to provide insight into the subject and to address more general questions about how local commerce functioned, emphasising the role of local investors in the grain trade.

This study focuses not only on investments deposited with the municipal town council's office, but also other investments which were covered by notarial contracts, mostly known as *societas* or *debitum* agreements. This illustrates the relationship between the Sicilian *caricatori*, who were Malta's main grain suppliers, and local importers of grain. It aims also to show how the commercial activity of peasants and landowners targeting niche products for the export market continued under the Knights and found a new injection of capital in order to grow.[12] The analysis may

7 NLM, Univ. 13, fols 247–247v. Fiorini, 'Demographic Growth', in Mallia-Milanes (ed.), *Hospitaller Malta 1530–1798*, 297–310: 298.

8 Again, one must be very cautious when interpreting such reports, since their main intention was to procure duty-free quotas.

9 Fiorini, 'Demographical Aspects', in Bugeja et al., *Birgu: A Maritime City*, 219–54: 238.

10 For a detailed list of the years of famine and scarcity of cereals in Malta and Gozo during the sixteenth century refer to Vassallo, 'Prices of Commodities', Table XIV, 80.

11 Fontenay, 'The Mediterranean World, 1500–1800', in Mallia-Milanes (ed.), *Hospitaller Malta 1530–1798*, 43–110: 62

12 As regards the grain trade between Malta and Sicily in the late Middle Ages refer to M. A. Aloisio, 'A test case for regional market integration? The grain trade between Malta and Sicily in the Late Middle Ages', in L. Armstrong, I. Elbl & M. M. Elbl (eds),

identify a model for similar patterns of trading relationships taking place in the same period between Sicily and other Mediterranean ports.

The chapter also deals with how the Hospitaller government and the two *Università* worked together, not only to procure the best possible wheat quotas from Sicily but also to try to control and stabilise the price and distribution of grain. Keeping staple food supplies affordable had one big benefit, that of filling empty stomachs and keeping the population content. At the same time, the taxation of a product for which demand was inelastic was a main source of revenue to sustain the expenses related to the defence of the island.

Land, its produce and use in the light of notarial acts 1467–1565[13]

Theories proposed by the *Annales* school of thought, implicating a slow, nearly static pace of life, argue that during the sixteenth century most economies of the Mediterranean region were bound to their own internal organisation, which did not permit countries to register an increase in levels of production and thus made them dependent on foreign trade. Such a hypothesis suggests a great lack of initiative and innovation and a situation that eventually led to these countries remaining largely unattached to the money economy.[14]

As already noted with regard to the economy of medieval southern Italy, Stephan Epstein argues against this theory of dependence on foreign trade, in which medieval peasants invariably pursued subsistence strategies. According to Epstein, social conflict and demographic change brought about significant changes whereby peasants became more commercialised through the relaxation of social constraints on commercial activities.[15]

During the medieval and early modern period Malta's agrarian-based economy was supported by barter, which became so important as a means of payment that it merited taxation. Land was an important source of wealth and its possession, whether by title or by lease, was a vital factor for subsistence. From a study of archidiaconal tithes for 1536, conducted by Godfrey Wettinger, it emerges that between one third and one half of the villagers, mostly peasants, owned a field, or at most two. This was quite different from the situation in neighbouring Sicily, where land was invariably owned by the king, the feudal lords or the ecclesiastical authority, and never by the peasants.[16] People were unwilling to sell property outright and instead they either rented it or sold it with a right of redemption,[17] the latter being recorded in notarial

Money, Markets and Trade in Late Medieval Europe: Essays in Honour of John H. A. Munro (Leiden, 2007), 297–309.

13 For problems relating to the difficutlies of deriving information from notarial acts refer to Epstein, *An Island for Itself*, 14–15.

14 Braudel, *The Mediterranean*, vol. 1, 382–3.

15 Epstein, *An Island for Itself*, 402–12.

16 Wettinger, 'Agriculture in Malta in the Late Middle Ages', 6–7.

17 The period stipulated for redemption differed, at times even set at after the death of the seller, the heirs being given the right to pay the redemption money within a stipulated time after his death.

acts as *cum gracia seu facultatis redimendi.*[18] A study of the acts of Notary Giacomo Żabbara for the years 1486–88 has identified a substantial difference in the totals of lands sold with the right of redemption and those sold outright. In fact, the latter amounted to only 10.2% of all land value sold.[19] Most land sales therefore represented no actual loss of patrimony. However, as is fully explained in this chapter, they emphasise the constant use of land as a means to obtain much-needed credit.

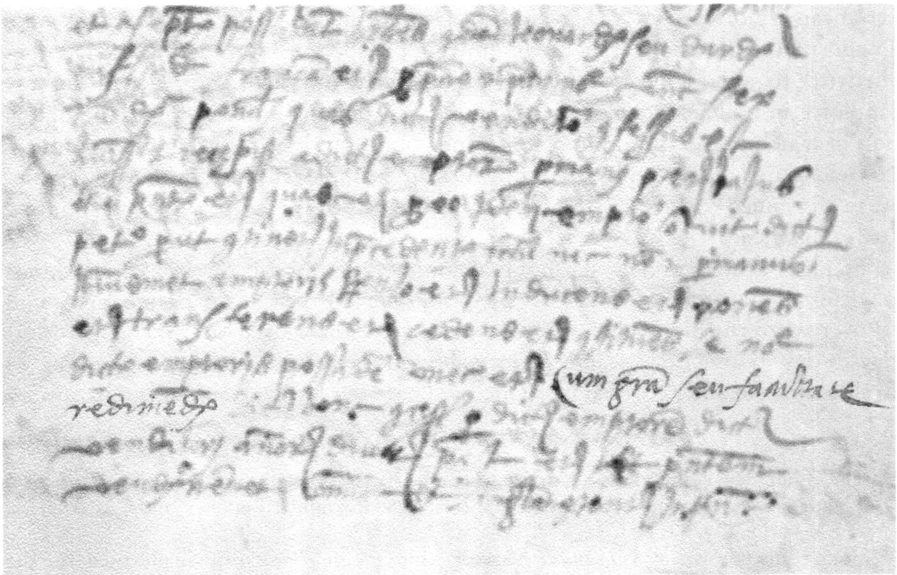

Fig. 2 Formula stating that the property could be redeemed by its original owner – *cum gracia seu facultatis redimendis*
Source: NAV, Notary Lorenzo Agius R 7/1, f. 5 (18.i.1524).

Malta's dependence on Sicily as its supplier of grain was accentuated when Maltese producers sought to reduce their grain production, particularly wheat, one

18 For a deeper insight into the sale or rent of property with the right of redemption clause refer to J. H. Munro, 'The Usury Doctrine and Urban Public Finances in Late-medieval Flanders (1220–1550): Rentes (Annuities), Excise Taxes, and Income Transfers from the Poor to the Rich', in S. Cavaciocchi (ed.), *Fiscal Systems in the European Economy from the 13th to the 18th centuries, Atti della Trentanovesima Settimana di Studi, 22–26 aprile 2007* (Florence, 2008), 974–1026. See also J. A. Lorenc, 'John of Freiburg and the Usury Prohibition in the Late Middle Ages: A Study in the Popularization of Medieval Canon Law' (PhD thesis, University of Toronto, 2013), 118–22, https://tspace.library.utoronto.ca/bitstream/1807/35887/1/Lorenc_John_A_201306_PhD_thesis.pdf (accessed 2 October 2016).

19 For a detailed breakdown of these transactions refer to S. Cachia, 'The Family and the Land in Late Medieval Malta: A Study of the Acts of Notary J. Zabbara, 1486–1488' (unpublished BA Hons dissertation, University of Malta, 2002), 53. This study analysed landholding in medieval Malta from a total of 340 notarial acts pertaining to Giacomo Zabbara. These had been previously transcribed by Fiorini in Fiorini (ed.), *Documentary Sources of Maltese History, Part 1, No.1.*

of the 'plants of civilization',[20] and instead to direct their efforts to producing cash crops. Cotton and cumin,[21] both of which were considered of high quality and were Malta's two principal export products, were in great demand in foreign markets.[22] In fact, Godfrey Wettinger even states that cotton from Malta and Alexandria formed the basis of the cotton industries of Genoa, Montpellier and Barcelona, and together with Sicilian production, it eventually replaced Turkish cotton at Barcelona in the fourteenth and fifteenth centuries.[23] This trend was also common in other Mediterranean regions where 'richer kinds of farming such as vines, and livestock were in constant competition with cereal growing',[24] especially considering the fact that the latter required large areas of land for relatively low yields. Evidence of the way landlords in Malta controlled the farmers' use of their land can be found in notarial acts in which the landlord imposed certain conditions when leasing out his land. A contract dated 24 December 1557 provides an example, stipulating that the farmer was constrained to sow only cotton in the last year of the lease, and could not sow barley or wheat.[25]

Stephan Epstein argues that notarial contracts are 'biased towards certain kinds of deferred transaction, which as far as commercial relations are concerned tend to over represent high-value, often foreign-based, trade over local exchange. Most day-to-day transactions, many informal work relations, and most patterns of livelihood were only recorded by chance and have left few written traces.'[26] Contrary

20 The other two being rice and maize. F. Braudel, *Civilization and Capitalism 15th–18th Century: The Structures of Everyday Life* (trans. S. Reynolds, Berkeley and Los Angeles, 1992), vol. 1, 107.

21 Botanically known as *Cuminum cyminum*, bitter cumin was principally used for the flavouring of food and drinks, for pharmaceutical preparations and for perfume. The sweet type, *Pimpinella anisum* (in Maltese *ħlewwa*, in English aniseed), was and still is used mainly as a condiment for food. Wettinger, 'Agriculture in Malta', in Buhagiar (ed.), *Proceedings of History Week, 1981*, 1–48: 22.

22 Wettinger, 'Agriculture in Malta', in Buhagiar (ed.), *Proceedings of History Week, 1981*, 1–48: 13–23. For the export of grain from Malta to other Mediterranean countries until 1437, and its abundance or shortage in the Maltese late medieval period refer to Wettinger, 'Agriculture in Malta', in Buhagiar (ed.), *Proceedings of History Week, 1981*, 1–48: 13–14.

23 Wettinger, 'Agriculture in Malta', in Buhagiar (ed.), *Proceedings of History Week, 1981*, 1–48: 16.

24 Braudel, *The Mediterranean*, vol. 1, 573. According to Horden and Purcell, various island societies contain highly renowned productive niches. P. Horden & N. Purcell, *The Corrupting Sea – A Study of Mediterranean History* (Oxford, 2000), 220. A drawback of wheat cultivation was the need for rotation, since it could not be grown on the same land for two consecutive years without serious harmful effects. It also required a space two or three times the surface area it occupied. Braudel, *Civilization and Capitalism*, vol. 1, 114.

25 '*In pacta et condictione quod dictus conductor non possit nec et liceat seminare in dicta clausura ordeum nec frumentum in ultimo locationis anno sed liceat ei seminare cottinis*' [sic]. NAV, R 4/1, fol. 124 (24.xii.1557). A document of 1449 stated that 'arable land of two crops, viz., land which is suitable for the production of wheat and barley and cotton ... is better and more valuable than land of one crop, that is land which is not suitable for the cultivation of cotton, and it is worth and usually valued if not by a half at least by a third more'. CAM, CEM, AO, vol. 2, fol. 25, as quoted in Wettinger, 'Agriculture in Malta', in Buhagiar (ed.), *Proceedings of History Week, 1981*, 1–48: 18 n. 100.

26 Epstein, *An Island for Itself*, 14–15.

to such a claim, from research carried out in the Notarial Archives, Valletta, it can be safely stated that daily petty transactions are rather abundant in the volumes for the period of this study, thus making the representation of villagers an important factor when analysing their contribution to economic activities. Although Epstein's argument may hold when studying deep rural transactions, on a small island like Malta the role of the market tended to be stronger, making notarial participation a much more common feature. The influx of foreigners into the island made notarial participation even more common, because the registration of notarial deeds acted as a safety mechanism in a highly cosmopolitan community.

The sale of cotton and cumin, even in small quantities, is a recurring subject in notarial acts.[27] Unfortunately, it is not often stipulated whether the produce was for local use or for export, although partnership agreements with a view to exporting small amounts of cotton were not uncommon, thus opening up this activity to petty investors.[28] A typical example is a *societas* agreement dated 1539[29] between Johannes Muscat from Lia and Petrus Muscat which states that Johannes was to invest 6 *uncie ponderis* as capital, while Petrus promised to provide his labour. It was further agreed that Petrus was to set sail on the first good weather and export the same amount of cotton.[30] The contract also stipulated that the two parties were to bear the same risks of the venture – '*ad commune lucrum et expensas*' [*sic*].

Various foreigners are also documented as buying small amounts of both cotton and cumin. In a contract dated 25 August 1541 Tommaso Bonnichi from Ħal Bisqallin[31] concluded a sale of bitter cumin with Giovanni Morsello from Pantelleria but residing in Bormla. A total of 1 *cantaro* and 40 *rotoli* of cumin were sold for 1 *uncia* 8 *tarì* 10 *grani*, at the rate of 27 *tarì* per *cantaro*. The stipulated sum was to be paid in Birgu when the said Giovanni returned from Messina aboard the *grippo*[32] belonging to Antonio Scarpello.[33] In yet another contract, Stefano Cafori, a Maltese citizen from Siġġiewi, stated that he received from the Greek Lorenzo Ros, and from Giovanni Sayti, 6 *uncie* 1 *tarì* 7 *grani* as payment for 93 *rotoli* of spun cotton.[34] This sale was first registered in the acts of Notary Giuseppe de Guevara on 3 March 1540. In an interesting contract dated 21 July 1543,[35] the Maltese *Hon.* Johannes Micallef

27 See as examples NAV, R 202/1, fols 23v–24 (28.iv.1536); R 202/4, fols 111–111v (20.i.1539 *ab inc*), fol. 153v (5.iv.1540), fols 161v–162 (8.iv.1540), fol. 168v (12.iv.1540), fols 170–171v (12.iv.1540), fol. 175 (19.iv.1540), fols 187–187v (27.iv.1540), fols 188v–189 (27.iv.1540), fols 194v–195 (29.iv.1540), fol. 199v (5.v.1540); R 224/13, fols 10v–11v (2.ix.1557), fol. 38v (7.ix.1557), fol. 46v (9.ix.1557), fol. 71v (11.ix.1557).

28 See also NAV, R 4/1, fols 132–132v (30.x.1557); NAV, R 224/17, fols 605v–607 (10.ii.1560 *ab inc*).

29 NAV, R 376/2, fols 29v–30v (10.ix.1539).

30 The actual price of the cotton *per cantaro* was not listed in the document.

31 Ħal Bisqallin forms part of Żejtun.

32 The *grippo* was one of the more important lateen-rigged merchant ships of the Order and of local *patroni*. It was similar to a brigantine and was mainly used by local masters for the transport of grain and other victuals. J. Muscat, *Sails Round Malta: Types of Sea Vessels 1600BC–1900AD* (Malta, 2008), 484.

33 NAV, R 224/1, fols 202v–203 (25.viii.1541).

34 NAV, R 224/1, fol. 180v (25.vi.1541).

35 NAV, R 206/7, fol. 190 (21.vii.1543).

received a total of 99 gold *scudi* in the form of cloth and other merchandise. This sum was part of a larger sum due to Micallef from *Magnificus* Johannes Charreta in respect of the sale of four sacks of spun cotton which the latter had sold for him in France, and also for an advance in cash amounting to 30 gold *scudi* which had been forwarded by Micallef. This contract shows how local producers of niche products were constantly trading their produce and seeking markets outside Malta. With the arrival of the Order, such opportunities were enhanced as a result of the great influx of merchants who not only acted as a link with merchants abroad but also conducted financial transactions in cash, encouraging the flourishing of a money economy.

Various innovations in shipping played a crucial role in the export trade, especially after 1350. Among these was the establishment of maritime insurance, which replaced the more antiquated sea loan agreements.[36] The well-documented use of such innovations by local merchants proves that they were in line with their European counterparts and thus attaining a level of comfort which made risk less dangerous.[37] A common form of insurance contract, highlighting the risks covered by such policies, is one concluded on 4 April 1536. This agreement covered a shipment of 18 *cantari* of spun cotton to be loaded at Birgu and shipped to Licata on the *fusta*[38] belonging to Giacomo Bonnichi. The said *fusta* was secured to travel to any other port which may have been deemed necessary for the purpose of this trade. It was further stated that should any misfortune covered by the said insurance take place, mainly fire, shipwreck or piratical attacks, the insurers were bound to pay the amount insured without any objection within four months, as was customary.[39]

Notarial acts also shed light on the relationship between the merchants and the local agrarian producers who delivered the essential commodities such as cotton and cumin, thus enabling the trade. Such was the case in an agreement between a priest from Żurrieq who sold 52 *scudi* worth of spun cotton to the Greek Georgio Gaglego.[40] In another instance, in February 1543, Johannes Michallef from Birgu agreed to load onto his ship a cargo of spun cotton weighing 89 *rotoli*, destined for Messina. He also promised his client, one Francesco Dearmenia, to sell the spun

36 Epstein, *An Island for Itself*, 269. The big insurance centre was Venice, even for ships or cargoes that never called at that port. R. de Roover, *The Rise and Decline of the Medici Bank* (Harvard and Oxford, 1963), 151.

37 See for example, NAV, R 202/1, fol. 87 (5.viii.1536), fol. 18 (21.iv.1536); R 202/1 Part II, fols 2v–3 (5.ix.1536), fol. 13 (15.ix.1536); R 202/1, fols 13 (7.iv.1536); R 202/4, fols 211–212 (21.v.1540), fol. 233v (28.vi.1540), fols 266–266v (29.vii.1540); R 202/5, fols 88v–89 (21.xii.1540); R 202/6, fol. 11 (7.ix.1541); R 4/1, fol. 135v (30.xii.1557), fols 41–41v (19.ii.1558); MS 778/4, fol. 133 (23.iii.1562), fols 166–167v ([?].[?].1562). For further reading on the use of insurance policies in sixteenth-century Malta refer to Abela, 'Port Activities', 88–95.

38 A *fusta* was 'slim, fast and low in the water, carried 18 to 22 benches or oars on both sides, one mast and a jib and was armed with two or three small guns. It was manned by 50 to 100 men who acted as soldiers, sailors and rowers when necessary. The *fusta* was smaller than a galleot.' Muscat, *Sails Round Malta*, 484.

39 NAV, R 202/1, fol. 8 (4.iv.1536). For further reading on the use of insurance policies in sixteenth-century Malta refer to Abela, 'Port Activities', 88–95.

40 NAV, R 224/1, fol. 410v (23.xii.1542).

cotton for the approximate price of not less than 5 *uncie* 10 *tarì* 4 *grani* per *cantaro*, since the prevailing selling rate was approximately 6 *uncie per cantaro*.[41]

An interesting recurring feature in almost all references to cotton is that it was described as being traded as *cutoni filati*, meaning that it was being sold or exported not in its raw form but already spun. Lack of documentation as to who was actually doing the spinning work means that we cannot determine the type of workforce. However, these documents can be used as broad economic indicators of activities that were being undertaken. It is possible that women were engaged in this type of domestic industry, either together with their husbands or else while the latter were employed in more strenuous work in the fields or at sea.[42]

It is perhaps in the light of factors such as those presented above that one should evaluate the use of general terms such as 'land of hunger' when describing the local economy in the early sixteenth century.[43] In the same way in which Epstein argues against the hypothesis that Sicily's economic backwardness resulted from lack of innovation and investment, Malta's economic backwardness needs to be evaluated in a far broader and deeper manner in which its shortage of grain production is seen in the context of a preference for specialisation in niche products such as cumin and cotton – in other words, the commercialisation of agriculture. As Godfrey Wettinger affirms in his study on late medieval Maltese agriculture, 'Maltese farming was sufficiently productive in one way or another to defray the expenses on wheat, on other foods as well as superior textiles and a whole range of other objects needed from abroad. It paid also, indirectly, for the island's normal needs of defence, and enabled substantial rents to be sent abroad regularly to absentee landlords.'[44] Such modifications in crop produce indicate that the investor or producer must have had more profitable returns which allowed him not simply to subsist but to enjoy extra rewards, minimal as these may have been. Concurrently, landlords' and farmers' preference for cash crops as against staples not only brought in much-needed foreign currency which balanced against trade payments in respect of grain imports,[45] but placed the island as a prime producer of specialised crops.[46]

41 NAV, R224/1, f. 243v (16.11.1543). It is interesting to note that in an earlier contract dated 1533 the quoted price per *cantaro* of spun cotton was 8 *uncie* 7 *tarì* 10 *grani*. NAV, R 439/9, fol. 27v (3.i.1533).

42 Wiesner-Hanks, *Early Modern Europe*, 196; O. Hufton, *The Prospect Before Her: A History of Women in Western Europe 1500–1800* (New York, 1998), 155–9.

43 Cassar, *Society, Culture and Identity*, 3.

44 Wettinger, 'Agriculture in Malta', in Buhagiar (ed.), *Proceedings of History Week, 1981*, 1–48: 3.

45 Wettinger calculates that to balance off the importation of 9,000 *salme* of wheat per year, the island needed to export well over 1,000 *cantara* of ginned cotton (cotton fibres separated from their seeds). However, other considerations must be evaluated, such as the income derived from the export of cumin and the fact that much of the exported cotton was spun into yarn before export, thereby raising its price by at least a third. Wettinger, 'Agriculture in Malta', in Buhagiar (ed.), *Proceedings of History Week, 1981*, 1–48 18.

46 The cultivation of cotton was widespread on the Maltese islands from classical times to the mid-nineteenth century. H. Bowen-Jones, *Malta Background for Development* (Durham, 1961), 225. The importation of cotton from Malta is mentioned in Genoa in the second half of the twelfth century. During the fourteenth century there is reference

This preference for cultivating niche products has also to be viewed in the wider European context. According to Epstein, a crucial factor directly affecting specialisation in the late Middle Ages was the redistribution of incomes, which was brought about by a loss of population in most western European regions, to the benefit of peasants, wage-earners and artisans. The low elasticity of demand for food grains provides only a marginal effect in income distribution. However, income distribution 'can have considerable effects on demand for manufactured goods and higher-quality foodstuffs ... during the late middle ages, the redistribution of incomes led to a considerable increase in demand for more and better non-staple foodstuffs and cheap manufactured goods, especially cloth, which in turn provided the main stimulus for specialization of agriculture and manufacturing'.[47]

The need for a credit market

People conceived of price as 'the relation between an amount of money and a quantity of a commodity, the former being variable and the latter fixed'.[48] By the sixteenth century, Sicily had established a sophisticated agricultural credit market, which had started to develop in the early fifteenth century. This enabled investors to advance capital to the producers or their agents at an agreed price (*meta*) per *salma* of wheat which was set after the following harvest. The operation of this credit system eventually helped to decrease uncertainty, while at the same time it stabilised production, prices and consumption.[49] Similarly in Malta ever since medieval times, extant documentation points to this having been a common trend. A case in point is an agreement drawn up in May 1525 between the Catalan merchant Melchiore Ferrer and Juliano Calabro, whereby Ferrer forwarded 11 *tarì* 12 *grani* while Calabro promised to sow bitter cumin in his fields and to deliver the equivalent amount of the advanced sum in this produce by the following August.[50]

Such practice is well documented during the period under study and one can safely say that the agricultural credit market was well established even in the initial years of the Order's stay on the island. Being a naval Order, the Knights hastened to create an efficient maritime communication system under their own control that eventually helped the harbour area to develop into a veritable centre of activity

to it being exported to various places such as Syracuse, Tripoli, Venice, Ancona, Bari and Barcelona. In the same period Pegolotti listed Malta among the six main cotton producing countries. During the sixteenth century, the French writer Rabelais used the phrase *blanc comme cotton de Malthe*, indicating the high regard which Maltese cotton enjoyed on the international market. Wettinger, 'Agriculture in Malta', in Buhagiar (ed.), *Proceedings of History Week, 1981*, 1–48: 16.

47 Epstein, *An Island for Itself*, 77. For a classic example of the preference to cultivate a cash crop over grains, see M. Fusaro, *L'uva passa. Una guerra commerciale tra Venezia e l'Inghilterra, 1540–1640* (Venice, 1997).

48 W. Kula, *Measures and Men* (trans. R. Szreter, Princeton, 1986), 102.

49 Epstein, *An Island for Itself*, 144.

50 NAV, R 7/1, fols 30–30v (27.v.1525).

comparable to any other south European coastal urban centre.[51] Good port facilities and the policing of the surrounding waters by the Order's navy attracted foreign merchants to the island and this, coupled with the increase in population, triggered a greater demand for local produce. Testimony to this demand are various notarial acts, like those found in the records of Notary Nicolò de Agatiis. Between 29 January 1540 and 5 May 1540 this notary recorded nine contracts regarding the sale of cumin[52] and three regarding the sale of cotton,[53] each of which represented a cash advance made by the investor to the producer. Notarial documents reflect that even members of the Order made much-needed financial advances to producers. The Knights seem to have started immediately to tap into small amounts of local sources of wheat to ensure the provision of sufficient supplies. Their worries about lack of supplies extended further than the supply of grain for local consumption, as they also had to ensure that their own galleys and other visiting galleys using Malta as a port of call were well provisioned.[54]

Evidence comes from various notarial sources. A case in point is a contract regarding a loan of 256 *tarì* advanced by the Knight *Fra.* Johannes Bonifacius Baulino to Johannes Vassallus from Attard on 5 November 1530, barely a month after the Order's establishment. This loan represented a 'friendly' advance in cash, to be repaid by the following July in the form of a supply of wheat estimated at 32 *tarì* per *salma*.[55] On the same day the same Knight drew up two similar contracts, one representing 128 *tarì* advanced from Casali di Girgor to *Hon.* Augustinus Borgius,[56] and another advanced to his co-villager Bartholomeo Borgius. The latter loan amounted to 96 *tarì*, equivalent to 3 *salma* of wheat to be delivered in July.[57] Thus, while in a particular contract this same Knight is found actively involved in buying shares in a corsairing expedition,[58] in the next he is investing in the local agricultural produce. Similarly, in February 1531 Melchiore Ferrer, a recurring name in notarial deeds connected to various trading activities, advanced a loan of 2 *uncie* to Inigo and Mattheo Camilleri from Żurrieq. These on their part were to provide Ferrer

51 C. Cassar, 'U Mulu de Malta: The Maltese Trade in Donkeys and Mules', *Storja* (1996), 12–20: 12.

52 NAV, R 202/4, fols 111–111v (29.i.1539 *ab inc*), fol. 150v (1.iv.1540), fols 153v–154 (5.iv.1540), fols 161v–162 (8.iv.1540), fol. 168v (12.iv.1540), fols 170–170v (12.iv.1540), fol. 178 (19.iv.1540), fol. 189 (27.iv. 1540), fols 194v–195 (29.iv.1540).

53 NAV, R 202/4, fol. 171 (15.iv.1540), fols 187–187v (27.iv.1540), fol. 199v (5.v.1540).

54 A case in point was the squadron of ninety strong vessels which were assembled in the summer of 1559 at Messina, whose objective was the fortress of Tripoli. These reached Malta on 2 December 1559; however, they were forced to spend most of the winter on the island due to bad weather. J. Abela '*De Uxore Proxima Futura Magistri Hieronymi Cassar*: New Light on Girolamo Cassar's Immediate Family', *Melita Historica*, 14:4 (2007), 375–85: 379 n. 13, 380 n. 18.

55 NAV, R 439/1, fols 1–2 (5.xi.1530). This would be equivalent to 8 *salme*. The word 'friendly' in loan contracts was invariably used as a safety valve to indicate that the debt was one of 'friendship'. It was affection that motivated the creditor to lend and no usurious profits were being sought. Lorenc, *John of Freiburg and the Usury Prohibition*, 75.

56 NAV, R 439/1, fols 2–3v (5.xi.1530).

57 NAV, R 439/1, fols 3v–5 (5.xi.1530).

58 NAV, R 439/1, fols 35v–36v (22.xii.1530).

with an equivalent amount of 'new cumin' [*sic*] (*cumini nuovum*), which was to be delivered by the following June.[59] A similar transaction by the same Ferrer on the same day was concluded with Nardus and Bertos Camilleri, also from Żurrieq. On this occasion the sum was 4 *uncie*, also described as a 'friendly' loan in respect of the future supply of cumin.[60]

Other interesting factors which illustrate how trade credit was increasingly becoming the way forward for various types of trading operations are reflected in various notarial contracts which shed light on the use of the services of money changers.[61] At least from the late medieval period[62] these are recorded as a source of trade credit used on the island, business partners finding it profitable to channel their work through the money changers' services. Such was the case of Petrus Muscat, who confessed to being indebted with Bertho Muscat in the amount of 15 *uncie* 15 *tarì ponderis*.[63] This sum was the amount remaining from the proceeds of a *societas* agreement which had been made between the two partners, wherein the objectives of the company included the carrying out of trade in *cuyrami barbantis*.[64] In this particular act Petrus was to pay back his partner *in pace et de plano ut bancus*[65] on his first visit to Sicily.[66] In yet another contract Georgius Cachie was indebted with Francesco Hajius for the sum of 2 *uncie* 5 *tarì argenti ponderis*, the price of thirty-four *canne*[67] of cloth (*dublecta et fustayna*) at the rate of

59 NAV, R 439/1, fols 41–42 (3.ii.1531).

60 NAV, R 439/1, fols 42–43v (3.ii.1531). Some other examples are NAV, R 439/1, fols 43v–44 (7.ii.1531), fols 44v–45v (7.ii.1531); R 439/2, fols 67–68v (24.ii.1531), fols 70v–71v (24.ii.1531); R376/3, fol. 472v (21.iv.1540), fols 472v–473 (21.iv.1540); R 376/4, fol. 13v (5.ix.1540); R224/1, fols 111v–112 (13.xii.1540), fol. 112v (16.xii.1540), fol. 114v (29.xii.1540); R 376/11 (no.2), fol. 504 (11.ii.1545); R 224/13, fol. 10v (2.ix.1557), fol. 11v (02.ix.1557).

61 The money changer formed the link between the public and the mint which was essential for the smooth operation of a money market. R. de Roover, *Money, Banking and Credit in Medieval Bruges – Italian Merchant Bankers, Lombards and Money Changers – A Study in the Origins of Banking* (Cambridge, MA, 1948), 220–1.

62 For example NAV, R 7/1 for the period 1524–28 holds a total of sixteen contracts mentioning the use of the money changer.

63 Fiorini explains that 'in pre-1530 Malta both Sicilian and local currencies were in circulation. The money of account for both was reckoned in *uncie* worth 30 *tarì*, the *tarì* worth 20 *grani* and the *grano* worth 6 *denari* or *pichuli (piccioli)*. When distinction between the two needed to be made, it was clearly indicated in the documentation by the use of the term *ponderis generalis* for the Sicilian currency and *pecunia Malte* or *Gaudisii* (as the case may have been) for the local currency.' Fiorini, 'Malta in 1530', in Mallia-Milanes (ed.), *Hospitaller Malta 1530–1798*, 111–98: 162.

64 Leather from Brabant.

65 Basically meaning that he will pay peacefully and in full. See V. Cusumano, *Storia dei Banchi Della Sicilia*, (Rome, 1887) 94–7. According to Trasselli this formula substantially meant that the person acting as surety or guarantor obliged himself to pay the creditor as if he (the guarantor) was a banker. C. Trasselli, *Note per la storia dei banchi in Sicilia nel XV secolo, Vol. II, I banchieri e i loro affari* (Cosenza, 1993), 55.

66 NAV, R 7/1, n.f. (2.i.1525).

67 Cloth was measured in *canne*, or *qasba* in Maltese, with one *canna* being approximately 2.06m long. Epstein, *An Island for Itself*, xii. Bowen-Jones translates one *canna* to 2.095m. Bowen-Jones, *Malta background for Development*, 13.

5 *carlini*[68] *per canna*. Once again, the debtor promised to pay *ut bancus* in Sicily by the coming Easter or on his first visit to the island.[69] Such cases indicate that local private entrepreneurs' links with Sicilian banks[70] existed even prior to the Order's arrival, albeit they area minimally recorded. These enabled merchants to make use of financial instruments such as bills of exchange and promissory notes, thus facilitating trading agreements. The arrival of the Order and the continual influx of foreign merchants greatly increased demand for such financial dealings. How did the Order's presence affect the transfer of money between Malta and other countries?

The transaction of large sums of money between the Order's commanderies scattered across Europe necessitated the establishment of a strong financial institution to pull in these revenues. As early as 1529 the Order began to take steps to provide for the easy flow of revenues, and its Receiver in Palermo was made responsible for collecting them. A study by Carmelo Trasselli established how, by 1570, this Sicilian depositary had already become an international bank.[71] Such an important institution could not but greatly facilitate financial transactions between Malta and other European countries, enabling the island's financial services to stand on a par with those of other southern European countries where this type of practice was very common.[72] Through the provision of this facility, more foreign merchants were attracted to the island, which now offered the necessary arrangements to cater for most of their business needs.

Often, the merchant who had correspondents overseas could offer the same services as a banker. A client might request him to transfer a sum of money overseas. This he could do, since he could order payment to be made by a correspondent of his who owed him money in respect of a particular agreement. In this way the merchant retrieved his money faster. Further, if the client who made the initial request was owed money by the merchant himself, he would not issue money but would limit himself to be legally covered by a contract or promissory note. By means of this practice, a current bank account may be said to have been established between the

68 The silver *Carlino* was worth 10 *grani*. This coin was available in either gold or silver. J. C. Sammut, *Is-Sistema Monetarja ta' Malta* (Malta, 2007), 86.

69 NAV, R 7/1, n.f. (2.i.1525).

70 Nowadays, to speak of banks conjures up images of prominent buildings reflecting the power of the private initiative, and of large regulatory agencies instituted to represent the interest of the state and of depositors. In the medieval and early modern period, most banks were miniscule in physical terms, but their importance in monetary terms was considerable. The tables of money changers and bankers were located in the centre of business districts. They took up little space: a booth or stall in a public square, or a small ground-floor room, perhaps connected to a small back room in a public building or in a private place. F. C. Lane & R. C. Mueller, *Money and Banking in Medieval and Renaissance Venice, Vol. 1 Coins and Moneys of Account* (Baltimore and London, 1985), 83.

71 C. Trasselli, as quoted in A. Giuffrida, *La Sicilia e l'Ordine di Malta*, 23. De Roover gives the following definition of an international bank: '*banchi grossi*, which did an international business and traded in bills of exchange'. De Roover, *Money, Banking and Credit in Medieval Bruges*, 151.

72 Abela, 'Port Activities', 39–48.

merchant and his correspondent.[73] When various clients left amounts of money owed to them by the merchant as deposit for future overseas payment, such as letters of exchange, the merchant could use this money to invest in other business affairs.

Another aspect of the need for money and how it could be generated is found in contracts which refer to the sale of land, particularly those which included the right of redemption, mentioned above. When analysing these documents, and in order to place them in their proper context, it is important to bear in mind the prevailing dogma of the Catholic Church, which prohibited the taking of any profits on loans which were considered 'small scale and "vile" forms of business assumed in general as sterile commerce of money or disreputable speculations performed by those who are called by canonists and jurists *viles personae* (persons of low degree) and *alienigenae* (foreigners) or *usurarii manifesti* (notorious usurers)'.[74] What separated honourable from deviant forms of credit was commercial risk; thus, in this case interest was a compensation for loss.

In order to carry out their trade at a profit and at the same time respect prevailing laws, money lenders had to find ways and means to circumvent such laws. Economic transactions in land were a preferred way by which such needs were addressed and met. Often, when landowners found themselves financially constrained, they would trade in their property for cash, while reserving the right to repurchase the property when economic conditions improved. As is shown further on, the inclusion of interest in the actual price, not only of land but also of various other commodities used to secure money loans, ensured that the creditor recovered the amount due, plus interest, without openly declaring a profit.[75] As is discussed in Chapter Three, from the records of ecclesiastical tribunals it may be safely stated that various persons who were charged with carrying out usurious practices were often accused of having forced their victims to draw up 'fictitious' contracts – such as those mentioned above containing 'hidden' interest – which at times were so exorbitant that the debtor could not rid himself of the debt.[76]

73 Trasselli, *Note per la storia dei banchi*, 63; R. S. Lopez & I. W. Raymond, *Medieval Trade in the Mediterranean World, Illustrative Documents Translated with Introduction and Notes* (New York, 1990), 16, 162.

74 G. Todeschini, 'Usury in Christian Middle Ages. A Reconsideration of the Historiographical Tradition (1949–2010)', in F. Ammannati (ed.), *Religion and Religious Institutions in the European Economy. 1000–1800, Atti della 'Quarantatreesima Settimana di Studi' 8–12 Maggio 2011* (Florence, 2012), 119–30: 125. In this study Todeschini provides an insight on the different meanings assumed in different periods by the word-concept *usura*. In the Byzantine empire this viewpoint never prevailed. Hence, interest on loans continued to be regarded as legitimate. See Lopez & Raymond, *Medieval Trade in the Mediterranean World*, 157.

75 Refer to NAV, R 7/1, fols 3v–4 (18.i.1525), fols 4–4v (18.i.1525), which relate to two contracts where the same piece of land changed hands more than once in just one day.

76 CAM, CEM, *Registrum Usuriarorum Melitae, Liber Primus 1570–1571.*

Local cereal production and consumption

Insufficient documentation hampers a detailed account of either local cereal production or the quantities imported during the period under study. Some statistical data after 1565 does provide a glimpse of local yields during the sixteenth century. In discussing local grain harvests, Bosio states that around 1566, when the population was approximately 20,000, local crops yielded about 25,000 *salme*.[77] Assuming annual *per capita* cereal consumption to be on the high side of 1.5 *salme*,[78] this quantity would have fed approximately 16,500 people, or 66% of the population. The yield figures indicate that the island was not as arid as most supplications to the Viceroy suggested it to be. It should be noted that Bosio's figures present an overall picture and do not provide a breakdown for the different cereal crops. In 1575 the Apostolic Delegate, Monsieur Pietro Dusina, reported that the island produced about 4,000 *salme* of wheat and 13,000 *salme* of barley, and noted that with greater efforts on the part of farmers higher yields might be obtained.[79]

A series of tax records for Birkirkara, Naxxar, Siġġiewi and Żebbug (all significant cereal producers) in the first half of the 1580s also provide a good indication on the general trend of agricultural activity in Malta[80] and indicate once again that there was an overwhelming preponderance of barley and meslin[81] production vis-à-vis wheat.[82] In 1546 twenty-three landowners of Naxxar,[83] who held twenty-nine holdings which were subject to decanal tithes,[84] paid a mere total of 1 *salma* 12 *tumuli* and 2 *mondelli* of wheat.[85] This indicates the small size of their landholdings. Most of their production must have been to provide for their own personal and family needs, such that little of it would have been offered for sale on the local market.[86]

77 Bosio, *Dell'Istoria della Sacra Religione*, vol. 3, 776.

78 NLM, Univ. 1, 'Relatione che fa il V. Re Conte d'Alva', fol. 189.

79 NLM, Libr. MS 433, 'Discorso di Mons Pietro Dusina su Malta', fols 18–24.

80 The figures do not include the total production output, since some producers may have been left out. Moreover, these declarations do not include the amount of seeds which were sown and the amount of cereal that was due to the 'metiture', since, as was customary in Malta, these were deducted from such tax declarations. Vassallo, 'Prices of Commodities', 64 n. 1.

81 'A mixture of cereal species that are sown and harvested together. The mixture wheat/rye is known as meslin, but in trade is usually classified with wheat.' Food and Agriculture Organization of the United Nations, http://www.fao.org/es/faodef/fdef01e.htm (accessed 24 February 2016). This type of grain is referred to by other names, like *maħlut* and *mixta*. Wettinger, 'Agriculture in Malta', in Buhagiar (ed.), *Proceedings of History Week, 1981*, 1–48: 13; Bowen-Jones, *Malta Background for Development*, 195.

82 Vassallo, 'Price of Commodities', 62–6.

83 In 1522, the Naxxar landowners held land which was spread out over the northern part of Malta. Wettinger, 'Agriculture in Malta', in Buhagiar (ed.), *Proceedings of History Week, 1981*, 1–48: 7.

84 Wettinger notes that 'tithes presumably originally represented tenths of the production of each holding'. Wettinger, 'Agriculture in Malta', in Buhagiar (ed.), *Proceedings of History Week, 1981*, 1–48: 7.

85 Wettinger, 'Agriculture in Malta', in Buhagiar (ed.), *Proceedings of History Week, 1981*, 1–48: 6.

86 Vassallo, 'Prices of Commodities', 66. Average annual consumption *per capita* of wheat was subject to wide variations.

Anthony Vassallo provides a good analysis of local cereal production in his study on commodity prices in Malta during the sixteenth century.[87] As already noted, production of barley and meslin was preferred in Malta to that of wheat. Vassallo builds his thesis through an examination of extant primary sources and shows that farmers' preference for meslin and barley was due to their higher seed:yield ratio.[88] Barley, a crop that commanded relatively low prices, was consumed mostly by the local livestock. The high transport costs and the risks of shipping made it uneconomic to export barley, but the island benefitted from the relatively higher yields of a crop that could be consumed locally.

In 1590 the Viceroy of Sicily, Conte d'Alva, commissioned Diego del Quadro to produce a detailed report on local cereal production and consumption.[89] The chief aim of del Quadro's four-month visit and subsequent report was to examine the basis for conceding duty-free quotas.[90] It is important to note that his report was produced at a time when Sicily was experiencing a crisis in cereal production and trying to compete with the supply of cheap grain from northern European countries.[91] It is no surprise that the authorities questioned Malta's demands, especially since del Quadro noted that the island produced a total of 34,976 *salme* and 9 *tumuli* of cereals, comprising 1,783 *salme* of wheat, 13,764 *salme* and 9 *tumuli* of meslin and 19,429 *salme* of barley.[92] From this he deducted 15,000 *salme* used as animal fodder, including for the Grand Master's cavalry.[93] Thus, del Quadro estimated that the *Università* was left with approximately 20,000 *salme* of cereal for a population of *ca.* 29,000. His calculations indicate that only 45% of the population was provided for by local yields and he reported that not only should present quotas be kept, but they should actually be increased.[94] Del Quadro also noted that the island had enough supplies to last it four months in time of siege, which would allow enough time for reinforcements to arrive from nearby countries.

The Order's needs were a very different story, since, according to del Quadro, the Grand Master and 'his house' (*sus casas*) needed a total of about 30 *salme* of wheat per year, while each Knight needed approximately 4 *salme* of wheat annually. In addition, high-ranking Knights were conceded extra quotas for their servants, as for

87 Vassallo, 'Prices of Commodities', 59–71.

88 Vassallo, 'Prices of Commodities', 59–60.

89 On the subject see also Giuffrida, *La Sicilia e l'Ordine di Malta*, 15–16.

90 He returned to Messina on 30 July 1590. Trasselli, 'Una Statistica Maltese', 475. NLM, Univ. 1, '*Relatione che fa il V. Re Conte d'Alva alla Ma. Del Re Filippo et sopra la numerazione dell'anime della Religione e popoli di Malta e Gozo, e del grano che queste producono un'ano' per l'altro, fatta da Diego Quadra, sopra l'aum.to delle tratte ...*', fols 183–186v. Trasselli informs us that another copy, presumably that which was presented to the Viceroy, is found at the *Archivio di Stato di Palermo, Patrimonio, n. provv. 2032, Recuperate di Materiali Diversi del 1590–91*, fols 195–200. Trasselli, 'Una Statistica Maltese', 476.

91 The year 1590 was one of great scarcity and famine in both Sicily and Malta. Braudel, *The Mediterranean*, vol. 2, 604; B. Dal Pozzo, *Historia della Sacra Religione de San Giovanni* (Verona, 1703), 326; Vassallo, 'Prices of Commodities', Table XIV, 80.

92 NLM, Univ. 1, 'Relatione che fa il V. Re Conte d'Alva', fols 184–189.

93 NLM, Univ. 1, 'Relatione che fa il V. Re Conte d'Alva', fol. 189.

94 Taking del Quadro's estimate of consumption *per capita* to be 1½ *salme*.

example the Knights of the Grand Cross who were allocated another 12 *tumuli* per month for a total of six slaves.[95]

In response to the report, the Sicilian Viceroy, Count d'Alva, informed the king of Spain that del Quadro had used incorrect estimates of consumption *per capita*, since he had assumed that all the population needed 1½ *salma* per head,[96] when in fact 'in order to know how many *tratte* may be exported the estimate of one *salma per capita* has always been used, and this with success'.[97] D'Alva further explained that the women,[98] who were approximately 45% of the population, did not require more than one *salma* since, unlike men, they did not perform a lot of heavy work (*essi non travagliare tanto corporalmente, che habbiano bisogno di estraordinario si come un homo*).[99] Men who worked in the fields, on the other hand, required 2 *salma* of wheat per year; however, it was noted that these did not make up more than 10% of the population. Moreover, children aged under five years and old people were said to require no more than ½ *salma* of wheat per year.[100] Thus, according to the Viceroy, del Quadro's report was erroneous in its conclusions and its findings could not be used as a basis for estimating duty-free grain quotas.

The exact number of mouths to be fed was not the only issue worrying the Sicilian authorities, who were also very much concerned when rumours began to spread that some of the supplies were being used illicitly by members of the Order who were smuggling duty-free grain abroad, to the detriment of the royal revenues.[101] This issue is dealt with below.

The price of wheat

Prices of local grain were usually, but not always, fixed by the *Università* towards harvest time, that is, by the end of June or early July.[102] At times, prices were also

95 It was stated that the Order needed about 8,551 *salme* of wheat. A breakdown of the members of the Order on the island reads as follows: 13 Knights of the Grand Cross, 61 Commanders, 422 Knights, 65 Chaplains and 69 brothers-servants-in-arms, bringing these to a total of 640. The Order also had four galleys with 1,417 sailors and 411 slaves, while the Grand Master had two galleys with 769 sailors and a total of 209 personal slaves. NLM, Univ. 1, 'Relatione del Calcola dell'Anime della Religione ...', fol. 183.

96 NLM, Univ. 1, 'Relatione che fa il V. Re Conte d'Alva', fol. 189.

97 NLM, Univ. 1, 'Relatione che fa il V. Re Conte d'Alva', fol. 189v, '*per sapersi quante tratte si possono estrare sempre si ha calculato una salma per anima e questo calculo sempre ha riuscito*'.

98 Del Quadro split the female population into those under and over five years of age. Thus, in this context, 'women' means the female population over the age of five.

99 NLM, Univ. 1, 'Relatione che fa il V. Re Conte d'Alva', fol. 190.

100 NLM, Univ. 1, 'Relatione che fa il V. Re Conte d'Alva', fol. 190.

101 NLM, Univ. 1, 'Relatione che fa il V. Re Conte d'Alva', fol. 183. On the subejct see Trasselli, 'Una statistica Maltese', 476. Similar instances of illicit use of export licences may be found in Braudel, *The Mediterranean*, vol. 1, 573.

102 See, for example, NLM, Univ. 13, fol. 64v (18.ii.1534), wherein a *bando* issued in February stated that nobody could sell wheat for more than 3 *tarí* per *tumino* on pain of being fined 4 *uncia* payable to the fiscal officer of the Grand Master, and fol. 126 (26.xi.1536), stating that no one could sell barley for more than 1 *tarì* and 1 *grano* per *tumino*. The

included in the official September price lists, such as that issued by the *jurats* in 1534 and entitled '*pandecta merche frumentij ordej carnum et aliarum rerum*'.[103] The latter were retail prices, while the prices fixed by the *Università* were generally of two kinds, one a retail price for the general public and the other a trading price to be used between merchants and farmers.[104] The grain merchants, who were not necessarily the official sellers of wheat,[105] advanced money to landlords or farmers and were paid back the equivalent of their loan in wheat or other grains. The advances were usually agreed in the presence of a notary and it was often, but not always, stipulated that the loan was '*nomine puri et veri mutui gratis*'.[106] A typical deed representing many other similar transactions would state as follows:

Die vigesimo nono mensis novembris primo Ind[iction]is Mill[esim]o Quinq[uagesi]mo Septimo.	(On the twenty-ninth day of the month of November of the First Indiction of the year one thousand five hundred and fifty-seven.
Hon[orabilis] Virgilius de Amato neapolitanus incola ville actard huius insule melite p[rese]ns coram nobis sponte vendidit hon[orabili] Mag[ist]ro Mariano Zaharia incole meliten[si] p[rese]nti etc. salmas tres ordei boni nitidi mercantibilis et receptibilis recollectionis proxime future prime indi[ctioni]s instantis. Quas quidem salmas tres ordei dictus hon[orabilis] Virgilius venditor dare et consignare p[ro]misit eidem hon[orabili] Mag[ist]ro Mariano emptori delatas et positas in hac nova civitate Melite in pace et de plano per totum mensem Junij p[ro]x[im]o venturum seminet ipse venditor aut no[n] [?] seminet recolligat aut no[n] recolligat, alias si defecerit	The Honorable Virgilius de Amato, a Neapolitan, resident in the village of Attard of this island of Malta, present before us, has, of his own accord, sold to the Honorable Mastru Mariano Zaharia, a resident of Malta, present, three salme of good barley, clean, tradeable and storable, of the next first coming harvest of the First present Indiction. Indeed, the said Honorable Virgilius, the seller, has promised to give and to consign to the same *Hon.* Mastru Mariano, the buyer, these three salme of barley, carried and placed in this new city of Malta; in peace and in full through the whole month of June, next coming, [whether] the seller himself sows or not sows, harvests or not harvests; at other times, if he shall have

Università of Gozo issued a separate price list which was usually determined by the prices prevalent in Malta. Vassallo, 'Prices of Commodities', 73.

103 Price list of commodities, wheat, barley, meat and other goods. NLM, Univ. 13, fol. 76v–78 (1534).

104 In Gozo these were distinguished by the words *meta* and *contrometa*, the latter being the retail price. Vassallo, 'Prices of Commodities', 74–5.

105 Official wheat sellers were referred to in documents as *magazinieri*.

106 NAV, R 376/2, fol. 58v (17.ix.1539). Literally meaning 'under the title of a pure and true exchange, free of charge', thus translating to 'what was thine becomes mine'. For a deeper insight into the usury doctrine and the Roman law concept of law as *mutuum* see Munro, 'The Usury Doctrine and Urban Public Finances', in Cavaciocchi (ed.), *Fiscal Systems in the European Economy*, 974–1026. See also Gaius, *Institutes of Roman Law*, Book III, para. 90, 'a loan for consumption … relates to things which are estimated by weight, number or measure, such as money, wine, oil, corn, bronze, silver, gold. We transfer ownership of our property in these on condition that the receiver shall transfer back to us at a future time, not the same things, but other things of the same nature: and this contract is called mutuum, because thereby meum becomes tuum', http://droitromain.upmf-grenoble.fr/Anglica/gai3_Poste.htm (accessed 28 February 2016).

teneatur et se teneri voluit ad co[m]munem valorem, quanti co[m]muniter valuerit ordeum In hac insula et nova civitate melite; et hoc p[ro] p[re]tio pretij nomine p[ro] ut seu quanti co[m]muniter In hac Insula dictu[m] ordeum constiterit in dicto mense Junij consignationis tempore, de quo quidem pretio dictus hon[orabilis] venditor confessus est habuisse et recepisse p[ro] ut p[resentaliter habuit et recepit a p[redic]to emptore untiam po[nderis ge[neralis] unam, Renuncians etc. Residuum vero quidquid et quantum fuerit dictus hon[orabilis] emptor dare solvere ac rea[li]t[e]r numerare p[ro] misit ipsi venditori In hac nova civitate Melite In pecunia numerata in pace et de plano ut bancus etc. In consignatione p[redic]ti ordei etc.

Actum in nova Civitate Melitae p[rese] ntibus nob[ilis] Vincentio Muscato et Hieronimo Romano testibus notis etc. [*sic*][107]

failed, he shall be obliged, and he has wished, that he be held to the common value, so much as barley shall be commonly valued in this island and in this new city of Malta. And this for the price, in the name of the price, or so much as the said barley shall have been fixed in this Island in this month of June at the time of consignment; concerning which price, indeed, the said honourable seller has declared that he had had and had received just as he has presently had and received from the aforesaid buyer one *uncia* of general weight. Renouncing etc. The rest of the sum, indeed, whatever and how much it shall have been, the honourable buyer has promised to pay and actually to number to the same seller in this new city of Malta, in cash, in peace and in full etc. in summary fashion etc. as a bank etc. on the consignment of the aforesaid barley.

Done in the new city of Malta, before the witnesses the Noble Vincenzo Muscat and Gerolamo Romano.)

Other contracts are more specific about price fluctuations. For instance, an agreement between two soldiers interested in trading in barley between Malta and Gozo states the following with regard to the consignment of 10 *salme* of Gozitan barley and the eventual payment of its value of 10 *scudi*:[108]

Et hoc pro precio quo valuerit ordeum generaliter in dicta insula Gaudisi in dicto mense et si valuerit tunc maioris precii, dictus emptor teneatur reficere dictum residuum in consignatione dicti ordei et si valuerit minoris preci dictus venditor teneatur restituere illud superfluum quod apparuerit habuisse Alias in casu dictus venditor defecisset in dicta consignatione ordej voluit se tenerij ad maiorem valorem et precium et ad omina alia damna et expensas quas propter ea subisse dictum emptorem constabit.

(And this for the price by which barley shall be generally valued in this island of Gozo in this month, and if it then shall be valued at a higher price, the said buyer is obliged to restore the outstanding on consignment of the said barley, and if it shall be valued at a lower price, the said seller shall be obliged to reimburse that excess which it shall have appeared to have had. At another time, in case that the said vendor had defaulted in the said consignment of the barley, he has wished that he be held for the higher value and for the price and for every other damage and expense which on account of this it shall be agreed that the said buyer had sustained.)

107 NAV, R 4/1, fols 69–69v (29.xi.1557).
108 NAV, R 4/1, fols 38v–39 (15.xi.1557).

This procedure of advance buying and selling of cereals gave rise to various abuses, especially when debtors found themselves in serious financial difficulties. Since the Catholic Church's teaching instructed that '*pecunia pecuniam non parit*',[109] businessmen found themselves in an ambivalent position: their profession and goals were morally acceptable, but the routine they had to follow to attain these objectives was censured. Financial advances were thus shrouded in a legal terminology by means of which the businessman could circumvent such prohibitions without appearing to be lending at a profit. Various forms of loans and agreements, such as the advance loans to farmers quoted above, made the loan contract a very widespread type of contract in medieval and early modern times.

What follows is an analysis of three hundred contracts categorised as *Debitum, Venditio* and *Mutuum* found in the acts of Notary Giuseppe de Guevara for the period September 1560 to August 1561. This register has been chosen because it is well preserved, is very legible and contains a substantial number of contracts of various types. It can thus be taken as providing very representative data on the different kinds of economic activity that were taking place. The register contains a total of 960 contracts, making this notary one of the most active in the harbour area. His clients included foreigners and members of all sections of Maltese society, from Knights to manumitted slaves. Furthermore, Notary de Guevara had been practising in Birgu since 1537 (and continued to do so up to 1574), so that by 1560–61 he was already well established. All of the contracts stipulate repayment in cash, *ut bancus*,[110] and, in the vast majority of cases, in the new town of Birgu. As can be seen in Chart 1, financial advances in the form of friendly loans made up 25% of the total number, second only to transactions related to the sale or purchase of real estate (31%). The data provides a clear indication that cash transactions were rapidly infiltrating the islanders' way of life and slowly, but surely, were partly substituting a barter economy.

Analysis of contracts involving farmers shows that these tended to borrow money in the first few months of the year. In so doing they would have been in a better position to buy seed or equipment, such as oxen, needed for cultivating land.[111] In most contracts it was stipulated that payment was to be made in July, that is, immediately after the harvest. If yields were good, farmers would be in a position to repay their loans in grain. But if the harvest was poor, or farmers had been the victims of raids,[112] they were often exposed to high interest rates. This is reflected by the

109 'Money cannot beget money.' In 1515 the Fifth Lateran Council authorised credit through the *Monti di Pietà*. H. Denzinger, *The Source of Catholic Dogma* (London, 1957), 238.

110 Refer to n. 65 in this chapter.

111 Braudel, *The Mediterranean*, vol. 1, 582.

112 See case quoted in Abela, 'Port Activities', 62, wherein a farmer was pleading not guilty to the accusations put forward by a priest in respect of the non-payment of a lease regarding a field named *Santa Catarina*. The farmer stated that although the lease was due on the previous Christmas day, he was hindered from effecting payment, due to the fact that the fruit of his work was consumed by the Turkish Armada during the siege of 1565. The commissioners decreed that in spite of such a loss, the contract still stipulated that he was obliged to pay even in case of '*pesti et armata et altri*', and thus in view of such clear conditions they had no other option but to order him to pay. CAM, CEM, AO, MS 46, fols 31–31v (5.iii.1566).

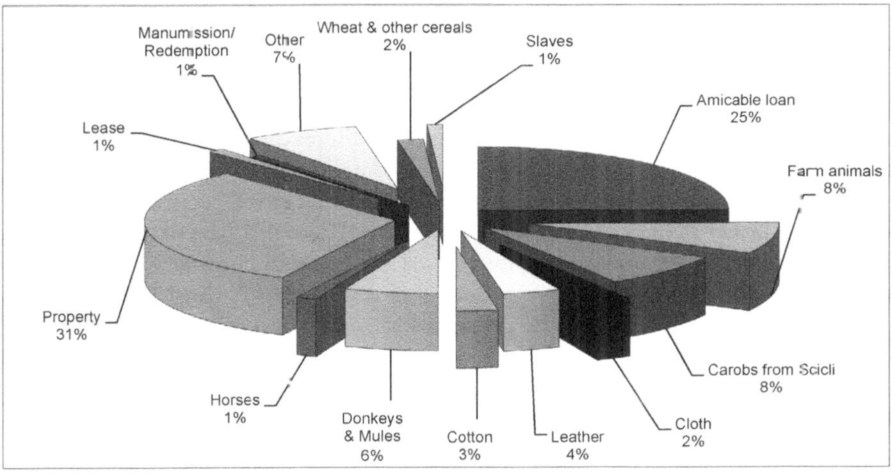

Chart 1 Selection of 300 contracts categorised as *Debitum, Venditio and Mutuum* to be repaid through a cash payment
Source: NAV, R 224/17 (1560–61).

insertion of clauses stating that in case the vendor defaults in consigning the product he will be obliged to pay for any damages and expenses incurred by the buyer.[113]

It is important to note the volatility of wheat prices. The price of local wheat was lower than that of the Sicilian grain,[114] not only because imported wheat carried with it extra transport costs, but also because the local wheat was inferior in quality. Still, in Malta the price of wheat depended very much on the outcome of the Sicilian harvest;[115] accordingly, the prices of local produce peaked in years of poor Sicilian harvest or political instability. As Vassallo shows in his analysis of prices of Sicilian wheat for the period 1523–1629,[116] prices escalated during years of famine and scarcity. For example, in October 1557,[117] due to famine, the cost price rocketed to 48 *tarì* 10 *grani* per *salma* of Licata (227kg), and then dropped back to 26 *tarì* 8 *grani* 2 *piccioli* a year later.[118] Periods of unrest also caused inflation, a case in point

113 NAV, R 224/17, fols 605v–607 (10.ii.1560 *ab inc*). For further reading on the circumvention of usury by means of technical terminology refer to Lopez & Raymond, *Medieval Trade in the Mediterranean World*, 105, 143–5, 157–61, 159, 396; Trasselli, *Note Per La Storia Dei Banchi*, passim.

114 Difference in prices between Maltese and Sicilian wheat did not follow an annual parallel trend, but differed according to the results of the harvest for that particular year. Vassallo traced a steady increase in local wheat prices between 1530 and 1630. Vassallo, 'Prices of Commodities', 84–6.

115 Sicily had a bad harvest every three to four years. For a detailed account of Sicilian exports of wheat during the period under study refer to Braudel, *The Mediterranean*, vol. 1, 598: fig. 51: Sicilian exports.

116 Vassallo, 'Prices of Commodities', Appendix II B.

117 NLM, Univ. 201, n.f. (1557).

118 Vassallo, 'Prices of Commodities', Appendix II B.

being the price of wheat for February 1565, almost three months before the arrival of the Turkish Armada. During this period the cost price of wheat stood at 37 *tarì* two *grani* 5 *piccioli* per *salma* of Licata, while it fell back to 22 *tarì* per *salma* a year later. It is also important to note that because of the high proportion of Sicilian imports, abundant harvests in Sicily meant that local crop failures did not have a drastic effect on prices.[119] The selling price for barley followed a different pattern because, unlike wheat, abundant local production of barley meant that prices were directly tied to local yields rather than dependent on Sicilian ones. The third type of grain produce, meslin, was chiefly local and was mostly used in the production of a type of bread called *pane misturato*. Since this produce was a mixture of wheat and barley, its pricing generally depended on the proportions of the two grains that it contained, and accordingly it price followed their same pattern.[120]

The *Università* and the importation of grain

Although the grain trade did not command the high profits that derived from the import of luxury goods such as pepper and spice, its enormous volume, supplying both main trading routes and secondary channels, provided investors from various strata of society with the possibility to invest even minimal sums of money. The market in wheat was the main reason for the existence of the three Maltese *Università* and, in line with the rest of Sicily, these sought to regulate business activities related to the wheat trade as best they could. By the sixteenth century Sicily enjoyed a leading position as exporter of wheat. It had a sophisticated and highly organised system of administration, with Palermo as the commercial centre.[121] As already discussed, throughout the Order's rule the Viceroy of Sicily conceded the annual provision of duty-free grain to the Maltese islands, albeit with continuing great difficulty. The opposition to conceding *tratte* should come as no surprise. As Braudel rightly explains, 'fiscal greed was as insatiable over grain as it was over salt. And the grain trade opened the door to a series of graces and favours. It was an instrument of power, a means of pressure, a way of repaying services and granting privileges.'[122] Accordingly, at times the Sicilian Viceroys conveniently turned Malta's dependence

119 Vassallo, 'Prices of Commodities', 83–4.

120 Vassallo, 'Prices of Commodities', 91–2. An eighteenth-century manuscript describing the method of how wheat and barley proportions were calculated states that a sample of one *tumulo* was taken and the wheat was separated from the barley. Additional documentation found in the records of the town council does not only confirm that such sampling was done, but that these samples were preserved at the town council's office. Vassallo, 'Prices of Commodities', 92 n. 5, 93.

121 Palermo did not handle loading or transport but had under its wing everything to do with the *negozio furmentario*. Braudel, *The Mediterranean*, vol. 1, 581.

122 Braudel, *The Mediterranean*, vol. 1, 572.

into a 'grain weapon'[123] which now and again they sought to exploit in order to fulfil expansionist ambitions in Africa.[124]

Throughout the Mediterranean, and Malta was no exception, the dire need to import wheat was a stimulus for both local and foreign investors who aspired to enhance their business activities by engaging in short-distance grain traffic. There were two ways in which one could invest in this sector. The predominant method was when the *Università* issued a call for interested investors to declare their intended share. The other method was by participating in a venture partnership. Although traditional seafaring skills and experience provided investors with a high degree of competence and the ability to operate independently, venture agreements were relatively riskier than the share capital investments commissioned by the *Università*, because the merchants were not accompanied on their voyages and protected by the Order's galleys.[125] There was thus a far greater risk of whole cargos of grain falling into enemy hands.[126]

The *Università* of Birgu, conveniently situated near Malta's main harbour, eventually enjoyed greater power than the other two *Università*.[127] As is documented in the various correspondence categorised as *lettere secrete* between the town councils and their representatives in Sicilian *caricatori*,[128] supplying the local market with duty-free wheat entailed much diplomatic and bureaucratic activity.[129] The documents provide a glimpse of the rather difficult and anxious life of the grain merchant. The *Università* had to ensure that a substantial sum of money was collected before any vessel was sent to import duty-free grain from Sicily. Through the issue of a *bando* it invited potential money lenders in the grain trade to declare their intended investment. This type of loan system carried a percentage of interest[130] and, since

123 This term was used by Abulafia to describe the political repercussions of Venice's dependence on Apulian grain in the fourteenth century. See D. Abulafia, 'Grain Traffic out of the Apulian Ports', in D. Abulafia, *Mediterranean Encounters, Economic, Religious, Political, 1100–1550* (Ashgate, 2000), 25–36: 26.

124 This was the case with the Viceroy Giovanni de Vega, who refused to furnish Malta with wheat and other victuals since he had been irritated by the Commissioners of the Order, whose report dated 30 January 1554 included negative comments on the possibility of the Order taking over Mehdia and protecting it against the infidels. J. Abela, 'Il-Gran Mastru Claudio de la Sengle', *Il-Mument,* 5 September 1999, 20–3. On Vega see also Braudel, *The Mediterranean*, vol. 1, 117; vol. 2, 910, 911–12, 974.

125 Refer to NAV, R376/11, fol. 701v (22.iv.1545), where, in a contract regarding the transport of 1,800 *salme* of wheat, it was specifically stated that the Order's galley was to be used.

126 The 'enemy' here implies not only Muslim attackers, but even unscrupulous sailors of the same religion

127 Its superiority to the other *Università* may be perceived even in the way it issued certain standards which had to be followed by the other two councils. For instance, on 14 October 1564 it informed the town council of Mdina that, with the Grand Master's consent, it was sending a *catapan* to standardise the Maltese *tumulo*. NLM, Univ. 202, fol. 180.

128 Mostly found in NLM, Univ. 202, which contains over 300 letters spanning from 1536 to 1579 dealing mainly with the wheat trade. The majority of these documents were sent from Licata by Maltese representatives in Sicily.

129 See also Giuffrida. *La Sicilia e l'Ordine di Malta*, passim.

130 Up to 1576 profit was fixed at 6 *tarì* per *salma* of wheat. However, starting from October

wheat was exempt from direct duty, the interest paid to the investors was a sort of indirect tax regulating the price of bread, on which excise duty by way of a stamp was also imposed.[131] Under the direction of the *Università*, the money advanced by these money lenders, together with a list of their names and the amounts of their investments, was sent with the *patroni* of vessels to Sicily,[132] Licata being the main supplier of grain for the Maltese islands.[133] The Maltese Consul in Licata kept a copy of the list.

Some of the most interesting contracts analysed in this study represent investments for the supply of wheat from Agrigento. In one such contract dated 26 January 1550, a year of great scarcity of grain[134] leading to famine,[135] Antonio Mihallef, a *patrone* from Birgu, was commissioned by the *jurats* of the Birgu *Università* to supply 320 *salme* of durum wheat.[136] Antonio had to buy the wheat from three different *magazeni.* Attached to the contract was the list of shareholders together with their respective investments, which totalled 78 *uncie* 22 *tarì* 6 *grani.* This sum covered the payment for 68 *salme* and 5 *tumoli* of wheat. Individual investments varied from 2 *uncie*, deposited by Antonio Calabro, to 29 *uncie*, deposited jointly by Matteo dello Re and his son Nicola.[137] It was further stated that the established price of wheat, fixed by the *ambaxatores*,[138] was 1 *uncia* 4 *tarì* 11 *grani* per *salma.*

On the same date a similar contract was drawn up between the *Università* and

of that same year each investor was entitled to 2 *tarì* on every *scudo* he contributed. NLM, Univ. 14 (10.x.1576), fol. 163; Vassallo, 'Prices of Commodities', 108.

131 Each loaf of bread was stamped to control and reduce illicit sale of the item. For the use of stamps as a means of control over abuse see Kula, *Measures and Men*, 57–8, 145.

132 NLM, Univ. 202, fols 11–12v (22.x.1555), fol. 15 (25.ix.1555). A typical example of the appointment of the *patrone* by the *Università* is found in NLM, Univ. 13, fol. 270 (23.x.1531), wherein Fernando Vella, who was *patronus* (ship master) of his *grippi*, was commissioned to load the said ship with wheat for the subsistence of the city and island of Malta. See also NLM, Univ. 5 (10.x.1556), fol. 17 for a list of Maltese *patroni* who were commissioned to import wheat. This list also includes the amount to be paid by each to '*lo signori baruni*' of Sicily for the purchase of wheat. See also NAV, R 376/11, fol. 501v (8.ii.1545), where the Mdina *Università* is commissioning Juliano Vella from Birgu to import 368 *salme* of wheat, hence forwarding him the sum of 233 *uncia.*

133 NLM, Univ. 202 contains over 300 letters spanning from 1536 to 1579, which deal mainly with the wheat trade. The majority of these documents, categorized as *lettere secrete*, were sent from Licata by Maltese representatives in Sicily.

134 Braudel, *The Mediterranean*, vol. 1, 604.

135 Bosio, *Dell'Istoria della Sacra Religione*, vol. 3, 277.

136 NAV, MS 778/1, fols 16–17v (26.i.1550). This refers to *grano forte*. The *Università* usually preferred to buy either this type of wheat or the *grano di rocella*. Cassar, *Society, Culture and Identity*, 38.

137 Nicola dello Re must have succeeded his father in the grain business, since his name recurs in the trade. He not only played the part of investor, but sometimes was also given the task of hiring out ships for the consignment of wheat. Such was the case in a particular contract wherein he hired the services of Antonio de Messina from Birgu to ship 370 *salme* of wheat from Licata to Malta. NAV, MS 778/1, fols 12–13 (2.ix.1549).

138 The *meta* established the maximum price at which a product was to be sold. However, this was not the market price but a rate which was fixed every year by the *Università* in each town to reflect the state of the harvest within its territory. Cassar, *Society, Culture and Identity*, 36. The *Università* bought grain supplies at going market prices.

merchant Michele Russo.[139] Russo was licensed to import a total of 462 *uncie* worth of wheat from Agrigento, of which Bernardo Cassar and Francesco Bonello received a balance of 83 *uncie* 8 *tarì*, covering 72 *salme* and 4 *tumoli* of wheat from various investors. Four separate lists,[140] comprising the names of *patroni* who were to embark on the voyage, investors and their shares, the amount to be purchased and the prevailing buying price of wheat, were attached to the contracts. Comparison of the four lists shows that most of the investors feature in each one. Thus, for example, Simone Bartulus invested 34 *uncie*, 14 *uncie*, 12 *uncie* and 21 *uncie*, respectively, in all four ventures. Likewise, Matteo Cassaro invested 8 *uncie*, 12 *uncie* and 10 *uncie*, while Stefano Bartalus and his son-in-law Blasio Borg invested 8 *uncie*, 8 *uncie* and 4 *uncie* 7 *tarì* 6 *grani*, respectively.[141] The money lenders who invested in the grain trade were paid their deposits and profits after the official wheat merchants had distributed all the Sicilian wheat supplies.

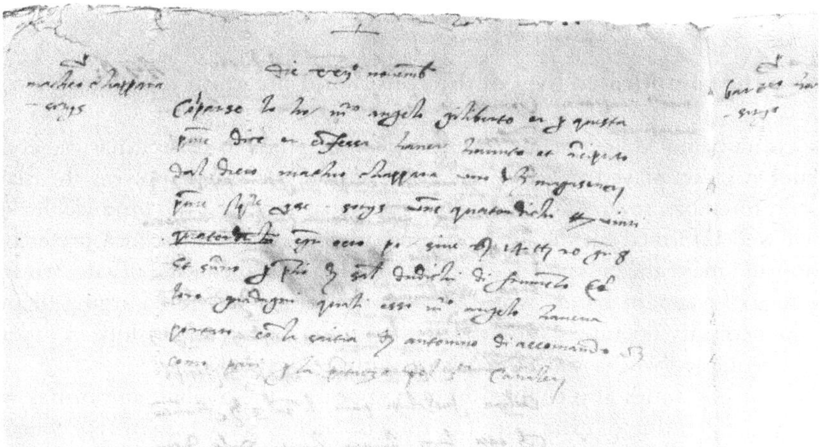

Fig. 3 A declaration made by an investor in the grain trade, namely *Mag.* Angelo Giliberto stating that he had been paid with profit by Matheo Chiappara, one of the official grain merchants

Source: NLM, Univ. 13, f. 446v (28.xi.1565).

139 NAV, MS 778/1, fols 25–26v (26.i.1550). Michele Russo and Paolo de Avola were captains of two grain ships which sank in autumn 1554. This was a tragedy for the Maltese, population since at the time the island was registering a great scarcity in its wheat provisions which was accentuated by various measures adopted by the Viceroy of Sicily, Giovanni de Vega who refused to supply Malta with wheat and other victuals. Abela, 'Il-Gran Mastru Claudio De La Sengle', 20–3.

140 These lists had no folio number but were inserted in NAV, MS 778/1 between fol. 16 and fol. 16v (26.i.1550).

141 Abela, 'Port Activities', 112–14.

Financing such a perilous journey was one of the major problems encountered by the *Università*. It seems that, prior to the arrival of the Order, at times the Crown made loans in favour of the *Università* of Malta and Gozo so that they could meet their financial burdens, as is recorded in a document dated 26 October 1531.[142] This makes reference to an earlier document dated 13 March 1527, in which the ambassadors of both *Università* obliged themselves to repay to the *Regia Curia* the sum of 1,400 ducats in gold, through the bank of *Mag.* Cosimi Xicorta. It was further stated that the sum was to be divided as follows: for the supply of wheat to Malta, 1,000 ducats, and to Gozo, 400 ducats[143] (*per accaptari frumenti per loro subsidio*). On 14 May 1530 the Crown informed the *jurats* that it was going to send *Nob.* Gio Battista Carusu, one of the Crown's bookkeepers (*rogituri*), to inspect the books of account relating to this transaction. An additional note at the end of the document indicates that by 28 January 1531 the matter had been settled and payment had been effected in Palermo.

The complicated lives of the consul and the grain merchant

With Licata being Malta's major grain supplier, it stands to reason that the consul of Malta in Licata played an active role in the entire process of supplying the island. First and foremost, several months before the actual export of the produce, he kept himself well informed on the current price of wheat so as to be in a preferential position and make the best possible bargain. On 19 December 1558 Luca de Armenia, the consul of Malta in Licata, wrote to the town council of Mdina urging them to send the necessary documentation together with the payment and ships in order to load the requested wheat, since the price was quite advantageous.[144]

The consul's duties also enabled him to appeal to the Sicilian authorities with regard to the granting of extra duty-free quotas. Such was the case in 1558, when de Armenia wrote to the town council of Mdina informing them that he, 'having been to His Excellency and lamenting of such small concessions to such a lot of people ... he granted me another one thousand *salme*'.[145] In addition, the consul took care of freight charges, port dues and the safety of the cargo ship, which required proper insurance coverage to guard against possible risks. He was also entrusted with the settling of bills, and to favour the Malta *Università* in regard to finding the necessary credit bills to ensure smooth transaction of the grain supply. It seems that this operation translated into differing percentage profits over the years. Thus, while in 1560 there was a commission of 15 *grani* per *salma* of grain which the consul bought,[146]

142 NLM, Univ. 12, fols 43–43v (26.x.1531).

143 NLM, Univ. 12, fols 542–543v (14.v.1530).

144 NLM, Univ. 202, fol. 20 (19.xii.1558).

145 NLM, Univ. 202, fols 26–26v (1.[?].1558). '*Essendo retrovato a sua eccelencia et lamentandome de la provista di tanto poco summa a tanto populo ... mi have provisto de altri salmi milli.*'

146 NLM, Univ. 202, fol. 46 (25.i.1560).

in 1575 '*le mie ragioni*' or 'my dues' were stated by the consul as being 5 *grani* per *salma*.[147]

Smaller supplies of wheat arrived also from other *caricatori*, particularly from Agrigento (Grigenti) and Terranova, which were other important suppliers of wheat from the south coast of Sicily.[148] As is shown in Fig. 4, apart from Castellamare there was no significant export port in northern Sicily. The concentration of export ports along the south coast benefitted Malta, since it facilitated communication and freight charges were considerably reduced.

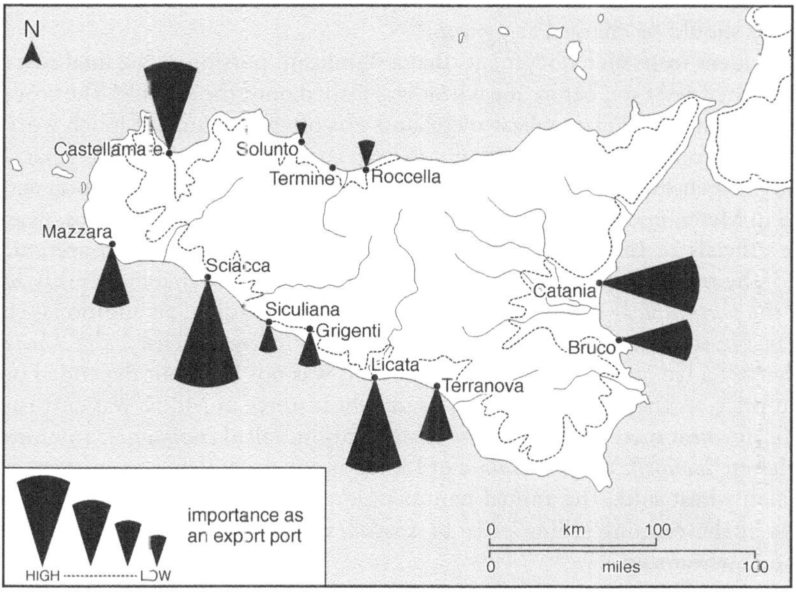

Fig. 4 Main Sicilian *caricatori* in 1532
Source: Braudel, *The Mediterranean*, vol. 1, 580.

Freight charges were additional costs on top of the cost price of the wheat. Consuls were reluctant to pay additional charges, even if a valid reason was given by the *patroni*. Such a situation was brought to the attention of the *Università* of Birgu when the consul claimed that the *patroni* had asked him for an additional *carlino* (10 *grani*) over and above the usual price because they had gone to Agrigento.[149] In another instance, in 1536, the Mdina town council issued a proclamation stating that nobody could charge more than 4 *carlini* (2 *tarì*) for wheat being imported from Licata and 5 *carlini* (2 *tarì* 10 *grani*) for wheat loaded from Terranova, on pain of being fined 1 *uncia*.[150]

147 Vassallo, 'Prices of Commodities', 102 n. 3.
148 For more information regarding ports and mercantile traffic in sixteenth-century Sicily refer to M. D'Angelo, 'Porti e Traffici Marittimi in Sicilia Tra Cinquecento e Seicento', in G. Simoncini, *Sopra i Porti di Mare, Vol. III Sicilia e Malta* (Florence, 1997), 71–110.
149 NLM, Univ. 202, fol. 66 (11.ii.1562).
150 NLM, Univ. 13, fol. 124v (26.xi.1536).

At times *patroni* were also harassed in Sicilian ports, where several dues were demanded on cargo which was supposed to be exempted from tax. Maltese envoys reported these abuses to the Sicilian authorities and reminded them that the privileges granted by the emperor to the Maltese were to be respected. In response to one such abuse, on 1 May 1536 the *Secretus* of Sicily[151] decreed that all those officials who abused of their office were to pay a fine of 1,000 florins.[152] A similar case of overcharging by Sicilian authorities is found in a letter dated 1542, in which the *Secreti* of Agrigento, Licata and Heraclia were instructed by the *Secretus* of Sicily, Knight Julianus Corbera, to stop charging Maltese seamen the fee of 1 *tarì* duty when this should be charged at 5 *grani*.[153]

It is evident from such documents that a significant portion of the final cost price had been incurred even before the wheat was loaded onto the ships.[154] The cost price as bought from the Sicilian wheat merchants was often the cause of much worry for the Maltese representatives, who sought to keep costs to the minimum.[155] Apart from the above expenses, other charges were incurred from the moment the wheat actually arrived in Malta, up to its consignment to the Mdina grain stores.[156] It was measured by the officials in Birgu and a charge on every *salma*, known as *misuratura*, was paid.[157] The transport from Birgu to Mdina was subject to a charge on every *salma*, called the *portatura*. If it was transported further from Mdina, an additional charge was payable to porters (*bastasi*). Apart from other petty expenses, the *Università* also charged a fee on every *salma* of wheat. This was not fixed but depended on the current price.[158] The sale and distribution of wheat stored at Mdina was entrusted to the official wheat merchants,[159] whose remuneration, called *cresimonia*, amounted to two Maltese *mondelli* on every *salma* of Licata or approximately 5kg on every 227kg of Sicilian wheat sold. The annual remuneration of these merchants was calculated at 2.2% of the running selling price of a *salma* of wheat multiplied by the annual volume of wheat sold.[160]

151 At the time the *Secretus* was Nicola Pollastra.

152 Del Amo García et al., *Documentary Sources of Maltese History, Part III: Documents of the Maltese Universitàs, No. 1*, Doc. 134.

153 Del Amo Garcia et al., *Documentary Sources of Maltese History, Part III: Documents of the Maltese Universitàs, No. 1*, Doc. 136, see also Doc. 120.

154 A good example providing a breakdown of the various expenses incurred in Sicily prior to shipment is found in a letter sent to the town council by the Consul of Licata, Leonardo Calava in 1556. NLM, Univ. 5, fols 17–18 (10.x.1556).

155 Anthony Vassallo noted that on 19 March 1575 about thirteen different expenses amounting to 25 *uncie* 26 *tarì* 10 *grani* were incurred on a consignment of wheat. Vassallo, 'Prices of Commodities', 102 n. 4.

156 As regards transaction costs and productivity gains, see F. C. Lane, 'The Economic Consequences of Organized Violence', *Journal of Economic History*, 18 (1958), 401–17; see also D. C. North & R. B. Homas, *The Rise of the Western World: A New Economic History* (Cambridge, 1973), 164.

157 Vassallo, 'Prices of Commodities', 103. It is not stated who the beneficiary of this income was.

158 Vassallo, 'Price of Commodities', 103.

159 These were also responsible for selling local grain and rice.

160 Vassallo, 'Prices of Commodities', 105–6.

The Order's Receiver in Sicily and the export of cereals

The establishment of the Knights in Malta necessitated a reorganisation of how revenues from their European priories reached the Common Treasury in Malta. Giuffrida states that once the Knights had settled in Malta, Sicily became their main financial centre, since all revenues incoming from the European priories were directed to the Sicilian priory. Further, the Order's Receiver[161] in Sicily was delegated with the huge responsibility of ensuring that all these cash inflows were transferred securely to the Common Treasury in Malta.

The person chosen to fill this post enjoyed special privileges, since not only was he often appointed as the Order's procurator in Sicily but he also had the right to select and appoint additional procurators to help him in his duties. Further, since Sicily was also Malta's main grain supplier, his responsibilities varied between having to keep good relations with the Viceroy and assure the continued granting of special *tratte*, and logistically supporting the Order's fleet. The Receiver was also responsible for overseeing the smooth export of all of the island's necessities and, when the need arose, for acting as the appointed legal representative in court cases concerning the Order.[162] Documents preserved at the Notarial Archives of Palermo shed light on the power delegated to the Order's appointed procurators with regard to the export of wheat and other victuals. Utilising his good knowledge of the Sicilian market, the procurator was authorised to:

> In the name and on behalf of the said Holy Order endeavour to export from the said city of Licata and its wharfs all and every quantity of wheat, barley, wood, meat live and dead, cheese, *equicasea*,[163] wine and any other victual or other necessary goods for the said Holy Order and make receipt or receipts of these exports.[164]

It was essential for the person holding such a prestigious position to have good relations with the Sicilian authorities, especially those higher up the hierarchy.

161 Until 1357 responsions were paid to the Priors. However, the Chapter General held in Rhodes during that year decreed that each priory must have commanders holding the title of Receivers responsible for the collection and eventual transfer of these responsions to the Common Treasury. Through this reform the Grand Master ensured stricter financial, administrative and political control. Giuffrida, *La Sicilia e l'Ordine di Malta*, 22.

162 Giuffrida, *La Sicilia e L'Ordine di Malta*, 85. He was also commissioned to deliver the annual falcon due in respect of the donation, a ceremony registered through a notarial deed. Giuffrida, *La Sicilia e L'Ordine di Malta*, 85.

163 This literally means horse-cheese. One of the most popular cheeses in Malta until the late eighteenth century was *cacio cavallo*, which is documented as early as 1590. The word may possibly be referring to this type of soft cheese, which is still very popular in southern Italy. (Thanks are due to Liam Gauci for this information forwarded on 3 September 2010.) See also S. Fiorini, *The 'Mandati' Documents at the Archives of the Mdina Cathedral, Malta: 1473–1539* (Malta, 1992), lix, where *cascavalli* or *cacio cavallo* is described as large, oblong cheeses produced in pairs.

164 '*Nomine et pro parte dicte Sacre Religionis, extrahendum et extrahi petendum et faciendum ex dicta civite Leccate et eius carricatorio omnia et singula frumenta, ordea, ligraminas, carnes vivas et mortuas, casea, equicasea, vino et alia quecumque.*' Quoted from Giuffrida, *La Sicilia e L'Ordine di Malta*, 87.

Whenever the need arose, the Maltese town council would refer any problems related to the shipment of goods from Sicily to Malta to the Receiver. From surviving correspondence between the Receiver and the Maltese *Università*, it is clear that most of the time the Receiver's functions overlapped with those of the Maltese consul. Because, as already noted, the Sicilian Receiver had good relations with Sicilian government officials, his intervention was often preferred to that of the consul. In fact, the Receiver often used his influence to speed up shipments of cargo or to remedy any injustices which Maltese *patroni* might have suffered at the hands of Sicilian officials. Such was the case in February 1536, when *Fra.* Simone di Bonanno,[165] one of the Order's most trusted receivers and procurators, presented a copy of the privileges enjoyed by the Maltese to the Sicilian Portulan and requested that the latter should order the Vice-Portulan of Licata to stop hampering Maltese ships from loading their cargo.[166]

The Order's Receiver in Sicily was also responsible for signing the necessary receipts authorising Maltese ships to load grain supplies and ship them to Malta, as well as for providing the necessary bills of exchange to facilitate payments between Malta and Sicily. In this regard, the Receiver was aided by other procurators who functioned on two distinct levels. On the first level were those in charge of the shipment of grain from specific *caricatori*, and on the second level was a procurator appointed to supervise and be accountable for all the shipments of grain from the different *caricatori*. The latter was thus empowered to 'issue receipts for the export of all wheat, barley and other pulses'.[167] It is clear that although the role of the Order's Receiver in Sicily has not attracted local scholarly attention,[168] his role in various transactions affecting the proper functioning of the Order in Malta merits serious investigation. This is especially so since his post also dictated that he represented the Order in commercial litigation and other disputes. Any surviving documentation relating to such litigation would broaden our perspective on how his office functioned and on relations between Malta and the Sicilian *caricatori*.

The miller and the baker

The work of the millers was a labour cost which was essentially tied to the cost of bread and biscuit.[169] There was a different price for grinding each of the three

165 The Sicilian *Fra.* Bonanno was a crucial link between Malta and Sicily, due to the high esteem in which his family was held by the Royal Crown. For a deeper insight into his life and work, especially the period when he was Receiver of the Order between 14 August 1529 and September 1537, see Giuffrida, *La Sicilia e L'Ordine di Malta,* 26–31.

166 NLM, Univ. 202, fol. 1 (21.ii.1536).

167 '*apocas extracionum omnium illorum frumentorum, ordeum et aliorum leguminum*', Giuffrida, *La Sicilia e L'Ordine di Malta,* 28.

168 Apart from Giuffrida, some other Italian scholars have tackled themes concerning the administrative organisation of the Order of St John in Sicily. See Giuffrida, *La Sicilia e L'Ordine di Malta,* 21 n. 2.

169 Biscuit was the main food on ships. It was flat bread that was baked twice for longer keeping. It was considered a provision of war and was prepared in the Order's bakeries.

cereals, wheat being the most expensive, and meslin midway between wheat and barley.[170] The prices charged by the millers were to be in accordance with those issued sporadically by the town council, though it is not clear on what criteria these prices were established.[171] Regulation by the town council ensured that millers did not demand excessive prices which then would be loaded onto the price of bread. In his analysis of grinding prices, Vassallo shows that they tended to fluctuate, just like the price of the grain itself, thus suggesting a strong link between the labour costs of the miller and the general price trend of grain.[172]

During the sixteenth century people from all strata of society consumed bread in its various forms, since it was a staple part of everyone's diet. Its different forms were representative of social inequalities. While the rich consumed white bread, which was both a rarity and a luxury,[173] the lower echelons of society ate bread made from inferior flour or from barley and rye. Similar to European countries, in Malta the price of bread was kept fairly stable throughout the sixteenth century. It was the weight of the individual loaf which varied according to prevailing prices, which, in turn, depended very much on the availability of the product.[174] The authorities knew very well that a rise in the price of bread often led to popular agitation.[175]

As can be seen from Table 3, throughout most of the sixteenth century the local price of a loaf of bread stood at 2 *grani* for a small loaf and 4 *grani* for a bigger loaf. The weight of a loaf of bread was determined by comparing a calculation of the *rotolos* of bread produced from one *tumulo* of wheat to the current price of wheat.[176] The year 1591 is of particular interest, since that was the year of the great southern famine in Europe, which resulted in general dearth of cereals. This resulted in a sharp rise in the price of bread.

Bakers were often warned to produce bread only of the official weight. This was stated in various proclamations, among them being one issued by the *Università* of Birgu in 1536 which declared that 'no baker or any other person may sell or dare to bake bread of lesser weight than that established by the *jurats* under a penalty of fifteen *carlini*[177] and the bread will be distributed to the poor as per orders given by the *jurats*'.[178] Furthermore, the *bando* stated that no tavern keeper should attempt

The Knights had large stores for provisions and munitions in Messina, Syracuse and Augusta in Sicily.

170 Vassallo, 'Prices of Commodities', Table XVIII, 114.

171 Refer to NLM, Univ. 13, fols 377–379 (28.ix.1562), where the price list issued by the town council ordered millers to charge 4 *grani* per *rotolo* for wheat, 5 *grani* per *tumino* for meslin and 4 *grani* per *tumino* for barley.

172 Vassallo, 'Prices of Commodities', 115.

173 Braudel, *Civilization and Capitalism*, vol. 1, 137.

174 Kula, *Measures and Men*, 71–8.

175 R. Cancila, *Il Pane e La Politica, La Rivolta Palermitana del 1560* (Naples, 1999); Braudel, *Civilization and Capitalism*, vol. 1, 43; Koenigsberger et al., *Europe in the Sixteenth Century*, 41–3.

176 Vassallo, 'Prices of Commodities', 117.

177 Equivalent to 7 *tarì* 10 *grani*.

178 '*Che alcuno fornaro o altro persona che sia posit vendir o sia ardito far lo pane manco de lo pezo che sira ordinate per li dicti S[igno]ri jurati soto pena di carlini xv et lo pani sera*

Table 3 Prices and weight of bread in Malta during the sixteenth century

Date	Price *Grani/piccioli*	Weight in ounces	Type of grain
December 1533	1.2	-	Wheat
December 1533[a]	1.00	-	-
September 1534	1.00	15	Wheat
September 1534	0.4	6	Wheat
October 1535	2.00	18	Wheat
October 1535	1.00	9	Wheat
September 1538	2.00	12	Wheat
September 1539	2.00	13	Wheat
September 1562	2.00	12	Wheat
September 1563	-	12	Wheat
November 1565	-	15	Wheat
September 1567	2.00	12	Wheat
September 1568	2.00	12	Wheat
September 1569	2.00	12	Wheat
October 1569	2.00	10	Wheat
September 1572	2.00	12	Wheat
April 1573	2.00	12	Wheat
September 1573	2.00	12	Wheat
September 1575	2.00	12	Wheat
October 1576	2.00	10	Wheat
September 1577	2.00	9	Wheat
June 1578	2.00	10	Wheat (Maltese)
December 1578	2.00	10	Wheat
April 1579	2.00	12	Wheat
January 1580	2.00	9	Wheat
November 1580	2.00	10	Wheat
November 1584	2.00	10	Wheat
September 1585	2.00	10	Wheat
September 1587	2.00	11	Wheat
December 1587	-	12	Wheat
September 1588	2.00	11	Wheat
September 1589	2.00	10	Wheat
September 1590	2.00	10	Wheat
September 1591	2.00	10	Wheat
December 1591	4.00	8.5	Wheat
December 1591	5.00	9.5	Wheat
December 1591	8.00	16.5	Wheat
September 1592	2.00	10	Barley
September 1592	4.00	14	Wheat
January 1595	2.00	7	Wheat
January 1595	4.00	14	Wheat
March 1595	4.00	14	Wheat
August 1595	2.00	10	Wheat
September 1596	2.00	10	Wheat

July 1596	2.00	10	Wheat
November 1596	2.00	8	Wheat (Sicilian)
November 1596	2.00	12	Wheat (Maltese)
September 1597	2.00	12	Wheat (Sicilian)
September 1597	2.00	12	Wheat (Maltese)
May 1599	2.00	12	Wheat (Maltese)
August 1599	2.00	12.5	Wheat (Maltese)
December 1599	2.00	11	Wheat (Sicilian)

[a] NLM, Univ. 13, fol. 62v (20.xii.1533).
Source: Vassallo, 'Prices of Commodities', 211–13.

to sell bread of a lighter weight.[179] In a price list of commodities dated 1562 it was declared that a loaf of bread weighing 12 ounces must be sold at 2 *grani*.[180] For comparative purposes, Table 4 shows some other commodities along with the price of bread.[181]

Licensed bakers were allowed different quantities of wheat from which to produce bread, and each loaf had to be stamped by the appointed official of the *Università*. By this means, the amount of bread produced from a given quantity of wheat could be calculated. If the result was a surplus in the amount of wheat supplied to the baker, he was advised that he owed that extra amount.[182]

The purpose of this tight control over wheat grinding and bread baking was to ensure the strict regulation of these commercial activities for the benefit of the authorities who sought to regulate the consumption of cereals. By this means the *Università* ensured not only that it had full control over a vital commodity such as wheat, but also that any surplus stocks would be utilised, and not go to waste to the detriment of the council's coffers and the public peace.[183] Heavy penalties were in force for any who dared to contravene official orders.

In fact, in 1568 Grand Master de Valette instructed the *Università* of Mdina to issue a *bando* which prohibited the sale of any type of wheat, barley or meslin from that year's crop and to warn bakers and grinders that this proclamation included their activities. Anyone caught breaking this law faced heavy penalties, including confiscation of the produce, and also confiscation of the mill and donkey used for grinding. The *Università* were reminded of their duty to check that the law was being enforced and adhered to, and those who informed the authorities of breaches

distribuito ali poveri per ordinationi de li s[igno]ri jurati.' NAM, MCC, Reg. AO, vol. 1, fols 46–47 (4.ix.1536).

179 '*Che nulla tavernaro sia ardito di vendere in sua taverna panis che non sia de justo pezo.*' NAM, MCC, Reg. AO, vol. 1, fols 46–47 (4.ix.1536).

180 NLM, Univ. 13, fols 377–379 (28.ix.1562).

181 NLM, Univ. 13, fol. 377–379 (28.ix.1562).

182 An excellent example is found in NLM, Univ. 201, *Primo Conto mandato dal Signor Commendator del Grano*. Unfortunately it is not dated, but it is bound in between documents dated 1545. It consists of a booklet containing a list of bakers, the amount of wheat they were supplied, the number of loaves of bread they produced annually and the surplus of wheat which was owed to the *Università*.

183 In 1577 the Birgu *Università* distributed 400 *salme* of old wheat to all bakers to be used prior to newer supplies. Vassallo, 'Prices of Commodities', 119 nn. 2 and 3.

Table 4 Pandetta or price list of various commodities issued in 1562[a]

Commodity	Weight / quantity	Value [price?]
Bread	12 ounce loaf	2 *grani*
Eggs	One dozen	10 *grani*[b]
Beef – ox (*La carni di bovi*)	One *rotolo*[c]	10 *grani*
Beef – cow (*La carni dela vacca*)	One *rotolo*	9 *grani*
Veal – up to one year old calf (*Vitella di uno anno infra*)	One *rotolo*	15 *grani*
Veal 12–18 month old calf (*Vitella di uno anno in sus*)	One *rotolo*	14 *grani*
Beef – heifer (*la carne de lo genicza*)	One *rotolo*	13 *grani*
Mutton – ram castrated (*lo castratu*)	One *rotolo*	13 *grani*
Mutton – ram (*La carne di muntuni*)	One *rotolo*	12 *grani*
Lamb (*la carne del agnello*)	One *rotolo*	12 *grani*
Meat – female kid (*La carne del agnelastra*)	One *rotolo*	12 *grani*
Lamb – weaned (*La carne del angello smamato*)	One *rotolo*	12 *grani*
Meat – she goat (*La carne della capra*)	One *rotolo*	15 *grani*
Meat – ewe	One *rotolo*	6 *grani*
Fish (*Scorchia*)	One *rotolo*	10 *grani*
Fish – yellow spotted eels (*Murini*)	One *rotolo*	8 *grani*
Fish (bestuni)	One *rotolo*	6 *grani*
Cheese (*Muxo di Sicilia*)	One *rotolo*	11 *grani*
Cheese (*Stagnato di Sicilia*)	One *rotolo*	23 *grani*
Cheese (*Stagnato de Malta*)	One piece (*pezia*)	3 *grani*

a The original listing is reproduced in brackets so as not to diminish the significance of the items. Translation of these commodities is taken from Vassallo, 'Prices of Commodities', 217–18.

b Six *dinari* or *piccoli* being equivalent to 1 grano. Thus one egg cost 5 *dinari* or *piccoli*.

c One rotolo being equivalent to 0.7934 kg. Vassallo, 'Prices of Commodities', 21.

Source: NLM, Univ.13, fols 377–379 (28.ix.1562).

of the law were to be allowed to keep half of the confiscated produce, while their names were to be kept secret.[184] The proclamation did not stipulate the reason for the enforcement of this law, but most probably the island's granaries contained a substantial surplus of grain from the previous year's harvest and the authorities wanted to use the supply before it rotted.

The Order's presence on the island, which served as a pull factor for merchants and sailors from neighbouring countries, created a heavy demand for wheat and its finished products, bread and biscuit. Consequently, the need for the services of bakers and millers also increased. It was not unusual for foreign bakers to set up business in Birgu and employ foreign staff. Such was the case with Ambrosio Tradeno from Trapani, who set up a bakery in Birgu and hired the services of the Genoese baker Thomasius Scala so that the latter might work '*in eius furno*' (in his bakery) for one continuous year for the salary of 1 *scudo* per month.[185]

Orders for supplies were also commissioned to bakers who operated outside the islands. Thus an agreement was entered into between *Fra.* Simone de Bonanno, the Order's Receiver in Sicily, and four Sicilian bakers stationed in the city of Palermo. The latter sold to the said *Fra.* Simone a total of 400 *cantari* (32,000kg) of biscuit bread which were '*bene cotti, asciupti, bene condicionati*'[186] for the price of 13 *tarì* 5 *grani* per *cantaro.* An interesting aspect of this contract is how certain clauses shed light on the ever-fluctuating price of wheat and other difficulties connected to supplying the biscuit that was necessary to the Order's fleet. Anticipating such difficulties, *Fra.* Simone agreed to reimburse any expenses which the bakers might incur in future if the tax on flour should be increased. It was also stipulated that, should the bakers be forced by the *Università* of Palermo or by the Royal Court to work for them instead, *Fra.* Simone promised to intervene on their behalf, while the bakers, in their turn, agreed to reimburse a deposit of 80 *uncie* which *Fra.* Simone had made in respect of the contract if negotiations to this effect should prove unsuccessful and they were not in a position to honour the agreement.[187]

Risks, contraventions and litigation

Since antiquity, the sea loan had been the only means of transferring risks in maritime transport from the shipper to another person.[188] By the late Middle Ages, however, mainly thanks to innovations by Italian merchants, marine insurance gradually replaced this type of agreement.[189] By this means both travelling and sedentary merchants tried to protect themselves as best as they could against pirates

184 NLM, Univ. 5, fol. 5 (19.vi.1568).
185 NAV, R 91/3, fols 126v–127v (16.ix.1568).
186 'Well-cooked, dry and in good condition.' Giuffrida, *La Sicilia e L'Ordine di Malta*, 89–90.
187 Giuffrida, *La Sicilia e L'Ordine di Malta*, 89–90.
188 F. E. de Roover, 'Early Examples of Marine Insurance', *The Journal of Economic History*, 5:2 (1945), 172–200: 175.
189 The big insurance centre was Venice, even for ships or cargoes that never called at that port. De Roover, *The Rise and Decline*, 151.

and other perils of the sea.[190] By the fifteenth century marine insurance was securely established and contracts adopted a rather stereotyped wording for the policies, the terms varying only when the needs of contractors demanded specific clauses or additional provisions. Such insurance contracts,[191] usually categorised by the notary as *Securitas*,[192] were also the means by which the *Università* sought to minimise risks. In official correspondence addressed to the Vice-Portulan of Licata, dated 1531, the town council promised to provide surety to a ship owed by a Maltese *patrone* which was at the time anchored in Licata and laden with wheat waiting to be shipped to Malta. They further confirmed that the ship, described here as a *fusta*, was to be *ad securitate et melioribus modo quo possunt.*[193]

The loss of capital for the *Università* in overseas ventures was of course a serious affair, since the *Università* operated with the capital of various investors. Practical and effective measures were taken in order to avoid losing a ship and its cargo due to mishap, one such measure being the way in which the *Università* distributed the collected capital to various *patroni* in order to spread the risk. A typical example of an insurance contract is an act dated 10 April 1545 which covers the round-trip voyage (*de intrata et de uxita*) of a ship of the Order commissioned by the *Università* to supply the island with 426 *uncie* worth of wheat from Licata. The opening lines of the contract list the names of the insurers and the guaranteed capital. Unfortunately, the insurer's premium is not stated. An extract from the contract reads as follows:

Presentes coram nobis sponte assecuraverunt et assecurant magnificos dominos Antonium Inguanes et Salvum Cumbo et Ioannem Cumbo tres ex juratis huius Civitatis et insule Melite presentes et se assecurari facientes nomini ipsius universitatis me Notario pro ea stipulante de intrata et de uxita[3] *videlicet:*

(These men, present before us, willingly, have insured, and do insure, the magnificent lords Antonio Inguanes and Salvu Cumbo and Giovanni Cumbo, three of the Jurats of this City and Island of Malta, present, and making themselves to be insured on behalf of the same *Università*, I, the Notary, stipulating on its behalf; concerning the entry and the exit, namely:

190 Lopez & Raymond, *Medieval Trade in the Mediterranean World*, 255. Refer to NLM, Univ. 202, fol. 76 (2.xii.1562), where it is stated that a shipload of 160 *salme* of wheat from Licata was wet and in bad condition, due to the rough weather.

191 From available documentation one may discern that various established merchants acted as insurers. Abela, 'Port Activities', 92–3.

192 According to Tenenti, it was only the increasing involvement of notaries in drawing up deeds of this nature which led to the categorisation of insurance contracts as *Noli e sicurtà*, starting from 1563. Prior to this date Ragusan notaries listed them under 'miscellaneous' acts. A. Teneti & B. Tenenti, *Il Prezzo del rischio: l'assicurazione mediterranea vista da Ragusa, 1563–1591* (Rome, 1985), 93. However, this does not seem to be the case in Malta, since various insurance documents prior to 1563 were already being grouped under *securitates*. Refer to NAV, R 202/1, fol. 7v (4.iv.1536); R 202/1, fol. 87 (5.viii.1536); R 202/1, Part II, fol. 13 (15.ix.1536).

193 Insured in the best possible way. NLM, Univ. 13, fols 40–40v (25.ix.1531). As regards insurance contracts drawn up in Malta during the period under study refer to Abela, 'Port Activities', 88–95.

de intrata supra uncijs quatrincentis viginti sex po[onderis] ge[neralis] consignatis no[bili] scribbe navis seu barchie sacre religionis Sancti Joanis Hierosolimitani nominate S[ancta] Maria capitaniczate per Rev[eren]dum Fratrem [vac.] seu per alios quosvis ad opus illas uncias 426 apportandi ad caricatorium civitatis leucatae et risicum incipiat et incipere debeat ex illa hora qua dicta barchia cum dictis pecunijs discedat a portu huius insule et durat et durare debeat donec et quousque dicta barchia una cum dictis pecunijs [applicaverit?] a bon salvamento in dicto caricatorio leucatae et dicte pecunie posite fuerint in terra a bon salvamento

de uxita vero super tanta quantitate frumenti emendi ex dictis unciis 426 ut supra assecuratis et totum risicum currat et currere debeat ex hora qua dicta frumenta incipient onerata super dicta [met?] barchia et durat et durare debeat ibi stando onerando ac disonerando et deinde recedendo eundo stando et navigando ad voluntatem capitanei seu aliorum quorumvis donec et quousque dicta frumenta erunt exonerata in portu suburbij maris melite in terra ad bonum salvamentum.

Itaque dicta barchia tam de intrata quam de uxita ...

concerning the entry [of port of destination] over the 426 *uncie* of general weight consigned to the noble Clerk of the ship or boat of the Holy Religion of St John of Jerusalem, called 'Santa Maria', captained by the reverend *Fra.* [vac.] or by whosoever others, for the task of carrying those 426 *uncie* to the wharf of the city at Licata, and the risk should begin, and ought to begin, from that hour at which the said boat with the said money should depart from the port of this Island and should last, and ought to last, until, and as far as, the said boat, together with the said money, shall have arrived safely in the said wharf at Licata and the said money shall have been safely deposited on land;

indeed, concerning the exit [of the port of destination] over the quantity of grain as much as [are] to be bought by the said 426 *uncie* as insured above; and the whole risk should run, and ought to run, from that hour at which the said grain shall begin to be loaded into the very said boat, and should last, and ought to last, for the lying-to over there, the loading and the discharging, and then, the departure, the going, the lying-to, and the sailing according to the disposition of the captain, or of whosoever others, until, and as far as, the said grains shall be safely discharged on land in the port of the suburb [of the Castle] of the Sea at Malta.

Consequently, the said boat, both concerning the entry and its exit ...)

Any claims forthcoming from the above insurance contract were to be honoured by the insurers within one month of the filing of the claim.[194] The time clause is interesting to note, since, as I have shown elsewhere, in the majority of insurance contracts of the same period, even those containing cargos of wheat,[195] the period of time allowed to the insurers for reimbursement of damages was generally

194 NAV, R 376/11, fol. 652v–654v (10.iv.1545).
195 NAV, R 202/1, fols 18–18v (18.iv.1536).

documented as being four months from the time of the filing of the claim, and this according to the local custom.[196]

Investors reaped the fruits of their investment after all expenses had been deducted and the wheat was distributed. However, investments were not always profitable. On 16 March 1548 the Grand Master and the town *jurats* issued a *bando* informing investors that, due to unforeseen difficulties, the wheat which was to be loaded from the *caricatori* of Licata had not yet been loaded.[197] Consequently, all those who had invested in the expedition were advised to declare their investment to the insurers, and if they were reluctant to be exposed to the risk they could retrieve either half or all of their investment from the office of the *jurats*. In the event that a claim was not filed by the investor, the *Università* would consider this as a show of the investor's intent to continue with the business of importing wheat, and this at their own risk, without prejudice to the *jurats*.[198]

Prior to setting out on a venture trip, *patroni* were always legally bound to accept responsibility for any damages which might result due either to carelessness on their part or to breach of contract. On 23 October 1531 *patronus* Fernando Vella was commissioned by the town council to go to Licata to load a consignment of wheat. The contract stipulated that should there be any damage to the cargo he, together with his partners Leonardis di Burdino and Bernardus Cassar, would be obliged to pay for it, plus any other interests which might accumulate.[199] On the same date two other *patroni*, Juliano Bellye and Jurlando Grini, were accused of not honouring an agreement according to which they were to import the necessary wheat as commissioned by the town council of Mdina.[200] Expenses for breach of contract could be quite heavy, as can be observed in a document stating that Matheus Vella, who had been commissioned by the town council to load a cargo of wheat from Terranova, was obliged to pay 100 *uncie* should he default in supplying the wheat.[201] Similarly, Johannes Mannara was commissioned to import 6 *salme* of wheat and was tied to the payment of a penalty of 2 *uncie*, payable to the fiscal officer, if he should default.[202]

Contracts were not always honoured, and various accusations were made in respect of breach of agreements. Litigation also arose over various unforeseen or unexpected expenses not agreed beforehand by both parties. Such was the case between Nicola Dello Re from Rabat and *jurat* Gregorio Xerri. Nicola declared that he had shipped 250 *salme* of wheat from Licata to Malta on Bartolomeo Xarricato's ship. Further, he stated that the *jurats* expected him to pay 2 *tarì per salma* as tax[203]

196 '*In lo tempo solito et consueto di mesi quatuor*'. NAV, R 202/1, fol. 8 (4.iv.1536). See Abela, 'Port Activities', 88–95.

197 It was not stipulated when it had to be loaded.

198 NLM, Univ. 13, fol. 250 (16.iii.1548).

199 NLM, Univ. 12, fol. 42 (23.x.1531).

200 NLM, Univ. 12, fol. 42 (23.x.1531).

201 NLM, Univ. 13, fol. 62 (4.xii.1533).

202 NLM, Univ. 13, fol. 67v (10.iv.1534).

203 The taxing of cereals offered a reliable source of income to the government's coffers and ensured that it covered various expenses incurred when undertaking works in respect of the upkeep of fortifications and the maintenance of soldiers. NLM, Univ. 13, fols 307–308v (13.viii.1552), '*che al presente non havemo ni de poter pagar dicti soldati che sia*

on the same consignment. Dello Re contested this, since he claimed that he was not obliged to pay it according to the agreement done with Gregorio Xerri.[204]

In a case presented at the *Magna Curia Castellania*,[205] Giovanpaolo Ros claimed that the *jurats*[206] of Birgu owed him the sum of 3 *uncie* 17 *tarì*, which were due to him in respect of expenses incurred following a consignment of wheat from Licata to Malta. Giovanpaolo explained that he had repeatedly asked them to effect payment, but to no avail. As a last measure, he was thus requesting the intervention of the court to help him recover the said sum.

Another case, which once again concerns the *jurats*[207] of Birgu, is that in which Paolo Canizaro appointed Alessandro de Randazo to act as his procurator and recover a sum of 300 *scudi* due to him in respect of a consignment of wheat which had been imported on the ship of Knight Romegas.[208] Alessandro stated that after distributing the wheat he had requested to be paid; however, the *jurats*, who were under obligation to make payment to his credit, insisted that on orders issued by the Grand Master the money intended for purchasing wheat had been allocated for the upkeep of the fortifications of the city. A disappointed Alessandro stated that the *jurats* had instructed him to wait until they had collected money from taxes.[209] By now a substantial amount of time had passed and he had still not been paid. Alessandro explained how some of the other partners who were with him on this deal by now either were dead, or were destitute due to this bad investment, since they had incurred much expense and interest. Alessandro insisted that he was convinced that the authorities would never fortify the city '*a spesi et con dinari d'altri*

facta una taxa supra li frumenti de Sicilia …' (since at present we are not in a position to pay the said soldiers let it be that a tax on Sicilian wheat is imposed). NLM, Univ. 201, n.f. (20.vi. 1560). See also A. Hoppen, 'Military Priorities and Social Realities in the Early Modern Mediterranean: Malta and its Fortifications', in Mallia-Milanes (ed.), *Hospitaller Malta 1530–1798*, 399–428: 402.

204 NAV, MS 778/1, fols 19–20 (28.ix.1547). The plea did not mention what kind of tax the importer was expected to pay.

205 NAM, MCC, 'Cedulae Supplicae et Taxationes', vol. 1. fols 83–83v (9.vi.1564).

206 The *jurats* who were notified of this claim were Giacomo Caloriti, Giovanni Domenico de Franchiscus Bartolomeo Habella and Giacomo Chilia. NAM, MCC, 'Cedulae Supplicae et Taxationes', vol. 1, fol. 83v (22.vi.1564).

207 In this case these were Ludovico Casata, Pietro Ros, Antonio Abela and Narducio Cassar. NAM, MCC, 'Cedulae Supplicae et Taxationes', vol. 1, fol. 36 (8.iii.1564).

208 NAM, MCC, 'Cedulae Supplicae et Taxationes', vol. 1, fols 36–39 (8.iii.1564). Romegas was one of the most renowned Hospitaller corsairs. For more published sources regarding his life and achievements see Bosio, *Dell'Istoria della Sacra Religione,* vol. 3, 389, 838, 847; Dal Pozzo, *Historia Della Sacra Religione,* 146; E. Rossi, *Storia della Marina dell'Ordine di San Giovanni di Gerusalemme* (Rome, Milan, 1926), 44, 51; U. Mori Ubaldini, *La Marina del Sovrano Ordine Militare di San Giovanni di Gerusalemme di Rodi e di Malta* (Rome, 1971), passim; Bono, 'Naval Exploits', in Mallia-Milanes (ed.), *Hospitaller Malta 1530–1798,* 351–97: 356, 359, 390. The latest work published is a biography by C. Testa, *Romegas* (Malta, 2002); see also J. Abela, 'A Window on Early Hospitaller Malta – A Study of the Acts of Notary Placido Abela, 1557–1558' (BA Hons dissertation, University of Malta, 2003), 62–5.

209 It was not specified to which taxes they were referring.

maxime di mercanti',[210] thus he was pleading for justice so that he might return home to Terranova and praise the righteousness of the Maltese court. He was given the opportunity to do so on 21 March 1564, when the court decreed that the *jurats* must make payment within eight days, or else they would be jailed.[211]

The local authorities' strict supervision of the local grain trade can be observed in the issuing of various *bandi* regulating the trade. On 17 October 1537 distributors of wheat were reminded that they needed an official licence from the *Università* of Mdina (*la licentia con la polisa deli dicti Signori jurati*) in order to carry out their trade;[212] while on 15 November 1538 the town council demanded a fine of 2 *uncie* from anyone who sold wheat in the villages without first taking it to the city.[213] In yet another *bando* issued by the Grand Master and the Castellan of Birgu on instructions of the Mdina Vice-Portulan in March 1536, it was proclaimed that all wheat imported from Sicily had to be covered by a licence issued by the Mdina *Università*, under pain of a fine of 50 *uncie* payable to the fiscal officer and another 5 *uncie* divided between the Castellan and the Vice-Portulan of Mdina. The merchant also had to pay *tratte* and any expenses and interest accrued from this contravention, plus any other fines which the Grand Master might choose to impose. Finally, the proclamation decreed that no person was allowed to sell any wheat to foreigners. Those in possession of wheat produce were reminded that they had to go with the said commodity to the office of the *jurats* for the wheat to be weighed, prior to any other business activity taking place.[214] On 19 March 1536 a *bando* stated that no one could sell wheat for more than 4 *carlini per tumino*, on pain of being fined 1 *uncia ponderis* payable to the *marammero* of the city, and eventual confiscation of the wheat.[215] Such documents reflect the consistent involvement of both the *Università* in trying to control the grain trade from the two main administrative centres of the island.

It is difficult to say how much of the duty-free wheat supplies were actually used for the island's necessities. As already noted, this issue deeply concerned the Sicilian authorities, since they suspected that part of the supplies were being smuggled rather than being used for the benefit of the population. The commissioning in 1590 of Del Quadro to investigate misappropriation does not seem to have shed any light on the matter. Although Del Quadro's report was quite detailed on the production and consumption of cereals, he did not tackle the issue of illicit trading in grain. On the contrary, his report painted a picture of an island that was insufficiently supplied to meet its daily needs, let alone use these *tratte* for economic gain. It is possible that Del Quadro could not establish the validity or otherwise of the rumours of illicit trading. The Sicilian authorities were quite rigorous in requesting that Maltese

210 (At the expense of the merchants.) NAM, MCC, 'Cedulae Supplicae et Taxationes', vol. 1, fol. 38v (20.iii.1564).

211 NAM, MCC, 'Cedulae Supplicae et Taxationes', vol. 1, fol. 39 (21.iii.1564).

212 NLM, Univ. 13 (17.x.1537), fol. 151v. On the same subject issued by the Birgu *jurats* see NAM, MCC, Reg. AO, vol. 1, fol. 21 (11.iii.1536).

213 NLM, Univ. 13 (15.xi.1538), fol. 171v.

214 NAM, MCC, AO, vol. 1, fols 20v–21 (11.iii.1536).

215 NLM, Univ. 13 (19.iii.1536).

vessels should produce evidence confirming that any tax-free grain supplies which were granted were truly intended for Malta.

Some interesting information which predates Del Quadro's report may shed light on situations which could have formed a basis for rumours about the illegal use of tax-free concessions. This is in the form of instructions to the Treasurer in Tripoli regarding a consignment of wheat to that North African fortress in 1544.[216] The instructions note that the amount of wheat to be exported from Malta to Tripoli amounted to 2,453 Maltese *salme*. This cargo was to be shipped on six *grippi* belonging to the Maltese *patroni* Brayto Burlo, Antonio di Messina,[217] Nardo Falson, Alfonso Habell and Luis Habell. The Treasurer was instructed to keep enough supplies from this consignment to supply the fortress for six months. What is most interesting is the mention of how he was to dispose of any 'extra' supplies. They were to be sold at an advantageous price to the Moors, who had to pay in good money.[218] Further, it was decreed that, should slaves be given as payment instead of money, these were to be bought on behalf of the Common Treasury. The Treasurer in Tripoli was also warned to strike the best deal possible with the Muslims, and if the latter should 'ask for exorbitant prices for these',[219] he, for his part, should ask for a higher price for the wheat. All income derived from the sale was to be placed in a box which was to be locked with two keys. Nobody could sell wheat outside the castle except for that sold on behalf of the Order, which had to be registered at the customs office as well.

Having sold all or most of this wheat for cash or in exchange for slaves, the Treasurer had to ensure that no more than 300 or 400 *salma* were left as surplus. Considering that on 17 February 1565 the Knights had to write to both the Portulan of Sicily and the Vice-Portulan of Syracuse to assure them that 100 *salma* of wheat had been loaded on their galleys for their use only '*et non ad altro effetto*', the sale of greater quantities of wheat to Muslims would surely have disturbed the Sicilian authorities.[220] Such documents do indeed pose a question as to whether all the duty-free wheat conceded by the Sicilian Kingdom to supply a supposedly 'hungry and barren island' was in fact being used for that purpose or whether, when the opportunity arose, parts of those supplies were traded for financial gain.

Another interesting document which sheds light on the probable clandestine re-export of duty-free imported grain is a joint proclamation released in 1536 by the Grand Master, the Castellan of Birgu and the Vice-Portulan of Notabile (Mdina).[221] It states as follows:

216 NLM, AOM, Lib. Bull. 418, fols 229v–230v (17.x.1544).

217 Antonio de Messina was also a jurat of the Birgu *Università* and had two *grippi* taking part in this expedition.

218 For a detailed explanation of the origin and use of the term 'Moor' in documentary sources of history see K. Baxter Wolf, 'The "Moors" of West Africa and the Beginnings of the Portuguese Slave Trade', *Journal of Medieval and Renaissance Studies*, 24:3 (1994), 449–69.

219 '*vi vorranno carricar tropo li precij de dettj negri.*'

220 NLM, AOM, Lib. Bull. 427 (17.ii.1565). It was agreed that these were to be deducted from the *tratte*.

221 NAM, MCC, AO, vol. 1, fol. 21 (11.iii.1536).

Che nexuna persona de qualsivolgia stato grado et conditione sia au[tori]zato et p[re]sumi ex dicta insula meliveti extrahir per altro loco frumento orgi ligumi et altri victuaglia che se extrahirano de lo regno de Sicilia ad nome de la Universitàti et qualo que sara lo contrario sia in pena di unci cinquanta alo fisco et unci cinquam per mediatate al dicto S[ign]or Castellano et sua corte et per alia medietate al dicto vice portulano e de pagar la tracta e tutti damni et interssi de tali frumenti et victuaglia et altra pena bene iusta reservata ala volunta de Mon[sign]or R[everendissi]mo.

(That no person of any state, grade or condition is authorised to export from this island of Malta to another place, wheat, barley, pulses or other victuals, which are exported from the Kingdom of Sicily on behalf of the *Università*, and if there is such an infringement he is obliged to pay a fine of 50 *uncie* payable to the fiscal office and five *uncie*, half of which are payable to the Castellan and the other half to the Vice-Portulan, and to pay the export licence and all damages and interests derived from this wheat and victuals and other penalties which are justly reserved to the discretion of the Grand Master.

Et similmenti che nexuna p[er]sona di qualsivoglia grado stato conditione sia au[tori]zato nec p[re]suma de li frume[n]ti venino ex regno sicilia ad opus bisogno et suburation de li citadini de dicta insula che vinda e p[re]suma vindiri a p[er]sona extranea qui [con]tranvinera sia i[n] pena [?]

And similarly that no person of any grade, state or condition is authorised to sell to foreigners wheat which is imported from the Kingdom of Sicily for the benefit and well-being of the citizens of this island on pain of being fined [?])

In the light of the above-mentioned *bando*, it is interesting to note the following contract entered into between Fra. Johannes Bonifacius Baulino and the *patrone* of a new galley which was to be armed for a corsairing expedition in 1530. Among other things, the agreement stipulates that the *patrone* was to receive 1,000 gold *scudi*[222] worth of wheat and other goods necessary for provisioning the said galley.[223] This was quite a significant amount of money, which translated into a considerable amount of wheat and victuals. Was this amount truly targeted at provisioning the galley,[224] or were ulterior motives of a commercial nature veiled in this agreement, whereby the *patroni* of galleys leased their ships and entered into agreements with members of the Order, thus combining economic motives with military factors?

Income derived from wheat and the upkeep of fortifications

The inelastic demand for cereals provided a significant and reliable means of revenue collection everywhere in Europe, and Malta was no exception. Income derived from

222 Approximately 400 *uncia* or 12,000 *tarì's* worth.
223 NAV, R 439/1, fols 5–14v (9.xi.1530).
224 According to Guilmartin, 'decks clogged with merchandise made a poor fighting platform'; J. F. Guilmartin, *Gunpowder and Galleys: Changing Technology and Mediterranean Warfare at Sea in the 16th Century* (rev. edn, London, 2003), 46.

the taxes ensured that various expenses incurred in the upkeep of fortifications and the maintenance of soldiers could be secured. In times of great scarcity, the income from the taxes was also used to subsidise the high prices of Sicilian wheat, especially when purchasing grain for the benefit of the poor.[225]

In the event of a general crisis in which both Sicilian and local wheat yields were drastically low, the *Università* had to resort to taxing real estate. Such was the case in 1556 when a tax of 5 *grani* on every *uncia* was imposed on '*li beni stabili*' (immoveable property). The terms of payment for these dues were stipulated, and it was resolved that half of the tax was to be paid by the coming Easter, while the other half was to follow by the next Easter. Those who had an income below 10 *uncie* were ordered to give six days' work per year in respect of the construction of the town walls.[226] The imposition of such taxes by a particular *Università* did not necessarily affect all the population, but was generally directed at collecting revenue from the villages which were subject to its jurisdiction.[227] For example, between 1552 and 1585 the *Università* of Mdina imposed a tax on both local and Sicilian grain on at least ten different occasions. This was chiefly directed at collecting revenue from Mdina, its suburb of Rabat and the four villages falling under its jurisdiction, namely Birkirkara, Siġġiewi, Naxxar and Żebbug (Table 5).[228]

Table 5 Various taxes imposed on cereals by the *Università* of Mdina 1552–88

	MALTESE In *tarì/grani per salma*			SICILIAN In *tarì/grani per salma*	
Date	**Wheat**	**Meslin**	**Barley**	**Wheat**	**Barley**
13/08/1552	*un tertio*[a]	*un tertio*	*un tertio*	2	-
15/03/1555	-	-	-	2	1
05/12/1557	2	1.1	1	2	-
21/09/1558	4	3	2	6	3
10/06/1563	2	1.1	1	2	1
14/05/1562	2	1.1	1	2	-
21/02/1570	1.1	1	0.15	1.1	-
04/10/1580	4	3.1	1.1	4	-
20/05/1582	6	4	2	6	-
19/06/1585	2	1.1	1	2	-

[a] It is not clear whether this tax meant the payment of one-third the price of a salma of wheat or the payment of the price of the amount of cereal of a dry measure called the tertio. Although this specific measure is hard to come by in documents, it is possible that it was one of the various sub-divisions of the salma and the tumulo. Vassallo, 'Prices of Commodities', 70.

Source: Vassallo, 'Prices of Commodities', 69.

225 Vassallo, 'Prices of Commodities', 67.
226 NLM, Univ. 201, n.f. (22.v.1556).
227 Vassallo, 'Prices of Commodities', 68.
228 Vassallo, 'Prices of Commodities', 68.

As can be seen from Table 5, even though Maltese wheat sold for much less than Sicilian wheat, it was taxed at the same rate as Sicilian wheat, which meant that tax was not calculated in proportion to the price of wheat but was blanket rate for all types. Barley was almost always taxed at half the amount of wheat, and meslin was approximately halfway between the two.

The general fear of a Turkish attack and the bad state of the islands' fortifications were the main justifications which were continuously exploited by the *Università* whenever it needed to impose additional taxes. Phrases such as '*si ha inteso com il turcho apparichia grandi armati in questo anno qualle mandari contra noj ... la Università et povera et non ha modo de farsi fortificare*'[229] were common enough in the minutes of the council meetings.[230] The stable demand for cereals meant that any taxes imposed on this product generated a good return for the town council's coffers from people of all strata of the population.

However, bread issues were a delicate matter which could provoke unwanted instability. Thus the *Università* was careful of the manner in which it established new taxes. On almost all occasions the threat of an imminent enemy attack (at times flavoured with the mention of the great number of Turkish ships reportedly on their way to lay waste to the island) was a convenient reason which seemed to coax the population into accepting new taxes on essential commodities. Frequent *razzias*[231] on Maltese coasts took place and must have weighed heavily on the minds of the inhabitants.

A case in point was the Muslim raid in May 1551, which is recorded as being one of the worst attacks on the island of Gozo, so much so that the island was literally depopulated.[232] People faced the reality that they had to live with the risk of becoming a slave. Most probably everyone had a relation or a friend who could recount the terrible ordeal of becoming a slave, and the great financial burden imposed on those who wished to acquire their freedom. Thus, any actions by the ruling and administrative bodies which were intended to provide a 'safer' home seem to have been tolerated.

The capture of grain ships

According to Fernand Braudel, during times of great famine 'if all else failed, the last great resource was to turn to the sea, to watch out for grain ships, seize them,

229 (It is known that this year the Turk is building up large fleets which he intends to send against us ... the *Università* is poor and does not have the means to fortify [the island].) NLM, Univ. 201. n.f. (4.v. 1556).

230 NLM, Univ. 201, n.f. (4.v.1556); see also Univ. 13, fol. 131v (28.ii.1537), Univ. 201, n.f. (15.iii.1555).

231 *Razzia* was a raid for plunder or slaves, especially one carried out by the Moors in North Africa. Circa nineteenth century from French from the variant of Arabic *ghaziah* war. *Collins English Dictionary – Complete and Unabridged 10th Edition*, Dictionary.com, http://www.dictionary.com/browse/razzia (accessed 22 August 2016).

232 S. Fiorini, 'The Resettlement of Gozo after 1551', *Melita Historica*, 9:3 (1986), 203–35.

then to pay the party concerned for the cargo later'.[233] Even in Malta's case, in order to address problems of acute cereal shortage, the Order resorted to seizing the grain ships[234] of co-religionists, a situation which generated much tension and litigation. Every time famine threatened, these ships, either anchored in the Maltese harbour or out at sea, became potential targets, a potential quick fix for feeding the starving population. One such case was that of the ship *Bellina*, in which the *Università* of Messina accused the two *Università* of Malta of illegally and forcefully unloading the ship's cargo of wheat at the Maltese harbour, to the detriment of the citizens of Messina.[235] Although the Knights of the Order generally paid for seized cargos, they were renowned for their cruel behaviour during such attacks,[236] which was often condemned and described as resembling that of the corsairs of Tripoli.[237] The minutes of the Mdina town council meeting of 27 December 1554 reported that '*perche nella insula havemo gran mancam[en]to de frumenti et al p[rese]n[t]i li galeri dela religionj sono andatj et si ret[trov]ano fora dela insula*'.[238] They further stated that if the Order's expedition was successful, any wheat which was made available up to a quantity of 4,000 *salme* would be purchased by the *Università* at its own risk, possibly meaning that it would pay for the expense incurred and would also deal with any legal issues arising from the capture. In the event that the Viceroy conceded extra amounts of wheat from Sicily, the captured cargo would be sold.[239]

The year 1559 was yet another year of scarcity in the supply of wheat and, as was the practice in such instances, a cargo of wheat from Terranova was captured by the Knights. Afterwards, the Mdina *Università* excused its actions by stating that it took this decision since '*questo populo al presente in gran fami havemo deliberato detta navi di scaricare*'.[240] In the year 1562, another year of great scarcity of wheat, a chancery minute stipulated that a letter had been sent by the Order to the Portulan of Sicily and to the Vice-Portulan of the *caricartorio* in Licata stating that, in view of the great shortage on the island, the Knights had ordered the unloading of 300 *salme* of wheat from the ship of *Hon.* Giovan di Giovanni and Martino di Trapani.[241] Such moves reflect how the Knights were quick to justify their actions in the eyes of Sicilian authorities, since Sicily was the island's main trading link and its granary. Difficult relations with Sicily would impede the easy flow of trade and place Malta in a critical situation. From the above-quoted documents it is also evident that at times when

233 Braudel, *The Mediterranean*, vol. 1, 331.

234 See, for example, Dal Pozzo, *Historia della Sacra Religione*, 524, where the author makes reference to the mission given to the galleys of the Order to search for wheat in the Levant.

235 Vassallo, 'Prices of Commodities', 82.

236 Braudel, *The Mediterranean*, vol. 1, 331.

237 Braudel, *The Mediterranean*, vol. 1, 331.

238 (Because the island is suffering from great scarcity of wheat at present the galleys of the Order have sailed out and are overseas.)

239 NLM, Univ. 201, n.f. (27.xii.1554). Presumably this would be done since, if the Viceroy had conceded the amounts requested, it would have been a problem to store great quantities of wheat, apart from the possibility that the wheat would rot.

240 (This people at present suffering from starvation we gave orders to the ship to unload.) NLM, Univ. 201, n.f. (15.xii.1559).

241 NLM, AOM, Lib. Bull. 427, fol. 250 (4.iv.1562).

the Hospitaller government faced great difficulties in provisioning the island the town council of Mdina supported the Knights in their endeavours to acquire the necessary grain by all possible means, thus contributing to both the economic and political stability of the island.

Conclusion

During the sixteenth century the constant increase in population throughout Europe made for difficulty in meeting the need for food supplies.[242] Similarly in Malta, the search for sufficient grain was a constant preoccupation for its rulers, both before and after the arrival of the Knights. Ever since medieval times, given the nature of the terrain and the relative infertility of the land, Malta's agriculture was primarily targeted at producing niche products that required less land than was needed for grain production. These crops yielded high-quality products which were in great demand in foreign markets, thus providing cash for the local population. This cultivation strategy was beneficial in offsetting the substantial payments which the island had to pay out to import almost all of its vital necessities.

Duty-free concessions on various staple products were a privilege from which the islands had benefitted since medieval times. Diplomatic efforts and bureaucratic procedures had to be followed in order to ensure their periodical renewal; consuls and merchants faced obstacles even after they had been officially granted. With the arrival of the Order, the island experienced a sudden increase of about 25% of the existing population, apart from another considerable inflow of foreign people, mostly merchants, traders, sailors and craftsmen, who were attracted to the island by the Order's establishment there. This flood of people meant more mouths to feed, and the Order was well aware that without the special concessions of the duty-free *tratte*, the governance of the island would prove difficult, if not impossible. It would also have been impossible for the Order to exist without the continuous inflow of its European revenues, since these supplied the financial underpinnings for its convent.[243] Consequently, any diplomatic negotiations with the Spanish Crown for the concession of duty-free quotas had to be agreed on neutral terms,[244] so as not to upset other European benefactors.

242 Sicily doubled its number of inhabitants during this century and, as already explained, even the Maltese islands' population increased considerably. Fontenay, 'The Mediterranean 1530–1800', in Mallia-Milanes (ed.), *Hospitaller Malta 1530–1798*, 43–110: 61; Braudel, *Civilization and Capitalism*, vol. 1, 104, 183.

243 Hoppen, 'Military Priorities and Social Realities', in Mallia-Milanes (ed.), *Hospitaller Malta 1530–1798*, 399–428: 400.

244 NLM, Lib. Bull. 425, fols 261v–262 (1.iv.1557). This document makes particular reference to the privilege of neutrality granted by the Spanish monarch to the Hospitaller Order. Specific instructions were issued to *Fra.* Bernardo de Guymaran, who was to embark on a mission to the king of Spain and had to '*procurarete ch'il privilegio di neutralità che sua M[aes]ta a concesso a nostra religion pervalersene in tempo di guerra, sia pubblicato nelle frontiere et che per accomodarne quelli che n'haveranno bisogno se ne facino molte copie authentiche sopra l'originale*' [sic]. (Ensure that the privilege of neutrality which

Malta's heavy dependence on Sicily as its major provider of staple commodities led to a situation in which market prices followed the general trend of prices in Sicily. The fluctuating price of Sicilian grain, with its many added costs, ultimately affected the weight of local bread, the growing cost of which was shouldered by consumers. Care is needed when interpreting the prices found in *pandette* (price lists). These were just the official retail market prices. The absence of relevant documentation which would help to better correlate these prices with the actual prices demanded on the market makes it very hard to establish the real selling price of a commodity.[245] In addition, just as in medieval times, grain proved to be an ideal commodity for the imposition of indirect taxes. The latter served mostly to provide the authorities with the necessary revenue for the proper upkeep of the town walls and the payment of various salaries, especially those of soldiers.

The steady encroachment on the medieval *Università's* privileges by the Hospitaller Order ensured that the new rulers controlled a crucial sector which was necessary for the smooth governing of the islands. The Hospitaller Knights knew well that 'bread and butter issues' were not to be left to the discretion of the administrative elite that made up the old town council of Mdina. On the other hand, the Order was careful not to upset old structures too much, since they were the key to the grain depositaries of Sicily.

His Majesty conceded to Our Religion prevails in time of war, and is published on all frontiers, and to accommodate those who would be in need of a copy, let it be that many of authentic true copies from the original be made.)

245 Fiorini, 'Malta in 1530', in Mallia-Milanes (ed.), *Hospitaller Malta 1530–1798*, 111–98: 167.

3

Women and Economic Activities

Women had a recognised role in pre-industrial European society which varied according to the geographic location and their social standing.[1] Although a substantial body of research is now available, secondary literature on the role of women in Maltese society and economic life is conspicuously absent. This is both an obstacle and a challenge for interpreting primary sources in legal archives.[2] The case study presented in this chapter aims to stimulate discussion on the subject and investigate how the change of ruler in 1530 affected the economic role of women in Maltese society.

In 1536 Jean Quintin d'Autun wrote about Maltese women: 'not at all ugly, but [they] live very much as if they were uncivilized; they do not mix with other people; they go out covered in a veil, as if to see a woman is here the same as to violate her'.[3] How much did prevailing attitudes towards women, who, from d'Autun's description, seem to have been quite secluded from the rest of society, affect their economic activity? Were they passive in the face of many exhortations to obedience? Is there any indication of the consequences of the Catholic Reformation, when women's obedience and role in the family underwent a significant transformation?[4] Can any distinction be detected between the elite and lower echelons, or between spinsters, married women and widows? What particular economic activities are

1 H. Kamen, *Early Modern European Society* (London, 2000), 157.

2 Carmel Cassar's work on the impact of the Council of Trent on women in Malta is still the only major work solely dedicated to women's studies. C. Cassar, *Daughters of Eve, Women, Gender Roles, and the Impact of the Council of Trent in Catholic Malta* (Malta, 2002). Works focusing on the religious roles of women in society include C. Muscat, *The Magdalene Nuns and Penitent Prostitutes, Valletta* (Malta, 2013); G. Aquilina, *The Jerosolimitan Nuns: The Church and Monastery of St Ursula, Valletta, Malta* (Malta, 2011). Other publications in the form of papers include the works of Y. Vella, 'Women Victims of Crime in Eighteenth Century Malta', in T. Cortis (ed.), *Proceedings of History Week 2003* (Malta, 2004), 17–23; Y. Vella, 'Earthly Madonnas? 18th Century Women Trouble-Makers', in *Storja 98* (University of Malta Historical Society, 1998), 33–40. Other unpublished material includes J. Sciberras, 'Women in Early Sixteenth-Century Malta' (MA dissertation, University of Malta, 2004).

3 J. Quintin d'Autun, 'Insulae Melitae Descriptio (Lyon, 1536)', in J. Quintin d'Autun, *The Earliest Description of Malta* (trans. H. C. R. Vella, Malta, 1980), 41.

4 G. Duby & M. Perrot (gen. eds) & N. Zemon Davis & A. Farge (eds), *A History of Women: Vol. III Renaissance and Enlightenment Paradoxes* (Cambridge, MA and London, 1993); Cassar, *Daughters of Eve*, passim.

Fig. 5 Maltese women drawn by the Knight of Malta *Fra.* Opizio Guidotti in c. 1600. *Source*: NLM, Libr. MS 413/I, f. 164a.

recorded for female foreign settlers? Did Maltese women have the same attitude to business undertakings as their foreign counterparts? The following discussion does not look at female slavery and prostitution. Although these were thriving activities in the harbour area, the subject merits study in its own right, due to its peculiarity.

In order to validate the arguments presented here and place them in context, the existing framework of women's legal persona needs to be constructed from notarial references and the prevailing laws. The sample of notarial registers consulted was chosen on the following criteria: the notary in question practised in Birgu; the volumes were in a good state of preservation; both Rhodiot and Maltese notaries are represented in the sample.

How much weaker in the eyes of the law?

The legal systems and law codes of early modern Europe reflected prevailing theories and perceptions of women, based mainly on traditional notions of the weaknesses of the female sex.[5] The main concern of lawmakers was the 'reproduction of family and

5 C. Opitz, 'Life in the Late Middle Ages', in G. Duby & M. Perrot (gen. eds) & C. Klapish-Zuber (ed.), *A History of Women: Vol. II Silences of the Middle Ages* (Cambridge,

kinship units', and there was no place for equality between the sexes.[6] Merry Weisner, however, points out that even though the law depicted women as mere shadows of their male counterparts, the ideal or desired situation that it was intended to create often did not reflect the real functioning of society.[7] Thomas Kuehn maintains that the effectiveness of the law in controlling women's actions is open to interpretation.

According to Kuehn, depending on their circumstances, some women were able to work around obstacles, such as the need to be represented by a *mundualdus*,[8] managing at times to reduce them to a mere formality.[9] Kuehn's study, which is heavily based on the operation and ambiguities of the law, challenges the analysis by Christiane Klapisch-Zuber, who arranged her subjects in a 'neat analysis' where there are no 'loose ends' and 'everything has its place in a structure, a function to fulfil and a meaning to express'.[10] Kuehn contends that when historians project an 'inalterable structure' onto the past, events may be omitted which, although infrequent, did actually take place, such as a remarried mother's donation of property to the family of her son from her first marriage.[11] Legal texts, such as those consulted in this study, are indispensable, and help us better to understand different forms of social behaviour since, as Kuehn explains, 'social behaviour took forms and meaning from norms, and social personhood rested on the substrate of legal personhood'.[12]

Late imperial Roman law placed fewer restrictions on women than did the laws promulgated during the high and late medieval period, even though the latter were mostly based on Roman law.[13] The limitations placed on a woman's legal persona

MA and London, 1992), 269–70. T. Kuehn, 'Daughters, Mothers, Wives, and Widows: Women as Legal Persons', in T. Kuehn & S. Seidel Menchi (eds), *Time, Space and Women's Lives in Early Modern Europe* (Kirksville, MO, 2001), 97–115: 97.

6 Kuehn, 'Daughters, Mothers, Wives', in Kuehn & Seidel Menchi (eds), *Time, Space and Women's Lives*, 97–115: 97.

7 M. E. Wiesner-Hanks, *Women and Gender in Early Modern Europe* (New York, 2008), 43.

8 The word *mundualdus* derived from the word *mundium*, found in the Germanic codes of law, which excluded all females from all public affairs and transactions. Women were represented by a *mundualdus,* a legally competent male who took a woman under his wing to represent her in a legal transaction where she could not appear by herself. The *mundualdus* was generally, but not always, a husband, father, brother, uncle or a friend of the woman. S. Fonay Wemple, 'Women from the Fifth to the Tenth Century', in Duby et al., *A History of Women: Vol. II*, 169–201: 174 (refer also to Section 4.4). For the legal function of the *mundualdus* refer to T. Kuehn, *Law, Family and Women, Towards a Legal Anthropology of Renaissance Italy* (Chicago, 1991), 212–37.

9 Kuehn, *Law, Family and Women,* 6; T. Kuehn, 'Person and Gender in the Laws', in J. C. Brown & R. C. Davis (eds), *Gender and Society in Renaissance Italy* (London and New York, 1998), 87–106: 87–91.

10 Kuehn, *Law, Family and Women*, 6.

11 Kuehn, *Law, Family and Women*, 5.

12 Kuehn, 'Person and Gender in the Laws', in Brown & Davis (eds), *Gender and Society in Renaissance Italy*, 87–106: 91.

13 During the early Middle Ages women were granted more freedom and certainly a greater portion of their families' assets. For example, restrictions to women's rights to inheritance in northern Italy can be observed after the 1130s with the *odium terciae* and *quartae* and the subsequent transition to a dowry system. (Thanks to Denise Bezzina for this electronic communication dated 12 March 2016.) For a discussion on the patrimonial rights of women during the early Middle Ages see the studies collected in F. Bougard,

restricted her from exercising the rights of *patria potestas* and from obligating herself for others, notably, standing as surety. Even though the *ius commune* excluded women from authoritative legal and political participation, it did not hamper in terms of marriage, holding property and the capacity to dispose of it, or much else. Beyond the impediment on standing surety for another, 'women were free in *ius commune* to own and dispose of property by all legal means and had equal inheritance rights with men'.[14] The influence of medieval canon law established that they could be guardians of their children after the father's death.[15] Women's right to dispose of their property without their husband's consent proved beneficial to the Church, especially after the reforms adopted by the Council of Trent, which emphasised the charitable aspect of the Christian soul.

The Lombard conquest of Italy brought with it the Germanic practice of the *mundualdus*, which limited women's legal capacities and required them to act with the consent of a male figure. Throughout the Middle Ages, across most of Europe, Roman law evolved in line with attempts to bring more uniformity to 'highly localized and often contradictory and conflicting law codes'.[16] Later, it played an important role in the legal reforms of the sixteenth century.[17] It guaranteed the absolute rights of the father (*patria potestas*), according an inferior status to women on the basis that they were not fully responsible for their actions, due to their 'fragility, imbecility, irresponsibility, and ignorance'.[18] Notwithstanding such legal prejudice, women 'did have rights and prerogatives in law, and in the life of virtually every woman who reached adulthood and [who] had some property certain occasions could bring these legal rights into action'.[19]

The situation in Malta was in the main similar to that found in the Italian and wider European context, although an important distinction between two different kinds of power is necessary: that is, power wielded by dynastic succession and the power acquired through elective means.[20] In the case of guilds and republics, there

L. Feller & R. Le Jan (eds), *Dots et douaires dans le haut Moyen Âge*, École française de Rome (Collection de École française de Rome, Rome, 2002), 295. For the transition to the dowry system in northern Italy see M. Bellomo, *Ricerche sui rapporti patrimoniali fra i coniugi. Contributo alla storia della famiglia medievale* (Milan 1961), 1–25 and A. Bartoli Langeli, 'Après le *Morgengabe.* Donations nuptiales et culture juridique dans l'Itali ecommunale', in Bougard et al., *Dots et douaires,* 123–30.

14 Kuehn, 'Person and Gender in the Laws', in Brown & Davis (eds), *Gender and Society in Renaissance Italy*, 87–106: 93.

15 Kuehn, 'Person and Gender in the Laws', in Brown & Davis (eds), *Gender and Society in Renaissance Italy*, 87–106: 93.

16 Wiesner-Hanks, *Women and Gender*, 43.

17 H. J. Berman, *Law and Revolution, II The Impact of the Protestant Reformations on the Western Legal Tradition* (Cambridge, M, 2006).

18 Additionally, it was stated that women were inept at keep secrets as well as being cunning and greedy. Wiesner-Hanks, *Women and Gender*, 46.

19 Kuehn, 'Person and Gender in the Laws', in Brown & Davis (eds), *Gender and Society in Renaissance Italy*, 87–106: 92. See also, M. Casola, 'Armatrici e Marinaie Nel Diritto Romano', in R. Pagano & F. Mastroberti (eds), *La Donna nel Diritto, nella Politica e nelle Istitizuioni, Quaderno del Dipartimento Jonico,* 1 (2015), 3–18.

20 N. Zemon Davis, 'Women in Politics', in Duby et al., *A History of Women*: *Vol. III*, 167–83: 168. As regards monarchies and the power of queens, Natalie Zemon Davis writes that

was no elective form of power which allowed an executive role to women. But when it came to the monarch, who was chosen by God, this choice had to be accepted even if the 'chosen one' were female. In Maltese society women were completely excluded from participation in local politics or service in public office. In accordance with the *ius commune* rule a woman could not serve as judge or lawyer, and the law debarred her from participating in the institutions of government, which included municipal and community assemblies. She had no right to testify in court in criminal cases or to serve as an oath helper, juror, guarantor or procurator.[21]

This situation was further buttressed by the arrival of the Order of St John, more so since the Order totally excluded women from participation in its hierarchy.[22] The Order was a governing body that was first and foremost a religious order of professed knights of noble origin[23] who took a vow of chastity. Unlike in countries where marriage was considered an important political strategy to determine strategic alliances between families, in Malta women did not feature in the political schemes of the ruling elite, the Knights of the Order of St John.[24]

Although women may have lost any political strategic influence which they had enjoyed through marriage alliances during the medieval period, indirectly, they did

'republics and monarchies gave different scope to the political role of women. The oligarchic republics, such as Florence of the early Renaissance, Venice, the Swiss cantons, and the German imperial cities, afforded the fewest settings in which women could enjoy political power publicly ... In contrast, those polities organized as kingdoms – France, England, Spain, the German principalities, and ducal Florence of the later Renaissance – had places formally reserved for women and arenas for public and semi public female action. Where power was acquired by dynastic succession rather than by election or cooperation, women were anointed as queens, and birth and marriage became matters of high politics.' Zemon Davis, 'Women in Politics', in Duby et al., *A History of Women: Vol. III*, 167–83: 169–70.

21 '"*feminae ab omnibus officiis civilibus et publicis remotae sunt, et ideo nec judices esse possunt, nec magistratum gerere, nec postulare, nec pro alio intervenire, nec procuratores existere*" (women can have no part in any civic and public office, and therefore may neither be judges, nor act as magistrates, nor plead in court, nor intervene on behalf of other, nor be *procuratores*).' As quoted in V. Oligiati, 'Professional Body and Gender Difference in Court: The Case of the First (Failed) Woman Lawyer in Modern Italy', in U. Schutz & G. Shaw (eds), *Women in the World's Legal Professions* (Oxford and Portland, OR, 2003), 419–36: 422.

22 While still in the Holy Land, the Order of St John 'incorporated a branch of sisters who lived according to the rules of the canonesses of St Augustine. These sisters were headed by a prioress who was directly subjected to the grand master. After the Order left Palestine, we find these sisters also in Aragon, England, Bohemia, and Germany, but in the fifteenth century this female branch had been reduced to a few sisters.' T. Freller, *Malta – The Order of St John* (Malta, 2010), 60. As regards the founding of the Jerosolimitan Nuns in Malta refer to G. Aquilina, OFM, *The Jerosolimitan Nuns, the Church and Monastery of Saint Ursula Valletta – Malta* (Malta, 2011).

23 During the chapter-general held in Rhodes in 1354, it was decided that serving brothers (*fratres servientes*) were to be excluded from being promoted to knights, and the latter were to provide proof of their noble descent. Freller, *Malta – The Order of St John*, 64.

24 This of course does not exclude the fact that some knights did indulge in sexual pleasures which at times bore illegitimate fruit. Such relationships were, however, regarded as illicit ones and had to be obliterated from the Order's history and shrouded from the public eye. However, it seems that at times the political influence of women through such personal relationships was not insignificant. G. Bonello, 'Knights and Courtesans', in *Histories of Malta: Versions and Diversions, Vol. 3* (Malta, 2002), 20–41.

participate in the political process through their right to own and transfer property. As McGough states, 'the transmission of property after death is, ultimately, a political problem'.[25] This was especially the case in Malta, where three different and autonomous heads of institutions were all accountable to the pope, these being the Grand Master, the bishop and, after 1574, the Inquisitor. In her study on women and the Reformation Elisja Schulte van Kessel notes that, 'women played an important part in the reform policies of the clergy, which had every reason to want to sabotage the all powerful kinship system'.[26] The majority of Maltese women who made wills left cash bequests in return for religious services for the repose of their soul, while richer women also left land endowments.[27] Several records dealing with land given as *juspatronatus*[28] reveal that the foundations of such *jus*, and the eventual nomination of rectors to administer such benefices, were carried out by noblewomen.

In her study on women in early sixteenth-century Malta Joanne Sciberras has shown that women featured extensively in contracts relating to the cession of land to members of the clergy. In fact, when a new rector was appointed to a benefice it was generally the daughter or wife of the founder of the benefice who presented him with the *juspatronatus*, a practice which seems to have been an important duty for women of noble origin.[29] The same study showed that the husband did not act on behalf of his wife in these cases, and seems not to have interfered in the presentation of benefices.[30] The bishop held the right to approve successive rectors or to appoint them himself in the event that the line of patrons died out. In his study on such bequests, Fiorini states that numerous documents reflect this situation, which is expressed in the following terms: '*beneficium devolutum ad manus nostras [id est, Episcopi] ob non presentationem patronorum*' (the benefice has been turned over to our hands [that is of the Bishop] due to the non presentation of patrons).[31]

The importance of women and their dowries in the economic life both of their

25 L. J. McGough, 'Women, Private Property, and the Limitations of State Authority in Early Modern Venice', *Journal of Women's History*, 14 (2003), 32–52: 33.

26 E. Schulte van Kessel, 'Virgins and Mothers between Heaven and Earth', in Duby et al., *A History of Women: Vol. III*, 132–66: 149.

27 Wives also appear alongside their husbands when a couple made such bequests. See S. Fiorini (ed.), *Documentary Sources of Maltese History, Part V: Documents in the Curia of the Archbishop of Malta, No 1: The Registrum Fundationum Beneficiorum Insulae Gaudisii: 1435–1545* (trans. Rev. Joseph Busuttil, Malta, 2006), Docs 9, 21, 58, 66, 70 as examples. For examples of bequests solely by women see Docs 15, 26, 82.

28 At times also called *animagium* in documents. According to Fiorini, the term is not encountered in canon law. However, it is 'used co-extensively with the term benefice or, in ecclesiastical jargon, a living, which in turn often translates as *beneficium* in Latin'. The term is descriptive of 'the single situation whereby members of the faithful (the founder or founders of the benefice) bequeath property (usually immobile, but pecuniary bequests are not unknown in the present records) on condition that a priest of their choice (called the rector of the benefice) reciprocates by praying (usually celebrating Masses) for the repose of the founders' souls ... After the demise of the founder, the patrons (usually the heirs) nominate successive rectors for canonical approval by the Ordinary, as required by Canon Law (Can. 1546).' Fiorini (ed.), *Documentary Sources of Maltese History, Part V, No. 1*, Introduction, liii–liv.

29 Sciberras, 'Women in Early Sixteenth-Century Malta', 81–3, especially Table 3.2, which lists those women who donated land as *juspatronatus* between the years 1506–54.

30 Sciberras, 'Women in Early Sixteenth-Century Malta', 83.

31 Fiorini (ed.), *Documentary Sources of Maltese History, Part V, No. 1*, Introduction, liv.

family and of society is best understood in a law promulgated by Grand Master Lascaris in 1640. This decreed that, since the Order was receiving reports of the exploitation of women's property by their husbands, women could no longer obligate themselves on behalf of their husbands without first obtaining permission from the Grand Master. This made it difficult for a husband to perform any kind of economic activity which might have been generated through use of his wife's dowry.[32] Opposition to the imposition of such restrictions was so great that the law was revoked later in the same year.

While the Hospitaller government tried hard to regulate women's legal rights and put a stronger patriarchal society in place, prevailing and long-established customs giving women property rights were well-engrained in Maltese society. There was a clear need for flexibility in this matter, allowing joint and equal participation in business by both husband and wife. Local customs presented strong resistance to the Knights Hospitaller, whose later schemes to further restrict the activities of Maltese women in the mid-seventeenth century seem to have failed. The revocation of Grand Master Lascaris's decree so soon after its promulgation shows how, a hundred years after the Knights' arrival, local Maltese structures of power remained far stronger than has previously been assumed.

The *mundualdus*

As has been noted, the Hospitaller Order was granted the right to rule over the islands on condition that the prevailing laws and customs of Maltese society were respected and observed. Vincenzo Bonavita makes an interesting observation on the Hospitallers' non-observance of local customs in relation to the validity of a woman's legal persona. He asserts that, contrary to the established local custom which subjected women to perpetual male tutelage, Rhodiot notaries who had moved to Malta with the Knights did not make use of the services of a *mundualdus*.[33] He maintains that, as was their own custom, they continued to follow the *Diritto Romano*, by which women had full rights of administration over their dowry and could enter into contracts of obligation on their own behalf without the consent of their husband. Thus, indirectly, women acquired greater legal rights under the Knights.

Bonavita substantiates his claim by reference to a contract drawn up on 25 March 1535 by the Rhodiot Notary Vincenzo Bonaventura de Bonetiis, in which the widow Agatha Zoppardi from *Casali Sancta Caterina* made a donation to her children without being represented by a *mundualdus*.[34] As was noted in Chapter

32 NLM, Libr. MS 439 Prammatiche Magistrali Lascaris 1640–1692 incluse quelle di Omedes 1553, fol. 48 (new pagination).

33 CAM, Misc. 273, V. Bonavita, *Dissertazioni Storico Legali su Malta e Gozo*, Introduction. Bonavita, *Dissertazioni Storico Legali*, fol. 327v. Roman law did not require unmarried adult women to have guardians but had known guardianship only for children. Wiesner-Hanks, *Women and Gender*, 46.

34 This contract still survives in NAV, R 206/1, fol. 195v (25.iii.1535).

One, the laws of Messina were the framework of Maltese civil law codes, and so it could be said that Agatha was acting within the parameters of the local law.[35] This is because, according to the prevailing law, *Mulier cuoque virum non habens se et sua obligare potest* (a woman who does not have a husband can obligate herself).[36] Thus, although a wife could not enter into contracts of obligation without the consent of her husband, a widow or a woman who did not have a husband could, in effect, enter into contracts of obligation.[37]

From analysis of late fifteenth-century Maltese documents, it can be seen that although the appointment of a *mundualdus* was a local custom,[38] it was not uncommon for a widow or a nubile to make a donation, will or contract of obligation without the presence of a male representative. An example is provided by the donation *inter vivos* which Ysmiralda, widow of Paulj Zarb, made to her daughter Johanna, whereby she gave her a third part undivided of a house with adjoining fields and courtyard. A clause in the contract stipulates that the transferor reserved part of the house for herself. It is further stated that the property formed part of the '*comunja substancia matrimonij Jpsius Ysmiralde cum dicto Paolo*' (the common assets of the marriage of Ysmiralde herself with the said Paolo), thus highlighting that it was part of the community of property from the said marriage, implying that Johanna was legally entitled to a portion of the inheritance, the *legittima*.[39]

35 G. La Mantia, 'Capitoli e Statuti Amministrativi Dell'Isola di Malta approvati dai Re o Vicere di Sicilia 1130–1530', *Archivio Storico di Malta*, 8:1 (1936–37), 1–17: 12.

36 V. La Mantia, *Antiche Consuetudini delle Città di Sicilia*, with an introduction by A. Romano (Messina, 1993), 41.

37 Under the earlier laws of Messina this section stated thus, '*Uxor cum marito susceptis filiis obligari potest, non susceptis filiis obligari similiter potest si pro communi utilitate vel necessitate obligationi facta fuerit. Mulier vero virum non habens se et sua obligare potest*' (A wife with a husband, if children have been born, can be laid under an obligation; if children have not been born, (the wife) can similarly be laid under an obligation, if the obligation shall have been made for the common benefit or necessity. A woman, indeed, not having a husband, can lay herselfand her descendants under an obligation). Thus, later laws which stated that a married woman could not obligate herself reinforced the authority of the husband over his wife's legal actions. V. La Mantia, 'Consuetudini di Trapani nelle quali e contenuto il testo antico delle consuetudini di Messina', in La Mantia, *Antiche Consuetudini*, 14. La Mantia also states that the laws of Palermo, Messina, Catania, Castiglione, Noto and Corleone restricted married women from acting as surety, from alienating property which was given to them as part of their dowry and from writing up testaments. Married women had to have their husband's consent in order to enter into contracts of obligation, appear in court and make donations. V. La Mantia, *Storia della Legislazione Civile e Criminale di Sicilia* (Palermo, 1866), 142 n. 2; see also La Mantia, *Antiche Consuetudini*, passim.

38 That this was the local custom may be proved by various notarial documents, such as the following which states thus, '*Jpsa mulier Catherina Jn presenti contractu cum provisione consilio et auctoritate Vincencij Barbar suj filij presentis etc. per eamdem Caterinam assumptj Jn procuratorem sive mundualdum ut morjs est mulierum*' [sic]. (The said woman Catherina [appearing] in this present contract with the counsel and authority of Vincentius Barbar her son, who is present, etc., adopted by the very same Catherina appointed as procurator or *mundualdus* as is the custom of women.) Fiorini (ed.), *Documentary Sources of Maltese History, Part I, No. 1*, Docs 11, 12.

39 Fiorini (ed.), *Documentary Sources of Maltese History, Part I, No. 1*, Doc. 128.

In another instance, in May 1487, *Domina* Clara de Stunica, a Maltese citizen resident in Mdina, promised to sell 35.8 *salme* of wheat to Peri Caruana, who also hailed from Mdina.[40] Domina Clara, who was a spinster, was not represented by a *mundualdus* and the contract stipulated that she 'has sold, and for the sake of this sale, has agreed and has laid herself under an obligation to the Honourable Perio Caruana her fellow-citizen' the said amount of wheat.[41] One should note that *Domina* Clara was a landed proprietor, since it was stated that the wheat was to be supplied from one of the territories which she held. A detail inserted in the marginal note of the contract stated that *Domina* Clara also gave some silver items as security, which she recovered on 30 August of the same year because she had honoured the contract. Such documents reinforce the hypothesis that emancipated women or widows had a legal persona and some options for exercising it, since they clearly did enter into contracts of obligation without a male representative. It is interesting to note that although in the majority of contracts husbands, sons and sons-in-law did serve as a *mundualdi*, giving their authority to the drawing up of a contract, they in no way ascribed it to themselves or to an inclusive 'we'.[42]

It is clear from the documents analysed for this study that the use of a male guardian was a local custom well-engrained in Maltese society even before the arrival of the Knights.[43] In a study by Emanuel Buttigieg on the acts of Notary Juliano Muscat for the year 1545, the author noted that out of a total of sixty-four contracts involving the participation of unmarried or widowed women, only nine women were not represented by a *mundualdus*. Out of these nine, three were unmarried and six were widows, some of whom were landed proprietors of noble origin.[44] Therefore, although according to the law single women or widows could act alone, it seems that they often opted to choose a *mundualdus* to represent them.[45] Such a preference is to be seen in the light of prevailing prejudiced attitudes within the society as a whole which sought to project that a 'woman is of the weaker sex than the male ... and the laws have less confidence in a woman'.[46] Psychologically, these women must have felt more 'protected' when commissioning a male representative.

In a number of deeds drawn up by notaries operating in Malta both before and during the first few decades of Hospitaller rule, it can be seen that although the use of the *mundualdus* was a local custom, in certain instances, such as when making wills, married women were not under obligation to have a male guardian. Thus, *Donna* Zarra de Brancato, wife of *Egregius* Gomes de Brancato from Mdina, left all her assets to her son, whom she nominated as her universal heir, while she left nothing

40 Fiorini (ed.), *Documentary Sources of Maltese History, Part I, No. 1*, Docs 183, 191.

41 '*vendidit et Jpsius causa vendicionjs dare et assignare promisit, convenit et se obligavit honorabili Perio Caruana suo concivj.*'

42 Kuehn, 'Daughters, Mothers, Wives and Widows', in Kuehn & Seidel Menchi (eds), *Time, Space and Women's Lives*, 97–115: 106–7.

43 Fiorini (ed.), *Documentary Sources of Maltese History, Part I, No. 1*, Docs 11, 23.

44 E. Buttigieg, 'Fifteen Years into Hospitaller Rule, A Study of the Acts of Notary Juliano Muscat 1545' (BA Hons dissertation, University of Malta, 2002), 81–7.

45 La Mantia, *Antiche Consuetudini*, 41.

46 Kuehn, *Law, Family and Women*, 218.

to her husband, who was still alive when the will was drawn up.[47] Supervision by male authority was also not always noted in other types of notarial deeds. This mostly depended on whether the woman was single, married or a widow, and also on her socio-economic status. A typical example is when the noble Katherina Romana, who was resident in Malta, received the large sum of 480 gold *scudi* in cash in the form of ducats, *doubloons* and gold and silver *scudi* as a 'friendly' loan from Antonio de Celestis. She was not represented by a *mundualdus*, but her title of nobility must have played an important part in the terms of this transaction.[48] A similar case is a contract drawn up in Messina, Sicily and later ratified in Malta. In this instance the most noble *Donna* Juana de Manuele, Duchess of Medina Celi and Vice-Queen of Sicily,[49] is documented to have been present for the drawing up of a contract in which she bought a third part of the shares in an armed ship at the cost of 680 *uncie.*[50] A copy of this contract is found among the acts of the Maltese Notary Placido Abela. In an additional note the notary states that he has read the contents of the contract word for word to the most noble Josephus de Alagona, one of the contracting parties who held another third part in the ship and its armaments. Josephus was in Malta at the time and he ratified the deed, while promising not to alienate his third part of the shareholding.

Other examples include those relating to the appointment of procurators,[51] money loan contracts,[52] donations, sale,[53] and purchase[54] and lease[55] of property. However, despite the fact that such cases were not uncommon, the general trend in business transactions concerning women indicates that they were accompanied by

47 NAV, R 229/29, fols 1934–1949 (14.v.1615); NAV, R 196A/1, fol. 1 ([?].i.1500).

48 NAV, R 206/7, fols 190v–191 (22.vii.1543). As a form of security to cover this loan the woman pledged a house and four slaves.

49 Juana Manuel de Noroña y Portugal (c. 1520–68) was the daughter of Sancho de Noronha, second count of Faro. In 1541 she married Juan de la Cerda (c. 1514–75), fourth duke of Medina Celi, who was appointed Viceroy of Sicily in 1557 by Philip II of Spain, a post he kept till 1564. S. Fink de Backer, *Widowhood in Early Modern Spain, Protectors, Proprietors and Patrons* (Leidon, 2010), Genealogy Chart XI, 268.

50 NAV, MS 514/1, n.f. (9.xi.1559).

51 NAV, MS 514/1, n.f. (19.iv.1560). Agatha, a widow from both her first marriage with Giovanni Caruana, and then from her second marriage with Notary Giovanni Rapa (whose registers are still to be found at the Notarial Archives, Valletta under MS 1033 (1535–47), appointed Giovanni Luca Abela as her procurator to act as a debt collector. NAV, R 224/1, fol. 76v (16.viii.1540), *Donna* Martina Deperalta, widow of Antonio appointed Pietro Deperalta and Pietro Decapdevilla as her procurators to carry out business for her in the Castle of Tripoli.

52 NAV, MS 514/1, n.f. (28.ii.1560), Giovanni Carlo Merulla declared to be in debt with respect to a friendly loan amounting to 80 *scudi* at the rate of 12 *tarí* per *scudo* which he borrowed from Lucia, wife of Georgio de Johane Curtina; NAV, R 202/5, fol. 87v (19.xi.1540), Johanna, wife of a captive and Guglirada, wife of Philippi, were in debt with Catherina, wife of Ambroxi Calabresi for the sum of 12 gold ducats.

53 NAV, R 202/2, fol. 81v (22.xi,1537); R 173/3, fol. 12v (8.iv.1538).

54 NAV, R 224/1, fol. 128 (29.i.1540 *ab inc*); R 202/11, fol. 122v (17.x.1546); R 202/7, fols 212–212v (13.viii.1543).

55 NAV, R 196/1, Section A, fol. 33 (15.iii.1533).

a male representative or, in the case of married women, that the husband usually appeared on behalf of his wife or gave his wife the authority to enter into contracts.

The marriage contract and its implications for women's economic activities

There may have been many reasons for the active and frequent participation of women in business deals. However, it is pertinent to note that marriage contracts were an important instrument, both before and after 1530, in giving women property rights which affected deals in trade and commerce. Women owned two types of property: dowries and paraphernal properties, the former being the woman's share of her parents' wealth and the latter being property over which she had complete control and which was not part of the dowry. The administration of the dowry was transferred to the husband upon marriage through a notarial act which regulated the parameters within which he could manage this asset. The terms and conditions set in pre-nuptial contracts entered into between the spouses' two families were crucial in establishing the extent to which a woman could control property received from a dowry.

The evidence contained in notarial acts points mainly to four customs which were mentioned by notaries when formalising marriage contracts: (i) those made *vel juxta leges Latinorum* or *alla Latina*, (ii) those contracted *vel juxta Graecorum leges* or *alla Greca*, (iii) those made *juxta usum Romanorum* or *alla Romana* and (iv) those which stipulated simply that the contract was made according to the marriage customs prevailing in Malta. Analysis of various marriage contracts reveals that those made *alla Greca* or *alla Romana* in actual fact referred to the same type of agreement. This may be confirmed from various marriage contracts drawn up at different periods, like that of Agatha Pace and Blasio Bezzina in 1562,[56] or that of Marietta Cassar drawn up much later in 1595, which stated that the marriage contract was made '*ad morem ritum et consuetudinem Romanorum quod vulgalitur dicunt alla greca sive alla Romana*' (according to the Roman ceremony and customs which in the common language is known as *alla greca* or *alla Romana*).[57]

A marriage contract made according to either of these customs did not carry a religious or cultural distinction, the main difference being an economic one. Although there were various regional variations, the laws of Palermo[58] give a good indication of the main distinction between a contract of marriage made according to the Latin custom and that made according to the Greek custom. In clause 41, under the heading *De prohibita alienatione dodarii et bonorum dotalium*, it is stated that in agreements made under the Greek custom, dowry goods which were given to the husband by the wife or her family could not be sold, even if the husband had the consent of his wife, since these did not belong to him but to his wife and her heirs. However, this prohibition did not apply to citizens who lived according to the Latin

56 NAV, R 376/44, Part I, fol. 114 (29.ix.1562).

57 NAV, R 508/8, fol. 701 (13.iv.1595).

58 G. Naso issued an edition of these laws in 1478 and they were subsequently re-issued in various other editions. See La Mantia, *Antiche Consuetudini*, 165 n. 1.

custom. Marriage agreements made according to the Latin formula established that if the couple had children, or else after the elapse of one year from the consummation of their marriage, the dowry goods could be mixed and consequently considered as part of the mutual possessions of husband and wife.[59]

An analysis of contracts which solely and specifically state that the contract was drawn up according to the Maltese custom established that this type of contract was halfway between the Greek and the Latin custom. Although, like the Latin pattern, it was based on the tripartite division of goods,[60] in most of the cases analysed the partition was not to take place before the children of the marriage had reached the age of fifteen. Thus it may be said that during the interim period, or if the couple were childless, just as in the Greek custom the separation of the couple's assets was a requisite.[61] It is pertinent to note that the formula '*secundum usum et consuetudinem Insule Melivetane*' seems to have been used frequently as a safety valve to safeguard the interests of both parties, and accordingly it is even found in contracts drawn up according to the Latin, Greek or Roman customs.

Notarial acts of the medieval[62] and early modern period indicate that in Malta the Greek or Maltese customs were the preferred types for marriage contracts. Analysis of marriage contracts taken from the registers of two notaries, namely Nicolò de Agatiis[63] and Placido Abela,[64] and others taken randomly,[65] points to this preference having grown much stronger after the arrival of the Order, since no contract explicitly documents the use of the Latin type of marriage agreement. Instead it is indicated that the contract was made according to either the Greek or Maltese custom. For example, Notary de Agatiis drew up three marriage contracts in the year 1539–40, two *alla greca* and one *secundum usum meliteum* [*sic*], while in the year 1540–41 he drew up another two, both made *alla greca*.[66]

59 La Mantia, *Antiche Consuetudini*, 189. One should note, however, that there were many regional variations. La Mantia, *Storia della Legislazione*, 156; La Mantia, *Antiche consuetudini*, 190.

60 Micallef, *Diritto Municipale di Malta*, vol. 1, 321.

61 Following these legal limitations, most contracts included similar clauses as the following: '*Quod quidem matrimonium presenti contrahentes declaraverunt et declarant illud contraxisse … Juxta usum melitesi hac tam conditione … quam hinc ad annos quindecim ad hodie numerates natis filijs ex ipso matrimonio vel non natis bona utrius [?] sponsi numquam interea confundantur*' (that indeed this matrimony the present contracting parties declared and declare that they contract … according to the custom of Malta here under the condition [that] … from henceforth to fifteen years from today whether children are born out of this matrimony or not the goods of anyone of the spouses [?] at no time must in the meantime be mixed). NAV, R 4/1, fol. 137v (30.xii.1557); see also R 202/6, fols 68v–70 (7.xii.1541); R 514/1, n.f. (24.iii.1558); R 4/1, fols 28–28v (1.xi.1557).

62 Fiorini (ed.), *Documentary Sources of Maltese History, Part I, No. 1*, Docs 139, 152, 234, 274, 302, 341.

63 These included R 202/4 (1539–40) and R 202/5 (1540–41).

64 NAV, R 4/1, fols 137–139 (30.xii.1557), fols 13–15v (10.x.1557), fols 127v–31 (1.xi.1557), fols 39v–42 (15.xi.1557), fols 22–26 (29.x.1557).

65 Once again the choice of registers was done on the aforementioned criteria, mainly that the notary practised in Birgu, that the volume consulted was in a good state of preservation and thirdly that both Maltese and Rhodiot notaries were represented in the sample.

66 NAV, R 202/5, fols 172v–173v (21.iv.1541), fols 268–274v (7.viii.1541).

All the contracting parties in the above contracts held the title of *Honorabilis* or *Honoratus* and transferred immoveable property as part of the promised dowry.[67] However, the donation of land as part of dowries can also be traced back to persons who did not hold a title. Of course, titles could have been omitted by the notary, and thus it is difficult to identify people's social standing in such contracts. The contracts of Placido Abela for the year 1557–58 include six marriage contracts: four made according to the Maltese custom and two according to the Greek/Roman custom. Once again, the contracting parties held the title of *Honorabilis* and transferred immoveable property, except in one contract, that entered into by a Knight of the Order, one *Fra.* Gullielmo Couppier who promised a lavish dowry to his manumitted slave Victoria amounting to 281 *scudi* and also including two slaves.[68]

The contracts analysed at random[69] were also found to be drawn up according to either the Maltese or Greek custom. Of particular interest were the records of Notary Nicolò de Agatiis for the period September to December 1546.[70] During this period this notary drew up five marriage contracts; three were made *alla greca*, one according to the Maltese custom and one according to the Rhodian custom.[71] The latter had similar conditions as contracts made by the Greek custom, so could well have been the same type of contract. The contracting parties in all cases, with one exception, held the title of either *Honorabilis* or *Nobilis*, and all but one included the transfer of immoveable property. The exception was an agreement drawn up according to the Greek custom between two Sicilians, the bride coming from Mazara and the groom from Syracuse. Although no immoveable property was transferred, the promised dowry consisted of various valuable items amounting to over 35 *scudi*. Preference for such contracts sheds light on the importance given by families to keeping the family patrimony within the respective lines of inheritance. The bride's family also imposed such conditions to make it difficult for the husband to alienate property without the consent of the wife. This resulted in the husband being more restricted in conducting any form of business with the goods brought over by the wife as part of her dowry.

The arrival of the Knights did not change the laws regarding dowries or inheritance which affected a woman's legal persona. However, the restrictions must have greatly affected the flow of commerce, especially when wives were not present to give their consent. As is shown below, even though these types of marriage contract restricted husbands from alienating property outright, husbands are still found to be drawing up contracts alienating the wife's property on condition that, according to a 'new law', the wife ratified the contract in the first instance. The preference for these types of marriage contract is to be seen in the light of the ever-increasing need for

67 NAV, R 202/4, fols 191v–193v (29.iv.1540), fols 237v–239v (4.vii.1540), fols 277–278 (11.viii.1540).

68 NAV, R 4/1, fols 22–26 (29.x.1557).

69 NAV, R 202/6, fol. 68v (7.xii.1541), fols 52–53 (7.xi.1541); R 224/1 fols 424 (17.i.1543); MS 514/1 n.f. (24.iii.1558), n.f. (14.viii.1558), n.f. (17.iv.1558), n.f. (13.vi.1558), n.f. (13.iv.1558), n.f. (28.xii.1559).

70 R 202/11, fols 19v–21v (26.x.1546), fols 23–25 (31.x.1546), fols 29v–31 (11.xi.1546), fols 40–41v (20.xi.1546), fols 55–57 (3.xii.1546).

71 NAV, R 202/11, fols 23–25 (31.x.1546).

ready cash that was created by the steady growth of a money economy, especially in the harbour area. The sale of immoveable property which often included the right of redemption was greatly increasing and was a common means of securing loans which at times were repaid against usurious gains.

From a court order referred to in an act dated 1487, it transpires that women knew well the rights which such contracts gave them; as a result, they defended the control which they enjoyed over their private property. This was especially so where payment of debts entered into by their husbands was concerned. In one particular contract Granata, the widow of Johannes de Falzono, was reported to have threatened to appeal against a court ruling which adjudged that a slave belonging to her late husband should be transferred to one of his creditors to make amends for bad debt relating to the sale of some oil. In her appeal Granata stated that her marriage had been contracted *alla Romana* and thus the slave was rightfully hers, since it had been part of her dowry, and could not be taken away from her.[72] The dispute was ultimately settled by the payment of a sum of money agreed to by both parties, and the slave returned to his rightful owner.[73]

In another court case Ysolda, widow of Zaccarias Bonnici, sued Stephanus Barbara regarding the division of a field which Ysolda had received as part of her dowry, part of which had been sold to the said Stephanus by her late husband. The Court of First Appeal heard the case[74] and its verdict was that Stephanus should give to Ysolda a half undivided part of the field, plus three *pensas cuctonj mahalugij*.[75] He was also ordered to construct a dividing wall at his own expense.[76] These settlement cases between women and their male opponents are revealing of the fact that late medieval and early modern Maltese women had property rights which they guarded jealously, notwithstanding the strong social bias of their legal disability. The contracts also highlight the legal limitations in terms of the alienation of a woman's dowry by the husband. Although the dowry was passed to the man upon marriage and he had the right to control and invest it, technically it was the sole property of the woman, and the husband was entitled to only half the interest it bore. He had no right to alienate it outright, and it was passed to the woman after his death, or else passed to her heirs after her demise.[77] Juxtaposing this element in Maltese marriage contracts and the English medieval concept of *coverture*,[78] one may note the advantage that Maltese

72 Fiorini (ed.), *Documentary Sources of Maltese History, Part I, No. 1*, Doc. 152. Also published in Wettinger, *The Jews of Malta*, Doc. 46.

73 Fiorini (ed.), *Documentary Sources of Maltese History, Part I, No. 1*, Doc. 274.

74 *Curiam primarum appellacionum*. Fiorini (ed.), *Documentary Sources of Maltese History, Part I, No. 1*, Doc. 64.

75 Carded cotton, cotton with seeds removed. Fiorini (ed.), *Documentary Sources of Maltese History, Part I, No. 1*, 342.

76 Fiorini (ed.), *Documentary Sources of Maltese History, Part I, No. 1*, Doc. 64.

77 McGough, 'Women, Private Property', 37–8.

78 While through marriage a woman's legal persona was engulfed by that of her husband, the unmarried woman had the right to make contracts in her own name and to own property. The weight played by *couverture* has been recently reappraised and fresh studies have in fact proved that this law could be manipulated. See T. Stretton & K. J. Kesselring (eds), *Married Women and the Law. Couverture in England and the Common Law World* (Ithaca, NY, 2013).

women had over their English counterparts. This is better explained in the following words from the writings of Sarah Kirkham Chapone, an eighteenth-century British feminist, who stated that 'a woman by our Laws alienates all her own Property so entirely by Marriage, that if she brought an hundred thousand Pounds in money, she cannot bequeath one single Penny'.[79]

Women in the economy of a port city

Debates about women's participation in the labour market have claimed that family functions attributed to women as child bearers, child carers and providers of domestic labour were the chief reason why it was hard, and at times even impossible, for women to pursue activities in highly skilled work which required specific training and experience.[80] An inability to provide continuity of service led to women taking lower-paid jobs which did not require particular skills, thus making it easier to fill a vacant job. John Hajnal argued in favour of the distinctive uniqueness of West European women, who married at a relatively later age than their counterparts in other regions.[81] Marriage was thus regarded as the point of formation of an economically independent household, unlike in other societies, where women married very young.[82] The latter usually moved directly from their father's household to that of their husband's father, their father-in-law still holding the headship. The woman thus retained a subordinate position at least until her widowhood.[83] Another feature which Hajnal associated with the tendency to marry later was that a good number of adolescent males and females worked as domestic servants.[84] In view of the above, the question arises whether the position of Maltese

79 S. K. Chapone, *Hardships of the English Laws in Relation to Wives* (London, 1735), 29–30, quoted from J. G. Sperling, 'Marriage, Kinship, and Property in Portuguese Testaments (1649–1650)', in J. G. Sperling & S. Kelly Wray (eds), *Across the Religious Divide, Women, Property, and Law in the Wider Mediterranean (ca. 1300–1800)* (New York and London, 2010), 158–74: 170.

80 R. M. Smith, 'Women's Work and Marriage in Pre-Industrial England: Some Speculations', in S. Cavaciocchi (ed.), *La Donna nell'Economia Secc. XIII–XVIII* (Florence, 1990), 31–55: 33.

81 J. Hajnal, 'European Marriage Patterns in Perspective', in D. V. Glass and D. E. C. Eversley (eds) *Population in History: Essays on Historical Demography* (London, 1965), 101–43. For a critical review of this theory see G. Fertig, *The Hajnal Thesis before Hajnal: The Pre-history of European Marriage Patterns* (2004), http://www.uni-muenster.de/imperial/md/content/hist_sem_swg/personen/fertig_g/download/hajnal.pdf (accessed 13 March 2016).

82 See also La Mantia, *Storia Della legislazione*, 141.

83 Smith, 'Women's Work and Marriage in Pre-Industrial England', in Cavaciocchi (ed.), *La Donna nell'Economia*, 31–55: 34–5.

84 Hajnal's theory was contested in the late 1970s for what concerns the Florentine context, see A. Molho, J. Kirshner & A. S. Morrison, 'Life Cycle Events in 15th Century Florence: Records of the Monte delle Doti', *American Journal of Epidemiology*, 106 (1977), 487–92. It has more recently been called into question again, especially with regard to the European marriage pattern and its impact on the economy: see, for example, D. Curtis, 'An Agro-town Bias? Re-examining the Micro-demographic Model for Southern Italy in the

women followed a similar pattern to that described by Hajnal, or whether the local scene offered different dimensions. To what extent were Maltese women involved in economic activities which went beyond their traditionally assigned roles?

Lack of contemporary data, such as tax records, which are an exceptional source for the history of labour,[85] makes it extremely difficult to estimate and categorise Malta's workforce during this period. Chancery and other official documents from the period of the Knights do not record the participation of women as part of the island's workforce. Therefore, although their contribution affected economic activities in various sectors, their voice in history is silent. Women's participation in various occupations such as agricultural labour, domestic help, as hostel keepers, retailers, weavers, petty financiers, administrators of their husband's affairs and in numerous other jobs is for the most part not recorded.

The female workforce thus tends to be invisible, except for some sporadic mentions or else when reference is made indirectly in legal documents. Notarial documents and court records provide a partial window onto women's place in the economic life of Malta in the sixteenth century, since in these instances women often declared their particular function and status in society. The pitfall in consulting such documents is that they provide no reliable statistical representation, and while some activities may have been recorded due to specific circumstances, others could well have been totally ignored. For this reason, it must be stressed that the cases presented here do not constitute the main picture. They are referred to here because they illustrate actual circumstances; although some may not have been numerous or common, the fact that they are documented means that they cannot be excluded from historical interpretation.

In spite of the prevailing patriarchal environment, cultural obstacles and various legal restrictions, numerous documents show that women played more than a passive role in business-related activities. It is important to note that great importance was given to feminine virginity, thus limiting women's freedom of movement and choice of work.[86] However, as noted above, the local law contained some compensatory features in terms of preserving women's property rights. The prevailing laws provided for a daughter to have a share in the property of her family of birth, through either inheritance or dowry.[87] According to the laws of Messina, if the father or mother

Eighteenth Century', https://www.academia.edu/7913631/An_agro-town_bias_Re-examining_the_micro-demographic_model_for_Southern_Italy_in_the_eighteenth_century (accessed 13 March 2016); P. P. Viazzo, 'What's so Special about the Mediterranean? Thirty Years of Research on Household and Family in Italy', *Continuity and Change*, 18:1 (2003), 111–37 and S. Ogilvie and T. Dennison's recent discussion in 'Does the European Marriage Pattern Explain Economic Growth?', *The Journal of Economic History*, 74 (2014), 651–93.

85 See for example D. Herlihy, 'Women's Work in the Towns of Traditional Europe', in D. Herlihy (ed.), *Women, Family, and Society in Medieval Europe: Historical Essays* (Oxford, 1995), 103–30.

86 Herlihy, 'Women's Work in the Towns', 119.

87 '*Viro et uxore dividere cum filiis, tercia pars bonorum debetur patri, altera matri, reliqua tertia filio vel filiis*' (The husband and the wife ought to divide [their property] with the children, one third ought to go to the father, the other (third) to the mother and the remaining one third to the son or children). La Mantia, *Antiche Consuetudini*, 35–42.

died intestate, all children living with the surviving parent had the right to an equal share.[88] A contract dated 16 September 1559[89] goes even further than this, since the property of the late Petrus Mifsud who died *intestato* was equally divided between his children, namely Leonore, Gaspare and Aghata, all of whom were married,[90] and Antonella, who was a widow. This illustrates a local scenario in which even married women living outside the family unit shared in the inheritance.[91] As discussed earlier, marriage laws provided for the protection of this property and did not permit its alienation by the husband without the consent of the wife; acquisitions or losses made by the couple during marriage were to be equally shared; and usually, widows were appointed as guardians of their minor children, giving them the chance to invest the inheritance.

When considering women's role in the Maltese economy during the first decades of the Knights' rule, it is important to remember that Birgu had been rapidly transformed from a mere hamlet into an overcrowded cosmopolitan port city which was home to one of the most active naval powers in the Mediterranean. Its population was in various respects different from that found in other villages and towns of Malta. Primarily, being the new seat of government it housed the members of the Order, a male community made up of approximately 500 knights[92] who had to accommodate themselves in an extremely small area. Further, Fiorini argues that the Rhodiot community which followed the Order to Malta was made up mostly of men. His calculations suggest that the Rhodiot population comprised nearly 300 males and approximately 120 females.[93]

The constant incoming wave of foreign merchants and seafarers further tipped the scale in terms of Birgu's predominantly male community. The sudden and heavy increase in Birgu's population created a variety of economic needs which presented employment opportunities for both genders, not only for the Maltese but also for

88 '*Praemortuo patre vel matre ab intestate, filio vel filiis viventibus cum patre vel matre superstite, tercia pars praemortui cedi filiis. Et sic iidem filii habent duas tercias partes bonorum unam debitam sibi iure naturae, alteram parentis praemortui*' (When the father or the mother has predeceased intestate, and the son or children are alive with the surviving father or mother, the third part of the predeceased is ceded to the children. And thus, these same children have two third parts of the goods, one part due to them by right of nature, the other of the predeceased parent). La Mantia, *Antiche Consuetudini*, 36.

89 NAV, MS 514/1, n.f. (16.ix.1559).

90 Another example which testifies that females had a share in their parents' inheritance is a late fifteenth-century contract wherein Catherina, the pregnant wife of Albanus de Urso, drew up her will since she feared the potentially fatal consequences of childbirth. Although Catherina had already mothered two sons by a previous marriage, as her universal heir she left the unborn child, be it male or female. To her other sons she left the '*comuni substancia bonorum matrimonij*' which she had enjoyed from her first marriage with their father. Fiorini (ed.), *Documentary Sources of Maltese History, Part I, No. 1*, Doc. 41.

91 Unfortunately, this was the only document encountered during this research relating to the inheritance of an *intestato*. Future research might confirm or disprove this hypothesis.

92 It is difficult to assess the exact number of knights stationed in Malta at any one time. Williams, '*Sacra Militia*', in Fusaro et al., *Trade and Cultural Exchange*, 139–56: 140.

93 Fiorini, 'The Rhodiot Community of Birgu', in Mallia-Milanes (ed.), *Library of Mediterranean History*, vol. 1, 183–241.

foreigners. As is discussed below, women were active participants in most areas and not only addressed the basic needs of the Birgu population but also contributed to the economic well-being of the new city. Further, through their consent in alienating property against cash payments they played an important role in providing the island's economy with a steady flow of cash.

Domestic service

Domestic service provided one of the links between the economies of city and countryside.[94] Rural residents travelled from the countryside to the city to sell their produce, or perhaps to hire out their labour as domestic servants. Unfortunately, contracts relating to the hiring of domestic help by both men and women are not common in notarial records for this period. Only the odd one or two are to be found in any volume of a particular notary.[95] Moreover, most people would not have chosen to regulate their employment through a legal contract, but through a verbal agreement, especially in the case of short-term jobs. However, the few records that have been identified give some limited insight on the conditions of work stipulated by employers of domestic help.

In the contracts analysed (only two for women), help was hired for a defined period of time and the servant was liable for any related expenses in case of breach of contract. The work required no training other than the personal experience acquired by the employee by helping with his or her family's daily chores. The two women's contracts stipulated that the employee should lodge at the employer's residence, clothes and food being provided by the employer. This type of work could be quite convenient, both for parents who hired out[96] their children and for married women, because although it was not well paid it was respectable and exempted the employee or her/his guardian from living costs. A better appreciation of these benefits can be noted in a contract dated 25 July 1558,[97] in which *Hon. Mulier* Angelina, wife of *Hon. Magistri* Francesco Romedio, hired out her services to *Discreta Mulier* Hyerene Vallistera, a resident of Birgu. The agreement was to last for the whole of Vallistera's life, provided that the work was performed honestly and licitly. In return, Angelina

94 Wiesner-Hanks, *Women and Gender*, 112; Cassar, *Daughters of Eve*, 152–7.

95 One here has to keep in mind that the abundance of notarial documentation and the difficulty which at times they present to the reader does not make it possible to give a complete analysis of these types of contracts, especially in view of the restricted time permitted for the research. One has also to keep in mind that notarial registers differ in their contents, in so far as one might come across a volume which has an abundance of a particular type of contract while another volume pertaining to the same period might not include even one contract relating to the same topic. Thus in these circumstances any generalisations are best avoided. The volumes chosen for this research were NAV, R 224/1 (1537–43); R 202/4 (1539–40); R 202/5 (1540–41); R 206/7 (1543); MS 514/1 (1557–60). These were selected because all four notaries practised in Birgu, two were Maltese and two were Rhodiot and the volumes are in a good state of preservation.

96 V. La Mantia, *Antiche Consuetudini delle Città di Sicilia*, with an introduction by A. Romano (Messina, 1993), 21.

97 NAV, MS 514/1, n.f. (25.vii.1558).

was allowed to live together with her husband and their son in her employer's house. The full and final payment for this work was 25 *scudi*, five of which were given as a down payment on the drawing up of the agreement. The remainder of the sum was to be paid after the employer's death.

The names of the persons involved in this particular contract are important indicators of Birgu's ever-growing community. The surnames of both the employer and the employee have a foreign connotation, which suggests that the contracting parties may have been attracted to the island by the presence of the Hospitaller Order. Other important indicators are the titles *Honorabilis* and *Magister*, since, as has been noted the former usually referred to landed proprietors while *Magister* was a title given to craftsmen. In this case *Magister* Francesco, Angelina's husband, could well have tried to establish himself in Birgu in order to carry out his craft. Angelina's work would have provided the family not only with extra income but also with the necessary shelter in a town where the exorbitant cost of property could compromise a family's standard of living.[98]

In another contract Marietta, daughter of the late Johannes Greci from Constantinople, and her mother Caterina, widow of the late Pancrati Derando, undertook to lease the services of eighteen-year-old Marietta to Lucretia de Caxaro, a Maltese resident in Birgu married to *Hon.* Constantini Zograf from Rhodes.[99] The agreement was to last six years, during which time Lucretia was to provide Marietta with food and clothes. At the end of the six years, by which time Marietta would have been twenty-four, Lucretia promised to give the servant 2 *uncie* (equivalent to 5 *scudi*) and various other items, including a cloak and a bed according to the Maltese market custom.[100] Another condition was that if Lucretia died before the end of the six years Marietta would still be entitled to the money and the goods. Marietta's mother stood surety for her daughter's obligation in this contract and elected a *mundualdus* in this respect. Marietta, who was not married, could well have entered into this agreement in order to make enough for a humble dowry. An interesting feature of this contract is the notary's inclusion of the place of origin of the contracting parties. This illustrates well the increasingly cosmopolitan society of Birgu, which contrasts sharply with the medieval Birgu described by Wettinger when he stated that it was probably 'a humdrum commercial, maritime and perhaps fishing centre without any particular, prestigious, social connotations'.[101]

What were men being offered as terms of employment as domestic servants? Were their conditions similar to those of the above-mentioned women? These questions are difficult to address and answer with any accuracy, particularly in view of the fact that cash payments were often combined with payments in kind. Although

98 For the housing problem in Birgu during the early period of Hospitaller stay, refer to Borg Cardona, 'The *Officio delle Case*', 39–69; Fiorini, 'Demographical Aspects', in Bugeja et al., *Birgu: A Maltese Maritime City*, 219–54: 228–43; Abela, 'Port Activities', 180–5.

99 NAV, MS 514/1, fol. 26–26v (21.i.1558).

100 Most probably this was a bed given to brides as part of their dowry, but the exact definition is not available.

101 Wettinger, 'The Castrum Maris', in Bugeja et al., *Birgu: A Maltese Maritime City*, 31–71: 59.

few sources are available, by adopting a comparative approach and evaluating the income and working conditions of both genders a wider perspective can be obtained. A contract from 1560 stated that a certain Mariano from Birkirkara, who was thirteen years of age, was hired out by his father to provide domestic services to *Hon.* Oliverios Felici.[102] The agreed wage was 2 *scudi* per year in addition to food, shelter and clothing. Mariano's father was also bound to guarantee the good and honest services of his son. In case of any breach of contract which obliged Oliverio to find a new servant, any expenses incurred were to be borne by the boy's father. In yet another contract a Neapolitan hired out his services as a domestic worker for 10 *scudi* per year in addition to shelter, food and clothes.[103]

In 1535 Alvarus Fernando from Lisbon hired out his services to Knight *Fra.* Antonio Tavares for two years at the monthly rate of 1 gold ducat.[104] Salvus Chabela, who came from the small Maltese village of Pasqualino, hired his services to Antonio Scarpello for eight months.[105] A significant difference in the conditions of work of this contract, setting it apart from the others, was that Salvus was bound to serve his master not only in his house but also on his ship when Scarpello was travelling. The agreed sum for this work was 4 gold ducats (4 *scudi* 3 *tarì*) together with food and shelter. This work involved much greater risks for the employee and the pay was considerably higher than that of any of the women whose contracts are analysed here. However, the pay was also much lower than that of the Neapolitan or Portuguese domestic servants mentioned above. Were Maltese workers paid less than their foreign counterparts? If this was the case, was it because they lacked particular skills? Further investigation of the primary sources might shed light on such matters.

From the above-mentioned contracts it seems that vacancies for domestic help in Birgu were mostly filled by foreign men and women, the latter most probably having followed their families to the island. One must also bear in mind that Birgu had a slave community which performed domestic duties, thus making such paid employment less available. Maltese women seem to have been much more secluded from society and averse to grasping the new job opportunities that presented themselves in Birgu. As was discussed in Chapter Two, most women would have been productive in their own families, either helping out in the fields or doing some other form of domestic work. The arrival of the Knights created an increased demand for agricultural products, so that farmers, labourers and their families benefitted from the establishment of the Knights, despite being cut off from the capital city. Young women had no choice of course; everything depended on the

102 NAV, MS 514/1, n.f. (3.i.1560).
103 NAV, R 206/7, fols 115 (23.iv.1543).
104 The exact words used in these contracts read 'locat operas servicia sue persone' and the type of work is described as 'sevicijs domesticis' [sic]. NAV, R 202/4, fol. 42 (22.x.1535). In NAV, MS 778/4, Part II, fols 96–97v (2.iii.1563), it is stated that one ducat was equal to 13 *tarì*. Similarly in NAV, R 202/1, fols 41–41v (7.vi.1536), where Didaco Hernandes, a Spanish merchant, sold a thirty-year-old black slave for the agreed price of 28 gold ducats, which were to be paid by the provision of four *cantari* of salted meat at the rate of 70 *tarì per cantaro*, and the remaining 6 gold ducats and 6 *tarì* in cash. This makes the gold ducat equivalent to approximately 13 *tarì*.
105 NAV, R 224/1, fol. 194v (4.viii.1541); see also fol. 172v (30.v.1540).

woman's family and on village traditions, and on whether work was available within a short radius.[106] Since Birgu was a male-dominated society comprised mostly of 'foreigners' – Knights, Rhodiots and merchants – families would have looked down on any jobs which could compromise a woman's honour, especially in an area where prostitution thrived.[107]

The business-oriented woman

Throughout sixteenth-century Europe the possibilities for women to acquire apprenticeship in some form of male-associated craft were very limited. Apart from restrictions imposed by the guilds, such limitations were mostly due to prejudiced perceptions of women's mental and physical abilities.[108] Further, it was perceived that a virtuous woman should be chaste, and once married she should dedicate herself to her family by providing companionship for her husband, looking after his household and raising his children. Virginity was a requisite for a blessed and honourable marriage, thus girls were kept under the close scrutiny of their relatives and had practically no opportunity to receive formal training in a trade or to expand their knowledge. Although women were viewed to be adequately suited to performing tasks such as midwifery and spinning, they were very often judged unfit to work in jobs which required concentration and strength.[109]

It is in this context that contracts relating to women skilled in particular crafts who ran their own business must be evaluated. One Clara Laspatara *alias* Donatalj who lived in Birgu in 1540 provides a striking example which questions the non-practising of men's crafts by women.[110] Clara, faithful to her name (or, most likely, nickname), was a sword maker (*spatara* from *spada*). Accordingly, before Notary de Agatiis she agreed to instruct Hieronymus de Paulo de Bluiso from Syracuse in the art of making and decorating swords. The apprenticeship was to last five years, during which time Clara was to provide her apprentice with clothes, food and lodging, in addition to 2 gold *scudi*. Thus, in addition to being self-employed in a traditional male job and supplying the market with such an important product targeted at an elite clientele, Clara also provided opportunities for paid trainee work.

106 Cassar, *Daughters of Eve*, 156.

107 Cassar, *Society, Culture and Identity in Early Modern Malta*, 134–5. Da Molin suggests the same for the Italian south, where it was almost 'better to starve' than to go into service, since this was considered a disgrace. G. Da Molin, 'Family Forms and Domestic Service in Southern Italy from the Seventeenth to the Nineteenth Century', *Journal of Family History*, 15 (1990), 504–27.

108 For what concerns the assumptions on restrictions on female labour refer to A. Bellavitis, 'Donne, cittadinanza e corporazioni tra Medioevo ed età moderna: ricerche in corso', in N. M. Filippini, T. Plebani & A. Scattigno (eds), *Corpi e Storia: Donne e uomini dal mondo antico all'età contemporanea* (Viella, Rome, 2002), 87–104. Bellavitis tends to underscore the differences between various geographical areas, and that in certain cities and trades women continued to play an important role.

109 Wiesner-Hanks, *Women and Gender*, 104.

110 Clara was not married. Bezzina, 'Early Hospitaller Birgu', 59.

Similarly to Clara, widows or single women are found involved in economic activities[111] and, at times, negotiated side by side with the men without the use of a male guardian.[112] One such example is Elena Morenam, a Rhodiot woman who was personally present for a contract of obligation in which she bought 3½ *scudi* worth of black cloth from Johannes Ghymes.[113] On the same day Ghymes sold 3 *scudi* worth of the same cloth to Domenica, daughter of Paulo Baldacchini, and on this occasion too the woman was not represented by a *mundualdus*.[114] In another instance Clara Pornicudine, a Rhodiot woman, lent 41½ *scudi* to Marchus Schembri from Zabbar, which was to be repaid on Clara's request.[115] What happened if women were not paid their dues? Did they present their case in court? The answer is in the affirmative, as is verified by a document wherein *Hon.* Helena Morena filed a case[116] at the *Magna Curia Castellania* in respect of the non-payment of a loan by *Hon.* Georgi Stupoglo.[117] The court ordered the immediate repayment of the loan. However, Georgi was not in a position to pay and so he was sent to row on the galleys of the Hospitaller Order. It seems that Helena was unhappy with the outcome of this case. She drew up a contract in which she absolved Georgi from all dues and stated that she had done so through a merciful act and *pro remedio anima sua* (to pay for her sins).

Widows are also found conducting various business deals varying from the sale or purchase of property or commodities to advancing cash loans. An analysis of these notarial acts shows the active participation of foreign women who had established themselves in Malta. Among a total of seventeen single women and widows found in the acts of Notary de Agatiis for 1538–40 the country of origin of four is not stated, two were Maltese and eleven were foreign, nine of these being Rhodiot.[118] One such Rhodiot was *Hon. Donna* Catherina, a widow who while in Syracuse had financially assisted her co-citizen Gaspare Balurdo to be redeemed from captivity. Just one month after the arrival of the Order of St John, on 26 November 1530,[119] the same Catherina is found in Birgu receiving a gold chain with 126 *maglieti*[120] and a gold ring with a pearl[121] as payment for redemption services effected through the work of Nicola Pirno as stipulated in an earlier contract drawn up in Syracuse.

Marriage for a woman did not necessarily mean the end of her life as a

111 The acts of Notary Nicolò de Agatiis for the years 1538–40 include a total of twenty-five contracts from a total of 665 involving widows or single women (3.8%). Bezzina, 'Early Hospitaller Birgu', Table 3.4, 57. The acts of de Agatiis for the year 1540–41 include a total 2.9% of acts involving widows or single women (excluding marriage contracts).

112 Bezzina, 'Early Hospitaller Birgu', 57.

113 NAV, R 202/5, fol. 21v (6.ix.1540).

114 NAV, R 202/5 fol. 21v (6.ix.1540).

115 NAV, R 206/7, fols 27–27v (13.ii.1543).

116 The Notarial act contains minimal information about the case, therefore it is not known whether the woman filed the case through a male representative.

117 NAV, R 206/7, fol. 292 (12.x.1543).

118 Bezzina, 'Early Hospitaller Birgu', 57.

119 NAV, R 439/1, fols 18–18v (26.xi.1530).

120 This could mean that it was worked in a weave or twist with three or more strands.

121 '*unam catenam auri cum maglietis centum viginti sex et unum anulum auri in quo est ligata una perla.*'

contributor to the financial well-being of her family. In early modern times many women acquired their husband's skills in a particular trade or else participated in a family-run business. In one notarial document *Donna* Lorenza, mother of the *aromatario Nob.* Franco de Nicolò, sought to hire the services of a shop assistant. She owned the shop jointly with her son, and the two undertook to give the employee 16 *tarì* per month together with food, drink and clothes.[122] In August 1545[123] *Hon. Mulier* Catherina bought a house in Birgu from *Hon.* Fava for the price of 35 gold *scudi*. The seller reserved the right of redemption – '*cum carta recuperanti*'[124] – a clear sign that the sale was triggered by a need for liquid cash, which Catherina was able to supply.

In another instance, on 8 November 1541 Madalena Ellum and her husband made a joint undertaking in front of Notary Nicolò de Agatiis in respect of a debt related to the consignment of a quantity of cloth which the couple had bought from a merchant from Lyon.[125] In this case the wife assumed a joint liability with her husband and therefore played the role of business partner more than that of traditional wife. Most probably the declaration of the wife's liability for any debts was necessary in case payment required the alienation of her personal property. The hiring of rooms must also have been a profitable business in an area which was struggling under the continuous inflow of foreign merchants and traders visiting the island on business trips. It seems that *Donna* Catherina, wife of Blasio Aquilina, offered such accommodation, since on 10 April 1560 she appointed Gabriele Codina, a citizen of Palermo, as her procurator and gave him the job of administering a hostel which she owned in the vicinity of the Magisterial Palace in Birgu.[126]

As has already been noted, women were often left in charge of their children's inheritance. This often meant that they had to act as debt collectors and at times even as investors of their children's capital. A case in point is *Nob. Donna* Beatrice de Modica, whose husband left her as the guardian of their son's inheritance. On 16 April 1541 she was recorded as having received part of a larger sum of money due to her late husband which she now had to safeguard for her son's future well-being.[127] Similarly, *Donna* Catherina, widow of Johannes Burlo, 'on behalf of herself and as guardian and on behalf of the son and heir of her late husband',[128] filed a declaration at the notary's office stating that on the first voyage of a ship to the castle of Tripoli she was going to send a fourteen-year-old slave named Maxama to be redeemed for the price of 100 ducats.[129] In another act, Johanna Buhagiar, also the guardian of her

122 NAV, R 4/1, fols 147v–148 (6.ix.1558).

123 NAV, R 439/36, fol. 151 (28.viii.1545).

124 With the right of redemption.

125 NAV, R 202/6, fol. 53 (8.xi.1541).

126 NAV, MS 514/1, n.f. (10.iv.1560). See also R 224/17, fols 510v–511v (14.i.1560). In the late sixteenth century a woman by the name of Louisa ran a hostel in Birgu and was described by her clients as being a 'clever and well dressed business woman'. T. Freller, 'Excellent Accommodation on Moderate Terms: Maltese Inns, Hostels and Hotels in Days of Old', *Treasures of Malta*, 12:2 (2006), 27–32.

127 NAV, R 202/5, fol. 171 (16.iv.1541).

128 '*tam nomine suo prop[ri]o q[ua]nti tutritio nomine filiorum et heredum dicti quondam olim sui virj.*'

129 NAV, R 202/5, fols 124–124v (30.i.1541).

son's inheritance, sold 18 canes' worth of cloth to Georgius Chilia,[130] making sure to mention specifically that she was acting on behalf of her son and her future heirs, and thus the proceeds of the sale benefitted all.

What of mothers who were not married? Do they appear in notarial acts? One such instance is the sale of a house which Margerita, the manumitted slave of the late *Rev.* Philippus de Guevara, sold to Manoli de Lindo.[131] Some details shed light on Margerita's life, as the deed informs us that she had a son, although the father is not mentioned. She is represented in the contract by a *mundualdus* and, although originally she had the status of a slave, having been set free she enjoyed all the privileges of a 'free' Maltese woman. Such documents bring some questions come to mind. Did she inherit the property from the priest, her ex-master? Was her son the son of the late *Rev.* Philippus who had manumitted her before he died? Was this how one section of the marginalised community acquired property and climbed the social ladder? It is perhaps in such cases that the ambiguity of the law comes out more clearly. Through manumission, a person who before had no legal rights was 'admitted' to society by the stroke of a pen. It just required the action of a benevolent master.

Women and transactions in property

Under the prevailing law women could own and inherit property, while husbands had to have the consent of their wives before alienating any property received as part of the wife's dowry or inheritance. These rights empowered women to transfer property through their wills, to make donations *inter vivos* and to authorise the legitimate sale of property. The great majority of women who held real estate did not own large holdings; nonetheless, they could negotiate their small possessions and be financial actors within the island's economy. Widows seem to have been the major benefactors, because they were in a more advantageous position than nubile or married women. Having outlived their husbands, they had more autonomy and were able to sell, purchase, invest, inherit or even remarry and enhance their financial assets.[132] Thus, a wife's role in the family's economic affairs was not confined to mere housewifely duties, nor constantly subordinate to her husband's, but could be invested with responsibilities crucial to her family's prosperity.

Evidence of the married woman's contribution in business deals, whether alongside her husband or as a widow acting alone or jointly with her siblings, is common in notarial acts. A typical case implying more than a simple act of sale is a contract drawn up on 6 May 1525, in which Catherina, wife of Amatore Delia, bought a house in Rabat from Johannes Saliba '*cum auctoritate dictus sui maritus*'

130 NAV, R 376/11, No. 2, fol. 521 (20.ii.1544).
131 NAV, R 206/7, fols 50–50v (19.ii.1543).
132 M. Chojnacka, *Working Women of Early Modern Venice* (Baltimore and London, 2001), 27. R. Braccia, 'Uxor gaudet de morte mariti', *Annali della Facoltà di Giurisprudenza dell' Università di Genova*, 30 (2000–1), 76–128.

(with her husband's authority).[133] The price was fixed at 10 *uncie*, to be paid 3 *uncie* on the drawing up of the contract, 4 *uncie* in kind in the form of a donkey and the remaining 3 *uncie* in cash *ut bancus* by the following Easter. A marginal note in the contract states that on the 13th of the same month Catherina resold the house to the same Johannes for 7 *uncie*, and on the same date a new contract was drawn up for the sale of the same house between the same contracting parties. This time the house was sold for 10 *uncie* and 20 *tarì* which, as in the previous sale, was to be paid in different forms of payment within a period of two years. Johannes held the right of redemption, fixed at nine years from the date of the contract.[134] Such successive contracts of sale and re-purchase of the same property, with their fluctuating values, reveal the fictitious nature of such transactions, in which agreed prices did not reflect the real value of the property, and which in all probability contained a hidden interest or intent to thwart creditors.[135]

Analysis of the three agreements shows that Catherina paid 6 *uncie* in cash the first time (excluding the donkey), received 7 *uncie* when reselling the property and bought the house once again for 10 *uncie* 20 *tarì*, with the seller retaining the right of repurchase. As already noted, the right of redemption in such contracts meant that in reality the seller retained possession of the property, while the buyer had the option to sell it if the time clause for redemption was not met, or even to rent it. This example clearly illustrates the importance of real estate as a tool for generating much-needed liquid cash, and also the important role played by married women in their husband's business cycle.

At times wives took on the same burden as their husband in contracts of debt and assumed the role of business partners. Two such partners were the *Argozzino*[136] of the bishop, *Nob.* Ferdinandus Montero, and his wife, who undertook to pay the sum of 7 *uncie* to *Hon.* Paolo Bellia. The couple invested this sum in a grinding mill, complete with two grinding stones and accessories.[137] In another act, a certain *Donna* Julia who was a widow gave her two brothers a special mandate permitting them to sell three oxen, a cow and a one-year-old sheep, a black donkey and 10 *salme* of hay which were in the territory of *Donna* Julia's late husband.[138] All these commodities were sold to *Hon.* Mariano Vella, who bought them for himself and on behalf of his wife, his son and his daughter-in-law Agatha. In an additional note the notary also stated that he had read the contract word for word in Maltese to Agatha, who in turn stated that 'out of her own free will she has ratified and does

133 NAV, R 7/1, fol. 28v (6.v.1525).

134 NAV, R 7/1, fols 29–29v (13.v.1525).

135 Refer to Abela, 'A Window on Early Hospitaller Malta', 99–103, Appendix I–VI which gives a detailed list of the nature of various types of transactions involving real estate. See also S. Cachia, 'The Family and the Land in Late Medieval Malta – A Study of the Acts of Notary J. Zabbara, 1486–1488' (BA Hons dissertation, University of Malta, 1999).

136 The *Argozzino* was an overseer of slaves. J. M. Wismayer, *The Fleet of the Order of St John – 1530–1798* (Malta, 1997), 337.

137 NAV, R 206/7, fol. 345 (20.xi.1543).

138 NAV, MS 514/1, n.f. (16.vii.1588).

ratify the said contract by obliging herself in an equal and joint share with the said *Hon.* Mariano the buyer and debtor'.[139]

A number of women appear in sixteenth-century documents as lease-holders either of land or of built-up property. As elsewhere in Europe and the Mediterranean, leases were very common in Malta. Farmers' wives were constantly involved in transactions related to the lease of land for a stipulated period which were paid either in cash or in kind, the latter most often being a share in the produce.[140] Another common type of transaction involving women and property was the sale of census.[141] The acts of Notary Placido Abela for the years 1557–58[142] indicate that out of a total of eight sales of census which had a right of redemption clause, five included women, three appearing together with their husband,[143] one being a widow[144] and another one being married but represented by her brother-in-law.[145] This type of transaction was also often carried out by creditors in order to hide usurious profits, the seller mortgaging the property but holding the right of redemption. An example of the latter case is a contract dated 22 November 1557[146] in which the Dutch *Hon.* Petrus Degisberto and his wife, Lucia, obliged themselves and their future heirs in a contract relating to the annual and free sale of 6 *tarì* of income deriving from a house which they held in Bormola, a suburb of the new city of Birgu.[147] The property in question was worth 2 *uncie* and thus the 6 *tarì* represented the 10% census allowed

139 '*de eius spontanea voluntate ratificavit et ratificat dictum contratum obligando se nomine proprio ac una eque principaliter et insolidum cum predicto Hon. Mariano emptore et debitore.*'

140 NAV, R 196A, Section I, fol. 6 (13.iv.1532), fol. 35 (11.i.1543). See also Sciberras, 'Women in Early Sixteenth-Century Malta', 90–8.

141 'A medieval term with various meanings, including the following: (i) An impost established by contract; this was introduced at a time when people were very sensitive to the evil of usury and adopted it as a way of making money short of imposing interest on loans, which was forbidden. (ii) A more restricted notion of the same idea of tax, which has survived, namely an annual payment in cash or kind that the owner of land imposed when leasing his property with full ownership rights and with no right of redemption. This second meaning is akin to, though not identical with, the classical concept of *emphyteosis, q.v.* The main difference from *emphytheosis* was that in census nothing really remained in the hands of the original owner.' S. Fiorini (ed.), *Documentary Sources of Maltese History. Part I: Notarial Documents, No.2: Notary Giacomo Zabbara: R494/1(II–IV) 1494–1497* (Malta, 1999), 422.

142 Data for the years 1557–58 derived from NAV, MS 514/1 and R 4/1.

143 NAV, R 4/1, fols 47v–49v (22.xi.1557); R 4/1, fols 142v–143v (31.xii.1557); MS 514/1, n.f. (28.vii.1558); R 4/1, fols 155–156v (16.ix.1558).

144 NAV, R 4/1, fols 148v–149 (16.ix.1558).

145 This was *Hon. Mulier* Agatha, wife of Johanni Raymondus Burlo, who was represented by Marianus Burlo. The Burlo were seafarers and thus most probably Johanni was at the time away from the island. NAV, R 4/1, fols 173–174 (24.ix.1558). As regards the Burlo family and their connection with seafaring refer to Wettinger, 'The Castrum Maris', in Bugeja et al., *Birgu: A Maltese Maritime City*, 31–71, passim. Fiorini, 'Demographical Aspects', in Bugeja et al., *Birgu: A Maritime City*, 219–54: 222–4.

146 NAV, R 4/1, fols 47v–49v (22.xi.1557).

147 The contract states '*Petrus de Gisberto olandensis bombarderius salariatus sacre religionis hierosolimitane et Lucie eius uxor incole melitensis*'. Thus it does not specify the country of origin of his wife. NAV, R 4/1, fols 47v.

by law according to the Royal Bull.[148] The contract also stipulated a condition that, should the present sellers or their heirs pay the 2 *uncie* in the future, the buyer must accept this price and return the property.

Likewise, *Hon.* Johannes Hagius and his wife, Agnetis, from the village of Mqabba sold the census of a house in Qrendi, while reserving the right to redeem it in a year's time.[149] More complicated was the contract entered into by *Hon.* Galceranus Randun in which he gave authority to both his wife, Oliveria, and his mother-in-law, Catherina, to enter into a contract of obligation relating to the sale of an annual census of a house. In this contract Catherina promised that her minor son would honour this obligation in the future if he was requested to do so, thus most probably this property was part of Oliveria's dowry.[150]

Outright sale of census without the redemption clause was less popular. In three examples the wife appeared with her husband as one of the vendors or as giving her consent.[151] Such contracts shed light on the legal position of married women, who on the one hand were prohibited from entering into contracts of obligation without their husband's authority, but on the other hand were considered equally accountable and capable of acting as guarantors of debts entered into by their spouses. They also shed light on the important and increasing role of women in consenting to the alienation of property as a means to generate cash in a society which was rapidly developing its money economy. The need for cash in hand was a direct result of the arrival of the Knights, since the increase in trading activities required a constant flow of cash, especially for trade with other merchants hailing from other parts of the Mediterranean.

Married women and contracts of obligation

Malta's heavy participation in corsairing activity meant that a good number of men were away from home for lengthy periods, died while fighting the enemy or were taken as captives by Muslim corsairs. These circumstances conferred particular functions on women, who had to administer and run the family's possessions, whether meagre or prosperous. Such cultural and political contexts are important when evaluating the plurality of indicators which determined Malta's economic needs. In a variety of situations and circumstances women were indispensable for keeping the wheels of

148 '*Uncijs duabus p[onderis] g[eneralis] censualibus supra venditionem ad rationem de decem pro centenario Juxta formam bulle apostolice et regie pragmatice*', MS 514/1, n.f. (10.i.1558). Most probably this refers to the papal bulls *Regimini* (1425 and 1455) which were in force at the time, in which credit through annuities was subject to the following conditions: the annuities created had to be assigned to a specific piece of real estate; it had to be possible to buy them back again if the debtor so desired; they might not represent a higher annual income than 10% of the capital invested. H. Van Der Wee, 'Monetary, Credit and Banking Systems', in E. E. Rich & C. H. Wilson (eds), *The Cambridge Economic History of Europe* (Cambridge, 1977), vol. 5, 290–393: 304.

149 NAV, R 4/1, fols 131–131v (5.x.1558).

150 NAV, MS 514/1, n.f. (10.i.1558).

151 NAV, R 4/1, fols 70–75v (29.ix.1557); MS 514/1, n.f. (10.i.1558), n.f. (16.ix.1558).

commerce turning, not only through their participation in traditional roles but also through their consent and participation in contractual obligations.[152]

Women thus had a peculiar and frequent role in Maltese society as representatives of their spouses, and undertook responsibilities which were traditionally associated with men. Thus, they are found among the main actors of society. Although they were legally restricted in their actions, in order for society to function smoothly the legal system needed to provide sufficient leeway for their participation. While the laws reflected male notions, law makers made concessions that enabled a woman to act independently.

For example, notarial acts demonstrate that the wife could enter into contracts of obligation if her husband was held in captivity. The acts of Notary de Agatiis register such a case on 10 March 1539 concerning Paula, wife of Jacobo Camilleri, the latter being noted as absent since he had been taken as a slave by Muslims – *servi hostium infedelium*.[153] Paula was concluding the sale of a house on her behalf and on behalf of her husband and their children in which it was stipulated that, upon his return, her husband was bound to comply with the 'new law' and ratify the said agreement, as were their children on their coming of age:

> According to the new rite, namely, that the said Jacobus, as soon as he shall have returned, and the said his sons, when they shall have come of age, shall ratify the present contract, being present before us all together equally individually and jointly.[154]

Paula held the right of redemption of the property, which was set at three years from the date of sale. In a marginal note dated 11 May 1539 she is reported to have received the money from the buyer, who was a Knight of the Order. A further marginal note, almost three years after the initial agreement and dated 7 February 1542, states that Jacobo is once again a free man. In line with notarial practice, the notary read the contract to Jacobo in Maltese and Jacobo ratified it, after confirming that he fully understood the obligations imposed by the agreement. Ratification of acts was also required in the case of the absence of a woman from the contract, thus pointing to wives holding a partial responsibility with their husbands in contracts of obligation.

As noted above, most probably such laws were enforced to protect against possible mismanagement of the wife's patrimony by her spouse, while giving the husband more flexibility if he wished to enter into a contract of obligation and his wife was not present for the agreement at the time. This was the case in a contract dated 29 September 1557 in which Paulus Barbara and his son-in-law Carolus Formosa[155] jointly entered into a contract of obligation on their behalf and on behalf of their respective wives. The men promised that, in line with the prevailing law, both their wives 'shall ratify and shall approve the present contract, and each and every item of its contents therein equally, individually and jointly with their aforementioned

152 This has been discussed in the analysis of the different type of marriage contracts.

153 NAV, R 202/4, fols 136–137 (10.iii.1539 *ab inc*).

154 '*iuxta formam novi ritus scilicet quam dittus Jacobus cum primum post liminij reversionem fecerit ratificabunt presentem contractum et ditti eius filii cum fuerint etatis perfectem presentes coram nobis una simul aeque principaliter et insolidum*' [sic].

155 NAV, R 4/1, fol. 70 (29.ix.1557).

husbands for the payment'.[156] From a contract dated 30 March 1543 it is clear that Malta was following similar patterns to those adopted in Sicily. The contract states that as per a previous contract drawn up in Palermo by Notary Theronimus Gittard on 8 January of the same year, Didacus Barbara acknowledges himself to be in debt to *Ma.* Fernando Decrinnas for the sum of 80 gold ducats, which he is obliged to pay in various ways, spread over a period of three years. In the 30 March contract Didacus's wife, Bartholomea, ratified this contract in Malta and guaranteed to renounce any property rights if there should be breach of contract.[157]

The wife of a captive could also issue receipts of payment on behalf of her captive husband. Such was the case of Imperia, wife of Bartholomeo Grima who at the time was held in captivity. Due to her husband's absence, Imperia issued a receipt to the Knight *Fra.* Jacobo De Aspramonte with respect to the rent of a house.[158] It is through such cases that one can appreciate just how much society needed women's participation in order to keep the economy running. Had women not had such powers, it would have been difficult for debts to be paid, for husbands to be redeemed and for the family's economic activity to continue. A woman whose husband was held in captivity found herself dealing with a collection of problems. At times she faced financial crisis in her endeavours to procure the necessary redemption money for her husband's release. Further, she had to find intermediaries to provide a link with the Muslim world and negotiate redemption terms.

It could be said that a woman assumed the leading role in her family at the most difficult times. Usurers were ready to capitalise on such situations and squeeze money out of desperate clients. Issues connected with corsairing and ransoming grew exponentially after the arrival of the Knights in Malta. This had a direct effect on the whole of the local population, while also pushing women to participate more in these types of transactions. Ultimately, the situation became unbearable and caused so many economic pressures that in 1607 the Knights established the *Monte di Redenzione*. This was a government institution funded by private bequests with the philanthropic aim of rescuing from slavery any of the natives who might have fallen prey to the enemy and had no means to ransom themselves.[159]

The arrival of the Knights increased opportunities for both Maltese and foreigners to work as soldiers or sailors on merchant ships or on corsairing ventures, the latter being privately armed or else flying the flag of the Order or the Grand Master. When the men fell into enemy hands their wives faced serious problems since there was no guarantee that they would ever be reunited with their families. But what happened if a husband died in captivity or out at sea?

A request deposited at the *Magna Curia Castellania* by the wife and daughter of Martino Vella, who presumably had died while in captivity, reveals that the local authorities were very cautious in declaring a person dead. In fact, they made sure to

156 '*presentem contractum ac omnia et singula in eo contenta ratificabunt et approbabunt, ac una eque principaliter et insolidum cum prenominatis eorum viris ad solutionem.*'

157 NAV, R 206/7, fol. 85v (30.iii.1543).

158 NAV, R 202/4, fol. 212 (22.v.1540). An approximate profit of 14%.

159 D. Rossi, 'The Monte Di Pietà in Hospitaller Malta' (BA Hons dissertation, University of Malta, 1998).

collect the testimony of eye-witnesses before officially proclaiming a person dead. It was thus that *Hon.* Nicolaus Demitiri, who had been taken as a slave with Martino, declared that the poor man had 'died and passed away from this present life at Brevisa where at the time he found himself slave, the slave being the witness, and the very witness himself had buried him [Martino]'.[160] Such precautionary measures are of course understandable because, on the one hand, a section of the population could face a situation where their assets were frozen and they could do nothing about it, while on the other hand a legitimate claim to assets by husbands who 'returned from the dead' would provoke much social and legal difficulty.

Loans – *sine aliquo usurarum*?

Consumption credit was an essential aspect of the temporary or continuous needs of the poor, the less poor and those in the higher echelons of society who, at some time or another, were compelled to seek cash advances at the exorbitant rates charged by usurers. In Rhodes the Order had set up the *Monte di Pietà* in 1505, making it one of the earliest *Monte* to function outside Italy. In Malta, gaining papal approval for this institution was a long drawn-out affair which gave rise to various protests by the Order. In fact, it was only in 1713 that consent for its establishment was given in the Bull *Inter Multiplices*. The Grand Master held exclusive jurisdiction *pro tempore* and there was a 2% rate of interest on amounts of over 10 *scudi* to offset the salaries of officials and other administrative expenses.[161] In the absence of an institutionalised lending organisation such as the *Monte di Pietà*,[162] usurers flourished and assumed a relevant economic role in sixteenth-century Malta. In effect, acting as a pawnbroker guaranteed the creditor full repayment, and often also a large profit margin. Whether or not they were licensed, a pawnbroker's services were essentially illegal and Christian usurers had to return illicit profits in order to gain absolution.[163] Women seem to have been well integrated into the entangled circle of usurers and performed well in the function of petty money lenders against the pawning of goods.

Two sixteenth-century registers in the Cathedral Museum Archives, known as *Registrum Usurariorum Melitae*, contain declarations received at the Episcopal Court relating to usurious practices in the port city of Birgu. In 1570 the then Vicar General, *Don* Antonio De Bartoli,[164] felt that the practice of usury in Birgu was a deep-rooted affair leading to much misery. In order to check and contain the practice, he issued an edict which was delivered at the Dominican Church of the

160 '*morse et trapasso della presente vita dentro Brevisa dove allora se trovava esso testimonio sciavo et esso proprio testimonio lo sottorro*' [sic]. NAM, MCC, AO. vol. 1, fols 209v–210 (1562).

161 Lane & Mueller, *Money and Banking in Medieval and Renaissance Venice*, 76.

162 Rossi, 'The Monte Di Pietà', 18, 31–2.

163 Lane & Mueller, *Money and Banking in Medieval and Renaissance Venice*, 76.

164 For a detailed description of the life of Antonius Bartolo STD (1533–1608) refer to Borg, *The Maltese Diocese during the Sixteenth Century*, 158–64.

Annunciation on 18 December 1570. The edict proclaimed that any person aware of any usurious dealings had a moral obligation to report them to the Episcopal Court and otherwise risked excommunication. The registers contain declarations and accusations made by various people in response to this edict and are not proper trial cases. Although they relate to the years 1570–75, various testimonies make reference to particular situations which occurred well before that period. The short time separating these records from the period of this study (1530–65) means that the large majority of names encountered in these lists are found also in pre-1565 notarial deeds.

The testimony of the Rhodiot Notary Bonaventura de Bonetiis[165] in the Episcopal Court on 22 December 1570 is of particular importance. It is evident from his testimony that various types of credit contracts often carried a hidden interest rate which permitted the creditor to make a good profit out of the issued capital, '*non obstante che li instrumento dice di semplice mutuo*' (notwithstanding that the contract stated that it was a simple loan).[166] Notary de Bonetiis's profession enabled him not only to be cognisant of actual situations but also to be a participant in the actual formulation and conclusion of such business deals through the careful manipulation of legal terminology. Here, reference could be made to the many money loan and trade credit contracts which ended in dispute, facing serious accusations of usury. Often, when concluding a loan contract, interest was included in the total sum due, since this measure assured that the creditor recovered the original capital plus the interest without openly declaring profit. Such instances were common all over the Mediterranean, as is evidenced by Notary de Bonetiis's deposition against the prosperous Greek merchant Johannes Callamia[167] in 1570. De Bonetiis stated that 'it has been some time that [Callamia] has been doing and has done exchange contracts in the acts of the said witness [Debonetiis], from Malta to Messina and Syracuse at the rate of 30 or 25%'.[168] Yet another witness stated that the same Callamia had forced his debtors to draw up fictitious contracts in order to conceal any signs of usury.[169]

Further, the *Vice-Comite* of the *Magna Curia Castellania* stated that once he had been constrained to borrow the sum of 100 *scudi* from the said Callamia; however,

165 NAV, R 206, Notary Vincenzo Bonaventura de Bonetiis's Register volumes seem to be all extant and the fifty-one volumes plus one index in his collection span the period from 1534 to 1576.

166 CAM, CEM, *Registrum Usuriarorum Melitae, Liber Primus*, fol. 6 (new enumeration in pencil).

167 Johanni Callamia came to Malta with the Knights in 1530. See, Fiorini, 'The Rhodiot Community of Birgu', in Mallia-Milanes (ed.), *Library of Mediterranean History*, vol. 1, 183–241: passim.

168 '*da piu tempo have usato et usati di fare contracti in li acti del revelantj di cambij a ragione di trenta p[er] cento o vinti cinqu[e] p[er] cento da Malta in Messina et Saragosa.*' CAM, CEM, *Registrum Usuriarorum Melitae, Liber Primus*, fol. 15v. Some examples of Callamia's contracts for the year 1543 found in the acts of Notary Debonetiis have the following reference NAV, R 206/7, fol. 114, fol. 151, fol. 162, fol. 166, fol. 255, fol. 261, fol. 313, fol. 406.

169 CAM, CEM, *Registrum Usuriarorum Melitae, Liber Primus*, fol. 4v (new enumeration in pencil).

the creditor made sure to document that the sum borrowed was 111 *scudi*, thus including a profit of 11%.[170] While Callamia was busy collecting his dues his wife, Zacalu, was busy washing her hair with a particular type of 'oil' which made her hair turn blonde.[171] Unfortunately for her, she ended up in front of the inquisitor, accused of practising witchcraft, a highly serious crime for a woman of her social standing.[172] Her accuser, Bartholomeo Faraone, declared that she had committed the crime eleven years earlier. Why had Bartholomeo spoken out now? Was Zacalu the victim of her husband's enemies?[173]

Women are also documented as makng 'friendly' loans, thus acting as important generators of much-needed liquid cash. Did women, as in Johannes Callamia's case, avail themselves of the legal possibilities which made usurious practice possible? Did the law permit them to lend money against the security of real estate? The answer to the latter question is yes, as is confirmed by various contracts which depict women as suppliers of liquid cash. In a contract dated 1558, *Nob.* Salvus Axac declared himself to be indebted to *Hon. Mulier* Venture, widow of *Hon. Mag.* Johannes Fallon, in respect of a loan of 10 *uncie.* In order to provide sufficient security for the borrowed sum Salvus hypothecated a field and a house which he held in Senglea.[174] The testimony of *Mag.* Leonardo Garibo confirms that some women missed no opportunities which came their way and even found ways of circumventing the law in their favour. Garibo stated that a certain Mariecta Falson, who according to him was a well-known usurer in the port area, concealed any profits made by drawing up fictitious contracts which included a 10% profit on sums of money lent.[175]

A detailed analysis of the first volume of the two registers in the Cathedral Museum Archives, pertaining to the years 1570–71, provides some interesting insights into women's active investment and the management of their property. Chart 2 shows that the testimony of fifty-nine witnesses (forty-five males and fourteen females) reveals a heavier participation in usurious practices by women.[176] In fact female participation exceeds male participation by about 65%. At the same time, the average amount of money issued by women was much less than that issued by men, the average sum loaned by men being 324% greater than that issued by women (Chart 3). It is important to note here that women's participation in commerce was restricted by their more limited access to capital, since this generally came to them from inheritances and dowries. Further, most married women

170 '*In pura rei veritate non havea havuto altro eccetto scuti cento e li altrj scuti undici se li piglo per guadagni di un anno*' [sic]. CAM, CEM, *Registrum Usuriarorum Melitae, Liber Primus*, fol. 7 (new enumeration in pencil).

171 It does not state what type of 'oil' this was.

172 Cassar, *Daughters of Eve*, 44.

173 CAM, AIM, Proc. Crim. vol. 3B case 26, fol. 453.

174 NAV, 514/1, fols 40–40v (18.ii.1558).

175 In particular, he mentions the acts of Notary Mattheo Briffa which are still extant and carry the reference, NAV, MS 612 and R 91 (1565–85). CAM, CEM, *Registrum Usuriarorum Melitae, Liber Primus*, fol. 17v.

176 In Chart 2 those usurers who were accused more than once or those who had the same general name to describe them, e.g. 'Jewish woman', were counted once. The same procedure was applied to men.

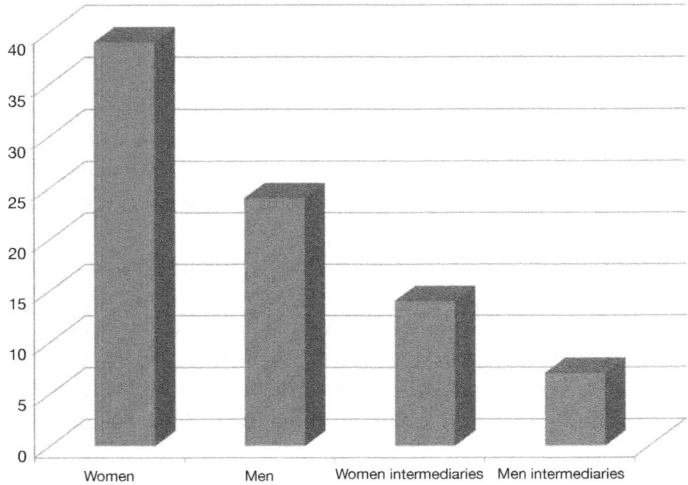

Chart 2 Individuals who were accused of usurious practice
Source: CEM, *Registrum Usuriarorum Melitae*, Liber Primus (1570–71).

needed their husband's consent in order to enter into contracts of obligation. Even if they found ways and means to act on their own they were still limited in their investment ventures.[177] Another striking feature is the number of male accusers: 76.3%, as opposed to 23.7% female accusers. Do these numbers point to a situation where women were viewed as upsetting the social order? As Merry Wiesner-Hanks explains, 'the maintenance of proper power relationships between men and women served as a basis for and a symbol of not only the larger political system but also for the functioning of society as a whole. Relations between the sexes often provided a model for all dichotomised relations that involved authority and subordination, such as those between ruler and subject'.[178]

The first woman mentioned in the *Registrum Usuriarorum Melitae* is a Sicilian widow named Domenica, resident in Birgu, who was accused of lending sums of money at the considerable profit of 12%.[179] The witness described the matter in the following terms: 'After a couple of days, talking with the same Domenica in her house which is situated in this new city, she recounted once again how she had given and lent to a Knight, one hundred *scudi*, and had pawned from him some gold items and had made him promise [to give her] twelve *scudi* for every hundred as profit.'[180] Another Maltese woman whose name was not disclosed was accused of lending money at a profit of 1 *carlino* per month, while *Hon.* Catherina Allegritta

177 Wiesner-Hanks, *Women and Gender*, 130–1.

178 Wiesner-Hanks, *Women and Gender*, 295.

179 CAM, CEM, *Registrum Usuriarorum Melitae, Liber Primus*, fols 1–2v.

180 '*Doppo alcuni giorni ragionando con la medesima Domenica in casa di essa testi posita in questa nova cita li hebbe a dire de novo come haveva dato et imprestato ad un cavaliere cento scuti con havere preso da lui pegni d'oro et esserli promesso da dicto cavaliere dodecj scuti per cento di beveraggio over di guadagno*' [sic].

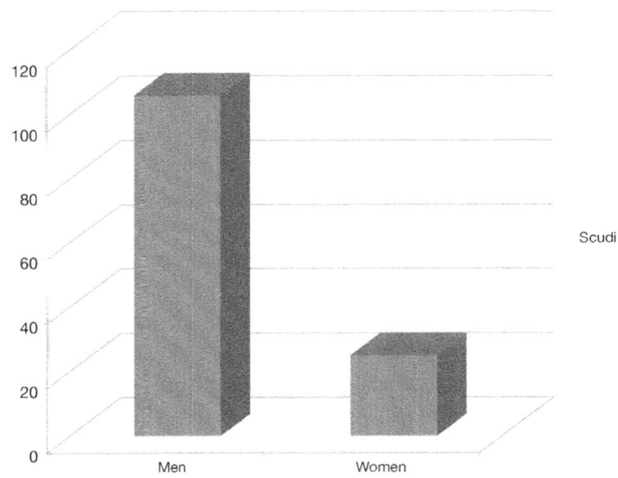

Chart 3 Average of credit advances in *scudi*
Source: CEM, *Registrum Usuriarorum Melitae, Liber Primus* (1570–71).

accused Angela di Manete of having lent money to her daughter Veronica and to a certain slave belonging to Carla Barberi at a monthly profit of 5 *grani* per *scudo*. When referring to women who '*donano a guadagno*'[181] (lent at a profit), the same Catherina testified that there were many women who lent at the same rate or even at the monthly rate of 1 *tarì* per *scudo*. Off-handedly, she recalled the names of Paula Dalli, Paula the mother-in-law of *Mag.* Paulo Haxixe, the mother-in-law of Juliano Vella from Bormla, a woman known as Angelina Latappera '*et multi altri degli quali non si arricorda*' (and a lot of others whom at the moment she did not remember).[182]

The benefits of pawning are made very clear in various statements such as that by Mariecta, the wife of Michaelis Manero, who said that she had needed to borrow the sum of 8 *scudi*, which she did through the intermediary service of *Mag.* Johannes Carolo Marullo. Marullo obtained the requested money from a certain Paula, who as security requested a number of items worth '*il duppio et triplo*' (double and triple) the sum lent and made her pay interest of 5 *grani* per month. Another statement, made by Marietta de Carli from Birgu, reveals that she had borrowed the sum of 10 *scudi* through the services of Antonella Chilia. As security she had to pawn a number of items worth 30 *scudi* and was obliged to pay monthly interest of 6 *grani* per *scudo*.[183] In this particular case Marietta further stated that apart from this loan she had borrowed another sum from Agatha, wife of Antonio Condo, who had lent

181 The verb 'donare' in Italian means to 'make a gift', but here it is used colloquially to mean 'to lend'.

182 CAM, CEM *Registrum Usuriarorum Melitae, Liber Primus*, fol. 4 (new enumeration in pencil).

183 CAM, CEM *Registrum Usuriarorum Melitae, Liber Primus*, fol. 4v (new enumeration in pencil).

her money at monthly profit of 10 *grani* per *scudo*. The witness further stated that she knew that a certain Thomasina Marrazza and Gianna di Monolj di Gratiana[184] from Birgu also lent at a profit, while the widow of Stephani Deassufunio had told her that she had lent money at a profit of 10% – '*con recupero diecj per cento di guadagno*'.[185]

It becomes very clear from various testimonies that a number of women accused before the Court were not the principal actors providing capital, but acted as intermediaries between the borrower and the lender (see Chart 2). In fact, these amounted to fourteen out of a total of eighty-four accused, and out of these thirteen were described as acting on behalf of female lenders, one of them also serving as an intermediary for both men and women. Male intermediaries amounted to seven, of whom four were intermediaries for women. These intermediaries were very careful in concealing their activities and warning their clients to keep silent, never mentioning or making reference to the principal agent in this complicated usurious cycle – most probably because they feared being prosecuted by the ecclesiastical authorities. The actions of the above-mentioned Antonella, an intermediary, were described in these words by her client:

> *non sapendo pure cui fosse la donna principale che e patrona di dectj denari anchi perche ... e stata pregata essa revelante da decta [Anto]nella che non la dovesse scoprire ... per non carricare sua conscientia* [*sic*][186]
>
> (not knowing who the main woman who was the owner of the said money was, even because ... she [the witness] was requested by Antonella [the intermediary] not to find out who lent her the money ... so as not to have a heavy conscience).

Of course, having a 'heavy conscience' meant that borrowers could be tempted to accuse their lenders in the Episcopal Court, which at times would turn out to be a profitable move, because if a money lender was found guilty of usury he or she would have to renounce any large profits.

The register also contains the testimony of a woman who actually admitted to having lent money at usurious gains. *Hon. Mulier* Hysabella, the wife of Michaelis de Christofaro, testified that she had lent money through the services of Madonna La Giorgentana. Hysabella stated that she did not know who the client was; however, she was given 3 *tarì* of profit, which she was ready to reimburse immediately.[187] Could the debtor have been a person of high social standing who wanted to conceal his or her identity? Intermediaries would have been useful in such instances. In any case, in a microcosm such as Birgu the spoken word carried a great deal of weight and was quick to circulate. It transformed, built or destroyed reputations, and being short of cash was not something to be proud of.

Hysabella's confession and her readiness to reimburse illicit profits reflect the doctrine of the Tridentine Church, which, according to Carmel Cassar, had 'mounted

184 Mentioned in the list of inhabitants of Birgu for the years 1538 to 1540. Bezzina, 'Early Hospitaller Birgu', 104.

185 CAM, CEM *Registrum Usuriarorum Melitae, Liber Primus*, fol. 5 (new enumeration in pencil).

186 CAM, CEM *Registrum Usuriarorum Melitae, Liber Primus*, fol. 4v (new enumeration in pencil).

187 CAM, CEM, *Registrum Usuriarorum Melitae, Liber Primus*, fol. 12.

a heroic response to the Protestant schism and in its efforts to revitalise the Church reached out in all directions to control and dominate the life of the faithful, including women'.[188] Raymond de Roover explains: 'usurers were excluded from the communion of the Faithful; they were not supposed to attend Divine service; they were not admitted to the sacraments; and they were denied burial in hallowed ground. This was the theory, at least. In practice things were a little different. Because of God's infinite mercy, usurers always could obtain absolution in *articulo mortis* provided that they repented their sins and offered to make restitution.'[189] In this case *Mulier* Hysabella was not 'at the point of death', but was convinced that she would be re-admitted to the Church's fold if she repented and restored the usurious gains she had received.

In another case Bernardina Milanesa confessed that she had borrowed a sum amounting to 30 *scudi* from Alexandro Abela[190] and hypothecated her house, which was situated in Birgu next to the Order's Infirmary. Bernardina's budget was obviously at a heavy deficit, and in her distress, or due to deceit, instead of cash she was given 30 *scudi* worth of cloth at 6 *tarì* per cane, which cost her an additional 4 *tarì* in making it whiter (*in fare bianchiari*). However, when she went to sell it in the town square she only got 2 *tarì* 10 *grani* per cane. She ended up borrowing more money and, in great financial difficulties and unable to pay the heavy debt, was constrained to draw up a contract and sell the house which she had hypothecated to her debtor.[191] The ruin and distress of Bernardina and others who testified before the bishop represents the everyday plight of a multitude of people who, like Bernardina, experienced financial difficulty and sought to remedy it by obtaining advances from unscrupulous money lenders. In Bernardina's case her imprudence is evidenced by the manner in which she accepted the terms imposed by her creditor. Little did she consider that the consequences of her deal would entangle her in a vicious circle of exploitation! Alexandro, on the other hand, not only got rid of some merchandise which seems to have been soiled, but at the same time capitalised on Bernardina's misfortune by adding her property to the deal. These money lenders were often called 'suppliers to the gallows', since their despairing victims often ended up in a vicious circle of delinquency and crime.[192] Indeed, as we see in the following case, some women may have ended up prostituting themselves.

At times women were the indirect victims of usurious practices, as in the case of the wife of Ambrosio Manero, a merchant from Birgu. In an ever-growing money economy, trade credit was an important tool for the merchant, enabling him to carry on with his business even when navigating in difficult waters. This is exactly what Ambrosio did at a time of cash shortage. In order to supply his business with the needed commodities, Ambrosio called upon his brother-in-law, *Magistro* Vincenzo Franzese, who was highly renowned in Birgu for his usurious practices.[193] Instead

188 Cassar, *Daughters of Eve*, 193.

189 de Roover, *Money, Banking and Credit in Medieval Bruges*, 151.

190 Alexandro Abela was a notary by profession and brother to Notary Placido Abela, whose acts still survive, although not in complete form. J. Abela, 'A Window on the Acts of a Maltese Sixteenth Century Notary – Placido Abela', in J. F. Grima (ed.), *60th Anniversary of the Malta Historical Society – A Commemoration* (Malta, 2010), 207–36: 212.

191 CAM, CEM, *Registrum Usuriarorum Melitae, Liber Primus*, fol. 22.

192 de Roover, *Money, Banking and Credit in Medieval Bruges*, 149.

193 The date of the document is 22 December 1570, but the witness stated that this case

of ready money, Ambrosio asked for a trade credit of 130 *scudi* worth of goods, a request which Vincenzo met without hesitation, on condition that Ambrosio paid a hefty interest rate. Being again in need of money, Ambrosio requested a further 60 *scudi* from his brother-in-law as he wanted to buy merchandise from a Venetian ship which had just anchored in the port. It seems that although Ambrosio did not default on his weekly repayments, the accumulated interest was so great that after some years he had paid back double the amount but still had not redeemed the debt. In an attempt to remedy the situation, Vincenzo's mother pleaded with her son to find the conscience to return the exorbitant profit to his brother-in-law, unless he wished to see his sister become a prostitute for the sake of his greed.[194] It seems that although Vincenzo was at the time in a very poor state of health, his mother's plea had no effect. On the contrary, the documents record that he cursed his mother, telling her that he neither held her as his mother nor considered his sister as one of the family since, as far as he was concerned, they were just trying to ruin him.

Catherina, the slave of *Nob.* Antonio de Via, also ended up as a victim of usury when her master pawned her in respect of a loan he had contracted with Lazzaro Bonnichi. Both contracting parties had agreed that Catherina was to work for Lazzaro for a period of three or four months at the most, giving him 1 *tarì* worth of work per day. However, it seems that Lazzaro was not content with her output and renewed her term each month for almost eight months. The miserable slave fled to her original master, begging him to release her from Lazzaro's possession because he was ill-treating her and even threatened to lock her up in jail if she failed to satisfy the debt in full.[195]

Such testimonies make clear the negative effects on the growth of a healthy economy that resulted from the Catholic Church's restrictions on the taking of interest, since merchants and traders, being in constant need of ready cash, at times had to resort to borrowing from usurers. Instead of reinvesting their profits in order to generate more work, their honest gains filled the pockets of usurers, with the result that many ended up bankrupt and their families were impoverished.

Notarial acts also provide evidence of women who were active participants in the credit market, and both locally and beyond the island's shores. In a particular act dated 1551[196] Giovanni Callamia and Giacomo Caloriti, both Rhodiot citizens of Malta, transferred a variety of gold items to Nicola Panthuineno, the appointed procurator of *Domina* Helena Gratiana. The contract stipulated that the procurator was to hand over the items to Emanuele Gatana, another Rhodiot merchant, who in turn was to deliver them to the said Helena in the city of Messina. In another instance, Clara La Carruba, who was resident in Birgu, found it opportune to lend capital to foreigners. On 15 December 1540 she is recorded to have lent 6 *scudi* to a Neapolitan merchant through the services of two Neapolitan intermediaries who, for their part, hypothecated their personal goods and promised that she would be repaid in three months' time in the port of Birgu.[197]

happened a few years earlier.

194 CAM, CEM, *Registrum Usuriarorum Melitae, Liber Primus*, fols 15v–16.

195 CAM, CEM, *Registrum Usuriarorum Melitae, Liber Primus*, fols 19v–21.

196 NAV, R 439/42, fols 15v–17 (21.vi.1551). All the persons mentioned in this act are Rhodiots.

197 NAV, R 202/5, fol. 101v (15.xii.1540).

Apart from illustrating the commercial interaction which existed between various negotiators throughout the Mediterranean, these contracts also highlight the fact that women such as *Domina* Helena and Clara, although adventurous in their dealings, sought to protect their capital when investing in risky overseas transactions. In order to ensure that their investment was safely guarded they usually drew up contracts and made use of the services of a male procurator who would be mainly responsible for collecting or paying debts and representing them in court cases if the need arose.

Knights of the Hospitaller Order are also documented as borrowing considerable sums of money from women, as in the case of the Knight *Fra.* Hieronymus Picullus, who borrowed 100 *scudi* from Beatrice de Adamo, relinquishing various goods as security.[198] Beatrice seems to have been quite an active business woman, since her name is encountered in various financial transactions. Her financial stability is also reflected in one particular act where she is recorded as having built a house in Birgu which was adjacent to the property of the Knight *Fra.* Rosset, a prominent Knight who oversaw dealings connected with the Order's slaves.[199] While highly successful business women like Beatrice are not the typical Maltese or foreign woman resident in Birgu, various women did participate directly in economic activities, either alone or as partners with their spouses.

Conclusion

Primary sources such as those found in the Notarial Archives bring to life the realities of everyday living and make it possible to study the multicultural society which had established itself in Malta, and how it mingled with the local population. This chapter has highlighted the possibilities and limitations which were afforded to women and the different ways in which women contributed to the island's economic development. During medieval times marriage alliances were an important and strategic tool for those who aspired to hold important positions among the ruling elite. Although women were excluded from political affairs, through their numerous charitable bequests and transfers of property to the Church they indirectly began to give more power to an institution which was a staunch opponent of the Order, namely the bishopric of Malta. Even before 1530, women enjoyed property and inheritance rights that allowed them to dispose of their dowries and their assets in such manner as they deemed fit. During the first decades of their rule the Hospitallers did not change or take away any of these rights, which were deeply rooted in old laws and customs.

The establishment of the Knights on the island created a ready market for goods, which reached unprecedented proportions. The economy boomed, especially in the retail sector, which now needed to cater for a larger community with a variety of needs, including the conspicuous consumption of the Knights. The influx of new arrivals created a variety of job vacancies for women which went beyond their

198 NAV, R 202/4, fols 34–34v (8.x.1539).
199 NAV, R 202/3, fols 36v–37 (15.x.1532).

traditional roles. Clara Laspatara manufactured swords, *Donna* Caterina owned a hostel, *Hon. Mulier* Angelina found work as a domestic servant and *Donna* Lorenza, with her son who was an *aromatario*, opened their own shop and even hired extra help. Notarial documents portray a situation in which, during the first decades of the Knights' stay, foreign women were more attracted than Maltese women to participate in economic activities in the harbour area. Maltese women possibly kept to the more traditional domestic work associated with village life, or went to the harbour area to sell their produce.

Cash was fast becoming the essential means for conducting business transactions, and lack of it hindered participation in the island's economic life. The need for money, which was often advanced through the hypothecation or sale of land, saw women take a greater part in their husband's business deals, since it was only through the wife's consent that land received as dowry could be sold or placed as security for much-needed loans. Lack of cash also created a steady market for the money lenders, some of whom soon sought to exploit those who were financially weak. This started a whole process in which weaker and poorer members of society ended up being sucked into an ever-growing spiral of debt. Usurers made sure to cover their loans not only through hypothecation of property but also by drawing up contracts which contained hidden interest. In the case of ransoming, circumvention of the law to hide exorbitant interest rates was not only adopted by Maltese money lenders but extended over a much wider area of the Mediterranean. Although they lent smaller sums of money than their male counterparts, women also lent at high rates of interest and seem to have had a good network of agents working for them. Catherina Allegritta remembered many of their names in front of the inquisitor. Angela, Paula and Angelina Latappera were among those whom she could recall, but she claimed that there were also many others. People like Bernardina Milanesa ended up as victims of a vicious circle in which usurers applied their own rules and imposed their own penalties on doubtful debtors, some of whom ended up prostituting themselves to pay for debts which they could never hope to settle with their meagre incomes. It was a situation in which the rich got richer and the poor got poorer.

The absence of a charitable institution like that of the *Monte di Pietà*, which in Rhodes seems to have been functioning by 1505, aggravated the situation.[200] While in Rhodes, the Knights knew that many problems related to usury and the exploitation of the poor would be considerably reduced by the establishment of a lending institution. Due to constant disagreement with the Roman curia,[201] this institution took a long time to develop.[202] The setting up of the *Monte* was yet another aspect of the Rhodian state which the Knights were not successful in transferring automatically to Malta, and it was only very late in their tenure of the islands that they managed to establish the institution there.

200 Rossi, 'The Monte di Pietà', 18.

201 The Roman curia was the administrative apparatus of the Holy See.

202 The approval of the *Monte di Pietà* by the Roman curia was a long drawn-out affair which generated a lot of protests from the Order. It was finally approved on 9 September 1713. Rossi, 'The Monte di Pietà', 31–2. See also de Roover, *Money, Banking and Credit in Medieval Bruges*, 150–1.

4

Trade with North Africa and the Levant

On a very superficial level the Mediterranean region during the first half of the sixteenth century could be described as comprising two opposing parts: to the north and west, Christian Europe; to the east and south, Muslim Africa–Asia. However, the Mediterranean cannot be defined in this over-simplified way. In the West, the *Moriscos*[1] in Spain were a unique cultural community and managed to conduct their business activities despite being severely persecuted. As Braudel notes, 'how could a hard-working people avoid becoming rich in a country flooded with precious metals and populated by an abundance of *hidalgos*[2] for whom any work was dishonourable?'[3]

Elsewhere, Jews[4] and Arab-Muslims, uprooted and expelled from their native land by the Spanish rulers, established themselves in North Africa and engaged in corsairing activities against the Spanish coasts and shipping. In the Eastern Mediterranean there were Christian communities composed of Genoese colonies in Chios, Lesbos, Phokaea and Pera, and Venetian colonies in Cyprus, Crete and other neighbouring islands. These competed with Greeks, Copts, Armenians, Jews and other non-Muslim subjects of the Ottoman sultan in trade and commerce.[5] As Molly Greene states, 'from the time of the Fourth Crusade in 1204 onward, the

1 From the beginning of the sixteenth century, baptised Muslims and their descendants were known as *Moriscos*. There were various *Morisco* societies scattered across Spain, and their conversion, which was generally forced, took place at different periods, starting with the Moors of Granada in 1499 in violation of the promise made to them by the Spanish Crown in 1492. The general expulsion of the *Moriscos* took place between 1609 and 1614. Braudel, *The Mediterranean*, vol. 1, 780–802; M. A. Ladero Quesada, '*Mudéjares* and *Repobladores* in the Kingdom of Granada (1485–1501)', in A. Meyuhas Ginio (ed.), *Jews, Christians and Muslims in the Mediterranean after 1492* (London, 1992), 53–77; N. Matar, *Europe through Arab Eyes, 1578–1727* (New York, 2009), 82.

2 Members of the Spanish aristocracy.

3 Braudel, *The Mediterranean*, vol. 2, 792.

4 The expulsion of the Jews from Spanish domains took place in 1492.

5 Suraiya Faroqhi explains that 'the Ottoman ruling elite was by no means hostile or even indifferent to trade: quite to the contrary, large-scale wholesaling traders were allowed to enrich themselves'. S. Faroqhi, 'The ruling elite between politics and "The Economy"', in İnalcik & Quataert (eds), *An Economic and Social History of the Ottoman Empire*, 545–75: 545–6; Fontenay 'The Mediterranean 1500–1800', in Mallia-Milanes (ed.), *Hospitaller Malta 1530–1798*, 43–110: 49. See also K. Fleet, *European and Islamic Trade in the Early Ottoman State: The Merchants of Genoa and Turkey* (Cambridge, 1999).

eastern Mediterranean was the point of intersection for not two, but three, enduring civilizations – namely, Latin Christianity, Eastern Orthodoxy, and Islam'.[6]

The Ottoman central government in Istanbul was supposed to hold a balancing control over its vast territories. However, this proved too difficult to accomplish, especially for far-away domains. As Suraiya Faroqhi explains, 'when we look more closely at day-to-day events in the borderlands it soon becomes clear that central regulation was only part of the story'.[7] The Barbary Regencies had more autonomy than other provinces of the Ottoman empire and during the sixteenth century Ottoman authority was delegated to provincial pashas who were, in Peter Earle's words, 'often the conquerors themselves, ambitious and powerful men, not likely to trouble themselves too much about the wishes of a superior so many miles away at the other end of the Mediterranean'.[8]

By the middle of the sixteenth century European officials and merchants enjoyed good relations with the Ottoman administration and were even allowed to travel to and live in the capital or provincial trading centres.[9] On the Christian side, Venice was a significant player and controlled important positions in the otherwise Ottoman-dominated eastern Mediterranean,[10] and was often accused of pursuing commercial interests with the Ottomans to an extent that ran counter to the Christian struggle against the Muslims.[11] As for the French, they drew up several agreements with Ottomans during the 1530s and 1540s;[12] as Peter Earle remarks,

6 M. Greene, *A Shared World: Christians and Muslims in the Early Modern Mediterranean* (Princeton, 2000), 4. See also B. Arbel (ed.), *Intercultural Contacts in the Medieval Mediterranean, Studies in Honour of David Jacoby* (London, 1996) which tackles the long-lasting convergence and intricate interaction between Christians, Muslims and Jews in its widest sense.

7 S. Faroqhi, *The Ottoman Empire and the World Around It* (London and New York, 2007), 27.

8 P. Earle, *Corsairs of Malta and Barbary* (London, 1970), 24. Earle further explains that the second generation of governors were appointed for a triennial period and these found it difficult to maintain power, due to frequent revolutions, and so they had to seek the help of the janissaries. The latter eventually wielded real power over the regencies which grew in their autonomy, with Constantinople mostly concerned with the region remaining Turkish, since it was a valuable part of the empire's defence system. The Barbary corsairs accepted the obligation of Turkish sovereignty, and when it came to supporting the Turks, they accompanied the empire in its naval warfare against the Christians. Earle, *Corsairs of Malta and Barbary*, 24. See also S. Faroqhi, 'Trade: Regional, Inter-regional and International', in İnalcik & Quataert (eds), *An Economic and Social History of the Ottoman Empire*, 474–530.

9 Due to lack of documentation it is difficult to give a quantitative analysis of such occurrences, and studies mainly depend on the writings of contemporaries, or else on perspectives adopted by modern historians. Faroqhi, *The Ottoman Empire*, 29.

10 These included Crete, which remained Venetian until the war of 1645–69, and Cyprus, which they kept until 1570.

11 V. Mallia-Milanes, *Venice and Hospitaller Malta 1530–1578* (Malta, 1992).

12 In 1525, during the battle of Pavia, King Francis I (b. 1494–d. 1547) was taken prisoner by the Habsburgs and subsequently liberated after the payment of a hefty ransom which included substantial political concessions. This situation led the king to conclude several deals with the Ottoman sultan, Süleyman. Such ententes remained a constant possibility, especially during the war years of the 1680s and 1690s. Faroqhi, *The Ottoman Empire*, 33.

'their concept of peace seems to have had a strange duality about it. On the one hand was the attitude of a trading nation who wanted to expand her commerce in the Mediterranean. Peace with Turkey and Barbary made good sense, and had the added advantage of encouraging hostility against Spain, often a common enemy.'[13] It is thus evident that both in Ottoman and Christian lands government policies most often reflected the political and economic interests of the country, rather than religious and ideological issues.

The full exploitation of lucrative trade opportunities was the common factor motivating all these participants in their daily struggle against religious ideologies which impeded the easy flow of trade. The Mediterranean region was indeed a complex space where sea-trade and sea-conflict co-existed,[14] a space which cannot be defined simply by its limits[15] or its religious beliefs. According to Nabil Matar, 'as much as [Muslim] jurists condemned such intercourse with the *nasara* [Christians], they stood as little chance of putting an end to it as did Christian clergy, princes, and even the papacy of curbing Christian trading with the Muslim world'.[16] Turning to Malta, to what extent did the island's Christian princes want to curb trading activities with the Muslim world? Were the restrictions imposed by the Hospitaller government aimed at cutting off Christian–Muslim trading contacts, or were they used as a means to control such trading and justify it in the eyes of the Christian world?

This chapter will provide a picture of the Mediterranean where different cultures found it opportune to trade along each other's shores, despite their traditional enmity.[17] Malta, the official base for Christ's militia, and as such considered the epitome of the Christian fight against the Muslim, is an excellent example of this paradox. This chapter looks at the individual trajectories of protagonists, whether merchants, knights, slaves, clergy or lay people and outlines the practical ways in which commercial and financial activities functioned in such circumstances. Such an analysis is essential in order to probe into the actions of the different stakeholders in Mediterranean trade, since they were very traditional and often bound by strong religious beliefs.

Primary sources shed light on the burgeoning local and foreign commercial activities in the Maltese harbour area, and the way in which they interplayed with the presence of the Knights Hospitaller. The Knights provided the essential institutional framework for commercial activities to flourish, strengthened existing maritime links and built upon local expertise, thus complementing the abilities of the local seafaring community. The paradox of the Knights' contrasting economic and spiritual needs is striking. On the one hand, they had to live up to their reputation

13 Earle, *Corsairs of Malta and Barbary*, 38.

14 Fusaro, 'After Braudel', in Fusaro et al., *Trade and Cultural Exchange*, 1–22: 7.

15 Abulafia, 'Introduction: What Is the Mediterranean', in Abulafia (ed.), *The Mediterranean in History*, 11–65: 11.

16 Matar, *Europe through Arab Eyes*, 10.

17 Salvatore Bono has even noted the presence in Tunis during the seventeenth century of Maltese merchants purchasing prize ships and cargoes. S. Bono, 'Guerra, Corsara e Commercio nel Maghreb Barbaresco (Secoli XVI–XVIII)', in G. Lopez Nadal (ed.), *El Comerç Alternativ. Corsaris i Contraban (ss XV–XVIII)* (Mallorca, 1990), 133–44: 141–2.

as Christendom's bulwark against the Infidel, and on the other hand, they had an interest in maintaining commercial links with Islamic trading posts throughout the Mediterranean. Thus, other realities existed aside from that of total hostility between the Cross and the Crescent, and these come to the fore when the daily operations of the different stakeholders in trade are examined.

This final chapter gives special attention to trading links between Malta, North Africa and the Levant and how such activities managed to survive, albeit at times on a very low level, in the environment of the different and independent policies adopted by the governors of the Ottoman states. The chief questions to be answered here are: was there a trading link between North Africa and Malta prior to the arrival of the Knights? How did the Knights exploit their dual presence in the two fortresses of Tripoli and Birgu? How did traders, both Christian and Muslim, operate successfully, often making trips to hostile ports in pirate-infested seas? Why were they attracted to trade in Maltese ports? How did the local population react to foreign players' involvement in the island's trading activities? How much did the shift of the main administrative centre of the island from Mdina, which was an inland city, to Birgu, a harbour city, affect Malta as a trading centre? Can it be said that the island's place in the Mediterranean was re-orientated through these changes?

It is hoped that fresh insights offered here will be a springboard to further in-depth studies in an area and period which until now has been neglected in Maltese historiography, and that the present study will complement others which have concentrated on commercial networks in the Mediterranean in the early modern period – thus providing a fuller picture of the maritime activities of the Mediterranean seafaring community.

The chapter first sets out to explain why, despite having a great potential for trade, Tripoli was considered a burden not only on the coffers of the Order but also on those of the Spanish Crown. It then looks at how administrative measures adopted by the Knights in Tripoli compare to those implemented in Malta, and the way in which trading activities connected to the castle of Tripoli were regulated. It then moves on to examine the mechanisms used by various merchants to fully exploit the Christian presence in Tripoli, and how different ethnic groups cooperated for the sake of their business interests. The chapter also aims to shed light on how the Order functioned in terms of the provision of victuals and other commodities from across the Mediterranean.

The castle of Tripoli under Christian rule

The Spanish conquest of ports along the Maghribi coast in the early sixteenth century was a direct response to the fear of a possible Ottoman advance in the Mediterranean.[18] This fear increased from the 1520s with Süleyman the Magnificent's accession to the

[18] A. Williams, 'Tripoli and the Knights of Malta Revisited', in P. Xuereb (ed.), *Karissime Gotifride – Historical Essays Presented to Godfrey Wettinger on his Seventieth Birthday* (Malta, 1999), 97–102: 97.

Ottoman throne in 1522.[19] His first act as sultan was to expel the Hospitallers from Rhodes, thus freeing a vital communication point between Istanbul and Cairo from a constant menace.[20] The establishment of the Barbarossa brothers in Djerba (1510), Djidjelli (1514) and Algiers (1516) triggered a major concern for Spain, especially since the political situation in the Mediterranean changed rapidly in the decade 1520–30.[21] It was as a consequence of this change that Malta acquired its full worth as a strategic outpost.[22] Tripoli was conquered by Ferdinand the Catholic in 1510. He then realised that his conquest could not finance itself and thus transferred full financial responsibility for the upkeep of this base to Sicily.[23]

According to Carmelo Trasselli, this was possible because the king knew that the viceroy would accept the heavy financial burden with little opposition.[24] On Charles V's accession to the Spanish throne one of his first decisions was to free Sicily from the financial and military burden of Tripoli,[25] thus putting an end to the Sicilian Viceroys' continual requests for financial aid. Similarly, just like the Sicilian Viceroys before them, the Order was presented with an option that it could hardly negotiate, since it was aware that the king knew very well how urgent, precarious and unstable its position was following the loss of Rhodes. After having reluctantly accepted the enclave of Tripoli, which was surrounded by a hostile hinterland, the Order managed to govern it for twenty-one years.

During the medieval period, Maltese corsairs operated from Tripoli against the Ottomans in the Aegean, and Malta served as a base for corsair vessels.[26] However, these activities were as nothing in comparison to the attacks suffered by Muslim

19 North Africa and the western Mediterranean in the earlier part of the sixteenth century had become as much of an Ottoman–Habsburg frontier as were the Balkans, and this continued to be the case under Süleyman's successors. Green, 'Resurgent Islam', in Abulafia (ed.), *The Mediterranean*, 219–49: 220–6; C. Heywood, 'A Frontier without Archaeology? The Ottoman Maritime Frontier in the Western Mediterranean, 1660–1760', *Crusades*, 2 (Society for the Study of the Crusades and the Latin East, Aldershot, 2003), 493–508.

20 M. Kunt, 'Introduction', in Kunt & Woodhead (eds), *Süleyman the Magnificent*, 3–38: 35.

21 Braudel, *The Mediterranean*, vol. 2, 855.

22 M. Fontenay, 'Charles Quint, Malte et la défense de la Méditerranée', *Revue d'histoire modern et contemporaine*, 50 (2003), 7–28.

23 The establishment of *presidios* along the North African coast as far east as Libya provided protection to Catalan and other ships navigating to the East, since it kept in check Muslim piracy. Abulafia, *The Great Sea*, 409.

24 Trasselli, *Da Ferdinando il Cattolico a Carlo V*, vol. 1, 205.

25 Before the transfer of Tripoli to the Knights in 1530, the Viceroy of Sicily, Ettore Pignatelli, received 12,000 *scudi* yearly for its upkeep. Other expenses such as the supply of ammunition or extraordinary expenses were the responsibility of the Spanish Crown. E. Rossi, *Il Dominio degli Spagnoli e dei Cavalieri di Malta a Tripoli* (Airoldi, 1937), 47. Carmelo Trasselli has also argued that the North African conquests led to grave economic repercussions in Sicily, as the country had to shoulder not only the financial expenses but also the presence of mercenaries employed by the Spanish Crown for North African campaigns. These were stationed in Sicily and were not averse to pillaging Sicilian towns. Trasselli, *Da Ferdinando il Cattolico a Carlo V*, vol. 1, 206.

26 Luttrell, 'Malta and Rhodes', in Mallia-Milanes (ed.), *Hospitaller Malta 1530–1798*, 255–84: 269–70.

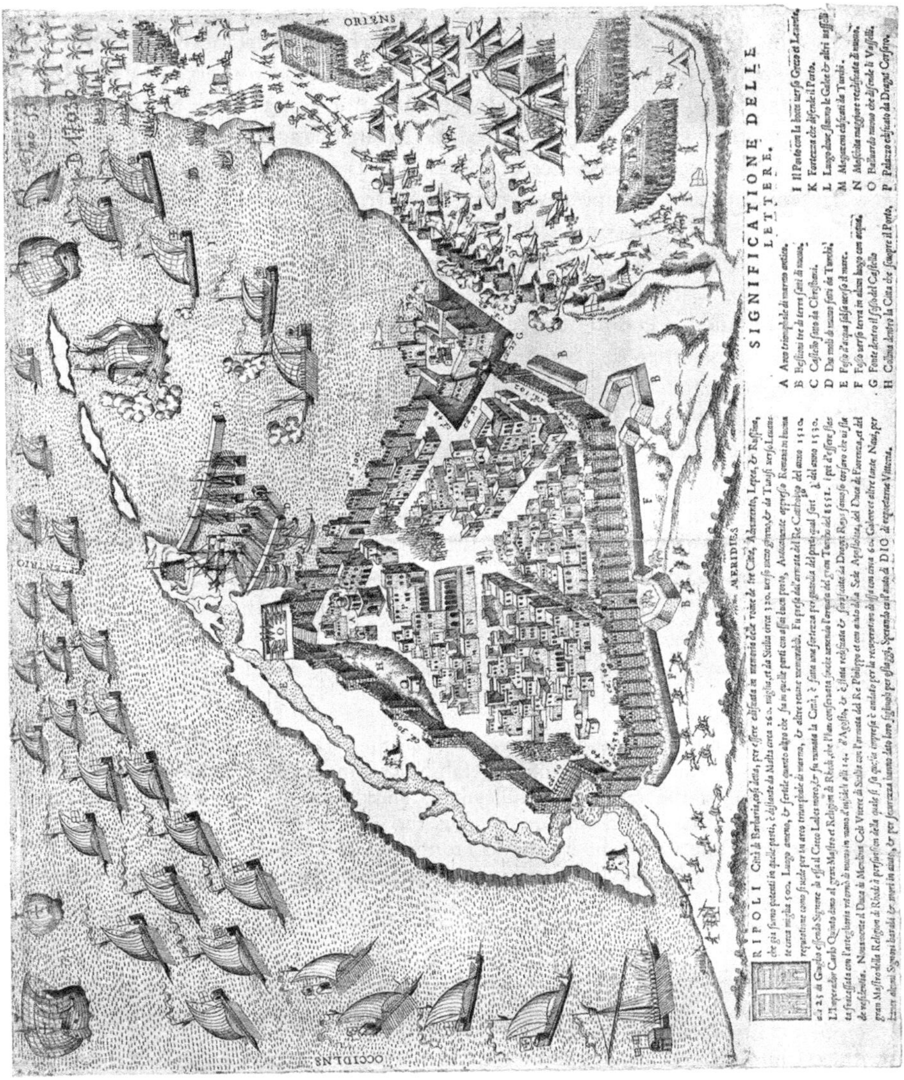

Fig. 6 Plan of the fortress of *Tripoli di Barbaria*
Source: Private Collection, Malta.

shipping as a result of the Order's establishment on the island. Trading links with Tripoli were already being exploited by Maltese merchants during the medieval period, but it was only after 1530 that Malta began to witness a substantial increase in economic activities, due to the presence of a Christian base in Tripoli. Corsairing was becoming the island's fastest-growing economic sector and the connection with Tripoli provided an important link for conducting slave redemption services which were coupled with transport of merchandise. Documentary evidence shows that the Tripoli outpost offered good trading prospects, and commercial links between Tripoli and Malta were retained even after the loss of the fortress by the Knights Hospitaller in 1551.[27]

Trade and taxation in Tripoli prior to the arrival of the Knights Hospitaller

Although there is a lack of documentation on the taxes in force during the Order's rule in Tripoli, the tax records for the Spanish period provide a good indication of how income was generated from Tripoli for the benefit of the ruling body. Research in the archives of the Order for the period 1530–51 has not turned up any relevant records additional to what has already been published.[28] It may well be the case that the Order chose to retain the existing taxation structures, since orders and instructions issued to newly appointed governors at Tripoli referred to the 'old customs' of the city and how they were to be respected.[29]

The Sicilian Viceroys acknowledged trade with the Moors as the most important

27 The main sources regarding Malta and the Tripoli fortress are G. Bosio, *Dell' Istoria della Sacra Religione* (2nd impression, Naples, 1684), vol. 3; E. Rossi, 'Il dominio dei Cavalieri di Malta a Tripoli (1530–1551) e i rapporti dell' Ordine con Tripoli nei secoli seguenti (1551–1798), *Archivium Melitense*, 6:2 (1925), 43–85; A. Vella, 'The Order of Malta and the Defence of Tripoli 1530–1551', *Melita Historica*, 6:4 (1975), 362–81; Williams, 'Tripoli and the Knights of Malta Revisited', in Xuereb (ed.), *Karissime Gotifride – Historical Essays*, 97–102.

28 The most extensive of these were those of 1548, which are dealt with later in this chapter. These *capitoli* were approved during the Chapter General of 1548 and duly recorded in the *Sacra Capitulum Generalia*. NLM, AOM 287. Other laws were incorporated within the various instructions given to the governors of the city recorded in the *Libri Bullarum*. When a new governor took possession of the city he was obliged to take with him a copy of the existing *bandi* and read them out to the population so that everyone knew how to respect the law. It was further stated that the city enjoyed many good customs which had been previously introduced.

29 '*Perche circa il governo del castello sono molte ordinatione antiche et moderne et bene costume quelle bene vederete et considerarete et conforme esse vi regirete, et si alcuna cosa dimportancia vi parera innovare darete prima aviso a noi et a nostro venerando consiglio accio che in quelle vi sia dato ordine*' [sic]. (Because regarding the governance of the castle there are a lot of ancient and modern ordinances and good customs, these you will observe and consider and govern according to them, and if in your opinion you think that you need to change [such laws] you will first notify us and our venerable council for the granting of permission.) NLM, AOM, Lib. Bull. 421, fol. 226v (9.xi.1549). Similar orders are found in NLM, AOM, Lib. Bull. 415, fol. 246v (10.vi.1533).

commercial activity in Tripoli.[30] Accordingly, all officials and residents of the city and fort were duty bound to accommodate the needs of all merchants so as to encourage them to enhance their trading operations.[31] The city's income was mainly derived from various taxes on trading activity, such as the customs tax imposed on all imported and exported commodities which is referred to in documents as '*di dohana*'.[32] This tax stood at 18 *grani* per *uncia* or 3% of the total estimated value of the merchandise.[33] Any goods imported into Tripoli which were not sold were exempt from export tax if the merchant chose to re-export them for sale elsewhere.[34] However, any goods which were bought directly from Tripoli for export purposes were subject to the tax. Other taxes included '*la caxa*', which amounted to 1 *tarì* per *uncia* or 33.3% on all goods sold within the fort and the city, and the '*cantarata*'.[35] The latter was imposed on both imported and exported items which were sold

30 This statement was made by the Viceroy himself when he stated in his *Capitoli* that '*li personi che portirano in dita cita li diti robbi et mercancij non li portirano ad altro efecto si non per vindirli alj morj perche conoxeno et sano chi in dita fortiliza tanti mercancij non si potevano per li genti chi stano in dita fortiliza comperarj*' [sic]. (The persons who bring to this city the said goods and merchandise do not bring them other than to sell them to the Moors, because these know that they could never sell so much merchandise to the residents of the fort.) NLM, AOM 6559, fol. 44 (6.iv.1523). The statement further stated that many merchants often declared that they were going to re-export their goods to Christian countries, but then, once they had avoided paying the export tax, they went to infidel countries and sold their wares there. Thus, any merchant who declared that he was exporting to Christian countries had to present the necessary documentation which substantiated his claims, this being stated as '*di fare li debiti responsali in fra legitima tempora como serrano portati in questi lochi*'. NLM, AOM 6559, fols 44–45 (6.iv.1523).

31 NLM, AOM 6559, fol. 40 (5.ix.1521). '*Per atrahiri lu comercio ad augmeto et utili di dita dohana, volimo et ordinamo chi li mercanti et persuni tratanti chi viniranno ad tratare et merci moniari in dita fortilizia siano ben tratate, visti et respectati, danduli stancia et locu, tanto per loro habitacioni como per la custodia et conservacioni di loru mercancij et robbi, non li fachendo alcuno ostaculo tanto in lo venire comu in lo comprari et vendirij azoche essendo ben tratate et onorati habiano causa di concurrirj et tratari in dita fortiliza in utili et aumento di la regia Corti*' [sic]. (In order to attract commerce and for the benefit of the said customs, we command that merchants and contracting persons who come to do business and trade in the said fortress are well-treated and respected, provided room and space both for their lodging as well as for the safeguarding of their merchandise and goods. They should not meet with any obstacle either in their arrival or their sales or purchases, since, if they are well-treated and honoured, they will have cause to return to this fortress and do business for the benefit of the *Regia Corte*.) See also NLM, AOM 6559, fols 54–55 (26.iv.1525).

32 The importing of wheat, armaments, iron, steel and other minerals was prohibited unless authorised by the governor. G. La Mantia, 'La Secrezia Dogana di Tripoli ed i Capitoli della sua Amministratione Approvati e Riformati dai Vicire di Sicilia negli anni 1511–1521', *Archivio Storico Siciliano*, 5:41 (1916), 466–90: 476. Other *Capitoli* included those issued on 6 April 1523, 26 May 1525 and the instructions given to *Nob.* Francesco Corsu, the fiscal officer (*credenciero*) of the *Regia Corte*, on 28 November 1528, a copy of which is found in NLM, AOM 6559. (It is to be noted that all enumeration of this manuscript was done in pencil at a later stage and at times it is not sequential.)

33 This was established as being 5% in the *Capitoli* of 1510–11, NLM, AOM 6559, fol. 8; La Mantia, 'La Secrezia Dogana di Tripoli', 472. Soldiers and guards of the fort were exempted from this tax, NLM, AOM 6559, fols 43, 45 (6.iv.1523).

34 NLM, AOM 6559, fol. 44 (6.iv.1523).

35 NLM, AOM 6559, fols 43–45 (6.iv.1523).

by weight, referred to in the documents as '*canna di peso*'. On importation, these types of goods were subject to the usual 18 *grani* per *uncia*. However, if they were eventually re-exported to Christian lands they were subject to an additional 1 *tarì* per *uncia* as *caxa* tax and another 1 *tarì* per *uncia* on the weight or *cantarata*.[36]

Both imported and exported merchandise had to be weighed and valued by the *Secreto* or his official before any further trading operations could take place.[37] All merchandise had to be imported or exported through two main gates, each of which had a guardian who kept a daily record of all imports and exports. One of these gates was known as *Porta della Marina* and, as the name implies, was used for sea-borne trade, while the other was known as *Porta della Vittoria*, used for all land trade.[38] As was the practice all over Europe, no merchandise could be exported during night-time, in order to ensure the transparency of all trading operations and avoid clandestine trading.

The sale and ransoming of slaves, both white and black, also carried a tax. Accordingly, each ransomed infidel slave had to make two kinds of payment, one of 5 gold ducats to the customs official and another of 1 gold ducat to the guard at the *Porta di la Victoria*.[39] Moreover, if a slave was returned to Tripoli from his place of captivity in the hope of being ransomed but was unlucky in his endeavour, the owner or *patrone* could 're-export' him without having to pay any tax.[40] Non-ransomed slaves could be sold by public auction even by Moors, and if such slave was eventually sold, a tax of 20 *tarì*, known as '*laxuta dela porta*' [*sic*],[41] had to be paid.[42] This tax was equivalent to that due on all black slaves who were exported. It is interesting to note that the laws (*capitoli*) make continuous and specific distinction between 'Moor slaves' and 'black slaves', the latter being referred to in documents as '*testa di nigru*'.[43] For example, Clause 12 of the 1521 *capitoli* stipulated that all 'black slaves' who entered the city had to pay a tax of 2 *doubloons* 1 *tarì*, while another 1 *doubloon* 4 *tarì* were to be paid on leaving the city, due to the *Regia Corte*.[44] This might be because 'black slaves' were sold in greater numbers since they were continually supplied by the Moors from the hinterland.[45] Moors were also allowed to sell any

36 NLM, AOM 6559, fol. 45 (6.iv.1523).
37 NLM, AOM 6559, fols 28, 37 (5.ix.1521).
38 La Mantia, 'La Secrezia Dogana di Tripoli', 472.
39 La Mantia, 'La Secrezia Dogana di Tripoli', 480.
40 The slave could stay in the fort for a period of six months, during which time he hoped to be ransomed – '*che qual si vogla moro che vinisi in dita fortiliza por rescatarsi non potisi in quilla star pio di misi sey*' [sic]. (After the elapse of this period he was to embark on a ship and return to his captive state.) NLM, AOM 6559, fols 64–65 (28.xi.1528).
41 In modern Italian this would be *l'uscita della porta* (the exit from the gate), meaning the tax paid on export.
42 NLM, AOM 6559, fol. 37 (5.ix.1521).
43 Baxter Wolf discusses the choice of the use of the terms Moors or Black slaves in Portuguese documentary sources of history. Baxter Wolf, 'The "Moors" of West Africa'.
44 NLM, AOM 6559, fol. 34 (5.ix.1521).
45 M. Fontenay, 'Routes et modalités du commerce des esclaves dans la Méditerranée des Temps Modernes XVIe, XVIIe et XVIIIe siècles)', *Revue Historique*, 4 (2006), 813–30: 815–17. Marcocci, 'Trading with the Muslim World', in Trivellato et al., *Religion and Trade*, 91–107.

'black slaves' not redeemed by public auction. Notarial contracts relating to the acquisition of slaves for eventual re-sale concluded in Malta by sedentary merchants and travelling partners almost always describe their 'commodity' as '*testa di nigru*'.[46]

The Tripoli *capitoli* stated that Venetian merchants who came to the fort to sell their commodities[47] should pay 1 *tarì* 18 *grani* for each *uncia* of the value of merchandise sold,[48] while the remaining balance to complete the 10% tax was to be paid by the purchaser. Additionally, any exports made by Venetian ships were subject to an extra '*tarì 1 per unza per raxuni di cantarata*'[49] over and above the 1 *tarì* 18 *grani*. Another clause stipulated that all merchandise bought from or sold to Moors was to pay a 10% tax.[50] However, Christian residents of the castle were exempted from this tax if their purchases related to essential items such as food and clothing.[51] Permission from the governor was required for the sale of wheat or barley to Moors. Such sales carried a tax related to *tratte* established in Sicily, which at the time amounted to 3 *tarì* per *salma*.[52]

In terms of corsair ships selling wheat to Moors, apart from having to obtain a licence from the governor, these had their tax charge doubled, to 6 *tarì* per *salma*, which was equivalent to the tax paid on these items if they were sold out at sea.[53] In 1528, in a set of instructions addressed to the newly appointed fiscal officer, *Nob.* Francesco Corsu, the Viceroy lamented that many traders were evading tax. Listing the various officers who were breaching regulations, the Viceroy lamented that

46 'The black slaves who were brought to Malta must have come by way of the Sahara, most of them having already been slaves of the Moors or Turks in North Africa before their capture by the knights or corsairs. However, great care must be taken in the interpretation of the Italian word *negro*, which could simply refer to a dark-coloured slave and have no particular racial significance.' G. Wettinger, *Slavery in the Islands of Malta and Gozo ca. 1000–1812* (Malta, 2002), 42.

47 The exact words used were '*ad fari fera*' (to do a fair). This tax excluded food and clothing sold to residents of the fort. NLM, AOM 6559, fol. 33 (5.ix.1521).

48 NLM, AOM 6559, fol. 33 (5.ix.1521). This was stated to be based on the customs of Palermo regarding Venetian shipping and was broken down as follows: 1 *tarì* due as tax – '*per raxione di caxa*' and 18 *grani* due to customs – '*per raxioni do dogana*', and was imposed on trade done with infidels as well as that with Christians, except those resident at the fort. NLM, AOM 6559, fol. 32 (5.ix.1521). It was noted by the present author that in La Mantia's transcript the following in the square brackets was not included: '*chi in casu chi li galiazi veneciani andassiro ad fari fera in la dita fortiliza [di Tripoli chi di tuti li mercantii chi si vendisiro in dita fortiliza] tanto ad Mori comu a Christiani*' (in the event that Venetian galleys went to do a fair in the said fortress [of Tripoli, that over all merchandise sold in the said fortress] both to Moors and to Christians). Refer to La Mantia, 'La Secrezia Dogana di Tripoli', 487. This suggests that there could have been some discrepancies between the different transcriptions.

49 NLM, AOM 6559, fol. 34 (5.ix.1521). This meant that they had to pay one *tarì* for every *uncia*'s worth of the commodity due to the *Regia Corte*.

50 NLM, AOM 6559, fol. 46 (6.iv.1523).

51 NLM, AOM 6559, fol. 51 (26.v.1525).

52 NLM, AOM 6559, fol. 46 (6.iv.1523).

53 NLM, AOM 6559, fols 32–33 (5.ix.1521). Moreover, if a corsair chose to sell his prize in Tripoli, he also had to pay a 10% tax. The relevant fees which were due to the Admiralty were not stipulated. In 1525, a 10% tax on any wheat brought in by corsair ships and sold to the Moors was introduced. NLM, AOM 6559, fol. 51 (26.v.1525).

fraudulent activities and rampant abuse of the taxation system were badly damaging the Crown's coffers. In order to remedy the situation, he was now placing full trust in Corsu and requesting all necessary measures to be taken to ensure proper functioning of the system.[54]

Thus, apart from all the other challenges which Tripoli posed to the Knights of the Order, which have been repeatedly echoed in Maltese historiography, such as the distance separating the two posts and the huge expense and effort of fortifying Tripoli,[55] it is here suggested that the outpost presented yet another problem. In taking over the administration of Tripoli, the Order inherited an administrative system which was corrupt and far from efficient in enforcing laws and collecting taxes. Tax evasion flourished, to the detriment of the governing body.[56] Were the Knights successful in suppressing malpractices, or were these engrained to such an extent that their administration found it difficult to eradicate them?

The governance of Tripoli – a forced 'option'

Once established in Malta and Tripoli in 1530, the Hospitaller Order immediately tried to strengthen the link between the two bases. In 1523 the commissioners' report identified that two-thirds of the Tripoli fortress was surrounded by sea, while the remaining third was surrounded by crumbling walls.[57] The fortress itself was small and had lodging for only the governor and a small number of Knights.[58] At the time, the entire population of the town consisted of not more than sixty Moorish families[59] who made use of a small and unsheltered port.[60]

54 *Nob.* Francesco Corsu was appointed fiscal officer (*credenciero*) of the *Regia Corte* on 28 November 1528. One of the instructions stated that at present the accounts of the customs were being kept in '*pitazzi*' which were carelessly kept. He was thus to keep all the books relating to imports and exports bound and in order, accompanied by an alphabetical index and covered in parchment. An account of all these activities was to be sent to the Viceroy every four months. If such books are still extant, their study would provide more detailed information on the type of trading activities taking place in this fortress. NLM, AOM 6559, fols 59–61 (28.xi.1528).

55 While the fort offered a good base for the lucrative trade in slavery, it lacked essential resources such as water, wood and lime, which were crucial for the proper upkeep of strategic bases.

56 For a more in-depth study of the corrupt administrative system in Tripoli under the Spanish refer to Trasselli, *Da Ferdinando il Cattolico a Carlo V*, vol. 1, Chapter IV, passim.

57 Bosio, *Dell'Istoria della Sacra Religione*, vol. 3, 29–30.

58 A. Williams, '"Stone or Wooden Walls?": The Problems of Land and Sea Defence in the Islands of Rhodes (1421–1522) and Malta (1530–1631)', in T. Cortis & T. Gambin (eds), *De Triremibus, Festschrift in honour of Joseph Muscat* (Malta, 2005), 415–26: 420.

59 A report dated 1522 reveals that over 150 Moorish families went to the fort, made friends with the soldiers and asked to set up a community there which would have been headed by their own Sheik. It seems this request was accepted and the Viceroy authorised the expedition of wood and lime for these families. Trasselli, *Da Ferdinando il Cattolico a Carlo V*, vol. 1, 231.

60 The Commissioners' report on Tripoli makes reference only to this port, which they described as small, insecure, molested by north-easterly winds and sheltered only to the

By 1530 the population had increased to about eighty families, mostly Moorish, living in the city. The authority of the governor did not extend beyond the city walls, with very minor exceptions such as the western villages of Zanzùr, Lmaia and Zuàga.[61] In fact, in Tagiura, twelve kilometres to the east of Tripoli, the Turkish lieutenant (*kialya*) Khair ud-Dìn had proclaimed himself king (*rais*).[62] In alliance with the Ottomans, he fortified the village and built a defence tower in its small port, which had by now become a nest of Muslim corsairs who constantly menaced the nearby Christian fortress of Tripoli.[63] According to Rossi, he managed to build another tower, known as *alqaide*, which was situated just one mile from the Christian fortress.[64] The end of Khair ud-Dìn's rule in about 1539 saw the establishment of the Turkish renegade Muràd Aghà as head of the rebels.[65] Muràd Aghà proved to be an even tougher opponent for the Hospitallers,[66] who tried hard, and unsuccessfully, to crush him.[67]

Although the Order had already experienced a similar situation in defending disparate posts while in Rhodes,[68] it now found it difficult to cope with the financial burden of defending two posts which were so far apart, increasingly menaced by the enemy and both lacking essential resources for their upkeep. The Hospitallers had tried more than once to persuade the emperor to grant them permission to destroy Tripoli and its port and abandon it. However, Charles V would not hear of such a plan and kept promising that he would intervene if his support was eventually required. But, in spite of the many promises, he was neither prepared to pour out any significant resources to the North African *presides*, nor ready to contribute in

west by the cliffs – '*piccolo, non sicuro, molestato dal grecale e solo riparato ad ovest da scogli*'. Rossi, *Il Domino degli Spagnoli*, 45.

61 Rossi, *Il Domino degli Spagnoli*, 53.

62 He was also known to Christians as Cacciadiabolo.

63 NLM, AOM, Lib. Bull. 415, fol. 215v (16.viii.1531), transcribed and reproduced in Rossi, *Il Domino degli Spagnoli*, Doc. I, 81.

64 Rossi, *Il Domino degli Spagnoli*, 55.

65 Referred to as Morataga or Muradaga by the authors of the period, among whom was Nicolò de Nicolai, who actually met and conversed with Muràd Aghà. Rossi, *Il Domino degli Spagnoli*, 56 n. 1; N. de Nicholai, *Le navigationi et viaggi nella Turchia* (Antwerp, 1576), 47.

66 Reference to the Knights' preoccupation with Mortaga and the problems he was creating for the Hospitallers in Tripoli through his constant attacks is found in NLM, AOM, Lib. Bull. 420, fols 217v–218v (8.i.1547).

67 Refer also to Vella, 'The Order of Malta and the Defence of Tripoli', 362–81. Various runaway Muslims from Tagiura are documented in the *Liber Bullarum*, since they would flee to the castle of Tripoli and afterwards make a request for a safe conduct pass to return to their homeland. There is no doubt that they would have been an important spying source for the Knights. See for example, NLM, AOM, Lib. Bull. 419, fol. 231v (5.i.1545); 420, fols 211–211v (17.viii.1546), fols 216–216v (31.xii.1546), fol. 221 (8.iii.1547); 421, fol. 204 (5.xii.1547); 422, fol. 207 (14.iii.1550), fol. 211v (4.viii.1550).

68 From 1344 until 1402 the Knights were also the appointed defenders of Smyrna castle, a task which cost them the hefty sum of around 3,000 florins per year. Once this important port was lost, they negotiated with Mehmet I for the port of Budrum. This too was another great drain on the Order's finances. Williams, 'Stone or Wooden Walls?', in Cortis & Gambin (eds), *De Triremibus*, 415–26: 416–17.

any way to ameliorating the Knights' increasingly vulnerable position in Tripoli.[69] Spanish rule had shown that human resources were the most difficult and costly item to supply in this outpost.[70]

As early as 1511 the Sicilian Viceroy Ugo Moncada felt it necessary to issue two *bandi*, one in January and another in August, in which he ordered, on pain of death, that all officials and soldiers who had fled from Africa to Sicily should present themselves at Trapani, from where they were to be given free passage to return to Tripoli.[71] In another instance, a group of about thirty-one high-ranking officials from Sicily were chosen to provide the necessary civilian set-up for Tripoli based on the Sicilian model. However, it seems that only one chose to take up residence and was eventually appointed governor.[72] A good number of Christians who came into contact with Islam, either as captives or as paid workers, often preferred to turn Muslim,[73] and this included numerous soldiers from the Spanish garrisons.[74] The Knights thus knew well that maintaining high morale was necessary to the successful manning of the fortress, and that in practice this meant that the soldiers must be well fed and adequately remunerated for their work.

In the Chapter General of 1548 the Knight and future Grand Master de Valette offered a possible solution for the good defence of Tripoli and suggested that the Hospitaller Order should transfer its seat of government from Malta to Tripoli. Although Malta was considered to be the frontier separating the two great ideologies, the move would have brought the Order one step closer in confronting the enemy of Christendom. Following the necessary evaluations, the project never materialised. The majority of the Order's members were of the opinion that it was best to wait and let things take their own course. However, the discussion of this issue and the ordinances which were subsequently promulgated for the better governance of Tripoli provide the historian with a clearer view of how the Hospitaller government functioned in this city.[75]

Just as in Malta's case, key positions would have been delegated to members of

69 Williams, 'Stone or Wooden Walls?', in Cortis & Gambin (eds), *De Triremibus*, 415–26: 421.

70 In fact, in 1511 a *bando* issued by the Sicilian viceroy invited people to settle in Tripoli and offered very tempting rewards to those who took up the offer, such as free land, exemption from tax and criminal impunity. However, only one person is recorded to have taken up the offer. Trasselli, *Da Ferdinando il Cattolico a Carlo V*, vol. 1, 208.

71 Trasselli, *Da Ferdinando il Cattolico a Carlo V*, vol. 1, 209.

72 Trasselli, *Da Ferdinando il Cattolico a Carlo V*, vol. 1, 209–10.

73 B. Bennassar & L Bennassar, *Les Chretiens d'Allah* (Paris, 2006), 19–20. The status of a slave did not impede a person from climbing the social scale in the Ottoman empire. What made one powerful was his closeness and good relations with the sultan. Earle, *Corsairs of Malta and Barbary*, 28–31; Fontenay, 'Routes et modalités', 817.

74 An example was provided in the instructions of the Sicilian Viceroy to Francesco Corsu, where the latter was instructed to find an appropriate guardian of the harbour since the previous one, namely Francesco Santande, after having defrauded the Crown, had deserted to the land of the Moors, leaving his office. NLM, AOM 6559, fols 63–64 (28. xi.1528). See also Braudel, The *Mediterranean*, vol. 2, 800, where he states that 'Spanish garrisons were decimated by epidemics of desertion.'

75 Document transcribed and published in Rossi, *Il Domino degli Spagnoli*, Doc. XI, 101–6.

the Order who also held full control of basic food supplies. The proposed transfer was to be effected in a gradual manner and the first Knights to settle there would have been required to pledge their loyalty to the governor of Tripoli, who was to be a Knight of the rank of Grand Cross. The governor would have ample powers which almost paralleled those of the Grand Master in Malta. However, he was bound to abide by the existing laws and customs of the castle and, should he feel a need to promulgate new laws, he had first to consult with the council of the Order in Malta and get their approval. The Common Treasury in Malta would ensure that the fort was well supplied with victuals to feed a garrison of about fifty Knights and 260 paid soldiers.[76] It was hoped that this exercise would give a clear indication of the feasibility of increasing the number of Knights to one hundred after the first year, and thereafter sending fifty Knights per year until all the members of the Order were settled in Tripoli. Should this exercise fail after the first, second or third year, it would be clear that the place was not adequate to house the headquarters of the Hospitaller Order.

Another important aspect of the plans for the possible transfer to Tripoli, and which tallies with the steps taken for the move to Malta, was the administration of the castle by the sea, for in Tripoli too it was stipulated that the harbour master was to be replaced by a Knight of the Order. Those who worked at the customs house would not be paid from the revenues of the castle, but would have to rely on what they received from the customs. Just as in earlier *capitoli* issued by the Sicilian Viceroys for the administration of Tripoli between 1511 and 1528,[77] there were limitations regarding commercial activity, and accordingly nobody was allowed to sell or buy wheat or biscuit, since this was to be the sole prerogative of the governor or the treasurer.[78] The Treasury would have the right of first refusal of any booty which corsairs brought to Tripoli, and for which profit fees due to the Admiral were to be paid.[79] Bakeries were to be administered and regulated by the government, and individuals would be permitted to bake bread only for their own personal use. At the time of the writing of these regulations it was highlighted that many Moorish families used to live in the city and go to the castle to buy their everyday necessities. This practice was repudiated by the Knights as early as 1533,[80] and again in the *capitoli* of 1548 the Hospitaller government complained of the Moors' easy

76 In 1528 the Viceroy of Sicily, Count de Monteleone, decreed that the city had to have a garrison of 200 paid soldiers. NLM, AOM 6559, fols 59–61 (28.xi.1528). In 1533 the city also had a garrison of 200 soldiers and officials, including the four chaplains of the Order. NLM, Lib. Bull. 415, fol. 415v (10.vi.1533).

77 NLM, AOM 6559 holds a copy of the *Capitoli* issued by the Sicilian Viceroys for the years 1511, 1512, 1521, 1523, 1525 and 1528.

78 Rossi, *Il Domino degli Spagnoli*, Doc. XI, 101–6: 103.

79 These excluded those corsairs who flew the flag of the Order. Rossi, *Il Domino degli Spagnoli*, Doc. XI, 105–6. The tax rate for Tripoli is not stipulated in the *Capitoli*. However, in Malta the *dretti di ammiragliato*, as they were known, amounted to 10% of the value of the booty. Earle, *Corsairs of Malta and Barbary*, 126–7.

80 NLM, Lib. Bull. 415, fol. 246v (10.vi.1533).

access to the castle and ordered that this was to be avoided in future, for the sake of the castle's security.[81]

Similar declarations had been made when the fort was under Spanish rule. It therefore seems that even though several orders had been issued since the conquest of the city to regulate the number of Moors who had full access to the castle, these were never seriously implemented. In their effort to establish more effective control, the Hospitallers decreed that to provide for the necessities of the Muslim population there should be a shop situated outside the castle which was to be adequately supplied with bread, wine, oil, cheese, vegetables, honey and other commodities,[82] thus completely excluding the Moors from the castle precincts.[83] Undoubtedly the exclusion of Moors from the castle would have served as a precaution for its safety. However, the Knights would have noted from the documentation handed over by the Spanish administration[84] the high level of tax evasion and fraud which existed in almost all trading operations, including those done with Moors. Therefore, another possible explanation for the Moors' exclusion from the castle could be that the Knights wanted to reduce the possibilities for them buy their necessities from Christian intermediaries who would have taken advantage of the tax-free regime[85] and sold their goods to the Moors at a lower price.[86]

It seems that this shop was never set up, since, notwithstanding all the prohibitions, Moors were still entering the castle to buy their daily necessities as late as 1551.[87] Further evidence of the lack of proper control in the organisational structure during the Knights' rule in Tripoli comes from a document dated 1533. The Maltese authorities were concerned that some Moors and Jews in Tripoli were being given a monthly ration of wine and bread similar to that given to the garrison. The Governor of Tripoli was instructed to investigate the situation and remedy any misappropriation of supplies.[88] The continuous breach of these regulations demonstrates that, just like its Spanish predecessors, the Order was not successful in enforcing its laws in Tripoli.

81 Rossi, *Il Domino degli Spagnoli*, Doc. XI, 104–5.

82 Apart from foodstuff, the document states '*et moltre* [sic] *alter cose minute che si vendono in detto loco*'. Rossi, *Il Domino degli Spagnoli*, Doc. XI, 104. All sales made to the Moors were to be noted down by the notary, who had to keep them in a good state. NLM, AOM, Lib. Bull. 415, fol. 246v (10.vi.1533).

83 Rossi, *Il Domino Degli Spagnoli*, Doc. XI, 101–6.

84 Here reference is made to the documentation contained in NLM, AOM 6559.

85 Although it is not certain if the *Capitoli* issued under Spanish rule were still applicable under Hospitaller rule, in the last set of *Capitoli* issued for Tripoli in 1551 it was stated that the soldiers in Tripoli were given a special price to buy their necessities. NLM, AOM, Lib. Bull. 422, fol. 223v (6.vii.1551). (Although this volume is dated 1549–50 it contains documents pertaining to 1551 as well. This is common in other volumes also.)

86 The Moors were free to negotiate with the Christians and they even had a market known as the çoco which was close to the castle. NLM, AOM, Lib. Bull. 415, fol. 246v (10.iv.1533).

87 NLM, AOM, Lib. Bull. 422, fol. 220v (28.iv.1551).

88 NLM, AOM, Lib. Bull. 415, fol. 246v (10.iv.1533). No report relating to the matter has yet been identified.

Tools of the trade

Evidence from notarial documents, although scanty and episodic for this early period, clearly shows that the commercial link with North Africa by merchants resident or anchored in Malta had been established prior to the advent of the Hospitallers in 1530, and even before the Spanish conquest of Tripoli in 1510.[89] On Wednesday 10 September 1494 Petrus Darmanin, *patronus* of a ship laden with barley and other merchandise intended for the North African region of the Mountains of Barqah, extended an existing partnership with another two Maltese, namely Notary Paulus Bonello and Peri Caruana, in respect of the same voyage.[90] Another deed, dated March 1495, informs us that a Catalan merchant resident in Malta was about to travel with his *caravella*, which was anchored in the Maltese port and laden with various merchandise,[91] to the region of the Mountains of Barqah.[92] Once there with the said cargo, the merchant was to acquire a slave for one of his creditors. This slave was to be shipped to Malta for eventual delivery to the buyer.[93] In May 1495 Franciscus Daudi of Syracuse chartered his vessel, which at the time was moored in the Maltese port of Benwarrad, to another citizen of Syracuse, one Masius de Marino. The ship was laden with wheat and other merchandise belonging to Marino and had to sail to the North African coast and the region of the Mountains of Barqah with the cargo.[94] Franciscus, on his part as captain of the ship, was allowed to carry five loads of fish free of charge. However, he was not permitted to carry any additional wheat or barley.[95]

In yet another notarial act, in view of the dangers of the pirates operating off the Barbary coast Vincentius Bestardes insured his ship before it sailed to the North African coast and again to the region of the Mountains of Barqah. The ship was laden with wheat, barley and other merchandise and the insurance cover was to last for a round trip, thus covering the journey Malta–North Africa–Malta.[96] Further evidence of trade between Malta and North Africa is found in a set of *capitoli* issued

89 In 1436 there was much debate in Malta about the percentage of tax to be paid on the importation of slaves from the 'mountains and other parts of Barbary'. Wettinger, *Slavery in the Islands of Malta*, 17.

90 Fiorini (ed.), *Documentary Sources of Maltese History, Part I, No. 2*, Doc. 5.

91 The document does not specify the type of merchandise but refers to it as '*mercancia super eamdem caravellum onusta*'. (The merchandise loaded on the said *caravella*.) Fiorini (ed.), *Documentary Sources of Maltese History, Part I, No. 2*, Doc. 107.

92 '*In partibus Moncium Barcarum de Capite Bono usque ad portum Trabus*' (in the region of Mountains of Barqah from Cape Bon and the Port of Tripoli). Fiorini (ed.), *Documentary Sources of Maltese History, Part I, No. 2*, Doc. 107.

93 Fiorini (ed.), *Documentary Sources of Maltese History, Part I, No. 2*, Doc. 107.

94 '*Jpsam fustam fore et esse onustam ordeo et alijs rebus ad opus Montis Barcarum*' (The said vessel being laden with barley and other goods intended for the Mountains of Barqah). Fiorini (ed.), *Documentary Sources of Maltese History, Part I, No. 2*, Doc. 115.

95 Fiorini (ed.), *Documentary Sources of Maltese History, Part I, No. 2*, Doc. 115.

96 Fiorini (ed.), *Documentary Sources of Maltese History, Part I, No. 2*, Docs 86, 87. For more references to the shipment of merchandise to North Africa see Fiorini (ed.), *Documentary Sources of Maltese History, Part I, No. 2*, Docs 74, 108, 200.

on 26 May 1525[97] by the Sicilian Viceroy, Ettore Pignatelli Count of Monteleone (r. 1517–34). This document highlights the Viceroy's concern over the fact that some merchants were selling cotton and linen[98] illegally to the Moors in Tripoli. It was further stated that these commodities had been either bought from corsairs or exported from the *Regno* or Malta without having paid the tax due to the *Regia Curia*.[99] Further complaints stated that some Moors resident in the city of Tripoli were stealing slaves and other merchandise[100] and selling them to Maltese and other individuals, to the detriment of the Crown's revenues.[101]

During the Order's rule the Hospitallers looked upon Tripoli not only as a strategic fortress but also as an important trading post where they could replenish a number of supplies.[102] The city and fort of Tripoli provided no resources to support the running of the fortress, but the lucrative market in slavery and corsairing made it an important meeting place for merchants of both religions. Tripoli offered the ideal set-up for the buying of slaves or redemption of captives, since it was close to Muslim lands.[103] Muslim traders found ways and means to extend commercial exchanges with Christian lands while conducting redemption services. Their strategies are evidenced in a number of safe conduct certificates and other instructions given to the galley captains of the Order's fleet, which were meticulously recorded in the *Liber Bullarum*[104] which is examined later in this chapter. Soon after the initial years of the Order's stay, Malta was fast becoming the ideal centre for conducting such transactions and notaries were kept busy drawing up agreements related to the slavery business.[105] In 1554 Yahaleph Zerbino, the slave of Honofrio Catanio, was granted permission by the Grand Master to leave for Tripoli to get the

97 *Capitula ordinacioni tenedi et observandi in regia secrecia dohana civitatis tripolis per secretum dohanetum credencerum et alios officiales dicte Regia Dohane.* NLM, AOM 6559, fol. 51–57 (26.v.1525).

98 The sale of linen to Moors was subject to a licence by the pope. However, it is not known why such a prohibition was imposed. La Mantia, 'La Secrezia Dogana di Tripoli', 472 n. 3.

99 NLM, AOM 6559, fols 51–52 (26.v.1525).

100 It is not said from whom they were stealing.

101 NLM, AOM 6559, fol. 54 (26.v.1525).

102 '*Vi partirete con nostre galere alla volta de Tripoli per che e necessaria nostra andata tanto per donar favore et animo al nostro castello de Tripoli comer per soccorrere ad altri bisogni che occorreramo*' [sic]. (You shall sail with our galleys towards Tripoli because our voyage is necessary for offering support and courage to our castle in Tripoli and also for addressing other needs which we will require.) NLM, AOM, Lib. Bull. 421, fol. 203 (13.ix.1547).

103 Trasselli argues that King Ferdinand's real interest in the conquest of Tripoli was due to its close proximity to Monti Barqha (Barca), which was a lucrative trading centre for slaves being supplied through the continuous arrival of the desert *caravane*. Trasselli, *Da Ferdinando il Cattolico a Carlo V*, vol. 1, 210–11.

104 These refer to magisterial bulls issued from the chancery by the Grand Master and his Council.

105 The register of Notary Nicolò de Agatiis for the administrative year 1543–44, NAV, R 202/8, contains the sale of a total of sixty-four slaves. For a detailed list of these sales refer to Wettinger, *Slavery in the Islands of Malta*, 242, 377–81. The private corsair vessels of Grand Master de Valette captured 3,020 slaves between 1557 and 1568, an average of 275 per year. Wettinger, *Slavery in the Islands of Malta*, 28–9.

necessary redemption money to free other Moors. He was also granted permission to return with a shipload of merchandise which was to be exchanged for slaves.[106] Similar licences were granted to Aoreibi de Alma[107] and Nasuph di Gallipoli,[108] the latter sailing to the Levant.[109] Such documentation illustrates the reality of a multi-religious, multifarious ethnic trading community which tried to benefit from trading links with North Africa and other countries. The work of historians like Goitein,[110] Abulafia[111] and Greene,[112] which spans different periods, has shown that despite the high levels of religious antagonism there was continuity over time in these trading relations. Religious divides were carefully dealt with, and merchants not only traversed the enclosed sea as subjects of their various sovereigns but also managed to create their own space and order.

The distance and perils separating the two posts did not seem to discourage foreign and local merchants from establishing themselves in the Tripoli fortress, and this thanks to the protection now being afforded to them by the Order.[113] The following investigation of sixteenth-century contracts linked to North Africa sheds light on the possible ways in which merchants conducted their activities. Analysis of the registers of Nicolò de Agatiis for the administrative year 1540–41[114] shows that out of a total of 416 contracts, 23 were linked to North Africa, either in respect of redemption services[115] or in connection with the transport of merchandise.[116] Eleven contracts deal with the sale of 'wild black slaves'[117] and three involve the sale of

106 NLM, AOM Lib. Bull. 424, fols 231v–232 (21.x.1554).

107 NLM, AOM Lib. Bull. 424, fol. 211v (5.iv.1554).

108 Gallipoli is a peninsula in north-western Turkey.

109 NLM, AOM Lib. Bull. 424, fols 235v–236 (16.vi.1554).

110 S. Goitein, *A Mediterranean Society: The Jewish Communities of the Arab world as Portrayed in the Documents of Cairo Geniza* (5 vols, Berkeley and Los Angeles, 1999).

111 Abulafia, *The Great Sea.*

112 M. Greene, *Catholic Pirates and Greek Merchants* (Princeton, 2010), 9.

113 Protection measures included the policing of the sea by the Order's galleys and the granting of safe conduct certificates.

114 NAV, R 202/5. De Agatiis extant registers are a total of thirteen registers spanning from 1535 to 1549.

115 As will be shown later in this study, redemption contracts translated themselves into profitable exchanges; a typical example taken from the register of Notary Vincenzo Bonaventura de Bonetiis refers to the redemption of Mahamet, a slave from *Capitis Bona Andria* (Cape Bon – a peninsula in far north-eastern Tunisia), whose redemption price was agreed at 300 gold ducats or else six black or white slaves aged ten years or more together with an amount of wax at the rate of 9 *uncia* per *cantaro*. NAV, R 206/7, fols 120v–121 (27.iv.1543). In another instance the Genoese Francescus Trinchera was redeemed from Tripoli by his co-citizen *Nob.* Honifirio Captanio Gerbini, described as '*Mercator et Januensis*', on instructions given by another Genoese, namely Baptista Pinelli Adorno. The agreed sum for his redemption was 150 gold ducats. The contract of redemption was ratified in Malta. NAV, R 202/2, fols 196v–197 (11.iv.1538).

116 These comprise twelve redemption contracts, four freight contracts, two contracts regarding the purchase of wool, a venture partnership agreement, procuration agreements and receipts of payments.

117 For example, the exact phrase for a black female slave would be '*unam servam nigram silvestram*', which referred to sub-Saharan slaves and often included also the specific mention of '*Ethiopiam*'.

two white slaves, a Moor and a Turkish slave. If slave-trading contracts which have insufficient data as to the actual place of origin of the 'commodity' are excluded,[118] this leaves a percentage of 5.5%. However, this is on the low side because the traffic in slaves from North Africa constituted an important activity for merchants.

The notarial register of Vincentio Bonaventura de Bonetiis[119] for the period January–December 1543 (R 206/7) contains a total of 391 contracts. Of these, eleven refer to the sale of slaves, while another eight refer to redemption contracts. Just one refers to a *societas* agreement with a view to conducting trade in Tripoli.[120] Although this indicates a mere 2.3% of the total agreements,[121] it compares well with the eight contracts referring specifically to trade with Sicily (2%), which was Malta's main lifeblood supply,[122] while there are none referring directly to other ports in the Mediterranean. Of course this does not mean that trading activities with the outside world which were taking place in Malta were limited to these contracts, since other contracts, especially those categorised as *Debitum*, often related to the sale or purchase of various commodities by both local and foreign merchants. However, because in most instances these did not stipulate the place of origin of the goods they were not included in calculating the percentages.

Register R 224/1, pertaining to Notary Giuseppe de Guevara[123] and covering the period 1537–43, records a total of 1,255 contracts. Out of these, fourteen refer to slave trafficking, seven of which mention specifically that the slaves were to be acquired from Tripoli. Two other contracts are in respect of redemption of Christian slaves from Tripoli (0.7%).[124] There are five *societas* agreements with the intent of trading with Sicily,[125] and two freight agreements for the importing of merchandise from Sicily[126] (0.6%). Register R 224/17 for the period 1560–61[127] records a total of 960 contracts. None of these has any reference to trade between North Africa or the Levant and only three refer to the sale of slaves (0.3%). Three relate to *societas* agreements to trade with Sicily and three others refer to freight services between

118 Some documents do stipulate that the slaves were to be acquired from North Africa, but others do not give the place of origin. Again, some slaves were acquired through corsairing activities.

119 This notary has a total of fifty-one registers spanning from 1534 to 1576.

120 It was not stipulated what kind of trade was to be conducted once in Tripoli. However, one of the partners was to provide the ship for the other shareholders to transfer themselves to Tripoli and wait for fifteen days. It was also agreed that any profits were to be equally divided. NAV, R 206/7, fols 231v–232 (24.viii.1543).

121 This percentage excludes those contracts which deal with the sale of slaves.

122 These are the following *naulum* (freight) contracts NAV, R 206/7, fols 86–86v (30.iii.1543), fols 183–183v (12.vii.1543), fol. 243 (29.viii.1543), fol. 42 (12.ii.1543), fol. 119 (27.iv.1543), fol. 283 (5.x.1543), fol. 341v (14.xi.1543), fols 180v–181 (7.vii.1543).

123 This notary has a total of thirty-eight registers spanning from 1537 to 1574.

124 Only those contracts in respect of the purchase/sale of slaves where Tripoli is specifically mentioned were taken into consideration when calculating the percentage. In all probability therefore this percentage would increase, had the notary included details of the place of acquisition of the slaves.

125 NAV, R 224/1, fol. 45 (6.iv.1540), fol. 47v (15.iv.1540), fol. 48v (16.iv.1540), fol. 65 (06.vii.1540). fol. 172 (25.v.1541).

126 NAV, R 224/1, fol. 91v (13.xii.1540), fol. 255 (13.xii.1541).

127 This register also belongs to Notary de Guevara.

Licata, Scicli and Terra Heraclia (0.6%).[128] Twenty-four contracts (2.5%) refer specifically to the purchase of carobs from Scicli in Sicily, twenty-three of them being drawn up in the month of February.[129]

This analysis indicates that most of the trade with North Africa related to human trafficking and merchants loading their ships with merchandise on both outgoing and home-coming voyages. This will be looked at in more detail below in discussion of safe conduct certificates issued by the Grand Master. As was highlighted in Chapter One, this analysis also shows that although individual notarial volumes offer rich insights and fascinating details of the workings and everyday life of a particular society, they are not an adequate source for quantitative analysis. A certain type of agreement that is absent from one register could be well documented in the registers of other notaries for the same year, some of which may not now be accessible; or indeed they might have not been registered in the first place.[130]

Who were the traders who were attracted to Malta? What exactly was their business and what tools did they use to cover their interests? In the absence of proper port registers, scrutiny of notarial acts held in Maltese archives helps to shed significant light on actual situations. Joint venture agreements with the main objective of trading with Tripoli-based merchants are found in various instances, and Birgu is clearly depicted as a town which was fast becoming an important meeting place for merchants from across the Mediterranean. One of the most important maritime activities was the transportation of all types of merchandise referred to in contracts as ***naulum*** or freight. A good number of contracts belonging to this category still exist for the period 1530–65, enabling a vivid picture of merchants' activities to be drawn.[131]

Specific phrases in these agreements, such as 'a *modo di mercanti*' or '*iuxta usum Rhodium*',[132] indicate that they represent a legal order based on internationally accepted norms and customs which were deeply rooted in the Mediterranean.[133] A

128 Also referred to in contracts as Terranova, present-day Gela in Sicily. An interesting document from these is NAV, R 224/17, fol. 332 (26.xi.1560), which refers to the transportation of animals from Gozo to Gela, among which there are eleven donkeys at the rate of 6 *tarì* per head.

129 The most frequent contracts are those referring to the sale/purchase of property, which total ninety-three (9.7%), and those referring to friendly loans, which amount to seventy-five (7.8%).

130 The registers of Notary Placido Abela are a case in point. This notary, who practised in Birgu and later on in Valletta, operated for at least thirty-four years, from 1557 to 1591. However, only one original volume, NAV, MS 514/1 (1557–60), and four incomplete register volumes, NAV, R 4/1 (1557–58); R 4/2 (1569–76); NAV, R 4/3 (1576–86, 1590–91) survive.

131 For a detailed description of these systems refer to W. Ashburner, *The Rhodian Sea-Law* (Oxford, 1909), clxxxix–cxcvii.

132 The phrase '*iuxta usum Rhodium*' is found in NAV, R 202/8, fol. 237v (3.iii.1543 *ab inc*); R 202/8, fol. 243 (4.iii.1543 *ab inc*); MS 514/1, n.f. (26.iv.1558); MS 514/1, n.f. (13.vii.1558) to quote some examples.

133 Studies on the institutional and legal order of international trade in the Mediterranean in the medieval and early modern period are still in their early stages. For a series of specific studies which explore the workings of economic processes, legal regimes and individual working lives in the maritime sector from the late sixteenth to early nineteenth centuries

contract drawn up in Birgu on 8 July 1555,[134] a few years after the fall of Tripoli to the Turks, guides the reader through the various stages of a typical venture agreement to be undertaken to the land of the 'infidels'. Here, the Ragusan merchant and *patrone Nob.* Marino de Johannes agreed to charter half the space on his ship, which had a capacity of one thousand *salme*[135] of wheat, to *Nob.* Paolo de Antonic, also from Ragusa. Here we have two merchants who were not citizens of Malta,[136] a clear indication that foreign merchants used Malta as their base to conduct business. The ship, which was to be well-equipped for the voyage,[137] had to leave the Maltese port in July, provided that the weather was good for navigating, and had to sail to the fortress of '*Tripoli de Barbaria*'. Once there, the space chartered on the ship had to be loaded with all kinds of merchandise within one month from its arrival. If for some reason there was a delay in the supply of merchandise, Marino must wait another ten days, known as days of grace or '*di stallia*'.[138] However, for these extra days Paolo had to pay 4 gold *scudi* per day. The merchandise was to be transported to either Malta, Brindisi, Otranto or any other destination which the client chose.[139] An interesting feature of this contract is the charge-out rate of the charter for each commodity, which was described as '*pro stipendio mercede et ragione de nolito*', and which was stipulated at the following rates:

see M. Fusaro, B. Allaire, R. J. Blakemore & T. Vanneste (eds), *Law, Labour and Empire: Comparative Perspectives on Seafarers, c. 1500–1800* (Basingstoke, 2015). See also Trivellato et al., *Religion and Trade.*

134 NAV, MS 778/1, n.f. (8.vii.1555).

135 It was specified that the weight of the *salma* corresponded to that of Messina '*salmj milli de grano dela missina generale*'.

136 Requests for the granting of Maltese citizenship to foreigners were to be approved by the Grand Master.

137 The exact wording used in the contract was '*ben in ordine ben accordata stagna con soj hominj velj et tuttj altrij cosi necessarj sufficienti a qual si vogla navigatione*' [sic]. (In good shape, with its proper tackle, well equipped with its men, sails, and all other things necessary and sufficient for any type of voyage.) This clause was inserted since no passage in the Sea-Law dealt 'explicitly with the obligation of the ship-owner to provide the ship in good state'. However, merchants were advised to make sure that 'the ship is "fresco e non vecchio", and that it is "bene concio" and "bene stagnate"'. Additionally, they had to ensure that it was well-equipped with armaments, depending on whether the voyage was in time of peace or war. Ashburner, *The Rhodian Sea-Law*, clxxxiii.

138 Chapters 25, 28 and 29 of *The Rhodian Sea Law* deal with the delay in loading by the merchant. If the agreed loading period was not maintained, the merchant was allowed an extra ten days' grace during which time he had to feed the sailors. If the merchant did not provide the cargo under the stipulated conditions, he was responsible for any damage to the ship. Ashburner, *The Rhodian Sea-Law*, clxxxvii.

139 These procedures follow the same pattern and directives as those described by Ashburner in examples he gives for the earlier medieval period. Ashburner, *The Rhodian Sea-Law*, clxxx.

Commodity	Quantity	Rate
Oil	30 *cavisi dela misura de Tripoli*[140]	7 *tarí*
Wool	3 *cantari a peso di Malta*	1 *ducato*
Li Muntunitij et Bestiami Pelosi (sheepskin and hairy livestock)	per 100	8 *tarí*
Li coiri Bovini (hides)	per 100	5 *scudi 6 tarí*

Thus, in this case, although the contract stipulated that half the ship was chartered, the charge-out rate was according to the unit of measure, which differed according to the type of commodity. An additional note stated that if the merchant chose to ship to Otranto or Brindisi, different charge-out rates were to be applied as follows:

Commodity	Quantity	Rate
Oil	Same as above	Same as above
Wool	2 *cantari a peso di Malta*	1 *ducato*
Li Muntunitij et Bestiami pelosi (sheepskin and hairy livestock)	per 100	12 *tarí*
Li coiri (hides)	per 100	8½ *scudi*

The higher prices quoted could have been due to the fact that the merchandise would have taken longer to reach southern Italy than Malta, thus increasing the risks and expenses for the service provider. The contract stipulated that Paolo was obliged to pay the freightage fees to Marino through the bank '*a modo di mercanti*'[141] within ten days of delivery. Marino was also bound to request Paolo's permission should he decide to carry other merchandise. Such precautionary measures ensured that the goods would not get mixed with other merchandise which could cause damage or loss. In case of a breach of contract, either of the parties was to be held personally liable to pay the related expenses according to the damage sustained.[142]

Another agreement between two Maltese merchants resident in Birgu, namely Antonius Scarpello as *patrone* of his *grippo*[143] and Matteo Habel, stipulates that

140 The weight of the *cafiso* varied from region to region. For example, in Sicily there were 105 different *cafisi* measures. Vassallo, 'Prices of Commodities', 42.

141 It is not stipulated what this method comprised, but in all probability it was in adherence to maritime usages as stipulated in the *Consolato de Mare*. This was a collection of maritime usages that was first written in fourteenth-century Catalonia. A printed edition was produced in 1494. It was inherited by the maritime states of early modern Europe and became 'the basis of all specific stipulations regarding matters of prize in the commercial treaties among the modern states until the latter part of the seventeenth century'. C. J. Kulsrud, *Maritime Neutrality to 1780; A History of the Main Principles Governing Neutrality and Belligerency to 1780* (Boston, 1936), 60–4.

142 'The parties to a contract may leave to the general law the determination of what shall happen if a provision of the contract is broken. They may, and generally do, prefer to settle the question for themselves, by imposing a penalty upon the transgressing party for the benefit of the other.' Ashburner, *The Rhodian Sea-Law*, ccii.

143 The *grippo* had a capacity of 70 barrels (*vegetum septuaginta*).

Antonius should go to Licata with his ship and, once arrived, wait for a period of not more than twelve days. During this time he was to receive a consignment of fifty barrels of wine, together with any other merchandise which Matteo might supply. After loading the cargo, Antonius was to set sail to Malta and wait for eighteen days, during which time he would receive instructions on whether he was to unload the cargo in Malta or in Tripoli. Should it be unloaded in Malta, the charge-out rate was stipulated at 7 *tarì* per barrel or per *cantarata*,[144] while if the *patrone* sailed with the cargo to Tripoli, the charge-out rate was doubled, stipulated at 15 *tarì* per barrel or *cantarata*. An interesting feature is the period stipulated for payment, which was ten days after consignment if the cargo was unloaded in Malta and fifteen days after consignment if unloaded in Tripoli.[145]

Various types of partnership agreement made it possible for businessmen from different spheres to come together and pool capital.[146] By the use of such basic legal instruments, the merchant protected himself by sharing the risks and dividing both the profits and losses derived from a particular business activity.[147] Contracts categorised as *accomandita*[148] were different from other partnership agreements, known as *societas* agreements. In an *accomandita* the financier provided money or merchandise or both for a merchant to ship abroad and to trade. For his part, the merchant bound himself to exploit the assets to best advantage while abroad, and on his return to divide the proceeds as agreed beforehand by the contracting parties.[149] Although the profits and risks were shared by the parties as in a *societas* agreement, the relationship between the parties resembled more that of a lender and borrower; and the lender did not become jointly liable with the borrower in any transactions with third parties. Contracts of this type lasted only for the duration of one voyage and were cancelled once the borrower had returned the capital plus any profits or less any losses.[150] Individual contracts differed in various details, since some specified the goods to be traded while others left this to the discretion of the merchant or travelling partner. It is evident from research in the Notarial Archives that this type of contract was still in use during the sixteenth century.[151] The particular features of these agreements become clearer through perusal of the original documents. An *accomandita* contract in the acts of Nicolò de Agatiis, dated 15 January 1537, refers to an agreement made by three men from Sicily. The investors, namely *Domnus* Michael Debuttino and Georgio Bucalan (the lenders), supplied one hundred pieces of Calabrian cheese to the travelling partner, namely Nicola Faga (the borrower). These were to be loaded onto the *grippo* of Andreotta Habel (the person providing freight) and delivered to the castle of Tripoli at the risk of the investors. Nicola, for

144 This meant merchandise which was valued according to weight.

145 NAV, R 202/5, fols 83–84v (13.xi.1540).

146 For the Maltese context refer to Abela, 'Port Activities', Chapter 3, passim.

147 Lopez & Raymond, *Medieval Trade in the Mediterranean World*, 174.

148 Also known by various other names such as *commenda, accomandita, accomendatio, collegantia, societas maris*, and many others. Lopez & Raymond, *Medieval Trade in the Mediterranean World*, 174.

149 Fiorini (ed.), *Documentary Sources of Maltese History, Part I, No. 2*, 420.

150 Lopez & Raymond, *Medieval Trade in the Mediterranean World*, 174.

151 Abela, 'Port Activities', Chapter 3.

his part, promised to give a true account of all business transactions, thus providing some sort of security to the investors by controlling the management of their venture. A marginal note dated 1 February 1537 informs us that Debuttino, one of the investors, declared that he had received the proceeds of this venture, which translated themselves into other commodities including three *rotolos* of pepper (*tribus rotulj piperis*).[152] Following this declaration the original contract was crossed out by the notary to show that the agreement had been fully honoured.[153]

In most contracts, although not in all cases, simple *societas* agreements, which were basic legal instruments with the chief aim of establishing a short-term partnership, would usually last for a single operation comprising a round-trip trading voyage. This type of agreement generally ended when the borrower returned the capital plus the profits after deduction of expenses.[154] However, due to the eclectic adoption of ideas from many different sources each contract had its own particular terms of agreement.[155] For instance, in a venture agreement drawn up in Malta on 9 February 1531[156] the Rhodiot *Hon.* Giovanni Ros, captain of a fifteen-bench *biremis* which at the time was anchored in Malta, was specifically described as having taken up residence in the fortress of Tripoli. He made an agreement with the Knight Giovanni Bonifar, who invested 55 gold *scudi* in a venture agreement which represented a share in the armaments of Ros's *biremis*.[157] In this particular case the contract was not for a single trip; instead it was specifically stated that the duration of the partnership was for an indefinite period and was to last for as long as the partners deemed fit. In line with the usual policy regulating these agreements, Ros was to account for the expenses incurred during the first voyage and every subsequent expedition. Any booty acquired was to be divided according to the initial share capital.[158] This agreement also reveals that although corsairing activities are not specifically mentioned in the contract they were so very much intertwined with trading that

152 According to Lopez & Raymond, at times payments in pepper and other spices, which were almost as durable and valuable as gold, were substituted for payment in coins, due to the insufficiency of the latter. Lopez & Raymond, *Medieval Trade in the Mediterranean World*, 145. See also NAV, R 206/1, fols 189–189v (19.iii.1535), where one black slave aged twenty-two years and valued at 36 gold ducats was exchanged for 18 pounds (*libris*) of saffron at the rate of 2 ducats per pound, provided that the slave was shipped to Malta.

153 NAV, R 202/2, fol. 117v (15.i.1537 *ab inc*).

154 Lopez & Raymond, *Medieval Trade in the Mediterranean World*, 175.

155 Alongside the Roman *societas* of labour and capital, Pryor also looks at various other contracts which may have contributed to the evolution of this type of contract. These include the *Nauticum fenus*, the Roman sea loan, the *Chreokoinōnia*, which was used at Byzantium for investment in maritime commerce (*chreos* signified debt and *koinōnia* partnership), the Jewish *'isqa'* contract and its Muslim counterpart the '*qirād*'. J. H. Pryor, *Commerce, Shipping and Naval Warfare in the Medieval Mediterranean* (London, 1987), 22–36.

156 NAV, R 439/1, fols 45v–47v (9.ii.1531).

157 During the fifteenth and sixteenth centuries the Mediterranean ship ownership was usually subdivided into twenty-four parts or *carati*. Ashburner, *The Rhodian Sea-Law*, clxiv; Abela, 'Port Activities', 85–8.

158 'After the return voyage was over, the *patronus* gave his account in Court in the presence of the mariners or partners, and the net profits were divided according to the shares.' Ashburner, *The Rhodian Sea-Law*, ccxlvii.

the necessary provisions were inserted in the event of the 'fortunate' capture of any booty.

In another *societas* agreement between two Genoese, namely *Hon.* Bernardinus Bonhomo,[159] who was employed on the Order's galley, and Johannes Antonio Payanum, who at the time was visiting Birgu, both men agreed to form a partnership which was to last for as long as Bernardinus deemed fit. The main trading activity of this *societas* was to traffic in several types of merchandise between Malta, Sicily and Tripoli in Barbary, usually including cheese, oil, wine, slaves and wool. Bernardinus invested 50 *scudi*, all in silver *aquile,* while Johannes Antonius pledged his work and also promised to serve the business faithfully and to the best of his abilities. Any profits or losses deriving from this agreement were to be shared equally by the two parties.

Debt contracts which registered a simple loan were also very common among merchants trading between Malta and Tripoli. A contract drawn up in Malta on 27 April 1541 refers to the repayment of a loan in respect of 16 *scudi* lent by Peiron Andreas *alias* Bux to Oliviero Jannoto. It is specifically stated in this act that the original deed regarding this debt was drawn up by Notary Pietro de Trugillo on 9 April 1541 '*in acre Tripolis*'.[160] In another instance, Pietro de Peralta was appointed as procurator of Antonio Chabela from Birgu on 16 December 1542.[161] Chabela specifically instructed him to recover the sum of 38 gold ducats[162] due from Giacomo Magro *alias* Causari, described as being a Maltese resident in the castle of Tripoli. This debt was covered by a previous contract drawn up in Birgu on 3 October 1542 by Notary Nicolò de Agatiis.

The above contracts illustrate a very simple point. Such agreements reveal not only that residents in the Tripolitan fortress were trying to enhance their income and broaden their business activities by acting as intermediaries for the local and foreign business communities, but also that agreements entered into with a view to trading in Tripoli were commonly drawn up and often honoured in Malta, which thus registered a substantial increase in the development of its financial services.[163] A case in point was the payment effected in Malta of a bill of exchange drawn up in Licata amounting to 75 gold *scudi*, which was originally to be effected in Tripoli. In order to honour this payment Petro Verasi was commissioned by the Spaniard Antonio Carisi to pay the bill of exchange by transferring the money to an intermediary, namely Raymondus de Palermo, who was in Malta. The latter was in turn requested to effect payment to two residents of Tripoli, namely Didacus Talavera and Petrus de Peralta, on his first trip to that city.[164]

159 NAV, R 202/4, fols 174–174v (15.iv.1540).
160 (in the castle of Tripoli) NAV, R 224/1, fol. 155v (27.iv.1541).
161 NAV, R 224/1, fol. 406v (16.xii.1542).
162 In almost all contracts the kind of ducat is not specified except for the mention that it was gold.
163 Abela, 'Port Activities', especially Chapter 2 and 4.
164 NAV, R 202/5, fol. 121v–122 ([?].i.1540 *ab inc*); see also R 202/2, fols 38v–39 (22.ix.1540); R 202/3, fols 223–223v (18.vi.1539); R 202/5, fols 224v–225 (1.vi.1541); R 206/7, fols 66 (3.iii.1543), fols 154v–155 (25.vi.1543), fols 192v (23.vii.1543), fol. 278 (2.x.1543) to quote some examples. Most of these related to redemption agreements.

Much preliminary work must have gone into the organisation of voyages such as those documented above. It would have included the drawing up of other types of agreements such as those concluded between the shareholders in the venture, the officers in charge and the sailors; the arming and provisioning of the ship; contracts for the necessary insurance to cover risks; and requests to both Christian and Muslim governments for permission to anchor in their ports.[165] All this work had to ultimately translate itself into profit for the merchant seafarer, but things did not always turn out as planned, since many obstacles awaited the merchant. These might take various forms, but the most frequent were pirate attacks, shipwrecks, fire, delays and, most common of all, commercial litigation.

Commercial litigation

Commercial litigation is part and parcel of the everyday running of business affairs. During the medieval period Mdina's town council citizen-judges were authorised by the Crown to dispense civil as well as criminal justice. Thus, any protests or claims made by local or foreign merchants had to be presented before the members of the Mdina *Università*. After having settled in Malta, and due to the substantial increase in the number of foreign merchants visiting the island, the Order well understood the need for an administrative and judicial set-up which was credible in the eyes of the major stakeholders in commerce.[166] This is clearly shown by the setting up of new tribunals in the port city of Birgu.[167] Unlike the medieval tribunal of the *Università*, on these tribunals sat *jurats* who represented the four main trading operators on the island, that is, French, Spanish, Greek and Maltese.

Foreign merchants exercised their legal rights in Malta either by filing a protest in court or else by drawing up a *compromissum* agreement. In general, throughout Europe, arbitration was substantially cheaper and quicker than any form of judicial resolution and was the preferred option when it was available. What made foreign claimants prefer either the one process or the other in Malta still needs to be fully investigated. There could have been many different reasons, including any or all of the following. The original contract might have been drawn up in Malta, or else one or more parties to the contract happened to be a resident or a citizen of Malta. The ship of the defendant could have been anchored in the Maltese port, so that the injured party sought to file their protest at the first possible opportunity so as to avoid further financial damage.

165 Abela, 'Port Activities', Chapter 2.

166 See for example NAM, MCC, Reg. AO, vol. 1, fols 102v–103 (1.ix.1537), where the newly appointed *jurats* for Birgu were the Catalan Melchiore Ferrer, the Greek Giovanni Callamia, the French Augustino Margallion and the Maltese Antonio de Messina, or NAM, MCC, Reg. AO, vol. 1, fols 146v–147 (4.ix.1538) which included the Catalan Melchiore Ferrer, the French Giovanni Charreton, the Rhodiot Giovanni Guascan and the Maltese Mattheo Habel.

167 See the Introduction.

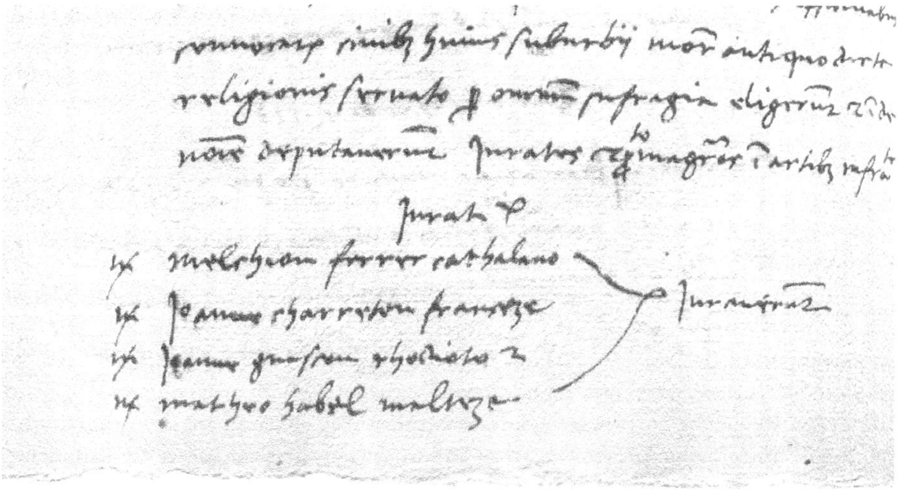

Fig. 7 The heterogeneous composition of *jurats* at the Birgu *Università* included Catalan, French, Rhodiot and Maltese representatives
Source: NAM, MCC, Reg. AO, ff. 146v-147 (4.ix.1538).

Valuable information can be gleaned from analysing these disputes. In one instance a protest was filed by *Don.* Thomaso Grasu in his capacity as the procurator[168] of *Don.* Bastiano Falere who, together with Pedro de Alonga, accused Christopharo Cantera of breaching port regulations or what they termed '*rompimento de porto*'. The protest stated that the merchants were seeking compensation because the accused owed them a total of 212 ducats due to them in respect of a consignment of wine to Tripoli. From their deposition it transpires that Cantera had secretly departed from Tripoli during the night without honouring his debts and without being granted the necessary departure documents from the governor.[169] Further investigation reveals that the merchants soon obtained a declaration from the governor of Tripoli attesting to their claims. The declaration permitted them to sue the fugitive debtor not only for breach of contract but also for violating port regulations. The need to obtain port clearance prior to departure is indicative of how the Order sought to eradicate abuses and control unregulated shipping. Similar regulations were adopted in various other European countries, such as in France, where a number of regulations were issued to this effect in 1553, and at various other times thereafter.[170]

After 1530, when the government of Tripoli passed to the Knights, protests regarding breach of port regulations by merchants, and at times other protests which were linked to trade with Tripoli and had previously been dealt with by the Sicilian courts, began to be addressed by the Maltese government. Thus, merchants in Sicily

168 In a world in which communication was slow, investors often empowered agents to act on their behalf.
169 NLM, AOM 6559, fols 397–405 (20.viii.1546).
170 Kulsrud, *Maritime Neutrality*, 21.

who prior to 1530 had operated directly between the Sicilian port and Tripoli were now sometimes constrained to stop at Malta in order to file or settle disputes. A case in point was a protest dated 13 July 1564 filed by Bartolomeo Michele from Marseilles as *patrone* of the *sayita* named *Santo Croce* [*sic*]. The said *patrone*, together with Martino Coet and Nicola Seger, all from Marseilles, denounced Francesco Boniet, another French merchant, for breaching an agreement they had concluded with the shipmaster and sailors in Marseilles regarding the transportation of merchandise from Marseilles to the now Ottoman fortress of '*Tripoli di Barbarie*'.[171] It seems that strong winds had forced the captain to anchor in Malta, consequently the ship was prevented from continuing its journey to Tripoli as it required the permission of the Grand Master to sail out of port. Several days had passed and the merchandise was stranded in the port, with the risk of rotting away. The merchants held Boniet responsible for any damages or additional expenses which were incurred due to the delay. Reference to the defendant was cautiously inserted by the notary, who refers to him as being 'present, hearing and understanding'.[172] An interesting detail emerging from this protest and which lends support to the hypothesis that Malta was quickly becoming a cosmopolitan centre hosting merchants from all over the Mediterranean is the fact that all foreigners in this litigation were declared to be present at the time when the protest was filed.[173]

The complex life of a merchant or his agent in a frontier outpost such as Malta is well attested in various legal documents. From a *compromissum*[174] agreement registered on 12 May 1541, one can form a good idea of just how complicated the negotiations for a single business deal could be. In this instance *Fra*. Aurelio Bottigella,[175] prior of Pisa, had consigned a net shipment of 191 *cantari* of wool coming from Tripoli in Barbary[176] to *Nob*. Francesco Corso,[177] who was a citizen of Syracuse. It was agreed between the two parties that Francesco should consign the

171 NAV, MS 778/4, fols 183–184 (13.vii.1564).

172 NAV, MS 778/4, fol. 183 (13.vii.1564).

173 Many cases involving foreign parties are present in Maltese Notarial Archives. See for example NAV, R 224/17, fols 887–888 (28.vi.1561), wherein *Nob*. Aloisius Meante from Marseille who was *patronus* of a ship anchored in Malta declared to be in debt of 40 gold *scudi* with *Hon*. Aloisius Vanoni, also a citizen of Marseille. This loan was in respect of a voyage and was to be repaid in Marseille, by the debtor's request. See also NAV, R 202/1, fols 32v–33 (8.v.1536); R 202/11, fols 21v–22 (27.x.1546); R 224/17, fols 826–826v (12.vi.1561), fols 806–807 (3.vi.1561).

174 A proceeding in which a dispute is resolved by an impartial adjudicator whose decision the parties to the dispute have agreed to be final and binding.

175 Bottigella was the first Governor of Malta, who came to the island to settle various matters prior to the official arrival of the Knights Hospitaller. He also held the post of Governor of Tripoli (1532–33), among other important positions within the Order's ranks.

176 Wool from Barbary is one of the most recorded commodities in notarial acts arriving from Tripoli. '*Di netto ex sacca in quibus insaccata erat*' [sic]. (Net out of the sack in which it was packed.) NAV, R 202/5, fol. 189 (12.v.1541).

177 In a document dated 15 February 1530, Francesco Corso is described as the appointed *dohaniero* and *secreto* of the Spanish Crown in the castle of Tripoli. NLM, AOM 6559, fol. 110v (15.ii.1530).

said merchandise to his procurator, *Nob.* Petrus Nalluni in Syracuse, who in turn was to export it to Venice on behalf of *Fra.* Bottigella.

It seems that only a portion of this wool reached the procurator of Bottigella, one *Hon.* Johannotto Bonanao,[178] in good condition. Bonanao in turn consigned it to Olivaro Locampesi and Antonio Guglielmo in the current net weight agreed by both. In the *compromissum* it was declared that the remaining consignment of wool was still in Petrus's possession since, because most of it was wet and rotten, Bottigella's procurator refused to accept it. It was further declared that the wool had been mixed with an inferior type during transport, and thus Bottigella was now requesting that Francescus Corsus should be made to pay compensation for the spoilt merchandise at the agreed rate of 2 *uncie* 3 *tarì* per *cantaro.*

The parties agreed to settle the dispute in an amicable way and thus they agreed that Franciscus was to bind himself to consign 145 *cantari* of wool to Bottigella or his procurator on his first trip to Syracuse. The wool had to be dry and in good condition as it was usually sold and bought in Tripoli of Barbary. It was to be weighed in Syracuse in the measure of the *rotoli* of Sicily at the expense of Francescus. Both parties were to appoint two experts, one from each side, who were to validate the fairness of the procedure under oath and were also duty bound to separate the good wool from the bad. Should there be disagreement, a third expert was to be nominated by the *Curia Consulatus* of Syracuse.[179] Both parties agreed that they would abide by the decision of the arbitrator and were forbidden to appeal against this decision or take each other to court. An important detail in this agreement refers to a new law promulgated in Sicily by which the parties promised to abide.[180]

Scrutiny of other deeds containing this condition supports the hypothesis that most probably this law referred to the obligation on the part of debtors to ratify agreements made abroad either in their country of origin or in any other city of their choice within a stipulated time. In the case in point,[181] Francescus Corsus's procurators had to ratify the current contract and oblige themselves to Bottigella within three days of the date of the current agreement. Furthermore, Francescus and

178 Bonanao seems to have been quite popular as a procurator who had connections with Tripoli. See, for example, NAV, R 202/5, fol. 138v (12.ii.1540 *ab inc*), where a carpenter appointed him to recover the sum due from a soldier stationed in Tripoli in respect of three *tabulas archibuxorum*. This could be referring to the wooden stock of the harquebus on which the barrel is mounted. It is also interesting to note that this contract reflects the possible lack of carpenters in Tripoli. Residents had thus to use the services of Maltese carpenters. (Thanks are due to Stephen C. Spiteri for this information, forwarded on 22 September 2011.) His connection to Bottigella, Governor of Tripoli, is also indicative of his close connection to the city.

179 '*dittus dominus prior ex una et [et] dittus no[bilis] franc[escus] partibus ex altera teneantur eligere duos expertos et tercium cau[sa] discordie eligendum per curiam consolatus ditte civi[ta]tis siracusar[um]*' [sic]. NAV, R 202/5, fol. 189v (12.v.1541).

180 '*formam novj ritus magne regie curie regnij cicilie*' [sic]. NAV, R 202/5, fol. 190 (12.v.1541).

181 Similar references to the ratification of contracts are found in various contracts drawn up in Tripoli and ratified in Malta regarding the redemption of slaves. Refer to NAV, R 202/2, fols 16v–18 (17.ix.1537); R 202/3, fols 223–223v (18.vi.1539); R 202/4, fols 182–182v (20.iv.1540); R 202/5, fols 16v–17 (7.ix.1540); R 202/5, fols 19v–20 (7.ix.1540); R 202/5, fols 22–22v (10.ix.1540); R 202/5, fols 26–27v (15.ix.1540).

his brother Ambrosius were to deliver an authentic copy of the ratified contract with the seal of the city of Syracuse or any other city of their choice to Bottigella with the first ship sailing to Malta. Either Francescus or Ambrosius was personally to consign the wool, and if it was not found to be of good quality they were to reimburse Bottigella for the loss incurred at the rate of 2 *uncie* 3 *tarì* per *cantaro* in cash, in the city of Syracuse, not later than four months from the date of consignment. It was further stipulated that these conditions had originally been agreed in a contract drawn up in Syracuse which also included the sale of slaves, oil, wheat and rope, among other commodities. Should there be another breach of contract, Ambrosius was to remain in Malta and be jailed until the agreement was honoured. Interest due for late consignment added up to 8 *tarì* per day, together with any other related expenses.

Even though the central point of arbitration was to settle disputes outside court, it was stipulated in the contract that neither Francescus nor Ambrosius could protest in any court, whether here in Malta or in Tripoli, Syracuse, Messina, Rome, Naples or any other place, nor could they ask for a safe conduct from other cities. This latter detail is highly interesting since it sheds light on how debtors in various countries tried to seek protection from their creditors by requesting the government to issue an order of immunity. In the case of Malta, for instance, safe conduct certificates sometimes make reference to the government's protection of foreign debtors. In such instances it was specifically stated that the Grand Master was protecting a particular debtor and, as such, his creditors could not harm him or hunt him down once he was under the Order's jurisdiction.[182]

The above contract shows how members of the Order, especially those who held important positions like Bottigella, kept good trading relations with Tripoli even after the end of their term. Merchants were attracted to do business with the Knights, since they facilitated trading activities through their connections with other senior officials of the Order posted to Tripoli. Although in the above case the merchandise was not to be consigned to Malta, ancillary activities related to this business, such as the registering of the *compromissum*, were conducted on the island. The need for merchants to visit the island not only to file protests but also to ratify contracts drawn up in Tripoli was enhanced by the Order's presence and this led to a substantial increase in Malta's connections with foreign merchants operating throughout the Mediterranean.

The *salvi conductus* – a passport to freedom of trade to 'all parts of the world'

Data derived from port registers, although very scanty for the period prior to 1565,[183] reveals that, just as in medieval times, merchants in Malta showed a particular

182 See, for example, NLM, AOM, Lib. Bull. 421, fol. 214 (5.vi.1548), where Loysio Aragonese came to live in Malta and was granted a safe conduct for a period of one year since, at the time, he could not pay his creditors.

183 These are NAM, MCC, *Registri Patentarum* vols I–IV. The only register which contains meagre data for the period under study is vol. I, which spans from 1564 to 1578.

preference for conducting business with and undertaking ventures to Sicilian ports. Where port registers are missing, notarial and Chancery[184] documents complement this information, as most shipping destinations intended for the procurement of staple goods such as grain, meat and wine reveal a hegemony of Sicilian products. A search in the acts of Notary Vincenzo Bonaventura de Bonetiis shows that all eight *naulum* contracts drawn up by this notary for the year 1534–35 represented trade with Sicily, mainly to procure wheat, wine and wood.[185] The *naulum* acts of the same notary for the year 1543 point again to a heavy dependence on Sicilian trade, since all services for the transport of merchandise were targeted to Sicily to import wine[186] wheat[187] and wood,[188] one even mentioning delivery of '*cottone in cochio*'.[189] Register R 224/17 for the period 1560–61[190] holds a total of 960 contracts.[191] Out of these, three relate to *societas* agreements to trade with Sicily and three others refer to freight services between Licata, Scicli and Terra Heraclia (0.6%),[192] while twenty-four contracts (2.5%) refer specifically to the purchase of carobs from Scicli, also in Sicily.[193]

Trade relations with other countries, especially France, did exist, although at a much lower level. The above preference must of course be evaluated in the sixteenth-century context. At the time, Malta was considered part of the royal domain of the Sicilian Kingdom and was eligible to import duty-free food supplies from Sicily, although at times this was not an easy task.[194] Such concessions led to the strengthening of links between the two islands and, as is clearly indicated in Tables 6 and 7, Malta still remained strongly attached to Sicily after 1530. In fact, the earliest available port registers found in Maltese archives give a clearer picture of shipping destinations after 1530 and indicate that four-fifths of the total amount of shipping registered between 1564 and 1600 was directed to Sicilian ports.[195]

184 See as an example AOM, Lib. Bull. 418 (22.ix.1542), fol. 193v, wherein Antonio Marmara was entrusted to procure all sorts of meat and victuals from Sicily for the use of the Order.

185 NAV, R 206/1, fols 14v–15v (4.xi.1534), fols 30–31v (12.xi.1534), fols 35–36 (23.xi.1534), fols 57–58 (4.xii.1534), fols 353v–354v (3.vii.1535), fol. 375 (9.viii.1535), fols 389v–390 (18.viii.1535).

186 NAV, R 206/7, fols 86–86v (30.iii.1543), fols 183–183v (12.vii.1543), fol. 243 (29.viii.1543).

187 NAV, R 206/7, fol. 42 (12.ii.1543), fol. 119 (27/iv. 1543), fol. 283 (5.x.1543).

188 NAV, R 206/7, fol. 243 (5.x.1543).

189 NAV, R 206/7, fol. 341v (14.xi.1543).

190 Notary Giuseppe de Guevara.

191 See above, n. 129 in this chapter.

192 See above, n. 128 in this chapter.

193 Twenty-three of these contracts were drawn up in the month of February.

194 Ever since 1526, the *Mastro Secreto* (Chief Fiscal Officer) of Sicily had ordered all *Secreti* of the Sicilian towns, Licata in particular, to supply Malta with duty-free merchandise. NLM, Libr. MS 1220, Notizie ed allegazioni diverse date in tempi diversi et in varie contingenze dell'Università di Malta dal notario Vittorio Griscti … 1747, fols 193, 195–196. Cassar, *Society, Culture and Identity*, 78.

195 Cassar, *Society, Culture and Identity*, 73.

Table 6 Shipping destinations from the Malta harbour 1564–1600[a]

Destination	Number of trips	Percentage
Sicily	4683	80.2
Italy (peninsular)	461	7.9
France[b]	309	5.3
Greece	115	1.9
Spain	75	1.3
Unknown	65	1.2
Piracy	28	0.5
Others[c]	102	1.7
Total number of trips	**5838**	**100**

a Data available for thirty-two years only, and in some cases a few months missing.
b Of the voyages made to France, 296 were directed to Marseilles.
c Others include: Alexandria, Tunis, Tripoli (Barbary), Tripoli (Syria), Alexandretta, Algiers, Smyrna, Constantinople, the Levant, Dalmatia, Flanders, England, and the West.

Source: Cassar, *Society, Culture and Identity*, 74. Cassar's sources for these figures are the *Registrum Patentarum* which contain the earliest known available information regarding shipping destinations and origins from and to Maltese ports.

The data shown in Table 6 indicates that trade with North Africa and the Levant was fairly minor in the second half of the sixteenth century, a situation which does not seem to have been much different for the period 1530–65. This may be due to the fact that, as is shown below, there was a 'close intersection between piracy and trade'.[196] Most of the goods acquired through piratical activity were ultimately traded and sold to merchants across the Mediterranean. Trade with North Africa was often combined with the redemption of slaves and, similarly, economic activities directed to the Levant were mostly tied to the redemption of slaves or related to corsairing activities.

Although *salvi conductus*[197] or safe conduct certificates issued to merchants from time to time by the Chancery of the Order[198] did not always assure a safe and swift

196 Abulafia, *The Great Sea*, 647.

197 *Salvi conductus* were issued to various other persons other than merchants. These included, among others, corsairs, knights who were dispatched on a diplomatic mission and freed slaves who wanted to return to their country. For example, see NLM, AOM, Lib. Bull. 424, fol. 212 (21.x.1553), where three slaves of the late Grand Master Juan D'Homedes (1536–53) where granted manumission by the Grand Master as per instructions left in his last testament.

198 NLM, AOM 6466 contains petitions for safe conducts for the period 1658–70, while AOM 625, 626 and 627 contain an alphabetical index of the items classified under the title '*Diverse Scritture*' in the *Liber Bullarum*. The dates of these volumes range from 1346 to 1695. See also Wettinger, *Slavery in the Islands of Malta*, 196, 206–7, 212–15, 291–2 and Brogini, *Malte, frontière de chrétienté*, especially Chapter 7.

Table 7 Shipping destinations to Italian ports 1564–1600

Destination	Number of trips	Percentage
Naples	248	4.3
Venice	52	0.9
Reggio	42	0.7
Leghorn	40	0.7
Genoa	27	0.5
Sardinia	20	0.3
Others[a]	32	0.5
Italy	461	7.9 of total

[a] Others include Rome (Civitavecchia?), Apulia (Bari?), Taranto, Ancona, Gallipoli.
Source: Cassar, Society, Culture & Identity, 75.

Table 8 Shipping destinations to Sicilian ports 1564–1600

Destination	Number of trips	Percentage
Licata	1050	18.0
Syracuse	912	15.6
Messina	572	9.8
Scicli	516	8.8
Pozzallo	504	8.6
Terranova (Gela)	258	4.4
Marsala	219	3.7
Vendicari	164	2.8
Grigenti (Agrigento)	163	2.8
Trapani	149	2.5
Others[a]	176	3.1
Sicily	4683 trips	80.2 of total

[a] Others include Palermo, Sciacca, Augusta and Catania.
Source: Cassar, *Society, Culture & Identity*, 75.

journey, they did provide merchants with a considerable amount of political and legal protection.[199] At the same time they offered their holders greater potential to extend their commercial activities in the Maghreb and Eastern Mediterranean.[200] Emperor Charles V had provided the Order with similar royal charters prior to their establishment in Malta.[201] The granting of these passes under the Order of St John did not follow a constant pattern. In fact, as can be seen in the Appendix, during the 1530s and 1540s rather low numbers of safe conducts were issued to merchants or prospective free slaves[202] about to sail to or from North Africa or the Levant. After 1552 around five safe conducts per year were registered. This increase may have been due to the fact that after the loss of Tripoli in 1551 the Order lacked a North African base to facilitate redemption negotiations for both Christians and Muslims, while at the same time corsairing activities were increasing and Malta was experiencing a constant steady flow of slaves.[203]

Not all voyages to North Africa or the Levant were covered by letters patent, or at least not all of them are found in the *Liber Bullarum*. According to Ann Williams this is also a problem with the Chancery records relating to the Rhodes period. She states that the records probably relate just to those letters patent that were presented to the Vice-Chancellor for registration. Further, she mentions the work of Nicolas Vatin, who 'in trying to assemble a statistic for foreign merchants trading in Rhodes, could only produce lists in single figures for each of the nations involved'.[204] This is very noticeable when the names of contracting parties found in notarial acts are compared with those for the same period in the *Liber Bullarum*.[205] In fact, with the exception of Bartholomeo Abela,[206] in all of the cases encountered in this study none of the merchant named in notarial acts with respect to trading activities in North Africa or the Levant is listed in the *Liber Bullarum* as being the holder of a safe conduct certificate. It can be safely assumed that the amount of trade between Malta, North Africa and the Levant was higher than what is officially registered in the Chancery documents.

199 Wettinger, *Slavery in the Islands of Malta*, 214.

200 On encountering a possible 'enemy' the holder of this patent would raise the flag of the Order and show the document to the captain to avoid being attacked. At times, however, captains ignored such patents. Wettinger, *Slavery in the Islands of Malta*, 214.

201 NLM, AOM 17, *Salva condotti di Carlo V alla Religione Geroslomitana.*

202 Safe conducts granted to free slaves who had already paid their ransom and were going back to their country without conducting further trade with Malta are not included.

203 Wettinger's account of the successes of Grand Master Jean de Valette's private corsairing vessels confirms just how much this economic activity was growing when he wrote: 'Thus in the twelve years of the magistracy of Jean de Valette (1557–1568), the private vessels of that Grand Master captured a total of 2,883 slaves, freed some 562 Christian slaves, and procured a total income in goods and slaves of some 400,000 ducats. They captured 13 oar-driven vessels, and captured or sank some 36 sailing ships. De Valette's corsair ships included a *galeotta* of 22 benches which he kept for six years, then two galleys for five years and a galeotta of 22 benches for another year, spending 9,000 *scudi* on the galleys and 6,000 *scudi* on the *galeotta*'. Wettinger, *Slavery in the Islands of Malta*, 34.

204 Williams, '*Sacra Militia*', in Fusaro et al., *Trade and Cultural Exchange*, 139–56: 142.

205 Some of which are mentioned passim in this chapter.

206 NLM, AOM, Lib. Bull. 426, fols 251–251v (1.xii.1556).

A typical safe conduct certificate would include the name of the merchant, his projected destination, often but not always the commodities he expected to buy and also the period for which the certificate was valid. Princes, admirals, governors and various other public officials were requested to 'let them travel freely in both their outgoing and incoming journey without inflicting any harm or giving them reason to be late in their journey', and 'on the contrary you should lend them any favour which you deem opportune'.[207] It is important to contextualise this latter clause, which demanded that ships be free from search and seizure within the parameters of the maritime law in force at the time. The latter was embodied in the rules defined in the *Consolato di Mare*,[208] according to which, 'once at sea an admiral had the right to stop and inspect even ships belonging to a friend, as long as he treated the captain fairly'.[209] This law also stipulated that merchandise on friendly shipping could be confiscated if it was identified as enemy cargo, provided that the Christian stakeholders were paid their rightful freight charges.[210] Thus, the most important considerations underlying the instructions found in safe conducts were as much social and political as economic, since the possible loss or damage of a cargo ship not only translated into great financial loss for the investors, but ultimately could even lead to shortages, especially during times of drought, which could in turn result in popular unrest.

Two merchants granted a safe passage in 1532 were Mabrayadi di Golena and Michaeli Cucagni, both of whom were instructed to sail to the Levant and beyond to procure much-needed commodities like salted meat, wax, candles, pulses and cheese, 'for our use and that of our Order'.[211] Voyages covered by letters patent in which economic activity was not linked to redemption services were mostly commissioned by the Order and directed to Christian lands.[212] This implies that the provisioning of the island depended heavily on private entrepreneurship[213] and was not limited to specific naval operations conducted by the Order's navy. The Order's

207 '*gli lassiate liberamente navigare andare venire & stare senza dargli impacchio danno disturbio ne causa de ritardare. Anzi prestarlj ogni opportuno favore.*'

208 The tribunal of the *Consolato del Mare* in Malta was established in 1697. C. Vassallo (ed.), *Consolati Di Mare and Chambers of Commerce* (Malta, 2000).

209 Greene, *Catholic Pirates*, 57.

210 Greene, *Catholic Pirates*, 60.

211 NLM, AOM, Lib. Bull. 415, fol. 232v (28.vi.1532).

212 These were not numerous and hardly ever exceeded three per year. See, for example, NLM, AOM, Lib. Bull 416, fol. 210v (3.iii. 1536); 418, fol. 193v (20.ix.1542); 419, fols 229v–230v (17.x.1544); 420, fol. 197 (20.x.1545), 423, fol. 203 (20.xi.1551), fol. 229v (7.ii.1553); 429, fol. 263 (30.iv.1563). Commissions to acquire commodities from Christian lands are also found in the form of instructions to galley captains of the Knights in the *Liber Bullarum*; see, for example, NLM, AOM, Lib. Bull. 417, fol. 255 (28.x.1538); 422, fol. 206v (27.ii.1550); 429, fol. 247 (19.i.1562), fols 253–253v (28.vii.1562); 430, fol. 266 (2.iii.1565).

213 Some safe conducts refer also to the personal business needs of specific merchants. See, for example, NLM, AOM Lib. Bull 418, fol. 200v (27.i.1543); 422, fol. 218 (28.ii.1551); 423, fol. 229v (7.ii.1553), fol. 230v (3.iv.1553). A typical example is the section entitled *Responsales* in Lib. Bull. 417, fols 283–283v, which lists a number of imported commodities, mostly wheat and cloth intended for the Order's use throughout the year May 1540 to May 1541. The ships used to transport these items belonged mainly to Maltese

commitment to establishing the essential framework for such negotiators to act within a well-regulated and efficient set-up under its control is well appreciated in this context. Such opportunities not only served as a pull factor for foreign economic actors but enhanced the trading operations of local traders with foreign partners and also encouraged them to respond favourably to emerging business opportunities.

Christian merchants or corsair ships that did not fly the flag of the Order, such as those of the Venetian nobleman Francesco Caena, also requested the granting of safe conducts in order to be able to cross over to Malta from North Africa with their loads of merchandise. In Francesco Caena's case, the Grand Master decreed that since Venice was a 'friend' of the Order, the said merchant, his ships, merchandise and men could travel freely to the Maltese harbours. Caena was of course aware that Venetian ships were a prime target for Maltese corsairs, who attacked them in hopes of seizing a friendly ship containing 'enemy' goods.[214] In Caena's instance it was further decreed that the licence was to remain in force for at least two months.[215]

Safe conducts and corsairing

The importance of safe-passage documents is also to be seen in the light of the great impact of piracy, whether licensed or not, on Mediterranean trade in the sixteenth century. The shipment of a vast number of valuable commodities around the Mediterranean, like gold, silk, spices and, crucially, grain, made piracy 'the land of opportunity'. Braudel describes piracy as 'eating the food of others in order to remain strong',[216] thus highlighting the heavy dependence of economic well-being on the incessant targeting of merchant vessels. This was especially so on islands such as Malta, which did not have a fertile hinterland. Plundering would of course result in shortages elsewhere in the Mediterranean and, as was discussed in Chapter Two, the capture of grain ships brought the most disastrous results, especially in times of famine.

Before the arrival of the Hospitaller Order, the Vice-Admiral of Sicily exercised a measure of control over corsairing activities by issuing licences, retaining the right to a percentage of the booty, defining the sectors of activity and providing for full legal satisfaction in case of infraction of the laws.[217] Such rules were aimed at preventing

merchants such as Alfonsius Habeli, Braytus Burlo, Bartholomeo Scarpello, Bartholomeo Habel, Petro Tabone and Luca Calafato.

214 Greene, *Catholic Pirates*, 59.

215 NLM, Lib. Bull. MS 415, fol. 208v (22.iv.1531), '*di poter venire intrare secura et saglire liberamente in nostro porto insula et terra senza che nessun de loro sia molestato ne impedito durantdo detto viagio qual declaramo et volemo essere in vigour et valore doi mesi a presso la revocatione se pure accadesse revocarlo*' (that they may enter freely and securely our port, island and land without any one of them being molested or impeded during this voyage, which [edict] we declare and want to be effective for a period of two months before revocation, if it is revoked).

216 Braudel, *The Mediterranean*, vol. 2, 869.

217 P. Cassar, 'The Maltese Corsairs and the Order of St John of Jerusalem', *The Catholic Historical Review*, 46:2 (1960), 137–41.

predatory warfare 'by forcing the privateer to give an account of his actions' and preventing him 'from concealing his capture, destroying the ship's papers, or making a reciprocal agreement with the merchantman to release ship and cargo'[218] while out at sea.[219] Thus, corsairing ventures were already regulated prior to the arrival of the Order, and kept under the scrutiny of the Sicilian admirals.

Once established in Malta, the Hospitaller Order took over these responsibilities from the Sicilian government. This transfer marks the granting of a highly important privilege to the Hospitaller government, something which has been greatly underestimated by local historians even though much has been written about the Maltese *corso* and its repercussions. According to Kulsurd, 'one of the chief aims of every powerful ruler at the opening of the Modern Era was to vest the Crown with the exclusive right to make war by land and sea. Once secured, this right was jealously guarded.'[220] To appreciate the importance of this right one must also keep in mind that the Order owed allegiance to the pope, who very often put pressure on the Knights to perform their role of holy warriors. Although Malta was granted to the Knights by Charles V as king of Sicily, the latter also held the title of emperor of Spain, and thus any form of war conducted from the island had to have the approval of the Spanish monarch. As Ann Williams states, 'the gift of a falcon each year, in itself a small gesture, nevertheless symbolised homage to the Spanish ruler', and the Order's position in the western Mediterranean was now much more delicate than it had been in Rhodes.[221]

The difficulties for the Order in asserting its position as a neutral ruling body are clearly evidenced in the first few years of its stay on the island, since it was prohibited by the Spanish monarch from minting its own coins. One therefore cannot assume that the right to license and regulate corsairing was something which was granted automatically. Taken in its proper context, the full extent of this privilege marks an important initial step towards the Order's future claim to sovereignty. The need for an efficient naval organisation required the state to mitigate or abolish irregularities in matters relating to *corso*. Later, this led to further specialisation in the adjudication process and it was thus that the year 1605 saw the setting up of the state's prize court or *Tribunale degli Armamenti* (Magistracy of Armaments), which was invested with the power to judge cases related to the proper implementation of and adherence to a system of legal codes related to piratical belligerency.[222]

218 Kulsrud, *Maritime Neutrality*, 22–3.

219 For an insight on the problems encountered by merchants while at sea refer to I. Katele, 'Piracy and the Venetian State: The Dilemma of Maritime Defense in the Fourteenth Century', *Speculum*, 63:4 (1988), 865–89.

220 Kulsrud, *Maritime Neutrality*, 23.

221 Williams, '*Sacra Militia*', in Fusaro et al., *Trade and Cultural Exchange*, 139–56: 150.

222 The *Tribunale degli Armamenti* had the specific intention of running the corsair business. One of the main concerns of this tribunal was 'the explosion in the corso and the problems it was creating'. M. Green, '"Victims of Piracy?" Ottoman Lawsuits in Malta (1602–1687) and the Changing Course of Mediterranean Maritime History', in Fusaro et al., *Trade and Cultural Exchange*, 177–201: 180. Similar developments took place in other countries in continental Europe, for example, France and the Netherlands, which jealously watched over their power and interests. Kulsrud, *Maritime Neutrality*, 11.

In asserting the right to make war, the state became the owner of all property acquired through corsairing, thus holding the right to dispose of prizes as was deemed fit. In fact, the practice in Malta dictated that prizes were to be divided into specific percentages, among which was 10% commission in favour of the Grand Master. Accordingly, just as was the policy adopted in Rhodes,[223] any ships flying the Hospitaller flag had to be covered by a licence[224] which specifically stated that the captain and crew of the licensed corsair ship were prohibited from molesting Christian shipping[225] or other ships considered friendly, even if Muslim. The mention of Muslim ships as 'friendly' points to the great ambiguity which was so very characteristic of the early modern Mediterranean.[226] While the Knights tried to circumvent the rules established by the *Consolato del Mare* as to what constituted a friendly ship, at the same time, when the need arose, and in order to replenish their resources, they protected that which, for them, would have otherwise been defined as 'eternal enemy'.[227] Corsairs were bound to ensure their adherence to these rules, as may be noted in the licence issued to Johannes Ros, a Rhodiot merchant and corsair,[228] or to the Maltese merchant Johannes Belia,[229] who, on obtaining their piratical licences, promised not to attack any Christian subjects or vassals. Such blanket prohibitions are easily understandable, since unrestricted attacks on friendly shipping could easily entangle the Order in an unwanted and costly confrontation.[230]

Corsairs had to present persons to act as surety, or *fidejussors* in legal terminology, who would guarantee their proper conduct. Hefty profits from this system encouraged the emergence of professional groups who took high risks with a view to making considerable gains.[231] How effective these injunctions were in protecting merchant shipping, or the extent to which they were actually enforced, is not

223 Luttrell, 'The Earliest Documents on the Hospitaller *Corso* at Rhodes', in Arbel (ed.), *Intercultural Contacts*, 177–88: 177.

224 Such licences, also known as letters patent, were granted for one or more years. Bono, 'Naval Exploits and Privateering', in Mallia-Milanes (ed.), *Hospitaller Malta 1530–1798*, 351–97: 391.

225 Particular emphasis was given to the ships of His Catholic Majesty and of the Venetian Republic. However, various disputes arose between the Hospitaller Order and Venice, since such instructions were often breached to the detriment of the Christian merchants. Mallia-Milanes, *Venice and Hospitaller Malta*, passim. English shipping was considered to be fair game, since it was known that these supplied the Barbary with arms and other goods. In accordance with papal instructions, Jews and Greek Christians were also to be respected, although official documentation from the seventeenth century attests to the continuous molesting of these Greek Christian subjects. Cassar, 'The Maltese Corsairs', 145–6; Greene, *Catholic Pirates*, passim.

226 Greene, *Catholic Pirates*, 60.

227 The issue of the *salvi conductus* to various Muslim merchants, already discussed, is a case in point.

228 NLM, AOM, Lib. Bull. 414, fol. 275v (10.viii.1530).

229 NLM, AOM, Lib. Bull. 414, fol. 286v (22.i.1530 *ab inc*).

230 A good example are the attacks carried out on Venetian shipping in 1554 and the consequential two *sequestri* of Hospitaller estates ordered by the Senate in a period of less than twenty-two months. Mallia-Milanes, *Venice and Hospitaller Malta*, 21.

231 Luttrell, 'The Earliest Documents on the Hospitaller Corso', in Arbel (ed.), *Intercultural contacts*, 177–88: 177.

known.[232] However, it is certain that 'illicit' attacks did take place, especially against Greek subjects of the Ottoman empire.[233] The detailed deposition of an enslaved Ottoman Greek sailor before the Maltese inquisitor illustrates how galleys flying the flag of the Order hunted down these Greek subjects, targeting commerce between Egypt and the Dodecanese.[234] During his deposition the Ottoman Greek sailor in question stated that most of the crew on board his ship, which he described as being composed of half Christians, half Muslims, managed to flee in small boats or took the risk of swimming to the shore, while the Maltese attackers got on board and took hold of the merchandise, irrespective of what belonged to the Christian sailors.[235]

In addition to the above pledge made when obtaining the licence to act as corsairs, notarial deeds relating to *societas* agreements which had specific clauses related to corsairing activities would also include clauses safeguarding the interest of the shareholders. In fact, all such deeds consulted for the present study always contained a personal pledge by the shareholders, which was intended to offset any damages or losses resulting from neglect or breach of contract.[236] Some of the investors were sedentary partners and thus made sure to include clauses wherein the *patrone* and captain would pledge to carry out their duties responsibly. Such clauses indicate that if corsairs did contravene their licence and were put on trial they were personally liable in law to compensate for any damages sustained by the sedentary partners.

The imposition of these prohibitions, as well as the official protection afforded by safe passages, created the necessary incentives for both Christian and Muslim merchants to undertake what would otherwise have been impossible trading voyages

232 In 1534 the knight *Fra.* Filippo Mazza was arrested by the Venetians for attacking Christian ships in the Adriatic and in the Gulf of Venice. After managing to escape he was eventually recaptured and beheaded and his ships were burned. In 1555 Pope Paul IV ordered the Grand Master to prevent the Knights from molesting Venetian shipping. Indeed, Venice took reprisals against the Order in 1582–83 on account of continuous attacks. This plundering forced the Venetian senate to order its navy to raid all Maltese ships which it encountered, since these were disrupting commercial traffic and hindered the victualling of the Island of Candia, apart from irritating the Turks, who vented their anger on Venetian possessions. Documentation pertaining to the seventeenth and eighteenth centuries reveals that these injunctions were not always observed. In fact, there are repeated official warnings and decrees prohibiting Maltese corsairs from molesting the inhabitants of the Greek islands, and punishments ranging from simple fines to the death penalty. During the war between France and Spain in 1637–38, French knights breached the Order's neutrality when they equipped their ships against the Spanish. Discipline was restored only after they were threatened with expulsion from the Hospitaller Order Cassar, 'The Maltese Corsairs', 146, 152–3. See also P. Falcone, 'Una relazione di Malta sulla fine del Cinquecento', *Archivio Storico di Malta*, 4:1 (1933), 2–51: 7.

233 Greene, *Catholic Pirates,* passim.

234 In this particular case the Ottoman-Greek merchant ship was caught off Damietta '*tra mare et salso*' – which refers to the point where the river Nile opens up to the sea – while it was making its way to Mcdon. J. Abela, 'Who was Georgio Scala?' in D. Agius (ed.), *Georgio Scala and the Moorish Slaves: The Inquisition Malta 1598* (Malta, 2013), 213–34.

235 Abela, 'Who was Georgio Scala?' in D. Agius (ed.), *Georgio Scala and the Moorish Slaves,* 213–34. As regards the seventeenth century, refer to Green, 'Victims of Piracy', in Fusaro et al., *Trade and Cultural Exchange*, 177–201.

236 A good example which goes into the specifics of such obligations is found in NAV, R 224/1, fols 438–439 (31.i.1543)

to hostile lands in pirate-infested seas, while ensuring the total control by the Hospitaller government over what would soon become the fastest-growing sector in the Maltese economy, namely corsairing and its ancillary activities.

Safe conducts and Muslim traders

Christian or Muslim owners of cargo vessels were both concerned to reach the same goal, which was to dispose of their merchandise in a profitable manner. Bargaining processes overcame religious and cultural divides and both parties tried as best they could to exploit all commercial possibilities open to them. Theoretically, the Knights were the sworn enemies of Muslims and, as such, Maltese merchants were not supposed to engage in trading operations with any Ottoman subjects or in any Ottoman territory. In practice, however, things were quite different. In view of Malta's lack of resources, and as an obvious move to entice new settlement to the island which would help to improve economic activity and stability, the Order petitioned Pope Clement VII to grant newly established traders on the island the necessary permission to trade with Muslims. It was thus on 1 October 1530 that the pope, having evaluated the precarious state of the island's provisioning, decreed that new inhabitants who settled in Malta, Gozo and Tripoli were allowed to trade in any kind of merchandise, including wheat, wine, oil and pulses, with the region of Barbary, Moors and the 'infidels'. As was noted in Chapter One, this Bull also granted those who had followed the Order from Rhodes exemption from the jurisdiction of the bishop of Malta, and instead they came under the ecclesiastical authority of the prior of the Conventual Church.[237]

While still in Rhodes, the Order had begun the policy of granting safe conduct certificates to Muslim merchants. As discussed, Muslim shipping considered 'friendly' due to the reciprocal benefits could not be attacked by Christian corsairs. These merchants were allowed to travel westwards, and at times they even made use of Hospitaller ships in order to ensure the safe arrival of various commodities at competitive prices.[238] As was discussed above, this practice was continued and further developed in Malta after the arrival of the Knights, through the granting of letters patent or safe conducts issued by the Order's Chancery.[239] These records bring to life the economic activities of some Muslim merchants who managed to find ways and means of penetrating the Christian market.[240] How did the Order justify

237 Paoli, *Codice Diplomatico*, 201–2.

238 D. Panzac, *La caravane maritime, marins européens et marchands ottomans en Méditerranée 1680–1830* (Paris, 2004), 10. See also Williams, '*Sacra Militia*', in Fusaro et al., *Trade and Cultural Exchange*, 139–56: 144.

239 A Bull issued in 1640 stated that those infidel traders who were caught trading without a safe conduct were captured and their wares confiscated. NLM, AOM, Lib. Bull. 439, 70v.

240 Bosio informs us that in 1529 some Turks who had been slaves of the Knights while still in Rhodes, and who were freed on the conquest of Rhodes by the Ottomans, still kept good relations with the Order and, after being granted safe conducts from the 'Turks'

its amicable relations with Muslim merchants? Why did it seek to protect them and how did it go about ensuring the smooth flow of commodities from hostile lands?

A good indication comes from documents such as those relating to the case of *Nob.* Bayz Mahmet Algnari, who is described as a merchant Moor resident of Djerba. In order to protect his interests, in 1534 this merchant applied to the Grand Master for the granting of a safe conduct.[241] The latter consented, but was careful to base his concession on the fact that many Christians were falling captive to Muslims, and thus Muslim merchants such as Bayz Mahmet would be excellent intermediaries for the redemption of such captives, since they were familiar with the region. The Grand Master's concerns thus portrayed an Order which was resolute in extending help to Christian captives in North Africa, a concern which in official documents was always given precedence over the benefit of trade. The chief motivation behind this was based on the fact that the Order had constantly to justify its claims to revenues that were extracted from all over Europe and could not risk appearing too lenient or co-operative towards the enemy of Christendom.

It was thus that Bayz Mahmet was permitted to travel freely with his men and his merchandise between Malta and the fortress of Tripoli, and there conduct the necessary business for the redemption of Christian captives in Tunis and Djerba.[242] At the same time, on his return voyage, together with his cargo of redeemed Christian captives he was permitted to bring back various other commodities in which he traded. It is interesting to note that in safe conduct certificates all those responsible for the safe passage of the merchants were not only requested to let the ship travel safely on her way without undue delay, but were also specifically requested not to permit her to be molested.[243] Such wording suggests that those to whom the instructions were addressed were also expected to extend their responsibility beyond their own actions and act accordingly if the protected ship was harassed by others.[244]

The following text is a typical example of a safe conduct certificate issued to a Muslim merchant (reproduced in Fig. 8).

Frater Claudius de la Sengle A tutti et qualimquam alle mani de iquali le presenti nostre perveniranno salute sia noto et manifestao qualmente l'eshibitor di esse Hagi buabdella de Chalipha Tripolino si parte al prensente di questa nostra isola di Malta con suo naviglio et marinari per andar alli Gerbi et tornar qua	(*Frater* Claude de la Sengle. To all and whoever in the hands of whom the present our [letter patent] will reach good greetings. Be it known and manifested that the exhibitor of this [letter patent] *Hagi buabdella de Chalipha Tripolino* is at present departing from this our island of Malta, with his ship

and from the Sicilian Viceroy, they were constantly trafficking in merchandise between Modon and Messina. Bosio, *Dell'Istoria della Sacra Religione*, vol. 3, 76.

241 NLM, AOM, Lib. Bull. 415, fol. 255v (8.i.1534).

242 This particular safe conduct did not stipulate whether it was granted for just one trip or more.

243 For examples relating to the last decades of the sixteenth century and the mid-seventeenth century refer to Brogini, *Malte, frontière de chrétienté*, especially Chapter 7.

244 NLM, AOM, Lib. Bull. MS 423, fol. 236v (17.vi.1553).

con alcune sue mercantie et robe per il che ci é stato supplicato gli volessimo dar et concedere nostre lettere patenti con le quali puotesse liberamente andar et tornar per l'effetto sopradetto. Per tanto commandiamo in virtu de Sancta ubedienza a tutti capitani et patroni de nostre galere et altri navigli di nostra Religione et di queste nostre Isole et dominij pregandovi Illustrissimi Principi Vicere locatenenti gubernatori armiragli generali proveditori Capitani giurati patroni et altri ufficiali de qual si voglia conditione nelle cui terre et giurisdictioni capitara detto Hagi Buabdella de Chalipha che lo lasciate liberamente andar passar et tornar con detto suo naviglio marinari et altre robbe et mercantie non permettendo che sia molestato impedito ne ritardato in modo alcuno anzi donarli et commandar esseli donato ogni aiuto et favore accio possa complir suo viaggo per il che restaremo obligati ad similia et multo maiora volendo che il prensente salvoconducto habbia vigore per un anno a contarsi dalla data delle presenti et oltre a nostra volunta et beneplacito. In cuius rei bulla nostra magistralis in cera Datum melitae die tertia mensis Octobris 1555.

to go to Djerba and come back here with some of his merchandise and goods, for which [purpose] we were requested that we would give and concede our letters patent, with which he could go and come freely to the effect of the above. Therefore we command in virtue of Holy Obedience to all captains and shipmasters of our galleys and other ships of our Religion and our islands and domains, praying to your Illustrious Princes, Viceroys, lieutenants, governors, admirals, generals, providers, captains, jurats, shipmasters and other officials of any kind and station in which lands and jurisdiction the said *Hagi Buabdella de Chalipha* will happen to be in, that you let him travel, go and come freely with his ship, sailors and other goods and merchandise, not permitting that he be molested, impeded or retarded in any way, but give him and command that he is given every kind of help and favour so that he could carry out his voyage for which (favour) we shall be greatly obliged. We order that the present safe conduct remains valid for one year from the present date together with our consent. Whereof our seal of government [is impressed] in wax. Given in Malta the third day of October 1555.)

In a similar way, Muslim merchants would come to Malta to redeem their fellow Muslim captives, at the same time taking advantage of the privilege granted to them to trade their goods. Mahometo Rayz, described as '*libero et franco turcho*',[245] was one such merchant who was granted a safe conduct permit for one whole year. He was requested to go to Djerba to redeem some Christian captives and was allowed to return to Malta with merchandise to be exchanged for the release of some Turks and Moors.[246] Similarly, Mechamet de Africa, who was once a slave but was now '*libero et manumesso*' (free and manumitted), was to go to Tripoli and Tazora and from there collect the necessary money, or its equivalent in merchandise, to redeem

245 A free Turk. NLM, AOM, Lib. Bull. MS 423, fols 213–213v (24.ii.1552).

246 '*Et anchora ritornar qua con alcune mercancie et robbe per il riscato de alcuni turchi et mori*' (and once again return here with his merchandise and goods for the redemption of some Turks and Moors). NLM, AOM, Lib. Bull. 423, fol. 213 (24.ii.1552).

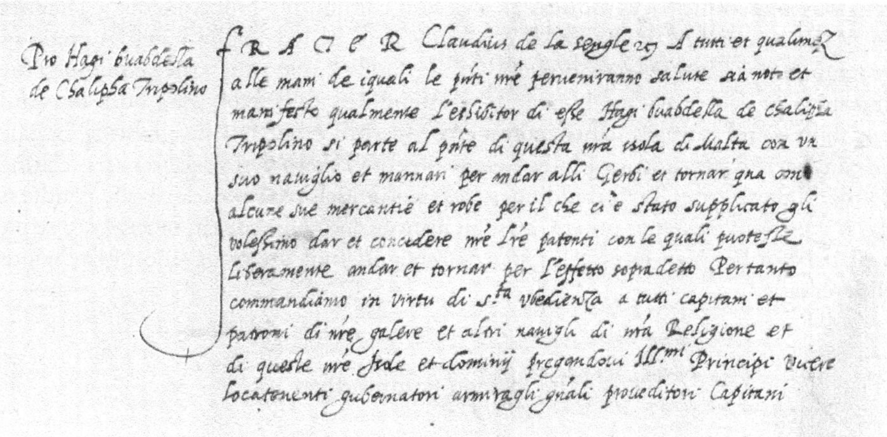
Pro Hagi buabdella de Csalipsa Tripolino

F. R. A. C. E. R. Claudius de la Sengle etc. A tutti et qualunque alle mani de iquali le pnti nre pervenirano salute et noto et manifesto qualmente l'essibitor di esse Hagi buabdella de Csalipsa Tripolino si parte al pnte di questa nra isola di Malta con un suo naviglio et marinari per andar alli Gerbi et tornar qua con alcune sue mercantie et robe per il che ci e stato supplicato gli volessimo dar et concedere nre lre patenti con le quali puotesse liberamente andar et tornar per l'effetto sopradetto Pertanto commandiamo in virtu di s.ta obedienza a tutti capitani et patroni di nre galere et altri navigli di nra Religione et di queste nre Isole et dominij pregandoci Ill.mi Principi Vicere locatenenti gubernatori armiragli gnali proveditori Capitani

Fig. 8 Extract from a typical letter patent issued by the Magisterial Palace and given to Muslim traders so that they could travel freely between Malta and North Africa
Source: NLM, AOM, Lib. Bull. 425 f. 207 (3.x.1555).

some Moorish slaves found in Malta.[247] In cases like this a slave who had spent considerable time on the island would have established various connections with the local population, which might at some point in time be translated into profitable operations. Murgian de Abdala from Aden[248] and Mahometo Hamidan Benalli de Zanzor[249] were two such merchants. They were freed as part of the joyous events celebrating the election of the Grand Master.[250] They then petitioned the Grand Master to give them a perpetual licence to travel with their merchandise between their own country and Malta. The Grand Master conceded on condition that their ships were not armed for corsairing. Rays Ahmet del Monesterio[251] was still the slave of Philippo Cilia when he was given a safe conduct to go to Golette and Tunis and return with his ship loaded with merchandise in order to ransom his own freedom and that of a number of other slaves.

In this way the Order tried to establish a balance between the projection of its image as the eternal enemy of the Muslim 'infidel' and the necessity to procure commodities from hostile territories to meet its daily needs. As has been shown,[252] the Order encouraged an indirect type of trade with North Africa that was mostly carried out by intermediaries, both Christian and Muslim. This brought to the island an ever-increasing number of heterogeneous merchants and adventurers of various

247 NLM, AOM, Lib. Bull. 423, fol. 236v (7.vi.1553).
248 NLM, AOM, Lib. Bull. 425, fols 198–198v (24.v.1555).
249 NLM, AOM, Lib. Bull. 425, fol. 199 (14.v.1555).
250 Although the name of the Grand Master is not mentioned in the document this must have been granted to them by Grand Master Claude de la Sengle (1553–57), and referred to in the document as supporting evidence of their current free status.
251 NLM, AOM, Lib. Bull. 425, fols 198–198v (15.ix.1556). Unfortunately, the safe conduct certificates do not go into much detail other than what has been quoted above.
252 Refer also to Appendix.

religious and ethnic backgrounds. This vibrant community found adequate facilities in Malta to conduct its business, especially that related to the lucrative trade in redemption of slaves. Merchants conducted round trips in which they combined the transport of people with shipment of commodities, fully exploiting both outward and homeward voyages. Their commerce was protected by the granting of safe conduct certificates and, as Molly Greene noted when analysing court cases relating to the Maltese *corso*, 'by forbidding attacks on infidels who possessed safe conducts from the grand master or other Christian princes, the court sought precisely to strike that balance between respect for state sovereignty and the recognition of religious difference'.[253]

The human commodity

Together with Livorno, Malta has frequently been referred to as the Christian version of Muslim Algiers, the North African capital renowned for its lucrative slave trafficking transactions.[254] Although Maltese seafarers and adventurers often resorted to corsairing ventures as a means of livelihood before 1530,[255] the arrival of the Hospitaller Order revolutionised the local framework for such ventures and attracted the participation of a myriad of *armatori* who invested in various expeditions.[256] The upsurge in naval activities encouraged local adventurers to combine their resources with those of the new settlers, as well as with those of various other foreign participants. This led to the meteoric expansion of the mercantile sector. The Birgu harbour area was constantly developed to suit the needs of these entrepreneurs, while the Order's fleet inspired some sense of protection through its constant patrolling of the surrounding seas.[257] Malta was soon recognised as a profitable centre for the common pooling of investments and the redistribution of goods, a pull factor which

253 Greene, *Catholic Pirates*, 114.

254 Michel Fontenay argues that the number of slaves found in Malta is not comparable to the greater number of slaves found in Algiers. However, one should consider the smallness of the island and the ratio of the slave population to that of the local inhabitants. M. Fontenay, 'Il mercato maltese degli schiavi al tempo dei Cavalieri di San Giovanni (1530–1798)', *Quaderni Storici*, 107:2 (2001), 397–8: 397.

255 M. Fontenay & A. Tenenti, 'Course et Piraterie Méditerranéennes de la fin du Moyen-Age au début du XIXème Siècle', in M. Mollat (ed.), *Course et Piraterie: Etudes preséntées à la Commission International D'Histoire Maritime à l'occasion de son XVe colloque international pendant le XIVe Congrès Interantional de Sciences historiques San Francisco, août, 1975* (2 vols, Paris, 1975), vol. 1, 78–136: 87. During the medieval period Malta served as a base for corsair vessels and these often recruited Maltese personnel for their expeditions. Cassar, 'The Maltese Corsairs', 137–41.

256 The *armatori* were the holders of the equity in a corsairing voyage. See Earle, *Corsairs of Malta and Barbary*, 127. For a detailed glossary regarding the various maritime activities and associated works and responsibilities see J. Muscat, *Il-Flotta ta' l-Ordni ta' San Gwann* (Malta, 2000), 197–211; J. Muscat & A. Cuschieri, *Naval Activities of the Knights of St John 1530–1798* (Malta, 2002), 209–19.

257 Abela, 'Port Activities', passim.

created an interrelated network of communities and encouraged the establishment of what Cassar terms a strong 'trade diaspora'.[258]

Traffic in slaves occupied a prime place in maritime trade in the southern Mediterranean, since it allowed for the profitable exchange of monies or commodities, the latter often being merchants' preferred means of exchange. They would receive cash deposits from the captives' families prior to their journey, which they could then invest in their business with good prospects for registering a net profit from their venture. On arrival in infidel territory they would usually trade their merchandise in exchange for Christian slaves, thus avoiding the risks of fluctuating exchange rates and making higher profits on the original deal. Brogini argues that it was only very late in the sixteenth century, with the proper establishment of corsairing activities, that commercial ties between Malta and the Muslim littoral were established.[259] However, Maltese notarial acts[260] prove the existence of such activities at a much earlier date.

Several medieval notarial references record agreements for the sale of black or Ethiopian slaves, the result of the trans-Saharan slave trade of the Moors of North Africa. Godfrey Wettinger has shown that this is similar to the pattern found in the Sicilian context, where slaves of African origin far outnumbered any others. He argues that several late fifteenth-century notarial references in Syracuse refer to the acquisition of slaves from the mountains of Barca (or Barqah), and these also include references to Maltese merchants resident in Syracuse. At times, they traded their wares in exchange for slaves and it is these African slaves who were easily brought to Malta. This hypothesis is further strengthened by the fact that in 1436 there was a long debate about the type of tax to be levied on the importation of slaves from North Africa.[261] As early as the first decades of the Order's rule, traffic in slaves was a pull factor which quickly gained momentum and saw merchants from all across the Mediterranean dealing in human traffic and other prizes. Countless businessmen and several knights commissioned their own corsair vessels or participated financially in corsairing expeditions under the Order's flag. The constant stream of slaves brought in by these corsairs created a network of commercial traffic and trade flourished between Christian and Muslim merchants who collaborated and interacted in the midst of a Holy War.[262]

As Fatiha Loualich explains, a slave was more than just a commodity or source of labour for the owner, since his or her value was assessed by taking various other

258 Cassar, *Society, Culture and Identity*, 76.

259 Brogini, *Malte, frontière de chrétienté*, 358.

260 Prize registers for the sixteenth century do not exist in Maltese archives and therefore notarial acts help to fill in this lacuna of information.

261 Wettinger, *Slavery in the Islands of Malta*, 17.

262 Genoese ships repeatedly challenged papal proclamations, hence continuing their trading ventures with infidel ports, the most precious merchandise being Tartar slaves obtained from their colonies of Caffa and Pera. This type of traffic continued even after the fall of Constantinople and well into the sixteenth century. C. Carosi, 'Redimere Captivos: Appunti sugli atti notaril di riscatto (Sec. XVI)', in V. Piergiovanni (ed.), *Corsari e riscatto dei captivi, garanzia notarile tra le due sponde del Mediterraneo, Atti del Convegno di Studi Storici Marsala, 4 ottobre 2008* (Milano, 2010), 47–74: 61 n. 46.

factors into consideration, such as the slave's socio-economic status and whether this allowed some sort of speculation which would permit a good profit for his or her redemption.[263] There are various examples of this in the Maltese context. The redemptions of knights are a case in point, and must have impinged heavily on the restricted financial resources of the Order.[264] A good example is an act drawn up on 18 February 1531,[265] just four months after the arrival of the Hospitaller Order. The receiver of the Order in Sicily, *Fra.* Simon de Bonanno[266] forwarded 50 gold ducats to *Fra.* Johannes Bresor to cover freight expenses incurred in respect of the transport of sixteen infidel slaves to Tunisia. Once they had arrived at their destination, the slaves were to be exchanged for another knight, namely *Fra.* Johannes Laura, Bailiff of Laureto. Although the prices of slaves varied considerably, various studies show that the average selling price of a slave during this period was in the region of 46 *scudi*.[267] Thus, these sixteen slaves would have brought in approximately 736 *scudi*, a hefty sum for the bartering of just one slave.

Similar redemption contracts concerning Knights of the Order reflect more or less the same prices as in the case of the knight *Fra.* Michael de Marsiglia, who was held captive in the castle of Tripoli in 1560 and redeemed for the price of 668 *scudi* 11 *tarì* 9 *grani*, which was paid through a bill of exchange issued by the Order's treasury.[268] Such prices can be better evaluated when they are compared to redemption contracts for captives lower down the social scale. For example, Josephus de Bonfiglio was redeemed at Tripoli through the services of *Nob.* Thoma de Leonti of Milan and Johannes de Alcida. Josephus had to pay a total of 114 *scudi* 10 *tarì*, which included the original asking price requested by the mediator, Chayd Chiabatio, plus all related expenses.[269] The debt was to be repaid '*in pace et de plano ut bancus*' in the city of Messina within eight days from when both the creditors and the debtor were to first visit the city. Should the debtor fail to honour this contract, the creditors retained the right to hold him as a prisoner both on land and at sea or on any ship.

From the above contracts it is clear that the notary's intervention regulated a whole series of situations, while guaranteeing the interests of the contracting

263 F. Loualich, 'In the Regency of Algiers: The Human Side of the Algerine Corso', in Fusaro et al., *Trade and Cultural Exchange*, 69–96: 72–3. See also S. Bono, *I Corsari Barbareschi* (Turin, 1964).

264 G. Bonello, 'Knights in Slavery: Captivi in manibus infidelium', in *Histories of Malta: Reflections and Rejections, Vol. 5* (Malta, 2004), 57–85.

265 NAV, R 439/1, fols 57–60 (18.ii.1531).

266 In notarial acts *Fra.* Simone de Bonanno is identified as '*Reverendus dominus frater Simon de Bonanno, miles hierosolomitanus, preceptor preceptoriarum Castellacii et Caltagironis prioratuum Lombardie et Messane et receptor in hoc regno comunis Thesauri Sacre Religionis Hierosolimitane*'. Giuffrida, *La Sicilia e l'Ordine di Malta*, 23–4.

267 Abela, 'A Window on Early Hospitaller Malta', 242. A study of the *Registro delle Prese* (Register of Prizes) for the years 1659 to 1663, conducted by Michel Fontenay, established the average price of a slave in that period to be 144 *scudi*, while the average price in the latter half of the eighteenth century was 208 *scudi*. Fontenay, 'Il mercato maltese degli schiavi', 397–8.

268 NAV, R 224/17, fols 730–730v (18.iv.1560).

269 NAV, R 44/7, fols 374–375 (19.iv.1564).

parties, especially those of his clients. Both before and during the Order's rule, Notary Pietro de Trugillo was the appointed notary at the Tripoli fortress[270] and was involved in various contracts regarding redemption of Christian slaves, both Maltese and foreign. These contracts reveal just how complicated the whole process of redemption was and how the parties involved went about assuring a positive outcome from their deal. Although Tripoli had been in Spanish hands since 1510, it was only with the establishment of the Knights Hospitaller that Malta witnessed an upsurge in transactions for the redemption of slaves from this fortress. At times, the Grand Master also issued safe conduct certificates to enemy ships to enable them to transfer captives to the port of Tripoli. This was the case for the knights and sailors of the *Catharinet*, a ship captured by Turgut Reis and taken with all her load to Djerba in 1548. Following this unfortunate capture, the knight Augustino Spagnol was sent as an envoy to negotiate the redemption of the captives. Once the prices were fixed, a Muslim ship was to carry them to the Order's port in Tripoli.[271]

Many foreigners too found the Malta–Tripoli connection a good link for co-ordinating human releases, as is evidenced by the case of Mundus Lapernich who hailed from the city of Palermo. From the notarial registers of Nicolò de Agatiis it transpires that while still in captivity Mundus drew up a contract through the services of Notary de Trugillo in which he promised to pay a total of 84 gold ducats to his creditor, Guglielmo Lufalato, or else to his agent.[272] The sum in question must have been higher than the original sum requested by the slave's master, since the prohibition on usury must be taken into consideration. As de Roover explains, 'one should not assume that the canonist doctrine on usury was merely a topic for academic discussion among theologians. The opposite is true: the usury prohibition had a tremendous effect on business practices all through the Renaissance, the Reformation, and even down to the French Revolution.'[273]

Compensation for loans was not licit if it translated into gain for the lender. However, if it was charged as reimbursement for loss or expense, it became licit.[274] Interest was considered as compensation due to a creditor in view of the loss he had incurred through lending, and therefore it was licit to claim *damnum et interesse* for other reasons not inherent in a loan, such as the failure to repay the principal on maturity.[275] According to Hunt and Murray, in certain cases repayment dates

270 NLM, AOM, Lib. Bull. 423, fol. 202 (7.x.1551) confirms that he was the Order's appointed notary up to the loss of Tripoli in 1551.

271 AOM, Lib. Bull. 421, fols 221v–222 (26.xi.1548).

272 '*Ad omnia simplicem requisitione ipsius creditoris seu persone legitime pro eo*' [sic]. NAV, R 202/2, fols 245v–247 (21.vi.1538). The inclusion of such a clause means that the debtor could thus validly pay a third person. However, it is to be noted that the creditor still held the right of recourse against the original debtor if his agent failed to forward him the payment. De Roover, *Money, Banking and Credit in Medieval Bruges*, 51.

273 R. de Roover, 'What is Dry Exchange?', in J. Kirshner (ed.), *Business, Banking and Economic Thought in Late Medieval and Early Modern Europe* (Chicago and London, 1974), 183–99: 185.

274 S. Hunt & J. M. Murray, *A History of Business in Medieval Europe 1200–1500* (Cambridge, 1999), 72–3.

275 De Roover, *The Rise and Decline*, 10–11.

were deliberately set earlier than actually planned in order to assess a charge for 'damages'.[276] Thus, as explained in Chapter Three, the manoeuvring of legal terminology provided ways and means by which to procure much-needed advances for commercial activities.[277]

Various other ancillary expenses were involved in the redemption process. These included administrative expenses, excise tax, food and transport costs. According to a study compiled by Paola Massa all these added up to about 26% of the original price.[278] Referring to the above case of Mundus Lapernich, it transpires that Lufalato, the creditor, had forwarded the requested sum of money to *Fra.* Francesco Ajaza, the Treasurer of the Order in Tripoli. Once free, most of these persons would have been transported to Malta, a service which at times was carried out by Muslim-owned ships.[279]

Notarial documents show that the debtor, once free, would have to ratify the contract made in Tripoli on his arrival in Malta, a condition which could have led to a renewed agreement stipulating a higher price than was originally agreed. The acts of Notary de Trugillo do not survive in the Maltese Notarial Archives and it is assumed that they were destroyed after the loss of Tripoli,[280] so it is not possible to compare the two contracts. In the case under analysis, once he was in Malta the freed slave Mundus promised to repay the debt in cash through the bank in either Syracuse or Palermo, according to the creditor's choice. If the payment was received late, the creditor had a right to any interest accrued through the late settlement.[281] He also reserved the right to be paid by a bill of exchange '*ad cambium et recambium*',[282] according to the rates of exchange prevailing at the time of the transfer of money in either Syracuse or Palermo.[283] If the debtor defaulted he was to be imprisoned '*cum*

276 Hunt & Murray, *A History of Business*, 72–3.

277 F. Braudel, *Capitalism and Material Life 1400–1800* (trans. M. Kochan, New York, 1973), 368; de Roover, *The Rise and Decline*, 108.

278 P. Massa, 'Il Riscatto dei "Captivi". Temi sociali e problematiche finanziarie', in Piergiovanni (ed.), *Corsari e Riscatto*, 135–50: 138.

279 Refer to the Appendix.

280 Electronic enquiries made at the Spanish National Archives on 22 November 2011 did not give any positive information as to the existence of these notarial acts.

281 NAV, R 202/2, fols 245v–247 (21.vi.1538).

282 This clause was mainly used to hide interest; a good example is provided in CEM, *Liber Usurarorum Melitae, Liber Primus* (1570–1571), where Francesco Rhochion was accused of lending money at an interest rate of 30% by hiding the profit in a *cambium et recambium* contract. Lopez & Raymond explain it as follows: 'This clause was often pure fiction, because it was understood from the very first that the borrower would avail himself of the option to repay the debt in local currency, so that the contract became a straight loan with interest disguised under another name.' Lopez & Raymond, *Medieval Trade in the Mediterranean World*, 163. See also de Roover, *Money, Banking and Credit in Medieval Bruges*, 81–2.

283 According to de Roover, the rates of interest were not the only factor which influenced the exchange rate, since this fluctuated in response to more powerful factors such as '(1) changes in the monetary standard either at home or abroad, (2) disturbances in the balance of payments between any two places, and (3) speculation based on the expectations of the exchange-dealers or on the criminal attempts of manipulators who some-

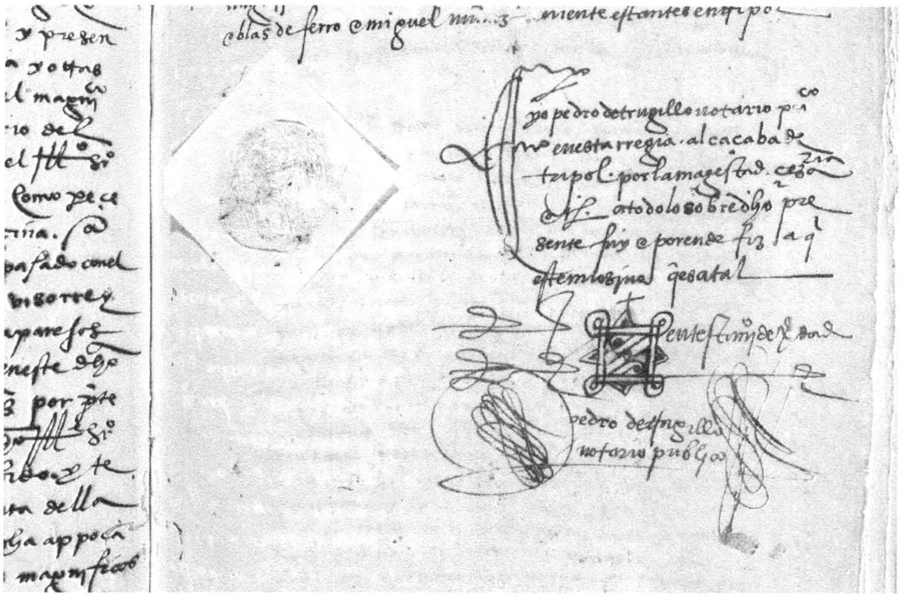

Fig. 9 The *signum* and seal of Notary Pedro de Trugillo, the notary who practised in the Tripoli fortress before and during the rule of the Knights Hospitaller, is found in a few certified true copies of his acts which were required by his clients and which are still extant in the Maltese archives

Source: NLM, AOM 7559, f.105 (new numeration in pencil) (24.xi.1529).

ferris quam sine' (with or without chains) until he settled his debt,[284] a shocking possibility for someone who had just been released from slavery. The borrower pledged both his moveable and immoveable property as security. On the other hand, in an authenticated copy of a contract drawn up in Tripoli for the redemption of Cola Petro Valestrero from Gozo, the captive undertook to be personally liable '*cum sua persona et benes*' to pay Alonso Peso 13 ducats in gold. Repayment was to be effected in Birgu in two separate payments, one half being due within four months from the date of the contract, and the other half within a year of the same date. As a security Cola hypothecated eight houses which he had in Rabat, Gozo and was liable to be imprisoned if there should be a breach of contract.[285]

This type of contract seems to have been quite common,[286] and in some cases once the captive had drawn up the deed in Tripoli things moved rapidly. This was the case with a contract done on 15 September 1540 by the Genoese Stephano Degaribaldo

times tried to corner the money market.' However, the lender was bound to gain in a stable market. De Roover, *Money, Banking and Credit in Medieval Bruges*, 63.

284 NAV, R 202/2, fols 245v–247 (21.vi.1538).

285 NLM, AOM 6559, fol. 575–577 (25.ii.1550).

286 See for example, NAV, R 206/7, fol. 66v (3.iii.1543), fol. 85v (30.iii.1543), fols 154v–155 (25.vi.1543), fol. 192v (23.vii.1543), fol. 269v (29.ix.1543); R 202/3, fols 223–223v (18.vi.1539); R 202/4, fol. 11v (7.ix.1539); R 202/5, fols 53–53v (28.ix.1540).

Fig. 10 The *signum* of Notary Selvagi de Via accompanies the signature of Notary Pedro de Trugillo. De Via is here confirming that this particular copy of a contract drawn up in Tripoli in respect of a redemption agreement was a true copy extracted from Trugillo's acts.
Source: NLM, AOM, 6559, f.576 (25.ii.1550).

and a redeemed captive from Gozo by the name of Matheus Sansun.[287] Degaribaldo seems to have been a very active merchant and redemption agent in Tripoli, since he is listed in various other acts as providing these services.[288] Sums due to Degaribaldo for redemption services varied from 38 ducats[289] to 103 ducats,[290] the repayment terms also varying in their due dates but never exceeding four months from the date of contract.

The aforementioned contract stipulated that the initial agreement relating to the redemption of Matheus had been made by Notary de Trugillo just twenty-one days before. Once again, a fixed date is set for repayment of debt which is approximately four months after release. It is also specifically noted that non-payment of the sum due on the specified date could translate itself into payment through *cambium* and *recambium* in any part of the world (*pro qualibus mundi partibus*) at prevailing or non-prevailing exchange rates (*quibus cambiis currentibus vel non currentibus*). Once

287 NAV, R 202/5, fols 26v–27v (15.ix.1540).

288 For example, in the acts of Nicolò de Agatiis five such contracts by Degaribaldo with captives held in Tripoli were done within a period of four days. Refer to NAV, R 202/5, fols 16v–17 (7.ix.1540), fol. 17v (7.ix.1540), fols 17v–18 (7.ix.1540), fols 19v–20 (10.ix.1540), fols 22–22v (11.ix.1540).

289 NAV, R 202/5, fols 16v–17 (7.ix.1540)

290 NAV, R 202/5, fols 19v–20 (10.ix.1540).

again in this instance, the inclusion of a possible future payment in *recambium* or through a bill of exchange necessarily involved an extension of credit and the parties to the exchange contract could make the profit certain and even eliminate all speculative risks due to unexpected fluctuations in exchange rates.[291]

Redemption appeals were very numerous and, as previously observed, the demand created a ready market for services.[292] Merchants were often the only point of contact between the captives, their masters and their families and fully explcited the situation, combining the transportation of merchandise with that of human commodity.[293] Stretched beyond his limits, the desperate captive would promise the world and more in return for his freedom. Fraught, anxious and uncertain of their future, captives were often exploited by shrewd dealers who made exorbitant demands in exchange for their hope of freedom.[294] The likes of such manoeuvres may be hinted at in a protest made by the Syracusan *Fra.* Marco Cannizaro in 1562. This Franciscan cleric protested in the Episcopal Court against the dealings of merchant Francesco Antonori and his partners. *Fra.* Marco claimed that his Muslim master had agreed to set him free for the price of 40 *scudi*, and in order to free himself he had asked the merchant and his partner, who were both in Tripoli at the time, to lend him the money required for his redemption. The merchant claimed that he did not carry any money with him, but if the slave's master consented, he would be prepared to give the equivalent amount in cloth.

This indicates that ready cash was not a method of payment favoured by travelling merchants, who preferred to barter their own merchandise for commodities with which they could supply their home markets, or else draw to up bills of exchange which they hoped to redeem at the desired profit.[295] Referring back to *Fra* Marco, the plaintiff stated that the final sum due to these merchants ended up an exorbitant 97 *scudi*. *Fra.* Marco also stated that the original sum should not have exceeded 50 *scudi*, since the rate of exchange used, 9 *reali* per *scudo*, was on the high side, and he insisted that such illicit profit was nothing less than usury.[296] He further stated that every freed Christian paid no more than 7 *scudi* '*per ragione della porta*'.[297] *Fra.* Marco claimed that after having been ransomed he was beaten and forced to sign a debt agreement amounting to 160 gold *scudi*, which was over and above the sum the merchants had paid for his release and which included the clause whereby he would

[291] Lopez & Raymond, *Medieval Trade in the Mediterranean World*, 163.

[292] See, for example, NLM, AOM, Lib. Bull. 424, fol. 212 (15.xii.1553), where a group of sixty Jews who were caught through corsairing activities had paid their redemption and were being jointly granted a safe conduct to go back to their countries.

[293] Some merchants even specialiaed in the redemption of slaves; see Carosi, 'Redimere Captivos', in V. Piergiovanni (ed.), *Corsari e riscatto dei captivi*, 47–74: 58–9.

[294] Carosi, 'Redimere Captivos' in V. Piergiovanni (ed.), *Corsari e riscatto dei captivi*, 47–74: 58.

[295] Abela, 'Port Activities', 39–42.

[296] He was thus insisting that he should have paid 450 *reali*, while the merchants were initially requesting 873 *reali* and after forcing him to sign a second agreement they were requesting 1,440 *reali*.

[297] CAM, CEM, AO, MS 42 1562, fols 91–94v (09.x.1652). This must have related to a tax imposed by the Ottomans on the export of redeemed slaves.

have been imprisoned if he had failed to honour his debt.[298] Once *Fra.* Marco had arrived in Malta, with the help of a certain Barresi *alias* Mancaruso[299] he managed to borrow 100 *scudi*, sixty of which he gave to his creditors and the rest of which he deposited at the Episcopal Court in order to file his protest. The merchants were now hunting him and Barresi down for an additional 100 *scudi* of illicit profit.

When analysing similar cases it is important to note that ecclesiastical privileges exempted a cleric from lay jurisdiction and from any liability to give evidence in the lay courts, at least not without the permission of their legitimate ecclesiastical superiors.[300] The merchants must have been aware of such laws, and instead of accusing Cannizaro they presented a case at the *Magna Curia Castellania* against Barresi, who, they claimed, was acting in breach of contract. Cannizaro and Barresi were now petitioning the bishop to pronounce the deal usurious and proclaim that all claims presented by Antonori should be declared illegal. Cannizaro was also insisting that Barresi should not be molested by the creditors.[301] It is interesting to note that the records of the *Magna Curia Castellania* contain the Episcopal Court's request to hold over all proceedings against Barresi which were presented by Antonori until the case was decided by the Court.[302] Although this case sheds light on the extensive power of ecclesiastical authorities over lay ones, one must be very careful in interpreting such exemptions, since these concessions did not exempt the clergy and religious from the legislative powers of the state.[303]

In a world with a great shortage of coins, coupled with the prohibition on lending money at a profit, repayment in cash was a difficult condition to honour. The Jewish community had been expelled from the Malta in 1492[304] and this deprived the Maltese economy of important actors who provided much-needed advances in financial transactions. The repercussions of this shortage are also reflected in how certain captives tried to negotiate their freedom through a mixed payment of cash and commodities. Redemption services were intimately tied to economic activities which translated themselves into lucrative business deals. An example of how a payment was honoured using different methods is a contract dated 10 February 1543[305] drawn up by Giuseppe de Guevara, in which Vincenzo Sirera declared that he had received the sum of 36 *scudi* 3 *tarì* from the captive Domenico Zahra from Ħal Lew.[306] This sum was only part of a larger amount of 61 ducats which Vincenzo had to pay in Tripoli for the redemption of the said Domenico, as per a contract drawn

298 NAM, MCC, Reg. AO, vol. 1, fol. 181.

299 NAM, MCC, Reg. AO, vol. 1, fols 181–182.

300 Such privilege was called the 'Privilegium Fori'. A. Depasquale, *Ecclesiastical Immunity and the Powers of the Inquisitor in Malta (1777–1785)* (Malta, 1968), 19. A full report of the operation of ecclesiastical privileges is given in the Report of Sir John Richardson dated 19 August 1826 as quoted in H. I. Lee, 'British Policy towards the Religion, Ancient Laws and Customs in Malta', *Melita Historica*, 3:4 (1963), 1–13: 2 n 12.

301 CAM, CEM, AO, MS 42, fols 91–94v (1562).

302 NAM, MCC, Reg. AO, vol. 1, fol. 182.

303 Depasquale, *Ecclesiastical Immunity*, 19.

304 Wettinger, *The Jews of Malta.*

305 NAV, R 224/1, fols 442–442v (10.ii.1543).

306 G. Wettinger, *Place-Names of the Maltese Islands ca. 1300–1800* (Malta, 2000), 282.

up by de Trugillo in Tripoli. The terms of agreement stipulated that the amount was to be reimbursed as follows: 26 *scudi* in cash and the rest in an equivalent amount of cotton, the latter presumably being supplied from Domenico's own produce. It was further agreed that the rest of the sum, 30 *scudi*, was to be repaid in cash through the bank at Birgu within a year's time.[307]

The above examples all refer to redemption of Christian slaves. However, Muslim captives in Malta are also recorded negotiating their redemption. Bali Hagi de Stambol, together with his wife and three children, was caught by the galleys of the knight Strozzi.[308] The captive was given permission to leave the island, go back to his home and then return with the requested redemption money with which to free all his family.[309] In another instance the Turkish slave Cussein, who was said to be from Coron, concluded a deal with his new master, Giorgio Serviantis del Zante, in which he promised to remit the sum of 9,500 silver Turkish aspers of good weight in exchange for his freedom.[310] This deal was to be concluded in the city of Zakynthos in a month's time, and the sum was to be forwarded to *Fra.* Baptista de Bellomo, who was also *patrone* of a *triremis* of the Order on which the slave was presently detained.

In April 1558 another slave, Busert Bin Hahmet de Casar, concluded the following agreement with his master Giuseppe Baldagno.[311] Busert was transferred to Antonio de Banda from Messina who was *patrone* of a ship belonging to Marco Antonio Delixandro, also from Messina. The ship was equipped to undertake a voyage to the Tripolitan fortress of Barbaria. Antonio was to conduct the slave to Tripoli, and from there retrieve 80 gold ducats, which was the stipulated price of redemption. This sum was to be remitted either in its value in dinars or in oil, wool or leather goods which the Arabs sold inside the fortress of Tripoli. An interesting detail is that the goods were to be exempt from duty. Busert promised to pay Giuseppe within twenty days of his arrival at the fortress, on condition that the *patrone* did not allow the slave to disembark unless he had received the said payment or its value in goods. The indispensable role of intermediaries, who very often were *patroni*, merchants or procurators,[312] is here set out quite clearly, since such conditions could only be met through the services of third parties such as Antonio, who would have been

307 Other examples of redemption contracts involving the same notary drawn up in Tripoli are found in NAV, R 222/1, fol. 132v (17.ii.1541); R 207/7, fols 154v–155 (25.vi.1543).

308 The document does not state the exact date when this family was taken into captivity. In 1530, Strozzi became Knight of the Order of Malta, for which he was Prior in Capua. In 1536, he was named commander of the galleys of the Order, a position he held again in 1552. Strozzi's biggest catch was that of 1537 when he seized two Turkish galleys and a *fusta* near the coast of Calabria, taking around eighty slaves. Bono, 'Naval Exploits and Privateering', in Mallia-Milanes (ed.), *Hospitaller Malta 1530–1798*, 351–97: 354.

309 NLM, AOM, Lib. Bull. 423, fols 227v–228 (12.xi.1552).

310 NAV, R 439/42, fols 8v–9 (20.vi.1551).

311 NAV, MS 514/1, n.f. (27.iv.1558). See also Abela, 'Port Activities', 172.

312 Refer to NAV, MS 514/1, n.f. (6.x.1559) wherein Bishop Domenico Cubelles (1540–66) appointed Gerolamo Cachialepori as his procurator and gave him the authority to free a Moorish slave for the price of 105 ducats at the rate of 14 *tarì* per ducat.

paid a percentage of the sum to be reimbursed by the slave.[313] Once arrived at their destination, the captive had to make the necessary connection with intermediaries in his own country who would be in a position to obtain the redemption money or its value in goods for him.[314] In this case, once the goods were supplied they had to be transported back to either Malta or Messina, depending on the destination of the vessel. If the sum was not paid, the slave was to return with the same ship and be consigned back to his master, Giuseppe.[315]

The acquisition of infidel slaves from Tripoli as a commodity for resale was one of the most profitable economic activities contributing to a boom in Malta's commerce.[316] There are many records in archival sources of the constant trade in slaves in Malta in the first decades of the Order's rule. The register of Notary de Agatiis for the administrative year 1543–44, NAV R 202/8, contains the largest number of slave sales registered by any notary in any one year during the period under study[317] – 39 out of a total of 496 deeds (7.9%). These documents record the terms of agreements concluded between trading partners and help us to understand their workings. Foreign merchants' stops in Malta before proceeding to Tripoli are mentioned constantly. A highly successful Rhodiot merchant was Johannes Callamia, who has already been referred to in connection with usurious practices (see Chapter Three). On 13 October 1544 Johannes made a deal with Petrus Antonius de Bona, a merchant from Syracuse, who was to sail to Tripoli in the following days. Petrus was to buy three male or female slaves not younger than fifteen years or older than twenty. The age bracket was an important detail in slave contracts, as the Grand Master prohibited the sale of Muslims younger than fourteen years, instructing that any such be educated in the Christian faith, in the hope that they would convert.[318]

Another common detail found in almost all contracts for the sale of slaves is the phrase '*ad usum magaseni ut vulgo dicitur testa de rasato*'. There existed various forms of such a phrase,[319] which were based on much older formulations which had

313 According to Brogini this oscillated between 10% and 30%. Brogini, *Malte, frontière de chrétienté*, 391.

314 For other such examples of intermediaries refer to Brogini, *Malte, frontière de chrétienté*, 388–92.

315 Similar contracts may be found in NAV, R 206/7, fols 120–121 (27.iv.1543).

316 For similar penetration of Europeans in West and North African slave markets refer to Marcocci, 'Trading with the Muslim World', in Trivellato et al., *Religion and Trade*, 91–107.

317 For example, the notarial volumes of the same notary for the year 1537–38 include 4.5% of acts relating to the sale of slaves, while those for 1538–39 include 4.3%; those for 1539–40 include 4.7% and those for 1540–41 include 4.1%. Some of these contracts involve the sale of more than one slave, but not more than three, e.g. R 202/5, fols 174–174v (21.iv.1541), fol. 225v (30.vi.1541), fol. 180–180v (29.iv.1541).

318 This law applied also to redemptions made in Tripoli, as is attested in the instructions given to the governor in 1559, where it was prohibited to '*alcuno moro o mora dela etta de anni catordecj inbasso si riscate per qual si voglia precio di riscate*' (that no Moorish boy or girl of the age of fourteen or below is redeemed for any price of redemption). NLM, AOM, Lib. Bull 421, fol. 227v (9.xi.1549). On this subject see also Wettinger, *Slavery in the Islands of Malta*, 465.

319 Other phrases with the same meaning were: '*pro tali quibus est*', see NAV, R 4/1, fol. 136v (30.xii.1557); '*cum omnibus eius defectibus latentibus vel apprentibus ac per tali qualis est*',

the main intention of protecting the buyer from defective 'goods'.[320] *Testa de rasato* suggests a reference to the captives' shaved heads, which made them stand out from the native Christian population. Referring back to the contract between Petrus and Johannes, the slaves were to be delivered in Malta, in good health, by the following December, that is, two months from the date of the agreement. The purchase price of the slaves was not to exceed 30 *scudi* per head, even if they were transported on a ship other than Petrus's. Thus, if the average selling price of a slave was 45 *scudi*, the gross profit derived by human traffickers was approximately 15 *scudi* per head. In this case, Johannes was to pay Petrus by different methods. On signing the agreement he delivered the equivalent of 60 *scudi* in oil and promised to pay the remaining 30 *scudi* in silver *aquile* on delivery.

A similar contract was concluded between six knights of the Order on the one part as shareholders in a corsairing expedition and Notary Vincenzo Bonaventura de Bonetiis on the other part. The six knights promised to deliver, either in Tripoli or else in Malta within six months, seven male or female 'negro' slaves over fifteen years of age.[321] Once again, the price for each slave, inclusive of all expenses, was 30 *scudi*, which the corsairs received before their voyage. It was further stated that they would be personally liable to cover this sum against any risk or peril. Of the agreed sum, 75 *scudi* were paid in the form of a well-equipped *sagitta*, while 30 *scudi* and 11 *scudi*, respectively, were paid by two of the notary's debtors and the remaining amount was paid in cash. However, one has to be cautious in the matter of prices. As has been highlighted by Michel Fontenay, prices depended on various factors, including the ethnic origin of the slave.[322]

Another interesting contract relates to an agreement between the Maltese *patronus* of a corsairing ship, Salvus Burlo, and the French merchant Johannes Carreton, who was also a citizen of Malta.[323] Carreton forwarded a total of 267 *scudi* 3 *tarì* 4 *grani* to Burlo in return for twelve slaves to be acquired by Burlo on his next corsairing expedition. The slaves could be white or black, male or female; however, their individual price was not to exceed 21 *scudi* 3 *tarì* 12 *grani*. Such contracts point to a situation in which the sedentary partner, in this case the French merchant Carreton, established a cost price for the 'commodity' before its actual acquisition. In this way he eliminated the possibility of future claims for additional payment which the travelling partner might make, due to a slave being worth more than the original agreed price.

Not only did the capture of slaves translate into financial rewards but, through

see MS 514/1, n.f. (4.v.1558): '*como uno sacco de ossa*', see R 4/1, fols 113v–115 (16.xii.1557); '*cum omnibus eius defectibus ad usum corsarium ut vulgo dicitur a sacco de ossa*', see NAV, R 224/1, fol. 43v (23.iii.1540); '*ut vulgo dicitur testa de rescaptito*', see R 202/11, fol. 16 (25.x.1546).

320 '*con quella fiducia di chi va a comprare nel magazzeno o nella casa altrui*'. L. Tria, 'La schiavitù in Liguria: ricerche e documenti', *Atti della Società ligure di storia patria* (Genova, 1947), vol. 70.

321 Here the notary uses the term '*dictis annis quindecim bene accaratos*' (the said age of fifteen being well apparent). NAV, R 202/11, fol. 16 (25.x.1546).

322 Fontenay, '*Il Mercato Maltese* degli schiavi', 397–8.

323 NAV, R 206/1, fols 293v–295 (20.v.1535).

the redemption intermediaries, commercial ties were established between subjects of the Cross and the Crescent. Both Christian and Muslim merchants successfully exploited this cruel trade in which hundreds of their co-religionists were captured. At times the exploitation was so excessive that plaintiffs appealed to the local authorities to annul the usurious agreements which desperate souls had been forced to enter into in return for their freedom. While various Christian, Muslim and Jewish captives adopted ways and means of negotiating their freedom with their masters, black slaves seem to have been the worst off. Documents rarely make any reference of their redemption, unless through the benevolent manumission of their masters. The almost non-existent ransom requests for this group made them the lowest-priced slaves on the market, while members of the Order were among the most highly prized human commodity on the Muslim market.

The Greek community of merchants

Pope Clement VII granted the new inhabitants of Malta, Gozo and Tripoli permission to trade with Muslims.[324] Many of those who left Rhodes after the Turkish victory were not Greeks but Latins who had good reasons for avoiding Turkish rule and settled elsewhere in the West.[325] They soon took advantage of the Order's presence in Malta and Tripoli and tried to penetrate into the various economic activities afforded by this new location.[326] This led to the creation of important trading networks with various other merchant communities scattered throughout the Mediterranean, especially those with Greek or Latin Rhodiot members.[327] The benefit of having such traders on Maltese shores can be appreciated from the efforts made by the Ottoman court in 1522 when it tried to convince these merchants to stay in Rhodes and refrain from departing with the Order.[328] Their decision to follow the Hospitallers into a rather bleak future points to their unwillingness to become Ottoman subjects and is proof of their loyalty to their long-time Latin masters.

However, from a purely economic point of view this decision went beyond the loyalty factor. Rhodiot merchants knew very well that there were huge benefits to

324 Paoli, *Codice Diplomatico*, 201–2. Fiorini states that at times members of the Rhodiot community who settled in Malta were described simply as 'Grecus' or 'Greca', and not specifically as '*Rhodius/Rhodia*'. Clear instances of Greek surnames prior to the arrival of the Knights are also found in Maltese archives. Fiorini, 'Demographical Aspects', in Bugeja et al., *Birgu: A Maltese Maritime City*, vol. 1, 219–54:, 233. Among other examples, confirmation of this statement is found in NAV, R 225/17, fol. 14 (3.ix.1560), which describes the Rhodiot Angelo Metaxi, an orthodox priest who came over to Malta with the Knights of St John, as '*Grecus habitatoris de questa nova civitatis Melite*'.

325 Luttrell, 'The Rhodian Background of the Order of Saint John in Malta', in Azzopardi (ed.), *The Order's Early Legacy*, 3–14: 5.

326 For more detailed information regarding the Rhodiot community of Birgu refer to Fiorini, 'The Rhodiot Community of Birgu', in Mallia-Milanes (ed.), *Library of Mediterranean History*, vol. 1, 183–241.

327 Fiorini, 'Demographical Aspects', in Bugeja et al., *Birgu: A Maritime City*, 219–54: 224–6: 230.

328 Greene, *A Shared World*, 15 n. 7.

be gained from supplying the Hospitaller Order with its daily worldly needs. Also, the Order's fleet provided Rhodiot Greek merchants with a sense of protection and belonging, something which their fellow Greeks who were Ottoman subjects lacked, due to religious divides which at times made them victims of both Christian and Muslim attacks.[329] Life for these Greek merchants was a continuous struggle because not only did they have to prove that they were Christian in faith but they also had to prove that their trade had a Christian identity.[330]

After 1530 the Greek Rhodiots who settled in Malta would have to share with their Maltese counterparts the rewards that came to them through their link with the Order. The Maltese were already renowned for their corsairing activities. In fact, reports dating back to the first decade of the sixteenth century show what great consternation the violent corsairing attacks of the Maltese caused to Christian and Muslim ships plying the Adriatic and the Levant, notwithstanding the fact that they were enjoined not to plunder Christian shipping.[331] Once settled in Malta, the Rhodiot Greek seafarers combined their expertise in seamanship with that of the Maltese and this, with the protection of the Order's fleet,[332] made them formidable traders on the Mediterranean coasts.

Notwithstanding the differences in judicial matters which were discussed earlier, Maltese traders soon capitalised on the plethora of opportunities which were injected into the local economy. Greek merchants were already present in Malta in the late medieval period, and so to a certain extent it must be assumed that business partnerships with the Greeks were not unknown in the local community. However, the sudden great increase in a skilled and experienced merchant community with strong commercial ties throughout the Mediterranean littoral enhanced the prospects of local seafarers whose ventures were still limited, due to the absence of a strong naval presence in their port.

Various notarial deeds offer striking examples of partnership agreements which reveal how both the Greek and Maltese communities exploited each other's maritime and trading abilities and capitalised on the interaction between Greeks who were established abroad and Maltese inhabitants.[333] For instance, in a contract dated 18 September 1536[334] the Greek Alessandro Arborei, who was a resident of

[329] The fear of being taken for Muslims is best appreciated in the various requests made by Rhodiots to the Grand Master to take up residence in Malta. Such requests refer to them being circumcised against their will, and therefore fearing that if captured during their voyage they would be automatically and erroneously listed as being of Muslim faith. NLM, AOM, Lib. Bull. 427, fol. 251 (14.4.1558).

[330] Greene, *Catholic Pirates*, 115.

[331] Mallia-Milanes, *Venice and Hospitaller Malta*, 11–12. Cassar, 'The Maltese Corsairs', 146.

[332] The ambiguity of Greek merchants is described by Greene, who states that they were 'Christians but of a rather dubious kind from the Catholic point of view, and many were also Ottoman subjects. Not surprisingly, then, issues of identity and representation followed Greek merchants around the ports of the Mediterranean, including Malta.' Greene, *Catholic Pirates*, 11.

[333] In this context 'inhabitants' refer not only to Maltese natives, but even to foreigners who had settled in Malta and obtained a Maltese citizenship and those who are referred to in documents as '*incola melitensis*', meaning that they were residents in Malta.

[334] NAV, R 202/1, fols 15–16 (18 ix.1536).

Messina, participated in an expedition to be conducted on the newly constructed *grippo* of the Maltese *Hon.* Leonardo Falzuni of Mdina. Another contract reveals that *Hon.* Stammato Papadopulo from the island of Zakynthos was indebted to *Hon.* Stammato Galanti, a Rhodiot resident of Malta, for the sum of 110 *scudi* due in respect of freight charges for the importation of twenty-seven barrels of wine from Zakynthos. This consignment was to be shipped by Angelo de Pasquali and payment was to be effected at Birgu, in cash, within four months from the date of the sale of the wine. Such a happy co-existence not only enabled the adequate provisioning of the island but ensured the Hospitallers' successful establishment there. Even though the island enjoyed a semi-autonomous rule before the Order's arrival, the Order knew that providing sufficient work opportunities and adequate food supplies for the population would ensure the diminution of the influence of the medieval ruling elite, thus limiting the risk of popular uprisings.

A typical example of the *modus operandi* of the Order, which provides good insight into how it exploited the trading potential of the Greek community, can be gleaned from Chancery records. On 8 December 1534 the Greek Sydero Metaxi, who was employed on one of the Order's galleys, was granted a safe conduct certificate to go to the Levant, Zante and Cephalonia in order to buy and import wine for the use of the Hospitallers.[335] He seems to have been an important middleman for the supply of the Order's needs from that area, since in another edict issued by the Order's chancellery in November 1530, *Fra.* Luys Broglia, captain of one of the Order's galleys (*galione*), was instructed to sail to Zante and Cephalonia where, upon arrival, he had to find out the going prices for wine and meat. Once he had done this work, any commodities purchased were to be acquired through the services of Sydero Metaxi, who was described as 'familiar to the region'.[336] Such partnerships allowed investors to take full advantage of the practical experience of particular merchants and their knowledge of the market, and aided the making of advantageous business deals. It is also clear that although merchants were engaged to negotiate on behalf of the Order, precautionary measures were taken to ensure that the prices paid were not inflated.

The accumulation of trustworthy information played a pivotal role in the Order's well-being, not only for purposes of espionage – as is well attested in various instructions given to officials and individuals who were ordered to spy on the movements of the Turks[337] – but also for the supply of commodities at competitive prices. Although there seem to have been good relationships between the Order and various merchants operating in different parts of the Mediterranean, these did not negate independent scrutiny by the Order in evaluating trading activities. The importance of this system of 'market intelligence', as Benjamin Braude defines it, needs to be evaluated in the contemporary context, where trading operations and

335 NLM, Lib. Bull. MS 415, fol. 194v (8.xii.1534).

336 NLM, Lib. Bull. MS 414, fols 282–282v (21.xi.1530), '*pratico in quelle parte*'.

337 A case in point is that of Giorgio Marino de Candia, who on 11 May 1532 was given a safe conduct to travel with his ship (*fregata*) in order to spy on the movements of the Turks. NLM, AOM, Lib. Bull. 415, fol. 231v.

prices were continually affected by such factors as regional conflict, epidemics and scarcity of food supplies.[338]

The Order's efforts to increase the safety of the waters around Birgu made it an ideal maritime centre hosting an interrelated network of commercial communities. Malta was not only evolving into a vibrant centre for trade, but was also fast becoming a centre for financial dealings by foreigners, including Greeks.[339] As a result of this co-operation and diversity, all those involved in trade thrived, and many foreign merchants who established a connection with the inhabitants provided cross-cultural contacts that facilitated trading activity.[340]

Conclusion

The arrival of the Knights Hospitaller in Malta in 1530 marked a turning point for both local and foreign commercial operators in the Mediterranean. Their establishment on the island, coupled with their cruising activities, both provoked and protected Muslim commercial shipping on the Mediterranean. Commercial activity in Malta was greatly stimulated and enhanced, since the Order served as a pull factor for a myriad of merchants from all across the Mediterranean littoral. Its presence on the island created an immediate and heavy demand for the supply of various commodities, ranging from the basic daily needs of the population, such as wheat and oil, to the most costly, such as slaves. In order to meet these demands both knights and merchants found it necessary to undertake voyages towards North Africa and the Levant, a necessity which saw the flourishing of a link between Christian and Muslim merchants. The Order sought to protect this trade by granting of safe conducts and by policing nearby waters. Although safe conducts did not guarantee the successful undertaking of ventures, they did provide both Muslim and Christian merchants with a considerable amount of political and legal protection.

The Order's short-lived presence in Tripoli and Malta's strategic position on the central axis of the Mediterranean were among the main ingredients helping to build bridges between Muslims and Christians. Prizes brought back to the island from corsairing activities, especially slaves, attracted merchants of diverse ethnic origins and placed Malta at the forefront of the traffic in human beings. David Abulafia argues, 'this darker side of Mediterranean history also encompasses the history of those already mentioned whom the pirates carried back and forth: male and female slaves and captives, though they too, like the historian Polybius, could play a notable role in cultural contact between the opposing shores of the Mediterranean'.[341] The reciprocal benefits generated by the transfer and redemption of slaves saw Muslim ships being allowed to import and export merchandise to and from the island, thus ensuring a good return for round trips and lucrative benefits for all those involved.

338 B. Braude, 'Venture and Faith in the Commercial Life of the Ottoman Balkans', *International History Review*, 7 (1985), 519–42: 528.

339 Refer to Abela, 'Port Activities', especially Chapter 2.

340 Cassar, *Society, Culture and Identity*, 75–6.

341 Abulafia, *The Great Sea*, 647.

The dynamic activity in the harbour area created a vibrant economy based on trade and the island witnessed an ever-increasing number of merchants and adventurers who, although of different religious and ethnic backgrounds, had the common goal of making a profit. Local businessmen responded favourably to the emerging opportunities, often investing their money, their property and even their work in the myriad of opportunities which were presented to them. Corsairing soon became the fastest-growing sector of the Maltese economy, and within a couple of years of the Order's establishment the island became known as an important centre for human trafficking and for the redistribution of goods acquired through such activities.

However, religious ideologies impeded the healthy growth of economic activity, especially due to the Catholic Church's embargo on lending at profit. Merchants had to be prudent, carefully concealing good returns on trade credit and exploiting loopholes which enabled the desired returns. Various forms of legal agreements made it possible for merchants across the Mediterranean to pool capital, share risks and enjoy rewards. The Greek community which established itself on the island became an important link between Maltese traders and other Greek or Latin Rhodiots scattered throughout the Mediterranean. All these external influences contributed to the gradual transformation of the harbour area, which, after 1530, took on a more cosmopolitan character and shed its medieval characteristics.

Conclusion

The recent opening up of the Maltese Notarial Archives marks an important step for Maltese and Mediterranean historical studies. Researchers had always found this archive difficult, if not at times impossible, to consult and this mostly due to its inaccessible state. Being legal in nature, the documents are a unique and veritable mine of information for the socio-economic historian. They not only provide evidence of an uninterrupted series of daily trading activities from the late fifteenth century to date but also shed light on various laws, customs and traditions which have moulded Maltese society through the centuries. The acts of notaries working in and around the harbour area are a significant source for establishing prevailing economic patterns.

This book has traced the impact of the arrival of the Knights Hospitaller on Malta's economic activity during the period 1530–65.[1] The focus has been on specific topics which both enlighten local historiography and allow for comparative analysis with similar issues in play in other countries. The paths chosen by particular sections of the local population have been traced, including a number of new settlers such as the Rhodiot community that followed the Order from the Dodecanese island of Rhodes. Additionally, wherever possible, it has followed the route of foreign traders, whether Christian or Muslim. The case studies support the central argument that the presence of a naval power, the Knights Hospitaller, generated a variety of economic activities which led to the creation of a vibrant, monetarised economy based on trade. The trade which flourished in the late sixteenth century and which is often referred to in Maltese historiography had a precedent which was interrupted only by the Ottoman siege of 1565.

Even though the fundamental reason for the existence of the Knights of St John had substantially diminished by the beginning of the sixteenth century, their naval presence and power in the Mediterranean were not an anachronism. With Malta as a base for their constant naval activities, especially those targeted against the Barbary corsairs, they managed to adapt themselves to the exigencies of the times. The acts of Notary Bartholomeo Selvagi de Via[2] drawn up in Malta in 1530 bear witness to

1 This book has built on an earlier study which was presented by this author for a Master's degree, and which was more concerned with the earliest forms of financial instruments in use in the harbour area in mid-sixteenth century Malta. Abela, 'Port Activities'.

2 NAV, R 439 (1530–51).

the Knights' immediate participation in an 'undeclared', low-level holy war[3] which justified their *raison d'être* in the eyes of their European benefactors. As Molly Green argues, 'the Knights of Malta were simply the most vicious and vocal practitioners of a set of practices and assumptions that structured a wide range of maritime encounters in the early modern Mediterranean'.[4]

The history of Malta under the Knights of St John offers a somewhat different case study than those of other feudal societies. Comprising some of the smallest inhabited islands in the Mediterranean, the archipelago lacked the essential resources to adequately feed a population which by 1530 numbered approximately twenty thousand.[5] Before the arrival of the Knights, the administration of the islands functioned through the workings of two independent municipal town councils, the *Università*, both of which enjoyed a semi-autonomous status under their Sicilian overlords.[6] Malta also boasted of its own set of ancient privileges and customs which it jealously guarded against usurpation. Consequently, when the islands were handed over to the Order of St John under their oath to honour and respect these rights and privileges, the new masters were not regarded by the Maltese notables of Mdina as 'conquerors' but, rather, as new governors who had agreed upon specific terms for the cession of Malta. This situation was later repeated in the nineteenth century, when the British agreed to honour the Declaration of Rights of the Maltese and act as protectors of the island, rather than as colonial rulers.[7]

Despite the declarations and promises, once the Knights of St John had established themselves on the island there was never any doubt as to who the true masters were. Deep down, the nobles of Mdina knew that they would never be given the opportunity to have a say in the government of the island. If there was ever the slightest illusion to the contrary before the arrival of the Knights, this was explicitly ruled out on their establishment when the Knights prohibited any Maltese from joining the ranks of the ruling elite within the Hospitaller Order – something which had been possible when Malta was under direct Spanish rule. Even so, the Knights endeavoured to tread carefully in asserting their power, and the game they played was shrewd. While on the one hand they seemed to honour and respect existing institutions, at the same time, in direct confrontation with the old system of administration, they set up new institutions with similar functions to those of the old town council. In contrast to the medieval institutions which were

3 J. Abela, 'Before Valletta: Port Activities Prior to the Great Siege' in N. Marconi (ed.), *Valletta, Città, architettura e costruzione sotto il segno della fede e della guerra* (Rome, 2011), 1–16: 6–9.

4 Greene, *Catholic Pirates*, 224.

5 Fiorini, 'Demographic Growth', in Mallia-Milanes (ed.), *Hospitaller Malta 1530–1798*, 297–310: 298; Cassar, *Society, Culture and Identity*, 122; Wettinger, 'Agriculture in Malta in the Late Middle Ages', in Buhagiar (ed.), *Proceedings of History Week, 1981*, 1–48: 13.

6 Dalli, 'Medieval Communal Organization', 1–10; R. Valentini, 'La sopravvivenza della "Universitàs Melivetana", fino alla cessazione delle infeudazioni dell'isola', *Archivio Storico di Malta*, 8:1 (Rome, 1935), 33–70; A. Mifsud, 'L'Approvigionamento e l'Università di Malta nelle passate dominazioni', *Archivum Melitense*, 3:5 (1918), 163–212.

7 H. Davis & B. Hough, 'The British Claim to Rule Malta', *Melita Historica*, 14:4 (2007), 387–408.

mainly the domain of a tightly knit group representing the nobles of the island who controlled annual elections, these new institutions were now partly administered by Maltese officials, most of whom came from the Birgu merchant bourgeoisie. With the coming of the Order, in line with developments taking place in Europe, where 'a bourgeoisie emerging from the background of trade was climbing by its own efforts to the highest place in contemporary society',[8] ambitious Maltese merchants were now given a golden opportunity to establish themselves and move up the social scale. It has been argued here that this merchant bourgeoisie contributed substantially to the successful establishment of the Knights, who through their naval activities revolutionised the mechanics of the port city and made it central to the island's commercial activities.

As explained in Chapter Two, the sudden influx of Greek and other foreign subjects, together with a sizeable number of slaves, turned the harbour area into a cosmopolitan city where people from various nations were shoulder to shoulder as they went about their daily activities. Just how real this picture was can be discerned from contracts for the sale of property in the area, where at times a house, a shop or a warehouse was described as situated adjacent to the property of people coming from two or three different countries.[9] Research on the chancery documents of the Order has also made it possible to suggest that the Knights were unsuccessful in establishing a common law for all their subjects. On at least two separate occasions they appointed a commission which was requested to amalgamate Maltese laws based on those of the Regno with the Rhodian laws, but it seems that this was unsuccessful.[10]

The 'uniqueness' of Malta as a case study lies in the relationship between governors and subjects. Although the Knights imposed their rule in an autocratic way, they did not fit the 'normal' conception of conquerors. For them, the island was not a mere fief which they had received from the Spanish Crown; it was a place to which they could relate, because after several years of wandering they could now rule in their own right. Despite the fact that in the early years they considered other options rather than Malta, the island immediately spurred a sense of belonging. Most importantly, it represented their only tangible hope for continued existence. If they lost Malta, the Knights knew that they would once again end up wandering from port to port. Considering the European political situation and their status of neutrality, this was not a comfortable position to be in.[11] Further, Malta was considered to be a frontier against the Ottomans and therefore its defence meant that they could still be actors in the fight against the Muslims.[12] The siege of 1565 proves the point, since it was this victory which put the Knights Hospitaller back on the military-political map of

8 Braudel, *Civilization and Capitalism*, vol. 2, 478.

9 Abela, 'Before Valletta', in Marconi (ed.), *Valletta, Città, architettura e costruzione*, 1–16: 8.

10 NLM, AOM 89, fol. 50 (new enumeration) (24.ix.1555).

11 Koenigsberger et al., *Europe in the Sixteenth Century*, 233–239; Kunt & Woodhead (eds), *Süleyman the Magnificent.*

12 See also Williams, '*Sacra Milita*', in Fusaro et al., *Trade and Cultural Exchange*, 139–56: 148–9.

Europe. On the local scene, however, this meant that it was now even harder for the local nobles to make any claims to their rights or privileges, which were gradually but steadily whittled away.

A vital factor contributing to the stability of the Hospitaller government was that the adequate provisioning of victuals, above all wheat, was a perennial preoccupation even before the Knights' arrival. The great increase in population created an even greater demand for wheat and its end products, making the role of private investors in the grain trade essential to the island's well-being. People from all strata of society invested in this trade, merchants engaging in a short-distance form of grain traffic which created a greater demand for ancillary services, such as freight handling and travel insurance. The Order, for its part, and despite repeated protests, immediately started to encroach upon the responsibilities of the Mdina and Gozo *Università*, whose main task had always been the provisioning of wheat for the islands' needs. The Knights established a harbour *Università* which gradually began to enjoy greater power than the other two *Università*. In time, it took over many of the functions of the old town councils, thus eliminating the risk of having a crucial sector for the islands' stability out of the direct control of the old ruling body. The concession of duty-free grain quotas was not automatically renewed each year, and most of the time both the Order and members of the Mdina *Università* took great pains to convince the Sicilian Viceroy to consent to the export of these supplies. When things were really tough, and in times of great scarcity, the Order set sail from the Maltese port on a mission to hunt down grain ships, be they Christian or Muslim. On the local scene, producers were continually engaged in advance buying and selling of cereals and niche products, which procured the necessary cash to invest in crops. However when the harvest was poor and debtors found themselves in such great financial constraints, they borrowed beyond their means.

Men were not the only actors partaking in the opportunities generated by the presence of the Knights. How this spill-over effect reached enterprising women, and how these women, despite legal limitations, tried to capitalise on various new opportunities which presented themselves, is a relatively novel topic in Maltese historiography. Analysis of various legal documents marking the different stages in a woman's life, such as daughter, emancipation, marriage, motherhood and widowhood, uncovers the legal persona of women in mid-sixteenth century Malta and the extent to which legal limitations impinged on the economic activities of the 'weaker' sex.[13]

[13] Exploiting the newly invented printing presses, at the beginning of the sixteenth century both the Protestant Reformation and the Catholic Counter-Reformation published works which instructed women how they should live the different stages of their lives. A highly popular book published in 1523 was the work of the Spanish humanist Jan Luis de Vives, entitled *De Institutione Feminae Christianae*, which is divided into three sections dealing with maidens, wives and widows. Throughout the work women are presented as being incapable of taking decisions or of saving their souls without the help of their husbands. Due to the lack of a man in their lives, widows, on the other hand, are advised not to remarry but to remain chaste so that their thoughts and prayers are constantly focused on their salvation. O. Hufton, *The Prospect Before Her: A History of Women in Western Europe 1500–1800* (New York, 1998), 35–7.

Marriage and dowry contracts are a rich source for the study of women's legal privileges and how these affected their involvement in economic transactions. In fact, different forms of marriage contracts did not carry religious or cultural distinctions; the main difference was an economic one. While the Greek and Roman custom provided for separation of assets, according to the Latin custom all the assets of the married couple were to be divided equally between them and their children. The tendency in Malta to draw up marriage contracts according to the Greek and Roman custom reflects a situation where most women remained in full possession of their assets on becoming wives and mothers. These rights were not abstract, but real rights which they could exercise, and included property rights, so that women are present in most economic activities concerning the transfer and sale of property.

Married women, with a few exceptions, could not enter into contracts of obligation without the consent of their husbands, but they could also be partially responsible for honouring agreements of debt contracted by their husbands. Thus, in the eyes of the law, these women were assuming the role of business partners. Widows were more autonomous and had more opportunity to sell, purchase, invest, inherit or even marry into financial assets. Even if the vast majority of women did not own large holdings of land, they could still negotiate their small possessions and become financial actors within the island's economy.

The role of women at times took forms different to that traditionally assigned to them. Women like Clara La Spatara, who manufactured swords, conducted an economic activity which was largely attributed to men, while Donna Catharina, a married woman, invested in the hospitality sector by opening an *Albergo*[14] in Birgu and commissioning a man to take care of its operation. Other women, like Paula Dalli, Angelina Latappera and Catherina Allegritta, were repeatedly accused of making usurious profits from financial loans advanced by them to people from various echelons of society, including knights. The collage of documents in the Notarial Archive frees these sixteenth-century women found in the harbour area from the traditional confines so often assigned to them, which tend to project them both as wholly dependent on male authority and as passive in grasping new opportunities generated by the new events occurring in the harbour area, other than that of prostitution.[15] Of course this does not mean that all women were enterprising, and most women were indeed tied to traditional roles. However, it is important to project the lives of those who were enterprising, because they did make a difference. Women's participation in economic activities, whether through their

[14] This was the exact word used to describe rooms for rent in the contract. NAV, MS 514/1, n.f. (10.iv.1560).

[15] See, for example, A. Brogini, 'Marginalités et contrôle social dans le port de Malte', http://cdlm.revues.org/index786.html (accessed 1 March 2016), which partly deals with the problem of prostitution in the harbour area. Although Cassar's work introduces a breath of fresh air into Maltese historical studies through his novel choice of subject, a cursory look at his primary sources makes it obvious that his thesis is built almost completely on evidence from inquisition records, which tends to make his work heavily dependent on information derived from persons whose testimonies were given under interrogation, and thus not performing under 'normal' circumstances. Cassar, *Daughters of Eve*.

consent in contracts of obligation or through physical work, was essential for the proper functioning of the machinery of credit.

Trade activity between Christian and Muslim ports during the first decades of the Order's stay in Malta is by far one of the most neglected areas of Maltese historiography. Similar to the situation in Rhodes,[16] one of the greatest impacts that the Order's presence had on Malta's economic activities was the increase in the island's economic importance, and this ultimately turned Malta into an important Mediterranean trading post. Due to the harbour area's ever-growing potential in generating new work opportunities, it became a draw to a great number of enterprising individuals, culminating in an unprecedented influx of new arrivals. Sicily still held its prime place as the island's main trading link, but trade and politics were carefully combined and the Knights soon sought to take advantage of the opportunities afforded to them by redemption services with Muslim lands.

It is clear from scrutiny of various chancery documents that the Knights of St John projected themselves as the main actors in the redemption of Christian slaves. Christian and Muslim merchants who were involved in ransoming services were granted safe conduct certificates by the Grand Master. This allowed them to make safer journeys both to North Africa and to the Levant. They often took advantage of such concessions, and on their round trips to and from hostile lands they managed to trade in various other wares. Interestingly, the extant documentation reveals that, once they had been freed, Muslim or Jewish slaves, such as Murgian de Abdalla and Mahometo Hamidan Benalli, who were Muslim, and Salomon Montesino and Michel Sacar de Patraz, who were Jews, also showed an interest in conducting trade between Christian and Ottoman lands and requested safe passage conducts to trade in merchandise without any link to redemption services.

Another profitable economic activity conducted between Malta and North Africa was the acquisition of slaves for resale, which was already documented as early as the late fifteenth century. The establishment of the Knights of St John in Malta strengthened the human trafficking and provided the necessary impetus for its steady growth and prosperity, merchants from all across the Mediterranean using Malta as a centre for this trade. The rapid increase in trading activity also led to development of Malta's financial services. The island offered visiting merchants not only the necessary commodities to replenish their ships' supply, but also the necessary legal and financial tools to conduct their business.

Historians who have focused on the early period of the Hospitallers' rule in Malta and their economic activities have furnished local historiography with a relatively sparse reading which is heavily based on primary sources in the archives of the Order. Their work reflects a traditional history which does not speak of more elusive topics, such as trading partners, business clients, agents, financial instruments, commodities, prices and the circumvention of legal structures in order to effect the swift circulation of money. This book has brought forth a different kind of historical interpretation by using largely untapped sources such as notarial acts and complementing the information derived from them with that found in other

16 Williams, '*Sacra Militia*', in Fusaro et al., *Trade and Cultural Exchange*, 139–56: 143.

archives such as those of the civil law courts, the Episcopal Court, the inquisitor's court and chancery documents.

Every folio provides a fresh reading and projects the daily trading activities of a Mediterranean world which would otherwise be lost to present generations. It is thus hoped that this contribution will be a springboard to trigger further studies in a topic which is so vital to the understanding of a people, its rulers and the economic patterns prevailing in its society.

Appendix

Salvi conductus given to various persons to trade in merchandise or to redeem slaves in North Africa or the Levant (1530–65)

Date	Beneficiary	Place of Origin	Destination	Reason for Pass	Validity	AOM Ref
22.01.1531	Mag. Francesco Chaena	Venice	Malta	Coming from Barbary with various merchandise	2 months	415, fol. 208v
11.03.1532	Mag. Visconte Cegala	Venice	Malta	Coming from Barbary with various merchandise	15 days	415, fol. 230
28.06.1532	Mabraydi Golena and Michael Cucayni		Levant	To bring salted meat, cheese, wax, candles, pulses and other goods for the Order		415, fols 232v-233
13.01.1534	Nobile Bayz Mahmet Algnari	Moor resident of Djerba	Tunis, Djerba and Tripoli	To redeem Christian slaves and conduct mercantile trade		415, fol. 255v
22.06.1542	Vincentio de Nadal	Venice	Malta, Tunis and other Infidel Lands	To be able to sell his goods in Malta and to carry on other business with Tunis and other infidel lands	6 months	418, fols 188-189
17.10.1544	Rabi Moyse	Jew of Azamor (a Moroccan city, on the left bank of the Oum Er-Rbia River, 75 km south-west of Casablanca)	Tripoli	To redeem himself and then go to Turkey to redeem his wife and children who are held captives there		419, fol. 228v
20.10.1548	Johanni Monghin	Marseille		To redeem some knights from Djerba		421, fol. 221

Date	Beneficiary	Place of Origin	Destination	Reason for Pass	Validity	AOM Ref
24.02.1552	Mahometo Rayz	Free Turk	Africa, Djerba	To redeem some Christian slaves and return E19 with merchandise and other goods for the redemption of Muslim slaves	1 year	423, fols 213-213v
12.11.1552	Samwel Ahadeph	Jew	Levant	To get the necessary ransom money for himself and other Jews		423, fols 227v-228
31.01.1553	Nasuff de Galipoli and two other accompanying Turks	Turk	Constantinople	To get money and merchandise to redeem himself and other Turks		423, fol. 229
01.03.1553	Emirech Zacaria de Caramisse, Synat Ayuat de Ayoli and Vassal Torres Casari	Armenians	To go back home	They came to Malta to conduct business and want to return home		423, fol. 230
05.04.1553	Emirech de Angori	Armenian	To go back home	He came to Malta to conduct business and wants to return home		423, fol. 230v
07.06.1553	Mechamet de Africa	Free African slave	Tripoli and Tazora	To redeem slaves and come back with merchandise		423, fol. 236v
21.10.1553	Andreoto Habel, Innocentio Tursimano and Matheo de Miguel		Tripoli	To make a round trip to Tripoli with merchandise which is not prohibited		424, fol. 211
21.10.1553	Aoreibi de Alma a freed slave		Tripoli	To go to Tripoli to get money and merchandise to redeem Muslim slaves		424, fol. 211v
09.02.1554	Monsur Moro del Monasterio	Moor	Tripoli	Paid for his redemption and now he is going to Tripoli to get money to redeem Muslim slaves		424, fol. 221v-222

Date	Beneficiary	Place of Origin	Destination	Reason for Pass	Validity	AOM Ref
07.02.1554	Andreota Habela	Maltese	Tripoli	To make a round trip to Tripoli with merchandise		424, fols 228v-229
20.03.1554	Cheder de Agras	Turk	Constanti-nople and Levant	Leaves with the permission of his master to go and redeem Maltese slaves		424, fols 230v-231
05.04.1554	Yahaleph Zerbino		Tripoli	Departs with the permission of his master to get money and mer-chandise to redeem some Moorish slaves		424, fols 231v-232
16.06.1554	Nasuph de Galipoli and two other accompanying Turks		Levant	Departs with a ship carrying both Turkish and Christian sailors to go to the Levant to redeem slaves		424, fols 235v-236
16.06.1554	Cassam Moro Gerbino	Djerba	Tripoli	To redeem his son		424, fol. 236
15.09.1554	Manduchai Hebreo	Lepanto	Lepanto	To negotiate the redemption of other slaves in Malta	two years	424, fol. 95-95v
14.11.1554	Nassuph di Galipoli	Turco di Ga-lipoli	Levant and other places	Is leaving Malta with an armed fregata on which there are Turks, Moors and some Christian sailors to get redemption money and other goods to redeem Turkish slaves and at the same time re-deem Christian slaves.		424, fol. 107v
26.01.1554	Andreoto Habel	Malta	Tripoli and Geluel	His ship has both Moor and Christian sailors. To carry out re-demption services and bring back merchandise.		424, fol. 63-63v

Date	Beneficiary	Place of Origin	Destination	Reason for Pass	Validity	AOM Ref
24.05.1555	Murgian de Abdalla a freed slave of the Grand Master	Aden from near the Red Sea		To traffic in various merchandise as was his trade		425, fol. 198
14.05.1555	Mahometo Hamidan Benalli a freed slave of the Grand Master	Zanzor		To traffic in various merchandise	For all his lifetime	425, fol. 199
18.08.1555	Andrea Marmara and a Turkish slave named Chisa de Galata	Malta	Constantino-ple and the Levant	To redeem his son and other Christian slaves		425, fol. 201
03.10.1555	Mahamet Zulat and six other Muslim slaves	Tunisia, Sfax	To go back home	To get the necessary ransom money		425, fol. 207
03.10.1555	Hagi Buabdella de Chalifo Tripolino	Tripoli	Djerba	To bring back merchandise	one year	425, fol. 207
16.11.1555	Zamaiaz Zaphartin	Jew of Algiers		To get the necessary money and goods to redeem himself accom-panied with one of his servants	two years	425, fol. 209
10.02.1556	Hianza Dorla	Turk	Djerba	To redeem slaves and come back with merchandise	8 months	425, fol. 209v
05.02.1556	Zalem Abez Esfachechino	Moor from Sfax	Djerba and Sfax	To bring back merchandise and redeem Muslim slaves	8 months	425, fol. 210v
15.09.1556	Ahmed del Monesterio slave of Philippo Bilia		Golette and Tunisia	To bring back merchandise on his own ships and redeem Muslim slaves	1 year	425, fol. 219v

Date	Beneficiary	Place of Origin	Destination	Reason for Pass	Validity	AOM Ref
06.11.1556	Amor Belbay Rays a slave of the knight Fra. Francesco de Lorraine, Prior of France		Djerba	To come back with his ship full of merchandise accompanied by seven sailors - 'compagni marinari' - and redeem himself and other slaves belonging to the Order and to private individuals	4 months	426, fol. 250v
01.12.1556	Bartholomeo Abela	Malta	Tripoli and Gcluel	To sell his merchandise and come back with other merchandise from North Africa		426, fols 251-251v
12.01.1557	Jacob Zamero de Tremesen, a slave of the knight Fra. Frences-to de Lorraine, Prior of France	Jew	Alexandria and other places	To bring back merchandise and redeem himself and other Jewish slaves		426, fol. 254
21.01.1557	Isuph Ali Ogli de Satalia slave of the knight Fra. Frencesco de Lorraine, Prior of France	Turk	Alexandria and other places	To bring back merchandise and redeem himself and other Turkish slaves	9 months	426, fol. 254v
21.01.1557	Agi Ibraim Ogli de Satalia, Memi Trevis Ogli and+B52 Thamuza Thsan Ogli, slaves of the knight Fra. Francesco de Lorraine	Turks from Alexandria	Alexandria and other places	To bring back merchandise and redeem himself and other Turkish slaves	9 months	426, fol. 254v
09.02.1557	Salmon Montesino, Sameul Alfarim, David Lerma, Joseph de Leve, Samuel Trangola, Samuel Casses all Jews, and, Ali D'Alessandria, Hagi Cossaim Daleppo, Saraph Caramet and Hagi Abdala de Lamech, Turks	Jews and Turks	To go back home	They were caught by the galleys of Fra. Jean de Vallette and had redeemed themselves		426, fol. 255v

Date	Beneficiary	Place of Origin	Destination	Reason for Pass	Validity	AOM Ref
10.02.1557	Salomon Montesino and Michel Sacar de Patraz, freed slaves of Fra. Jean de Vallette	Jews from Tripoli in Syria	Venice and Zakynthos (Giante)	To traffic in merchandise between Zakynthos and Malta	14 months	426, fol. 256.
13.03.1557	Alli Binabi du Dalem	Moor from Tripoli in Syria	Alexandria and other places	To bring back merchandise and redeem himself and other Moorish slaves	9 months	426, fol. 257v
22.03.1557	Mag. Nicolo Guspare	Merchant from Zakynthos	Zakynthos	To come to Malta from Zakynthos to traffic in merchandise.		426, fols 261-261v
11.05.1557	Ismael Alfarin a freed slave of de Vallette	Free Jew	Tripoli in Syria, Cairo and other places	Wants to traffic in merchandise between Malta, Tripoli in Syria, Cairo and other places	2 years	426, fol. 264.
22.05.1557	Agi Sinan a freed slave of Fra. Francesco de Lorraine	Free Turk	Constantinople and other places	To redeem his son and other Turks and come back to Malta with merchandise	1 year	426, fol. 264v
25.05.1557	Ali son of Mahometo Alessandrino a freed slave	Free Moor from Alexandria	Levant and other places	To come to Malta with merchandise	1 year	426, fol. 264v
31.05.1557	David Lerma a freed slave		To go back home	This was an extension of the safe-conduct found in AOM 426, fol. 255.		426, fol. 264v
10.06.1557	Joseph de Leave a freed slave	Free Jew from the Levant	Tripoli in Syria	To traffic in merchandise between Tripoli in Syria and other places and Malta	1 year	426, fol. 267v
26.06.1557	Hagim Cossoem de Alepo, Hagi Cassan de Alepo, Abraim bin Hagi Cossein, Babasurif de Carahamet		To go back home	Were freed slaves		426, fol. 271v

Date	Beneficiary	Place of Origin	Destination	Reason for Pass	Validity	AOM Ref
09.12.1557	Rocho Butino Chioto		Zakynthos and Cephalonia	To go to Zakynthos and Cephalonia with a shipload of merchandise and come back with wheat and other victuals which were necessary for the provisioning of the island		426, fol. 195v
09.12.1557	Isaac Stella a freed slave	Free Jew	Levant	To go to the Levant accompanied by another Jew named Samuel and come back to Malta with merchandise to redeem other Jews	1 year	426, fol. 196
19.02.1559	Franculi Bisbeli a chemist		Soria, (Syria)	To buy drugs, medicine and other goods which the Order requires for its infirmary+E68	9 months	427, fol. 262v
02.12.1559	Rays Cashen a slave	Sfax	Djerba	To bring back merchandise and redeem himself	10 months	428, fols 256v-257
09.02.1560	Rays Cashen a slave	Sfax	Djerba	To bring back merchandise and redeem himself		428, fol. 259
23.04.1560	Mahamet de Razit Ben Halij	Djerba	Malta	Wants to come to Malta and bring his goods accompanied by the galleys of the Order		428, fols 266-266v.
23.04.1560	Gioseph Guideo and other Jews	Djerba	Malta	Want to come to Malta from Djerba with the galleys of the Order with their goods and money and return when they please.		428, fol. 266v.

Date	Beneficiary	Place of Origin	Destination	Reason for Pass	Validity	AOM Ref
31.05.1560	Joan Lorenzo de Lango, five Turks, Two Moors and a Turkish woman		Constantinople and other places in Turkey	To redeem some Christian slaves and return with merchandise		428, fol. 269v
21.09.1560	Rays Cashen a slave	Sfax	Djerba	To extend his safe conduct for another four months		428, fol. 277v.
11.04.1561	Rays Cashen a slave	Sfax	Djerba	To transfer this safe conduct to Rays Taylo Oil Cassar, should Rayz Cashen die. He was to go to Djerba and come back with his ship laden with merchandise and 9 sailors		428, fol. 230
06.10.1561	Giosepho de Seccha, Francesco Antamri and Giovanni Compiano	Lucca and Florence residents in Marseille	Tripoli of Barbary	To redeem slaves and carry out other business and come back to Malta		429, fol. 240v
13.11.1561	Stamate Papadopolo and Josuph Abdulla Ogli Cerches	Modon and Constantinople	Malta	To get the necessary redemption money for slaves and return with merchandise to Malta		429, fol. 245v.
09.03.1562	Hallij Tunisino ferrero	Moor from Tunisia	Golette and Tunisia	To bring back goods and merchandise		429, fol. 248v.
20.07.1562	Salomon Guideo	Jew from Rhodes	To go back home	To redeem himself and other Jews		429, fol. 252v
27.07.1562	Nicolo Crusso Clonari detto Chayon		Levant	To negotiate the redemption of Christian slaves who were in Constantinople and other parts of Turkey		429, fol. 253

Date	Beneficiary	Place of Origin	Destination	Reason for Pass	Validity	AOM Ref
04.08.1562	Benor de Sfacz, a slave	Sfax	Tripoli in Barbary	To negotiate his redemption and that of other Muslim slaves		429, fol. 253v.
07.08.1562	Haggia Fatima de Xontena	Moor	Tripoli in Barbary	To get the necessary money to redeem one of her sons, Haggia Cashem and come back with merchandise.		429, fol. 253v.
02.12.1562	Davi Lindo	Free Jew	Levant	He redeemed himself and was going back to his country and other parts of the Levant with the intention of coming back with merchandise.		429, fol. 258v
30.04.1563	Hon. Beneditto Boenjo		Golette	Brought merchandise to Malta		429, fol. 263
11.06.1563	Joanettino Melissino	Lindos	Rhodes	He had brought about 200 redeemed Christians and was now requesting to go back to Rhodes.		429, fol. 264
15.06.1563	Christofino Forestieri, Yousif Ogli Turco and Satalia slaves of the Order		Levant	To redeem slaves and bring back money and merchandise+E91		429, fol. 264
13.06.1563	Cusseyn Abdulla Ogli di Bosna and+B88 Ciaschia di Achmet Mustafa Ogli Turco slaves of the Order		Levant	To redeem a slave		429, fol. 264
16.06.1563	Jochuda Albo	Jew of Constantinople	Levant	To get redemption money for other Jews		429, fol. 267

Date	Beneficiary	Place of Origin	Destination	Reason for Pass	Validity	AOM Ref
06.05.1564	Abraam Simaria	Jew	Tripoli in Barbary	To load from Tripoli in Barbary goods and merchandise to be exchanged for the redemption of other Jews		430, fol. 253
10.06.1564	Cacan Rays Turco	Turk	Tripoli in Barbary	To load from Tripoli in Barbary goods and merchandise to be exchanged for the redemption of other slaves.		430, fol. 255
28.06.1564	Stamato Papdopoli and 6 Turks	Modon	Modon	To go to Modon and redeem the said slaves and come back with goods, money and merchandise	1 year	430, fol. 255v
27.06.1564	Christofino Forestieri and Hieronymo Foretieri and 3 free Turks		Satalia	To negotiate the redemption of Muslim slaves who were in Malta and come back with goods, money, letters and merchandise	1 year	430, fols 255v-256
13.07.1564	Mensur el Nichaili a slave	Sfax	Alexandria	Leaving with the ship of Christofino Forestieri to go to Alessandria to negotiate his and other slaves' redemption (travelling on the same ship), and return to Malta with merchandise, goods and money	1 year	430, fols 256-256v
07.12.1564	Nicolo Crusso Clonari detto Chayon and+B1 some Turks		Constantinople and other parts of the Levant	To negotiate the ransom of some Turkish slaves found in Malta		430, fol. 263

Bibliography

Primary Sources

Manuscript Sources

CATHEDRAL ARCHIVES OF MALTA, MDINA

Archives of the Inquisition, Malta

AIM, Proc. Crim. vol. 3B

Curia Episcoplis Melitensis, Acta Originalia

CEM AO MS 2 1400–99
CEM AO MS 6 1502–20
CEM AO MS 8B 1527–30
CEM AO MS 9 1530
CEM AO MS 10 1531
CEM AO MS 15 1536
CEM AO MS 23B 1543
CEM AO MS 28 1548
CEM AO MS 36 1556
CEM AO MS 38 1558
CEM AO MS 40 1560
CEM AO MS 41 1561
CEM AO MS 42 1562
CEM AO MS 46 1566

Curia Episcoplis Melitensis, Other

CEM Registrum Usurariorum Melitae, Liber Primus 1570–71
CEM Registrum Usurariorum Melitae, Liber Secundus 1574–75

Miscellanea

Misc 28 Miscellanea Notitiarum: Miscellanea Notitiarum: Notizie dei privilege dei Re di Sicilia in favor di Malta (1218–1588)
Misc 34 Privileggi, Capitoli, Lettere, 1404–1570
Misc 273 Bonavita, V., Dissertazioni Storico Legali su Malta e Gozo

Misc 440 Conti dell'Ospedale di Santo Spirito dell'anno 1540 sino all'anno 1562

NATIONAL ARCHIVES OF MALTA (Legal Section, Mdina)

Magnia Curia Castellania
Acta Originalia
Vol. I 1543–66
Vol. II 1567–70

Cedulae Supplicae et Taxationes
Vol. I 1564
Vol. II 1565–66

Comune Aerarium
Vol. I 1552–97

Registri Patentarum
Vol. I 1564–78

Registrum Actorum Originalium
Vol. I 1535–41
Vol. II 1551–54

Registrum Depositorium
Vol. I 1560–88

Suprema Appellationis Curia et Tribunalis Publicae Audientiae Causae
Vol. I 1539–98

NATIONAL LIBRARY OF MALTA, VALLETTA

Archives of the Order of Malta
AOM 17 Salva Condotti di Carlo V alla Religione Gerosolimitana

AOM 70 Original Deed of Donation of the Maltese Islands and Tripoli by Emperor Charles V to the Order of St John, 1530
AOM 85 Liber Conciliorum (1526–35)
AOM 86 Liber Conciliorum (1535–43)
AOM 87 Liber Conciliorum (1543–48)
AOM 88 Liber Conciliorum (1548–53)
AOM 89 Liber Conciliorum (1554–57)
AOM 90 Liber Conciliorum (1558–60)
AOM 91 Liber Conciliorum (1561–67)

AOM 153 Recodification of the customs and statutes of the town of Rhodes – 24 February 1510 (seventeenth-century copy)

AOM 286 Sacra Capitula Generalia annorum (1526–38)
AOM 287 Sacra Capitula Generalia annorum (1548)
AOM 288 Sacra Capitula Generalia annorum (1555)

AOM 410 Liber Bullarum (1522–24) M. Magistri Fratris Philippi de Villiers L'Isle Adam
AOM 411 Liber Bullarum (1524–25) M. Magistri Fratris Philippi de Villiers L'Isle Adam
AOM 414 Liber Bullarum (1528–30) M. Magistri Fratris Philippi de Villiers L'Isle Adam
AOM 415 Liber Bullarum (1531–34) MM. MM. Philippi de Villiers L'Isle Adam et Petrini de Ponte
AOM 416 Liber Bullarum (1534–37) M. Magistri Fratris Petrini de Ponte
AOM 417 Liber Bullarum (1537–42) M. Magistri Fratris Joannis de Homedes
AOM 418 Liber Bullarum (1541–43) M. Magistri Fratris Joannis de Homedes
AOM 419 Liber Bullarum (1543–45) M. Magistri Fratris Joannis de Homedes
AOM 420 Liber Bullarum (1545–47) M. Magistri Fratris Joannis de Homedes
AOM 421 Liber Bullarum (1547–49) M. Magistri Fratris Joannis de Homedes
AOM 422 Liber Bullarum (1549–50) M. Magistri Fratris Joannis de Homedes
AOM 423 Liber Bullarum (1551–53) M. Magistri Fratris Joannis de Homedes
AOM 424 Liber Bullarum (1553–55) M. Magistri Fratris Claudii de La Sengle
AOM 425 Liber Bullarum (1555–56) M. Magistri Fratris Claudii de la Sengle
AOM 426 Liber Bullarum (1556–57) MM. MM. Claudi de La Sengle et Joannis de Valette
AOM 427 Liber Bullarum (1558–59) M. Magistri Fratris Joannis de Valette
AOM 428 Liber Bullarum (1559–61) M. Magistri Fratris Joannis de Valette
AOM 429 Liber Bullarum (1561–63) M. Magistri Fratris Joannis de Valette
AOM 430 Liber Bullarum (1563–64) M. Magistri Fratris Joannis de Valette
AOM439 Liber Bullarum (1579–81) M. Magistri Fratris Joannis Levesque de la Cassiere
AOM 469 Liber Bullarum (1639–41) M. Magistri Fratris Joannis Pauli Lascaris Castelar

AOM 625 Indice di molte notizie contenute nei Registri delle Bolle di Cancelleria 1345–1662

AOM 626 Repertorio di varie materie contenute nei Registri delle Bolle di Cancelleria 1346–1695

AOM 627 Indice alfabetico di diverse materie contenute ne libri delle Bolle sotto il titolo Diverse Scritture

AOM 740 Libro dei contratti del Tesoro (1620–1794)

AOM 1651 Raccolte di varie Ordinazioni sanzionate tra l'anno 1404 e 1636

AOM 2079 Benefici di Giuspadronato del G. Maestro

AOM 2080 Differenze giurisdizionali tra I Vescovi di Malta e l'Ordine Gerosolimitano

AOM 6421 Tratte e provisioni alla Religione ed Università di Malta

AOM 6466 1658–1670 (contains petitions for safe conducts)

AOM 6559 Ordinationi & Altre Scritture concernenti il Governo di Tripoli

Archives of the Università (Municipality of Malta)

Univ. 1 Tratte concesse alla Religione ed all'Università di Malta 'Tomo I' che racchiude diplomi ed altre scritture originali sottoscritti dall'Imperatore Carlo V e da Filippo II Re di Spagna tra gli anni 1500–1599

Univ. 3 Volume contenente quindici originali Diplomi in pergamenta nei quali sono descritti i Privilegi concessi da diversi Sovrani ai Maltesi 1397–1725

Univ. 5 Lettere dal 1523 al 1600

Univ. 7 Diverse Scritture e Privileggi dei Maltesi

Univ. 9 Privilegji dell'Isola di Malta 1350–1585

Univ. 12 Registro degli Atti dell'Università della Città Notabile 1450–1498 (also contains documents from 1512 to 1531)

Univ. 13 Atti dell'Università della Notabile, 1531–1570 (starts from 25 September 1531 and includes some documents from 1467)

Univ. 14 Atti dell'Università della Notabile 1570–1589

Univ. 201 Volume marcato C.N.3 contenente varie scritture antiche tra le quali alcune del Consiglio Popolare e relazioni dei procuratori dell'Università della Notabile spediti all'estero per comprare frumento, 1589–1594 (includes pre-1589 correspondence which dates to the 1550s)

Univ. 202 Volume contenente lettere originali dei consoli e proucratori della Città Notabile e dei giurati della Vittoriosa concernenti l'amministrazione della Massa frumentaria, 1536–1579

Univ. 206 De insulis Meliveti et Gaudisii eiusque secretia, feudis et iuribus. Capibrevium, concessiones et Privilegia prout in Regia Cancelleria Regni Sicilie

Library Manuscripts

Libr. MS 148 Prammatiche Magistrali pubblicate l'anno 1640 per comando del serenissimo Principe Fra Paolo Lascaris Castellar

Libr. MS 153 Pragmaticae Rhodiae, F. Emerici D'Amboyse Magni Magistri Sacrae Religionis Hierosolymitanae (seventeenth-century copy)

Libr. MS 433 Discorso di Mons. Pietro Dusina su Malta

Libr. MS 439 Prammatiche Magistrali Lascaris 1640–1692 incluse quelle di Omedes 1553

Libr. MS 672	Processus super gabella scutorum centum millium auri pto perfection munimentorum Florianae Stae Margaritae et de Ursis
Libr. MS 704	Untitled volume containing miscellaneous documents dating from c. 1500 to 1765
Libr. MS 740	Costituzioni di Malta 1509–1681
Libr. MS 1214	Ragguaglio de' Pubblici Notari antichi di Malta e Gozo dei quali non si trovano i registri, per essere porzione trasportati in Constantinopoli e porzione in Catania, dall'anno 1312, con una cronologia de' Pubblici Notari i registri di quali esistono nell'Archivio della Città Notabile
Libr. MS 1220	Notizie ed allegazioni diverse date in tempi diversi et in varie contingenze dell'Università di Malta dal notario Vittorio Griscti ... 1747
Libr. MS 1365	Indice dei Notari che attegiarono in Malta e Gozo 1400–1686
Libr. MS 1408	Leggi e Costitutioni Pragmaticali ordinate dal Ser.mo e Rev.mo Signore Il S. Fra. D. Gregorio Carafa ... pubblicate sotto li 11 Settembre 1681

Publications

Del Dritto Municipale Di Malta, Nuova Compilazione con Diverse Altre Costituzioni (Malta, 1784)

Leggi e Costituzioni Prammaticali, Rinuovate, reformate, ed ampliate dal Serenissmo, ed Ementissimo Signor Fra D. Antonio Manoel de Vilhena de Conti di Villaflor: Gran Maestro della Sacra Religione Gerosolimitana, e dell'Ordine Militare del S. Sepolcro, Principe di Malta, e Gozo, & c: Colle Pandette, ed Inidice de Titoli, e delle materie (Malta, 1725)

De Nicholai, N., *Le navigationi et viaggi nella Turchia* (Antwerp, 1576)

NOTARIAL ARCHIVES, VALLETTA

R 4/1	1557–58	Notary Abela Placido
MS 514/1	1557–60	Notary Abela Placido
R 44/4	1560–61	Notary Baldacchino Giacomo
R 44/5	1561–62	Notary Baldacchino Giacomo
R 44/6	1562–63	Notary Baldacchino Giacomo
R 44/7	1563–64	Notary Baldacchino Giacomo
R 48/2 (Bastardello)	1565–67	Notary Bartolo Angelo
R 48/7	1563–68	Notary Bartolo Angelo
R 206/1	1534–35	Notary Bonaventura de Bonetiis Vincenzo
R 206/2	1535–36	Notary Bonaventura de Bonetiis Vincenzo
R 206/7	1543	Notary Bonaventura de Bonetiis Vincenzo
R 206/10	1546–47	Notary Bonaventura de Bonetiis Vincenzo
R 206/13	1549–50	Notary Bonaventura de Bonetiis Vincenzo
R 206/35	1564	Notary Bonaventura de Bonetiis Vincenzo

R 69/1	1517–31	Notary Bondino Giacomo
MS 585/1	1516–31	Notary Bondino Giacomo
MS 585/2	1517–31	Notary Bondino Giacomo
MS 588/1	1467–21	Notary Bonello Paolo
R 91/3	1568–69	Notary Briffa Matteo
R 105/1	1531–54	Notary Buttiegieg Don Giorgio
R 123/3	1599–1601	Notary Calleja Pietro
R 140/12	1528–31	Notary Cancur Don Consalvo
R 160/8	1561–62	Notary Cassar Antonio
R 173/3	1676–77	Notary Cauchi Tommaso (Jr)
R 187/2	1601–02	Notary Chiappara Marc'Antonio
R 196A/1	1501–26	Notary Cumbo Gulio
R 202/1	1535–37	Notary de Agatiis Nicolò
R 202/2	1537–38	Notary de Agatiis Nicolò
R 202/3	1538–39	Notary de Agatiis Nicolò
R 202/4	1539–40	Notary de Agatiis Nicolò
R 202/5	1540–41	Notary de Agatiis Nicolò
R 202/6	1541–42	Notary de Agatiis Nicolò
R 202/7	1542–43	Notary de Agatiis Nicolò
R 202/8	1543–44	Notary de Agatiis Nicolò
R 202/9	1544–45	Notary de Agatiis Nicolò
R 202/11	1546–47	Notary de Agatiis Nicolò
R 214	1559–73	Notary de Brincat Matteo
R 224/1	1537–43	Notary de Guevara Giuseppe
R 224/2	1544	Notary de Guevara Giuseppe
R 224/4	1546–48	Notary de Guevara Giuseppe
R 224/13	1557	Notary de Guevara Giuseppe
R 224/17	1560–61	Notary de Guevara Giuseppe
R 224/23	1564–1656	Notary de Guevara Giuseppe
R 224/24	1565–66	Notary de Guevara Giuseppe
MS 778/1	1546–55	Notary de Guevara Giuseppe
MS 778/4	1562–64	Notary de Guevara Giuseppe
MS 778/5	1564–65	Notary de Guevara Giuseppe

R 229/29	1614–15	Notary de Lucia Giovanni Simon
R 248/1	1557–59	Notary Falzon Giovanello
R 7/1	1524–28	Notary Hagius Lorenzo
R 376/2	1539–40 (Sept–March)	Notary Muscat Juliano
R 376/3	1539–40 (March–Aug)	Notary Muscat Juliano
R 376/4	1540–41	Notary Muscat Juliano
R 376/11	1544–45	Notary Muscat Juliano
R 376/44 Part I	1562–63	Notary Muscat Juliano
R 414/1	1512–37	Notary Rapa Antonio
R 439/1	1530–31	Notary Selvagi de Via Bartolomeo
R 439/2	1531	Notary Selvagi de Via Bartolomeo
R 439/3	1532	Notary Selvagi de Via Bartolomeo
R 439/9	1532–33	Notary Selvagi de Via Bartolomeo
R 439/15	1535	Notary Selvagi de Via Bartolomeo
R 439/20	1536	Notary Selvagi de Via Bartolomeo
R 439/22	1537	Notary Selvagi de Via Bartolomeo
R 439/25	1538	Notary Selvagi de Via Bartolomeo
R 439/30	1540–41	Notary Selvagi de Via Bartolomeo
R 439/35	1543–44	Notary Selvagi de Via Bartolomeo
R 439/36	1544–45	Notary Selvagi de Via Bartolomeo
R 439/39	1547	Notary Selvagi de Via Bartolomeo
R 439/42	1550–51	Notary Selvagi de Via Bartolomeo
R 439/43	1551	Notary Selvagi de Via Bartolomeo
R 439 (unreferenced)	1549–52	Notary Selvagi de Via Bartolomeo
MS 1069/1	1538–39	Notary Sillato Bartolomeo
R 508/8	1594–95	Notary Zelivo Giorgio

Printed Sources

Abela, G. F., *Della descrittione di Malta isola nel mare siciliano con le sue antichità ed altre notitie* (facsimile edn, Malta, 1984)

Aquilina, G., & Fiorini, S. (eds), *Documentary Sources of Maltese History Part IV Documents at the Vatican No. 1 Archivio Segreto Vaticano Congregazione Vescovi e Regolari Malta: Visita Apostolica no. 51 Mgr Petrus Dusina, 1575* (Malta, 2001)

Barz, W. D., 'The Maltese Statuti e Ordinamenti of 1533' (trans. J. Sammut, *Id-Dritt*, official organ of the Law Society-Universtiy of Malta), 15 (1990), 5–20

Bosio, G., *Dell'istoria della Sacra Religione et Ill.ma militia di S. Gio. Gerosolimitano* (3 vols, Rome, 1594–1602) (2nd impression, Naples, 1684; Venice, 1695)

Cassola A., with the collaboration of I. Bostan and T. Scheben, *The 1565 Ottoman Malta Campaign Register* (Malta, 1998)

Dal Pozzo, B., *Historia Della Sacra Religione Militare di S. Giovanni Gerosolimitano detta di Malta* (Verona, 1703)

de Nicholai, N., *Le navigationi et viaggi nella Turchia* (Antwerp, 1576)

de Vertot, R. A., *The History of the Knights of Malta* (2 vols, London, 1728, facsimile edition, Malta, 1989)

Del Amo García, J., Fiorini, S. & Wettinger, G. (eds), *Documentary Sources of Maltese History, Part III: Documents of the Maltese Universitas, No. 1: Cathedral Museum, Mdina, Archivum Cathedralis Melitæ, Miscellanea 33: 1405–1452* (Malta, 2001)

Fiorini, S. (ed.), *The 'Mandati' Documents at the Archives of the Mdina Cathedral, Malta: 1473–1539* (Malta, 1992)

— *Documentary Sources of Maltese History, Part I: Notarial Documents, No. 1: Notary Giacomo Zabbara: R494/1(I) 1486–1488* (Malta, 1996)

— *Documentary Sources of Maltese History, Part I: Notarial Documents, No. 2: Notary Giacomo Zabbara: R494/1(II–IV) 1494–1497* (Malta, 1999)

— *Documentary Sources of Maltese History, Part I: Notarial Documents, No. 3: Notary Paulo Bonello: MS. 588: 1467–1517, Notary Giacomo Zabbara MS. 1132: 1471–1500* (Malta, 2005)

— *Documentary Sources of Maltese History, Part II: Documents in the State Archives, Palermo, No. 1: Cancelleria Regia: 1259–1400* (Malta, 1999)

— *Documentary Sources of Maltese History, Part III: Documents of the Maltese Universitas, No. 3: Acta Juratorum et Consilii Civitatis et Insulae Maltae, II: 1512–1531* (Malta, 2016)

— *Documentary Sources of Maltese History, Part V: Documents in the Curia of the Archbishop of Malta, No. 1: The Registrum Fundationum Beneficiorum Insulae Gaudisii 1435–1545* (trans. Rev. Joseph Busuttil, Malta, 2006)

La Mantia, G., 'Capitoli e Statuti Amministrativi Dell'Isola di Malta approvati dai Re o Vicere di Sicilia 1130–1530', *Archivio Storico di Malta*, 8:1 (1936–37), 1–17

La Mantia, V., 'La Secrezia Dogana di Tripoli ed i Capitoli della sua Amministraione Approvati e Riformati dai Vicire di Sicilia negli anni 1511–1521', *Archivio Storico Siciliano*, 5:41 (1916), 466–90

— *Antiche Consuetudini delle Città di Sicilia*, with an introduction by A. Romano (Messina, 1993)

— 'Consuetudini di Trapani nelle quali e contenuto il testo antico delle consuetudini di Messina', in *Antiche Consuetudini delle Città di Sicilia*, with an introduction by A. Romano (Messina, 1993)

Luttrell, A., 'The Earliest Documents Transcribed in the Cathedral Archives Mdina: 1316–1372', in Azzopardi, J. (ed.), *Archives of the Cathedral of Malta Misc. 32A: 1313–1529* (Malta, 1977), 29–52

Micallef, A., *Diritto Municipale di Malta Compilato Sotto De Rohan G.M. Or Nuovamente Corredato di Annotazioni* (2 vols, Malta, 1841)

Mifsud, A., 'Le Franchigie Costituzionali Alfonsiane e l'invasione dei Mori del 1429', *Archivum Melitense*, 3:8–12 (1918–19), 332–40

— 'L'Approvigionamento e l'Università di Malta nelle passate dominazioni: Documenti Inediti', *Archivum Melitense*, 3:6 (1918), 223–34

Paoli, S., *Codice Diplomatico del Sacro Militare Ordine Gerosolimitano, oggi di Malta* (2 vols, Lucca, 1737)
Patinella, J. A., *Tyrocinium sive, Theori-Practica tabellionatus officii [...]* (2nd edn, 4 vols, Palermo, 1777)
Quintin d'Autun, J., 'Insulae Melitae Descriptio (Lyon, 1536)', in *The Earliest Description of Malta* (trans. H. C. R. Vella, Malta, 1980)
Testa, F. (ed.), *Capitula Regni Siciliae que ad hodiernam diem lata sunt* (Palermo, 1741)
Valentini, R., 'I Cavalieri Di San Giovanni da Rodi a Malta: Trattative Diplomatiche', *Archivum Melitense*, 9:4 (1935), 137–237
— 'Gli Ultimi Re Aragonesi ed i primi Castigliani in Malta', *Archivio Storico di Malta*, 8:1 (1936–37), 72–101
— 'Documenti per servire alla Storia di Malta', *Archivio Storico di Malta*, 13:4 (1937), 462–99
— 'Documenti per servire alla Storia di Malta', *Archivio Storico di Malta*, 9:1 (1937–38), 97–123
— 'Documenti per servire alla Storia di Malta', *Archivio Storico di Malta*, 10:1 (1938–39), 58–76

Secondary Sources

Published Sources

Abela, J., 'Il-Gran Mastru Claudio De La Sengle', *Il-Mument*, 5 September 1999, 20–3
Abela, J., '*De Uxore Proxima Futura Magistri Hieronymi Cassar*: New Light on Girolamo Cassar's Immediate Family', *Melita Historica*, 14:4 (2007), 375–85
— 'A Window on the Acts of a Maltese Sixteenth-Century Notary: Placido Abela', in Grima, J. F. (ed.), *60th Anniversary of the Malta Historical Society – A Commemoration* (Malta, 2010), 207–36
— 'Before Valletta: Port Activities Prior to the Great Siege', in Marconi, N. (ed.), *Valletta, Città, architecttura e costruzione sotto il segno della fede e della guerra* (Rome, 2011), 1–16
— 'Who was Georgio Scala?' in Agius, D. (ed.), *Georgio Scala and the Moorish Slaves: The Inquisition Malta 1598* (Malta, 2013), 213–34
— 'The Great Siege of 1565: Untold Stories of Daily Life', in Camilleri, M. (ed.), *Besieged* (2 vols, Malta, 2015), vol. 2, 97–115
Abulafia, D., *The Western Mediterranean Kingdoms 1200–1500: The Struggle for Dominion* (London, 1977)
— *Frederick II: A Medieval Emperor* (London, 1988)
— 'Lo stato e la vita economica', in Toubert, P. & Paravacini, A. (eds), *Federico II e il mondo mediterraneo* (Palermo, 1994), 165–87
— *A Mediterranean Emporium: The Catalan Kingdom of Majorca* (Cambridge, 1994)
— 'Grain Traffic out of the Apulian Ports', in Abulafia, D., *Mediterranean Encounters, Economic, Religious, Political, 1100–1550* (Ashgate, 2000), 25–36
— *Mediterranean Encounters, Economic, Religious, Political, 1100–1550* (Ashgate, 2000)
— (ed.), *The Mediterranean in History* (London, 2003)
— 'Introduction: What is the Mediterranean?', in Abulafia, D. (ed.), *The Mediterranean*

in History (London, 2003), 11–65
— *The Great Sea: A Human History of the Mediterranean* (London, 2011)
Aloisio, M. A., 'A Test Case for Regional Market Integration? The Grain Trade between Malta and Sicily in the Late Middle Ages', in Armstrong, L., Elbl, I. & Elbl, M. M. (eds), *Money, Markets and Trade in Late Medieval Europe: Essays in Honour of John H. A. Munro* (Leiden, 2007), 297–309
Aquilina, G., OFM, *The Jerosolimitan Nuns, the Church and Monastery of Saint Ursula Valletta – Malta* (Malta, 2011)
Arbel, B. (ed.), *Intercultural Contacts in the Medieval Mediterranean, Studies in Honour of David Jacoby* (London, 1996)
Ashburner, W., *The Rhodian Sea-Law* (Oxford, 1909)
Bartoli Langeli, A., 'Après le *Morgengabe*. Donations nuptiales et culture juridique dans l'Itali ecommunale', in Bougard, F., Feller, L., Le Jan, R. (eds), *Dots et douaires dans le haut Moyen Âge*, École française de Rome (Rome, 2002, Collection de École française de Rome, 295), 123–30
Baviera Albanese, A., *Diritto pubblico e istituzioni amministrative in Sicilia. Le fonti* (Rome, 1974)
Baxter Wolf, K., 'The "Moors" of West Africa and the Beginnings of the Portuguese Slave Trade', *Journal of Medieval and Renaissance Studies*, 24:3 (1994), 449–69
Bellavitis, A., 'Donne, cittadinanza e corporazioni tra Medioevo ed età moderna: ricerche in corso', in Filippini, N. M., Plebani, T. & Scattigno, A. (eds), *Corpi e Storia: Donne e uomini dal mondo antico all'età contemporanea* (Viella, Rome, 2002)
Bellomo, M., *Ricerche sui rapport patrimoniali fra i coniugi. Contributo alla storia della famiglia medievale* (Milan, 1961)
— *Società e istituzioni dal mediovo agli inizi dell'età moderna* (9th edn, Rome, 1999)
Bennassar, B. & Bennassar, L., *Les Chretiens d'Allah* (Paris, 2006)
Berman, H. J., *Law and Revolution, II The Impact of the Protestant Reformations on the Western Legal Tradition* (Cambridge, MA, 2006)
Blackburn, B. & Holford-Stevens, L., *The Oxford Companion to the Year* (Oxford, 1999)
Bonello, G., 'Knights and Courtesans', in *Histories of Malta: Versions and Diversions, Vol. 3* (Malta, 2002), 20–41
— 'Knights in Slavery: Captivi in manibus infidelium', in *Histories of Malta: Reflections and Rejections, Vol. 5* (Malta, 2004), 57–85
Bono, S., *I Corsari Barbareschi* (Turin, 1964)
— 'Guerra, Corsara e Commercio nel Maghreb Barbaresco (Secoli XVI–XVIII)', in Lopez Nadal, G. (ed.), *El Comerç Alternativ. Corsarisme i Contraban (ss XV–XVIII)* (Mallorca, 1990), 133–44
— 'Naval Exploits and Privateering', in Mallia Milanes, V. (ed.), *Hospitaller Malta 1530–1798: Studies on Early Modern Malta and the Order of St John of Jerusalem* (Malta, 1993), 351–97
— *Corsari nel Mediterraneo. Cristiani e musulmani fra guerra, schiavitù e commercio* (Milano, 1993, 2nd edn, 1997)
— 'La schiavitù e la storia del Mediterraneo', in *La schiavitù nel Mediterraneo*, in Fiume G. (ed.), *Nuove Effemeridi. Rassegna trimestrale di cultura*, XIV (2001), 4–19
— 'Slave Histories and Memoirs in the Mediterranean World: A Study of the Sources (Sixteenth–Eighteenth Centuries)', in Fusaro, M., Heywood, C. & Omri, M. S.

(eds), *Trade and Cultural Exchange in the Early Modern Mediterranean: Braudel's Maritime Legacy* (London & New York, 2010), 97–115

Borg, V., *The Maltese Diocese during the Sixteenth Century, Melita Sacra II* (Malta, 2009)

Borg Cardona, S. R., 'The *Officio delle Case* and the Housing Laws of the Earlier Grand Masters, 1531–1569', *The Law Journal*, 3:1 (University of Malta, 1951), 39–69

Bowen-Jones, H., *Malta background for Development* (Durham, 1961)

Braccia, R., 'Uxor gaudet de morte mariti', *Annali della Facoltà di Giurisprudenza dell' Università di Genova*, 30 (2000–01), 76–128

Braude, B., 'Venture and Faith in the Commercial Life of the Ottoman Balkans', *International History Review*, 7 (1985), 519–42

Braudel, F., *La Méditerranée et la Monde Méditerranéen à l'Époque de Philippe II* (Paris, 1949, 2nd rev. edn, 1966)

— *Capitalism and Material Life 1400–1800* (trans. M. Kochan, New York, 1973)

— *Civilisation matérielle, Economie et Capitalisme, XVe-XVIIIe siècle* (3 vols, Paris, 1979)

— *Civilization and Capitalism 15th–18th Century: The Structures of Everyday Life, Vol. I* (trans. S. Reynolds, Berkeley & Los Angeles, 1992)

— *Civilization and Capitalism 15th–18th Century, The Wheels of Commerce, Vol. II* (trans. S. Reynolds, Berkeley and Los Angeles, 1992)

— *The Mediterranean and the Mediterranean World in the Age of Philip II* (trans. S. Reynolds, 2 vols, Berkeley, Los Angeles and London, 1995)

Bresc, H., 'The "Secrezia" and the Royal Patrimony in Malta: 1240–1450', in Luttrell, A. (ed.), *Medieval Malta: Studies in Malta before the Knights* (London, 1975), 126–62

— *Un Monde Méditerranéen, Économie et Sociéité en Sicile 1300–1450* (2 vols, Palermo, 1986)

— (ed.), *Figures de l' esclave au Moyen-Age et dans le monde moderne* (Paris, 1996)

— 'Reti di scambio locale e interregional nell'Italia dell'alto Medioevo', in Romano, R. & Tucci, U. T. (eds), *Storia d'Italia*, Annali, VI, 135–78

Brogini, A., *Malte, frontière de chrétienté (1530–1670)* (Rome, 2006)

Brown, J. C. & Davis, R. C., *Gender and Society in Renaissance Italy* (London & New York, 1998)

Bugeja, L., Buhagiar, M. & Fiorini, S. (eds), *Birgu – A Maltese Maritime City* (2 vols, Malta, 1993)

Burke, P., *The Renaissance – Studies in European History* (2nd edn, Basingstoke and New York, 1997)

Buttigieg, E., 'Social Relationships in Mid-Sixteenth-Century Malta: An Analysis through Notary Juliano Muscat's Register R 376/11, *Storja 2008* (Malta, 2009), 47–66

— *Nobility, Faith and Masculinity: The Hospitaller Knights of Malta, c. 1580–c. 1790* (London and New York, 2011)

Calleja Schembri, H., *Coins and Medals of the Knights of Malta* (London, 1966)

Cancila, R., *Il Pane e La Politica, La Rivolta Palermitana del 1560* (Naples, 1999)

Carosi, C., 'Redimere Captivos: Appunti sugli atti notarili di riscatto (Sec. XVI)', in Piergiovanni, V. (ed.), *Corsari e riscatto dei captivi, garanzia notarile tra le due sponde del Mediterraneo. Atti del Convegno di Studi Storici Marsala, 4 ottobre 2008* (Milano, 2010), 47–74

Caruana Galizia, A., 'The Maltese Nobility during the Hospitaller Period: Towards a Reappraisal', *Symposia Melitensia*, 7 (2011), 89–102

Casola, M., 'Armatrici e Marinaie Nel Diritto Romano', in Pagano, R. & Mastroberti, F. (eds), *La Donna nel Diritto, nella Politica e nelle Istituzioni, Quaderno del Dipartimento Jonico*, 1 (2015), 3–18

Cassar, C., 'Popular Perceptions and Values', in Mallia-Milanes, V. (ed.), *Hospitaller Malta 1530–1798: Studies on Malta and the Order of St John of Jerusalem* (Malta, 1993), 429–73

— 'U Mulu De Malta: The Maltese Trade in Donkeys and Mules', *Storja* (Malta, 1996)

— *Society, Culture and Identity in Early Modern Malta* (Malta, 2000)

— *Daughters of Eve, Women, Gender Roles, and the Impact of the Council of Trent in Catholic Malta* (Malta, 2002)

— 'La Valette Bl-Assedju Riesaq', in Bartolo, E. (ed.), *Min Kien Callus?* (Malta, 2003), 55–62

— 'State intervention in the Grain Trade of Malta (16th–20th Century), *Mediterranean Review*, 6:2 (2013), 59–89

Cassar, P., 'The Maltese Corsairs and the Order of St John of Jerusalem', in *The Catholic Historical Review*, 46:2 (1960), 137–56

Cassola, A., *The 1565 Ottoman Malta Campaign Register* (Malta, 1998)

Cave, R. C. & Coulson, H. H., *A Source Book for Medieval Economic History* (Milwaukee, 1936, reprinted, New York, 1965)

Chapone, S. K., *Hardships of the English Laws in Relation to Wives* (London, 1735)

Chojnacka, M., *Working Women of Early Modern Venice* (Baltimore and London, 2001)

Cusumano, V., *Storia dei Banchi Della Sicilia* (Rome, 1887)

Da Molin, G., 'Family Forms and Domestic Service in Southern Italy from the Seventeenth to the Nineteenth Century', *Journal of Family History*, 15 (1990), 504–27

Dalli, C., 'Medieval Communal Organization in an Insular Context: Approaching the Maltese *Università*', *The Making and Unmaking of the Maltese Universitas* (Heritage Supplement, Malta, 1993), 1–10

— 'In Fronteria Barbarorum: Waiting for the Turks on late Medieval Malta', in Fiorini, S. (ed.), *Proceedings of History Week 1994* (Malta, 1996), 115–26

— 'Capitoli: The Voice of an Elite', in Fiorini, S. (ed.), *Proceedings of History Week 1992* (Malta, 1994), 1–18

— 'Enlightening the Middle Ages', in Xuereb, P. (ed.), *Karissime Gotifride – Historical Essays Presented to Godfrey Wettinger on his Seventieth Birthday* (Malta, 1999), 3–16

— *Iż-Żmien* Nofsani Malti (Malta, 2002)

— *Malta, The Medieval Millennium* (Malta, 2006)

D'Angelo, M., 'Porti e Traffici Marittimi in Sicilia Tra Cinquecento e Seicento', in Simoncini, G. (ed.), *Sopra I Porti Di Mare III, Sicilia e Malta* (Florence, 1997), 1–110

Davis, H. & Hough, B., 'The British Claim to Rule Malta', *Melita Historica*, 14:4 (2007), 387–408

Davis, R. C., *Christian Slaves, Muslim Masters: White Slavery in the Mediterranean, the Barbary Coast, and Italy, 1500–1800* (New York, 2003)

De Bono, P., *Sommario della Storia della Legislazione in Malta* (Malta, 1897)

de Giorgio, R., *A City by an Order* (Malta, 1985)

Denzinger, H., *The Source of Catholic Dogma* (London, 1957)

Depasquale, A., *Ecclesiastical Immunity and the Powers of the Inquisitor in Malta (1777–1785)* (Malta, 1968) de Roover, F. E., 'Early Examples of Marine Insurance', *The Journal of Economic History*, 5:2 (1945), 172–200

de Roover, R., *Money, Banking and Credit in Medieval Bruges – Italian Merchant Bankers, Lombards and Money Changers – A Study in the Origins of Banking* (Cambridge, MA, 1948)

— *The Rise and Decline of the Medici Bank* (Harvard and Oxford, 1963)

— 'What is Dry Exchange?', in Kirshner, J. (ed.), *Business, Banking and Economic Thought in Late Medieval and Early Modern Europe* (Chicago and London, 1974), 183–99

Earle, P., *Corsairs of Malta and Barbary* (London, 1970)

Epstein, S., *Speaking of Slavery: Colour, Ethnicity, and Human Bondage in Italy* (New York, 2001)

Epstein, S. R., *An Island for Itself. Economic Development and Social Change in Late Medieval Sicily* (Cambridge, 1992)

Falcone, P., 'Una relazione di Malta sulla fine del Cinquecento', *Archivio Storico di Malta*, 4:1 (1933), 2–51

Faroqhi, S., 'The Ruling Elite between Politics and "The Economy"', in İnalcik, H. & Quataert, D. (eds), *An Economic and Social History of the Ottoman Empire 1300–1914* (Cambridge, 1994), 545–75

— 'Trade: Regional, Inter-regional and International', in İnalcik, H. & Quataert, D. (eds), *An Economic and Social History of the Ottoman Empire 1300–1914* (Cambridge, 1994), 474–530

— *The Ottoman Empire and the World Around It* (London and New York, 2007)

Federuci, G. & Malanima, P., 'Progress, Decline, Growth: Product and Productivity in Italian Agriculture, 1000–2000', *Economic History Review*, 57:3 (2004), 427–64

Fink de Backer, S., *Widowhood in Early Modern Spain, Protectors, Proprietors and Patrons* (Leidon, 2010)

Fiorini, S., 'Demographic Growth and the Urbanization of the Maltese Countryside to 1798', in Mallia-Milanes, V. (ed.), *Hospitaller Malta 1530–1798: Studies on Malta and the Order of St John of Jerusalem* (Malta, 1993), 297–310

— 'Demographical Aspects of Birgu up to 1800', Bugeja, L., Buhagiar, M. & Fiorini, S. (eds), *Birgu: A Maltese Maritime City* (2 vols, Malta, 1993), vol. 1, 219–54

— 'Malta in 1530', in Mallia-Milanes, V. (ed.), *Hospitaller Malta 1530–1798: Studies on Malta and the Order of St John of Jerusalem* (Malta, 1993), 111–98

— 'The Municipal Councils in the Maltese Islands: 1530–1800', *The Making and Unmaking of the Maltese Universitas* (Heritage supplement, Malta, 1993), 13–24

— 'The Resettlement of Gozo After 1551', *Melita Historica*, 9:3 (1986), 203–35

— 'The Rhodiot Community of Birgu, A Maltese Maritime City: 1530-c.1550', in Mallia-Milanes, V. (ed.), *Library of Mediterranean History* (Malta, 1994), vol. 1, 183–241

— 'The Vice-Admiracia Insularum Meliveti et Gaudisii', in Vassallo, C. (ed.), *Consolati Di Mare and Chambers of Commerce* (Malta, 2000), 29–44

— 'X'Nafu dwar Callus', in Bartolo E. (ed.), *Min kien Callus?* (Malta, 2003), 15–53

Fleet, K., *European and Islamic Trade in the Early Ottoman State: The Merchants of Genoa and Turkey* (Cambridge, 1999)

— 'The Mediterranean', *Journal of Early Modern History*, 6:1 (2002), 63–72

— 'Turks, Mamluks, and Latin Merchants: Commerce, Conflict, and Cooperation in the Eastern Mediterranean', in Harris, J., Holmes, C. & Russell, E. (eds), *Byzantines, Latins, and Turks in the Eastern Mediterranean World after 1150* (Oxford, 2012), 327–44

Fonay Wemple, S., 'Women from the Fifth to the Tenth Century', in Duby, G., Perrot, M. (gen. eds) & Klapish-Zuber, C. (ed.), *A History of Women, Silences of the Middle Ages* (London, 1992), 169–201

Fontenay, M., 'La place de la course dans l'economie portuaire: l'exemple de Malte et des portes barbaresques', in Cavaciocchi, S. (ed.), *I porti come impresa economica (sec. XII – XVIII)* (Florence, 1988), 1321–47

— 'The Mediterranean World, 1500–1800: Social and Economic Perspectives', in Mallia-Milanes, V. (ed.), *Hospitaller Malta 1530–1798: Studies on Early Modern Malta and the Order of St John of Jerusalem* (Malta, 1993), 43–110

— 'L'esclave galérien dans la Méditerranée des Temps Modernes', in Bresc, H. (ed.), *Figures de l'esclave au Moyen-Âge et dans le monde moderne* (Paris, 1996), 115–43

— 'Il mercato maltese degli schiavi al tempo dei Cavalieri di San Giovanni (1530–1798)', *Quaderni Storici*, 107:2 (2001), 397–8

— 'Pour une géographie de l'esclavage méditerranéen aux Temps Modernes', in *Atti del convegno L'esclavage en Méditerranée à l'*époque moderne (2002), 17–52

— 'Charles Quint, Malte et la défense de la Méditerranée', *Revue d'histoire moderne & contemporaine*, 50 (2003), 7–28

— 'Routes et modalités du commerce des esclaves dans la Méditerranée des Temps Modernes XVIe, XVIIe et XVIIIe siècles)', *Revue Historique*, 4 (2006), 813–30

— 'Esclaves et/ou captives: préciser le concepts', in Kaiser, W. (ed.), *Le commerce de captives: les intermediaries dans l'*échange et le rachat des prisonniers en Méditerranée, XVe–*XVIIIe siècle* (Rome, 2008), 15–24

— & Tenenti, A., 'Course et Piraterie Méditerranéennes de la fin du Moyen-Age au début du XIXème Siècle', in Mollat, M. (ed.), *Course et Piraterie: Etudes presentées à la Commission International D'Histoire Maritime à l'occasion de son XVe colloque international pendant le XIVe Congrès Interantional de Sciences historiques San Francisco, août, 1975* (2 vols, Paris, 1975), vol. 1, 78–136

Freller, T., 'Excellent Accommodation on Moderate Terms: Maltese Inns, Hostels and Hotels in Days of Old', *Treasures of Malta*, 12:2 (2006), 27–32

— *Malta – The Order of St John* (Malta, 2010)

Friedman, E. G., *Spanish Captives in North Africa in the Early Modern Ages* (Madison, WI, 1983)

Fsadni, M., 'The Dominicans', in Bugeja, L., Buhagiar, M. & Fiorini, S. (eds), *Birgu: A Maltese Maritime City* (2 vols, Malta, 1993), vol. 2, 663–715

Fusaro, M., *L'uva passa. Una guerra commerciale tra Venezia e l'Inghilterra, 1540–1640* (Venice, 1997)

— 'After Braudel: A Reassessment of Mediterranean History between the Northern Invasion and the *Caravane Maritime*', in Fusaro, M., Heywood, C. & Omri, M. S. (eds), *Trade and Cultural Exchange in the Early Modern Mediterranean: Braudel's Maritime Legacy* (London & New York, 2010), 1–22

— *Political Economies of Empire in the Early Modern Mediterranean: The Decline of Venice and the Rise of England 1450–1700* (Cambridge, 2015)

— Heywood, C. J. & Omri, M. S. (eds), *Trade and Cultural Exchange in the Early Modern Mediterranean: Braudel's Maritime Legacy* (London, 2010)

Giambruno, S. & Genuardi, L. (eds), *Capitoli inediti delle citta demaniali di Sicilia approvati sino al 1481* (Palermo, 1918)

Giuffrida, A., *La Sicilia e l'Ordine di Malta 1529–1530, La centralità della periferia Mediterranea* (Palermo, 2006)

Goitein, S., *A Mediterranean Society: The Jewish Communities of the Arab World as Portrayed in the Documents of Cairo Geniza* (5 vols, Berkeley and Los Angeles, 1999)

Green, M., *A Shared World: Christians and Muslims in the Early Modern Mediterranean* (Princeton, 2000)

— 'Resurgent Islam: 1500–1700', in Abulafia, D. (ed.), *The Mediterranean in History* (London, 2003), 219–49

— *Catholic Pirates and Greek Merchants* (Princeton, 2010)

— '"Victims of Piracy?" Ottoman Lawsuits in Malta (1602–1687) and the Changing Course of Mediterranean Maritime History', in Fusaro, M., Heywood, C. & Omri, M. S. (eds), *Trade and Cultural Exchange in the Early Modern Mediterranean: Braudel's Maritime Legacy* (London and New York, 2010), 177–201

Guilmartin Jr., J. F., *Gunpowder and Galleys – Changing Technology and Mediterranean Warfare at Sea in the Sixteenth Century* (rev. edn, London, 2003)

Hajnal, J., 'European Marriage Patterns in Perspective', in Glass, D. V. & Eversley, D. E. C. (eds) *Population in History: Essays on Historical Demography* (London, 1965), 101–43

Halevi, L., 'Religion and Cross-Cultural Trade: A Framework for Interdisciplinary Inquiry', in Trivellato. F., Halevi, L. & Antunes C. (eds), *Religion and Trade: Cross-Cultural Exchanges in World History, 1000–1900* (Oxford, 2014)

Heller-Roazen, D., *Enemy of All, Piracy and the Law of Nations* (New York, 2009)

Herlihy, D., 'Women's Work in the Towns of Traditional Europe', in Herlihy D. (ed.), *Women, Family, and Society in Medieval Europe: Historical Essays* (Oxford, 1995), 103–30

Heywood, C., 'A Frontier without Archaeology? The Ottoman Maritime Frontier in the Western Mediterranean, 1660–1760', *Crusades*, 2 (Society for the Study of the Crusades and the Latin East, Aldershot, 2003), 493–508

Hoppen, A., 'The Fortification of Malta, 1530–1798: The Impact on the Maltese', in Mallia Milanes, V. (ed.), *Hyphen*, 2:3 (1980), 103–14

— 'Military Priorities and Social Realities in the Early Modern Mediterranean: Malta and its Fortifications', in Mallia-Milanes, V. (ed.), *Hospitaller Malta 1530–1798: Studies on Early Modern Malta and the Order of St John of Jerusalem* (Malta, 1993), 399–428

Horden, P. & Purcell, N., *The Corrupting Sea – A Study of Mediterranean History* (Oxford, 2000)

Hufton, O., *The Prospect Before Her: A History of Women in Western Europe 1500–1800* (New York, 1998)

Hunt, S. & Murray, J. M., *A History of Business in Medieval Europe 1200–1500* (Cambridge, 1999)

İnalcik, H. & Quataert, D. (eds), *An Economic and Social History of the Ottoman Empire 1300–1914* (Cambridge, 1994)

Kaiser, W., 'L'économie de la rançon en Méditerranée occidentale (XVIe–XVIIe siècle)', in Cavaciocchi, S. (ed.), *Ricchezza del mare, ricchezza dal mare* (secc. XIII–XVIII) (2 vols, Florence, 2006), vol. 2, 689–701

— 'La exceptión permanente. Actores, visibilidad y asimetrías en los intercambios comerciales entre los países europeos y el Magreb (siglos XVI–XVII)', in Martinez Torres, J. A. (ed.), *Circulación de personas e intercambios en el Mediterréneo y en el Atlántico (siglos XVI, XVII, XVIII)* (CSIC, 2008), 171–89

— & Calafat G., 'The Economy of Ransoming in the Early Modern Mediterraean', in Trivellato, F., Halevi, L. & Antunes, C. (eds), *Religion and Trade: Cross-Cultural Exchanges in World History, 1000–1900* (Oxford, 2014), 108–30

Kamen, H., *Early Modern European Society* (London, 2000)

Katele, I., 'Piracy and the Venetian State: The Dilemma of Maritime Defense in the Fourteenth Century', *Speculum*, 63:4 (1988), 865–89

Klapisch-Zuber, C., *Women, Family, and Ritual in Renaissance Italy* (Chicago, 1985)

Koenigsberger, H. G. Mosse, G. L. & Bowler, G. Q., *Europe in the Sixteenth Century, A General History of Europe* (London and New York, 1989)

Koenigsberger, H. G., Mosse, G. L. & Bowler, G. Q., *Europe in the Sixteenth Century* (2nd edn, London and New York, 1992)

Kuehn, T., *Law, Family and Women, Towards a Legal Anthropology of Renaissance Italy* (Chicago, 1994)

— 'Person and Gender in the Laws', in Brown, J. C. & Davis, R. C. (eds), *Gender and Society in Renaissance Italy* (London and New York, 1998), 87–106

— 'Daughters, Mothers, Wives, and Widows: Women as Legal Persons', in Kuehn, T. & Seidel Menchi, S. (eds), *Time, Space and Women's Lives in Early Modern Europe* (Kirksville, MO, 2001), 97–115

Kula, W., *Measures and Men* (trans. R. Szreter, Princeton, 1986)

Kulsrud, C. J., *Maritime Neutrality to 1780; A History of the Main Principles Governing Neutrality and Belligerency to 1780* (Boston, 1936)

Kunt, M. & Woodhead, C. (eds), *Süleyman the Magnificent and His Age* (London & New York, 1995)

Ladero Quesada, M. A., '*Mudéjares* and *Repobladores* in the Kingdom of Granada (1485–1501)', in Meyuhas Ginio, A. (ed.), *Jews, Christians and Muslims in the Mediterranean after 1492* (London, 1992), 53–77

La Mantia, V., *Storia della Legislazione Civile e Criminale di Sicilia* (Palermo, 1866)

Lane, F. C., 'The Economic Consequences of Organized Violence', *Journal of Economic History*, 18 (1958), 401–17

— *Venice and History, The Collected Papers of Frederic C. Lane* (Committee of Colleagues and Former Students eds, Baltimore, 1966)

— & Mueller, R. C., *Money and Banking in Medieval and Renaissance Venice, Vol. 1 Coins and Moneys of Account* (Baltimore and London, 1985)

— 'The Venetian Galleys to Alexandria, 1344', in Kohl, B. G. & Mueller, R. C. (eds), *Studies in Venetian Social and Economic History* (London, 1987), 431–40

Lee, H. I., 'British Policy towards the Religion, Ancient Laws and Customs in Malta', *Melita Historica*, 3:4 (1963), 1–13

Leopardi, E. R., 'The Island of Gozo (1432–1453)', *Melita Historica*, 3:3 (1962), 77–80

Lopez Nadal, G. (ed.), *El comerç alternatiu. Corsarisme i contraban (ss. XV–XVIII)* (Palma de Mallorca, 1990)

Lopez, R. S. & Raymond, I. W., *Medieval Trade in the Mediterranean World, Illustrative Documents translated with Introduction and Notes* (New York, 1990)

Loualich, F., 'In the Regency of Algiers: The Human Side of the Algerine Corso', in Fusaro, M., Heywood, C., Omri, M. S. (eds), *Trade and Cultural Exchange in the Early Modern Mediterranean: Braudel's Maritime Legacy* (London and New York, 2010), 69–96

Luttrell, A., 'The House of the Castellan of Malta', *Heritage*, 9 (Malta, 1978), 161–5

— 'The Rhodian Background of the Order of Saint John in Malta', in Azzopardi, J. (ed.), *The Order's Early Legacy in Malta* (Malta, 1989), 3–14

— 'The Fourteenth-Century *Capitula Rodi*', in Luttrell, A. (ed.), *The Hospitallers of Rhodes and their Mediterranean World* (Aldershot, 1992), 204–11

— 'Malta and Rhodes: Hospitallers and Islanders', in Mallia-Milanes, V. (ed.), *Hospitaller Malta 1530–1798: Studies on Early Modern Malta and the Order of St John of Jerusalem* (Malta, 1993), 255–84

— 'The Earliest Documents on the Hospitaller *Corso* at Rhodes: 1413 and 1416', in Arbel, B. (ed.), *Intercultural Contacts in the Medieval Mediterranean* (London and Portland, OR, 1996), 177–88

— 'Giliberto Abbate's Report on Malta: c. 1241', in *Proceedings of History Week 1993* (Malta, 1997)

— 'Approaches to Medieval Malta', in Luttrel, A., *The Making of Christian Malta, From the Early Middle Ages to 1530* (Aldershot, 2002), II, 1–70

— 'Hospitaller Birgu: 1530–1536', *Crusades*, 2 (Society for the Study of the Crusades and the Latin East, 2003), 121–50

— *Studies on the Hospitallers after 1306, Rhodes and the West* (Aldershot, 2007)

Mack Smith, D., *A History of Sicily: Medieval Sicily 800–1713* (London, 1968)

Mahoney, L., *A History of Maltese Architecture from Ancient Times up to 1800* (Malta, 1988)

Malanima, P., 'Urbanization and the Italian Economy during the Last Millenium', *European Review of Economic History*, 9 (2005), 97–122

Mallia-Milanes, V., *Venice and Hospitaller Malta 1530–1798 – Aspects of a Relationship* (Malta, 1992)

— 'Introduction to Hospitaller Malta', in Mallia-Milanes, V. (ed.), *Hospitaller Malta 1530–1798: Studies on Early Modern Malta and the Order of St John of Jerusalem* (Malta, 1993), 1–42

— 'The Birgu Phase of Hospitaller History', in Bugeja, L., Buhagiar, M. & Fiorini, S. (eds), *Birgu: A Maltese Maritime City* (2 vols, Malta, 1993), vol. 1, 75–96

— 'Frà Jean de La Valette 1495–1568', in Cortis, T. (ed.), *The Maltese Cross* (Malta, 1995), 117–29

— 'Was Early Modern Malta an "Isolated World"?', in Marullo di Condojanni, F. (ed.), *Conference at Fort St Angelo of the SMOM* (Malta, 2000), 23–8

— 'La donazione di Malta da parte di Carlo V all'Ordine di S. Giovanni', in Anatra, B. & Manconi. F. (eds), *Sardegna, Spagna e Stati Italiani nell'Età di Carlo V* (Urbino, 2001), 137–48

— 'A Trial of Hospitaller Strength: From Rhodes to Malta via Nice and Villefranche, 1523–1530', in Salvatore, G. (ed.), *La Navigation du Savoir: Réseau des arsenaux historiques de la Méditerranée. Actes du Colloque: Premières journées internationals du patrimoine maritime méditerranéen, 27 au 30 mars 2003, Villefranche-sur-Mer* (Nice, 2006), 73–81

— 'A Pilgrimage of Faith, War, and Charity: The Order of the Hospital from Jerusalem to Malta', in Carvalho, J. (ed.), *Religion, Ritual and Mythology: Aspects of Identity Formation in Europe* (Pisa, 2006), 83–96

— (ed.), *The Military Orders, History and Heritage, Vol. III* (Aldershot, 2008)

Marcocci, G., 'Trading with the Muslim World: Religious Limits and Proscriptions in the Portuguese Empire (ca.1480–1570)', in Trivellato, F., Halevi, L. & Antunes, C. (eds), *Religion and Trade: Cross-Cultural Exchanges in World History, 1000–1900* (Oxford, 2014), 91–107

Martini, A., *Manuale di metrologia, ossia misure, pesi e monete in uso attualmente e anticamente press tutti i popoli* (Turin and Loescher, 1883)

Massa, P., 'Il Riscatto dei "Captivi". Temi sociali e problematiche finanziarie', in Piergiovanni, V. (ed.), *Corsari e riscatto dei captivi, garanzia notarìle tra le due sponde del Mediterraneo, Atti del Convegno di Studi Storici Marsala, 4 ottobre 2008* (Milano, 2010), 135–50

Matar, N., *Europe through Arab Eyes, 1578–1727* (New York, 2009)

Mathiex, J., 'Trafic et Prix de l'Homme en Méditerranée aux XVII° et XVIII° Siècles', *Annales*, ESC, 9 (1954), 157–64

McGough, L. J., 'Women, Private Property, and the Limitations of State Authority in Early Modern Venice', *Journal of Women's History*, 14 (2003), 32–52

Mercieca, S., 'The Spatial Mobility of Seafarers in the Mediterranean: A Case Study based on *Status Liberi* Documentation (1581–1640)', *Journal of Mediterranean Studies*, 12:2 (2002), 385–410

Micallef, A., *Trattato delle Procedure Civili nel Foro di Malta* (Malta, 1839)

— *Dritto Municpale di Malta* (2 vols, Malta, 1843)

Mifsud, A., 'Appunti sugli archvi di Malta', *Archivum Melitense*, 2:13 (1912–13), 9–67

— 'La Cattedrale e l'Università, ossia, il Comune e la Chiesa in Malta', *La Diocesi*, 2:3 (1917), 34–44

— 'L'Approvigionamento e l'Università di Malta nelle passate dominazioni', *Archivum Melitense*, 3:5 (1918), 163–212

— 'Papi, Fortificazioni e Tasse nel Passato di Malta', *Archivum Melitense*, 3:1 (1919), 399–430

Molho, A., Kirshner, J. & Morrison, A. S., 'Life Cycle Events in 15th Century Florence: Records of the Monte delle Doti', *American Journal of Epidemiology*, 106 (1977), 487–92

Montalto, J., *The Nobles of Malta 1530–1800* (Malta, 1980)

Mori Ubaldini, U., *La Marina del Sovrano Ordine Militare di San Giovanni di Gerusalemme di Rodi e di Malta* (Rome, 1971)

Mortilla, V., *Nuovo Dizionario Siciliano-Italiano* (2nd edn, Palermo, 1853)

Munro, J. H., 'The Usury Doctrine and Urban Public Finances in Late-medieval Flanders (1220–1550): Rentes (Annuities), Excise Taxes, and Income Transfers from the Poor to the Rich', in Cavaciocchi, S. (ed.), *Fiscal Systems in the European Economy from the 13th to the 18th centuries, Atti della Trentanovesima Settimana di Studi, 22–26 aprile 2007* (Florence, 2008), 974–1026

Muscat, C., *The Magdalene Nuns and Penitent Prostitutes, Valletta* (Malta, 2013)

Muscat, J., *Il-Flotta ta' l-Ordni ta' San Gwann* (Malta, 2000)

— *Sails Round Malta: Types of Sea Vessels 1600BC–1900AD* (Malta, 2008)

— & Cuschieri, A., *Naval Activities of the Knights of St John 1530–1798* (Malta, 2002)

North, D. C. & Homas, R. B., *The Rise of the Western World: A New Economic History* (Cambridge, 1973)

Ogilvie, S., and Dennison, T., 'Does the European Marriage Pattern Explain Economic Growth?', *The Journal of Economic History*, 74 (2014), 651–93

Olgiati, V., 'Professional Body and Gender Difference in Court: The Case of the First (Failed) Woman Lawyer in Modern Italy', in Schutz, U. & Shaw, G. (eds), *Women in the World's Legal Professions* (Oxford and Portland, OR, 2003), 419–36

Opitz, C., 'Life in the Late Middle Ages', in Duby, G., Perrot, M. (gen. eds) & Klapish-Zuber, C. (ed.), *A History of Women: Vol. II Silences of the Middle Ages* (Cambridge, MA and London, 1992), 269–70

Panzac, D., *La caravane maritime, marins européens et marchands ottomans en Méditerranée 1680–1830* (Paris, 2004)

Patterson, O., *Slavery and Social Death: A Comparative Study* (Harvard, MA, 1985)

Perry, M. J., *Gender, Manumission, and the Roman Freedwoman* (Cambridge, 2013)

Pryor, J. H., *Commerce, Shipping and Naval Warfare in the Medieval Mediterranean* (London, 1987)

Ressel, M., 'The Hanseatics in Southern Europe: Structure and Payment of German Long-Distance Shipping, 1630–1700', in Fusaro, M., Allaire, B., Blakemore, R. J. & Vanneste, T. (eds), *Law, Labour and Empire: Comparative Perspectives on Seafarers, c. 1500–1800* (Basingstoke 2015), 141–57

Rodger, N. A. M., 'The Law and Language of Private Naval Warfare', *Mariner's Mirror*, 100:1 (February 2014), 5–16

Romano, A. (ed.), *Cultura ed istituzioni nella Sicilia medievale e moderna* (Soveria Manelli, CZ and Messina, 1992)

— (ed.), *Consitutiones Regum Regni Siciliae* (Messina, 1992)

— 'Note sull'ordinamento giudiziario del Regno di Sicilia', in Romano, A. (ed.) *Cultura ed istituzioni nella Sicilia medievale e moderna* (Soveria Manelli, CZ & Messina, 1992), 197–225

— 'Bastardelli, protocolli e registri. La registrazione notarile degli atti in Sicilia fra medioevo ed eta moderna', *Archivi per la storia*, 6:1–2 (1993), 61–78

Rossi, E., 'Il dominio dei Cavalieri di Malta a Tripoli (1530–1551) e i rapporti dell'Ordine con Tripoli nei secoli seguenti (1551–1798)', *Archivium Melitense*, 6:2 (1925), 43–85

— *Storia della Marina dell'Ordine di San Giovanni di Gerusalemme, di Rodi e di Malta* (Rome and Milan, 1926)

— *Il Dominio degli Spagnoli e dei Cavalieri di Malta a Tripoli* (Airoldi, 1937)

Sabillion, C., *On the Causes of Economic Growth: The Lessons of History* (New York, 2008)

Sammut, J. C., *Currency in Malta* (Malta, 2001)

— *Is-Sistema Monetarja ta' Malta* (Malta, 2007)

Savaglio, A. (ed.), *Guerra di corsa e pirateria nel Mediterraneo*, Atti del convegno (Crotone-Cariati 30 novembre–3 dicembre 1995) (Cosenza, 1999)

Schulte van Kessel, E. 'Virgins and Mothers between Heaven and Earth', in Duby G. & Perrot, M. (eds), *A History of Women: Vol. III Renaissance and Enlightenment Paradoxes* (Cambridge, 1993) 132–66

Setton, K. M., *The Papacy and the Levant (1204–1571)* (4 vols, Philadelphia, 1984)

Simoncini, G. (ed.), *Sopra I Porti Di Mare III, Sicilia e Malta* (Florence, 1997)

Smith, R. M., 'Women's Work and Marriage in Pre-industrial England: Some Speculations', in Cavaciocchi, S. (ed.), *La donna nell'economia secc. XIII–XVIII* (Florence, 1990), 31–55

Sperling, J. G., 'Marriage, Kinship, and Property in Portuguese Testaments (1649–1650)', in Sperling, J. G. & Kelly Wray, S. (eds), *Across the Religious Divide, Women, Property, and Law in the Wider Mediterranean (ca. 1300–1800)* (New York & London, 2010), 158–74

Spiteri, S. C., *The Great Siege – Knights vs Turks MDLXV* (Malta, 2005)

Spufford, P., 'The Role of Entrepreneurs in State Formation', in Cavaciocchi, S. (ed.), *Poteri Economici e Poteri Politici Secc. XIII–XVIII, Attti della 'Trentesima Settimana di Studi', 27 aprile – 1 maggio 1998* (Florence, 1999), 483–500

Strayer, J. R., *On the Medieval Origins of the Modern State: With New Forwards by Charles Tilly and William Chestar Jordan* (Princeton, 2005)

Stretton, T. & Kesselring, K. J. (eds), *Married Women and the Law. Couverture in England and the Common Law World* (Ithaca, NY, 2013)

Teneti A. & Tenenti, B., *Il Prezzo del rischio: l'assicurazione mediterranea vista da Ragusa, 1563–1591* (Rome, 1985)

Testa, C., *Romegas* (Malta, 2002)

Todeschini, G., 'Usury in Christian Middle Ages. A Reconsideration of the Historiographical Tradition (1949–2010)', in Ammannati, F. (ed.), *Religion and Religious Institutions in the European Economy. 1000–1800, Atti della 'Quarantatreesima Settimana di Studi' 8–12 Maggio 2011* (Florence, 2012), 119–30

Trasselli, C., 'Una statistica maltese del secolo XVI', *Economia e Storia*, 9 (1966), 474–80

— *Il Mediterraneo e Sicilia all'inizio dell'epoca moderna* (Cosenza, 1977)

— *Da Ferdinando il Cattolico a Carlo V, L'esperienza siciliana 1475–1525* (2 vols, Soveria Mannelli, CZ, 1982)

— 'Note per la storia dei banchi in Sicilia nel XV secolo', in *I banchieri e i loro affair Vol. II* (Cosenza, 1993)

Tria, L., 'La schiavitù in Liguria: ricerche e documenti', *Atti della Società ligure di storia patria*, 70 (Genova, 1947)

Trivellato, F., 'Jews of Leghorn, Italians of Lisbon, and Hindus of Goa: Merchant Networks and Cross-Cultural Trade in the Early Modern Period', in Curto, D. R. & Molho, A. (eds), *Commercial Networks in the Early Modern World* (European University Institute, Florence, 2002), 59–89

— *The Familiarity of Strangers: The Sephardic Diaspora, Livorno, and Cross-Cultural Trade in the Early Modern Period* (New Haven, CT, 2009)

Valensi, L., 'Esclaves Chrétiens et Esclaves Noirs à Tunis au XVII° Siècle', *Annales*, ESC, 9 (1967), 1267–88

Valentini, R., 'Il Patrimonio della Corona in Malta fino alla venuta dell'Ordine', *Archivio Storico di Malta*, 5:1–4 (Rome, 1934), 3–32

— 'I Cavalieri di S. Giovanni da Rodi a Malta: Trattative diplomatiche', *Archivum Melitense*, 9:4 (1935), 137–237

— 'La sopravvivenza della "Universitàs Melivetana", fino alla cessazione delle infeudazioni dell'isola', *Archivio Storico di Malta*, 7:1 (Rome, 1935), 33–70

— 'L'Espansionismo aragonese nel Mediterraneo come causa della decadenza di Malta', *Archivio Storico di Malta*, 12:2–3 (1941), 99–130

— 'Funzione storica e dispersione del patrimonio demaniale di Malta', *Archivio Storico di Malta*, 13:1–3 (Rome, 1942), 1–39

Van Der Wee, H., 'Monetary, Credit and Banking Systems', in Rich, E. E. & Wilson, C. H. (eds), *The Cambridge Economic History of Europe*, 5 (Cambridge, 1977), 290–393

Vassallo, C. (ed.), *Consolati Di Mare and Chambers of Commerce* (Malta, 2000)

Vella, A., 'The Order of Malta and the Defence of Tripoli 1530–1551', *Melita Historica*, 6:4 (1975), 362–81

Vella, Y., 'Earthly Madonnas? 18th Century Women Trouble-Makers', in *Storja 98* (Malta, 1998), 33–40

— 'Women Victims of Crime in Eighteenth Century Malta', in Cortis, T. (ed.), *Proceedings of History Week 2003* (Malta, 2004), 17–23

Viazzo, P. P., 'What's so Special about the Mediterranean? Thirty Years of Research on Household and Family in Italy', *Continuity and Change*, 18:1 (2003), 111–37

Wettinger, G., 'The Distribution of Surnames in Malta in 1419 and the 1480s', *Journal of Maltese Studies* (University of Malta), 17–18 (1987–88), 104–38

— 'Early Maltese Popular Attitudes to the Government of the Order of St John', *Melita Historica*, 6:3 (1974), 255–78

— 'Honour and Shame in Late Fifteenth Century Malta', *Melita Historica*, 8:1 (1980), 65–77

— 'Agriculture in Malta in the Late Middle Ages', in Buhagiar, M. (ed.), *Proceedings of History Week, 1981* (Malta, 1982), 1–48

— 'The Archives of Palermo and Maltese Medieval History: A First Report', in Buhagiar, M. (ed.), *Proceedings of History Week, 1982* (Malta, 1983), 59–68

— *The Jews of Malta in the Late Middle Ages* (Malta, 1985)

— 'The Nature of Maltese Politics, c. 870–1964', in Mallia-Milanes, V. (ed.), *The British Colonial Experience 1800–1964: The Impact on Maltese Society* (Malta, 1988), 19–34

— Acta *Iuratorum et Consilii Civitatis et Insulae Maltae* (Palermo, 1993)

— 'The *Castrum Maris* and Its Suburb of Birgu during the Middle Ages', in Bugeja. L., Buhagiar, M. & Fiorini, S. (eds), *Birgu: A Maltese Martime City* (2 vols, Malta, 1993), vol. 1, 31–71

— 'The Origin of the "Maltese" Surnames', *Melita Historica*, 12:4 (1999), 333–44

— *Place-Names of the Maltese Islands ca. 1300–1800* (Malta, 2000)

— *Slavery in the Islands of Malta and Gozo ca. 1000–1812* (Malta, 2002)

— 'L-attitudni tal-Maltin Lejn il-Kavallieri', in Bartolo, E. (ed.), *Min Kien Cailus?* (Malta, 2003), 7–14

Wiesner-Hanks, M. E., *Early Modern Europe 1450–1798* (Cambridge, 2006)

— *Women and Gender in Early Modern Europe* (New York, 2008)

Williams, A., 'Constitutional Development of the Order of St John in Malta, 1530–1798', in Mallia-Milanes, V. (ed.), *Hospitaller Malta 1530–1798: Studies on Early Modern Malta and the Order of St John of Jerusalem* (Malta, 1993), 285–96

— 'Tripoli and the Knights of Malta Revisited', in Xuereb, P. (ed.), *Karissime Gotifride – Historical Essays Presented to Professor Godfrey Wettinger on his Seventieth Birthday* (Malta, 1999), 97–102

— '"Stone or Wooden Walls?": The Problems of Land and Sea Defence in the Islands of Rhodes (1421–1522) and Malta (1530–1631)', in Cortis, T. & Gambin, T. (eds), *De Triremibus, Festschrift in Honour of Joseph Muscat* (Malta, 2005), 415–26

— '*Sacra Militia*, the Order of St John: Crusade, Corsairing and Trade in Rhodes and Malta 1460–1631', in Fusaro, M., Heywood, C. & Omri, M. S. (eds), *Trade and Cultural Exchange in the Early Modern Mediterranean: Braudel's Maritime Legacy* (London and New York, 2010), 139–56

Wismayer, J. M., *The Fleet of the Order of St John – 1530–1798* (Malta, 1997)

Zachariadou, E., 'Monks and Sailors under the Ottoman Sultans', *Oriente Moderno*, new series, 81:1, 'The Ottomans and the Sea' (2001), 139–47

Zemon Davis, N., 'Women in Politics', in Duby, G. & Perrot, M. (gen. eds) & Zemon Davis, N. & Farge, A. (eds), *A History of Women: Vol. III Renaissance and Enlightenment Paradoxes* (Cambridge, MA and London, 1993), 167–83

— & Farge, A., 'Women as Historical Actors', in Duby, G. & Perrot, M. (gen. eds) & Zemon Davis, N. & Farge, A. (eds), *A History of Women: Vol. III Renaissance and Enlightenment Paradoxes* (Cambridge, MA and London, 1993), 1–7

Unpublished dissertations

Abela, J., 'A Window on Early Hospitaller Malta – A Study of the Acts of Notary Placido Abela, 1557–1558' (BA Hons dissertation, University of Malta, 2003)

— 'Port Activities in Mid-Sixteenth Century Malta' (MA dissertation, University of Malta, 2007)

Bezzina, D., 'Early Hospitaller Birgu – A Study of the Acts of Notary Nicolò de Agatiis, 1538–1540' (BA Hons dissertation, University of Malta, 2001)

Bezzina, V., 'The Administration of the Maltese Islands, A Study of the Acta Iuratorum et Consilii Civitatis Insulae Maltae' (MA dissertation, University of Malta, 1999)

Borg, V., 'Birgu: A Demographic Overview 1558–1658' (BA Hons dissertation, University of Malta, 1999)

Buttigieg, E., 'Fifteen Years into Hospitaller Rule – A Study of the Acts of Notary Juliano Muscat, 1545' (BA Hons dissertation, University of Malta, 2002)

Cachia, S., 'The Family and the Land in Late Medieval Malta – A Study of the Acts of Notary J. Zabbara, 1486–1488' (BA Hons dissertation, University of Malta, 1999)

Mercieca, S., 'Community Life in the Central Mediterranean. A Socio-Demographic Study of the Maltese Harbour Towns in Early Modern Times: Bormla 1587–1815' (PhD thesis, University of Paris-IV Sorbonne, 2001–2)

Rossi, D., 'The Monte Di Pieta' in Hospitaller Malta' (BA Hons dissertation, University of Malta, 1998)

Sant, M. A., 'Coinage Problems Facing the Order of St John in Malta' (MA dissertation, University of Malta, 1967)

Sciberras, J., 'Women in Early Sixteenth-Century Malta' (MA dissertation, University of Malta, 2004)

Vassallo, A. M., 'Prices of Commodities in Malta and Gozo, 1530–1630' (BA Hons dissertation, University of Malta, 1976)

Internet Sources

Alfani, G. & Sardone, S., 'Long Term Trends in Economic Inequality in Southern Italy. The Kingdom of Napes and Sicily in the 16th–18th Centuries: First results', http://

eh.net/eha/wp-content/uploads/2015/05/Alfani.pdf (accessed 9 August 2016)

Bibliographical reference to the role of slavery in European economic growth, http://www.oxfordbibliographies.com/view/document/obo-9780199730414/obo-9780199730414–0091.xml (accessed 30 January 2016)

British History Online, http://www.british-history.ac.uk/report.aspx?compid=92249 (accessed 9 May 2016)

Brogini, A., 'Marginalités et contrôle social dans le port de Malte à l'époque moderne (XVIe–XVIIe siècles)', *Cahiers de la Méditerranée*, 69 (2004): http://cdlm.revues.org/index786.html (accessed 26 April 2016)

Cassar, M., 'Vestiges of Arabic Nomenclature in Maltese Surnames', 22nd International Congress of Onomastic Sciences, Pisa, 4 September 2005, https://www.academia.edu/183114/Vestiges_of_Arabic_Nomencalture_in_Maltese_Surnames (accessed 21 August 2016)

Collins English Dictionary – Complete and Unabridged 10th Edition, Dictionary.com, http://www.dictionary.com/browse/razzia (accessed 22 August 2016)

Curtis, D., 'An Agro-town Bias? Re-examining the Micro-demographic Model for Southern Italy in the Eighteenth Century', https://www.academia.edu/7913631/An_agro-town_bias_Re-examining_the_micro-demographic_model_for_Southern_Italy_in_the_eighteenth_century (accessed 13 March 2016)

Fertig, G., 'The Hajnal Thesis before Hajnal: The Pre-history of European Marriage Patterns' (2004), http://www.uni-muenster.de/imperia/md/content/hist_sem_swg/personen/fertig_g/download/hajnal.pdf (accessed 13 March 2016)

Food and Argiculture Organization of the United Nations: http://www.fao.org/es/faodef/fdef01e.htm (accessed 24 February 2016)

Government of Malta Libraries Department, http://www.libraries.gov.mt (accessed 10 May 2016)

Hershenzon, D. B., 'Early Modern Spain and the Creation of the Mediterranean: Captivity, Commerce, and Knowledge' (unpublishded PhD thesis, University of Michigan, 2011), http://deepblue.lib.umich.edu/bitstream/2027.42/89664/1/hershenz_1.pdf (accessed 5 April 2015)

Lorenc, J. A., 'John of Freiburg and the Usury Prohibition in the Late Middle Ages: A Study in the Popularization of Medieval Canon Law' (PhD thesis, University of Toronto, 2013), https://tspace.library.utoronto.ca/bitstream/1807/35887/1/Lorenc_John_A_201306_PhD_thesis.pdf (accessed 2 October 2016)

Malanima, P., 'The Italian Renaissance Economy (1260–1500)', International Conference at Villa La Pietra, Florence May 2008, http://www.paolomalanima.it/default_file/Papers/RENAISSANCE_ITALY.pdf (accessed 8 August 2016)

Mainoni, P., 'I mundoaldi nella Puglia medievale: alcuni quesiti dalla lettura dei documenti (secc. XII–XIV)': https://www.academia.edu/19861050/Patrizia_Mainoni (accessed 29 April 2016)

Mendola L., 'Translation of the Deed of Donation of Malta, NLM, AOM, 70 with Additional Historical Material by Mallia-Milanes, V.': https://www.orderofmalta.int/wp-content/uploads/archive/pubblicazioni/Charlesv_donation.pdf

New Advent Catholic Encyclopedia: http://www.newadvent.org/cathen/03738a.htm (accessed 9 May 2016)

Index

Printed and bound by CPI Group (UK) Ltd, Croydon, CR0 4YY

15/09/2026

14962416-0005